THE
APPREHENSIVE GARDENER

MANAGING GARDEN PLANTS

THE
APPREHENSIVE
GARDENER

MANAGING GARDEN PLANTS

GRISELDA KERR

Griselda Kerr

PIMPERNEL
PRESS LTD
www.pimpernelpress.com

For our children, Robbie,
Cordelia and Walter

Pimpernel Press Limited
www.pimpernelpress.com

The Apprehensive Gardener
Managing Garden Plants
© Pimpernel Press Limited 2019
Text © Griselda Kerr 2019
Photographs © William Kerr 2019
Design by Becky Clarke Design

A catalogue record for this book is available
from the British Library.

Typeset in Gotham and Memphis LT

ISBN 978-1-910258-23-1

Printed and bound in China
By C&C Offset Printing Company Limited

9 8 7 6 5 4 3 2 1

All the photographs in the book were
taken by William Kerr in his and Griselda's
Derbyshire garden.

Title page: *Clematis urophylla* 'Winter Beauty'
(flowering December–February)
Right: *Achillea* 'Summerwine'
(flowering June–August)

CONTENTS

INTRODUCTION

This book is about how to look after the plants already in your garden – what to do when and how. It is based on the wisdom and expertise of those gardeners whose articles, books and lectures I have devoured over the last twenty years. Some of it has been put into practice in our own garden – and a great deal has not; nobody without an army of gardeners could do everything in this book. It is to be dipped into when a reminder is needed: when might I prune this cotinus, how shall I make my lemon tree happy, when and how should I prune my climbing rose, or rambler (quite different), when ideally should the hydrangea heads come off, how can I encourage this monarda to stay longer in flower, should I deadhead this canna, is it all right to cut back this juniper, how can I get the best from my fig tree, what else should I consider this month? It is a book for the apprehensive gardener who, as confidence develops, discovers there is an instinctive flexibility in gardening that makes calendars quite unnecessary. Until that time, this book is a crook to lean upon.

The book can be used in two ways. A plant can be looked up in the index to see, by casting an eye across the months of the year, when to do something. Or a month can be viewed as a whole to select any plants of interest. If the name of the plant in question is unknown, the section 'Areas to consider' at the start of each month will give a good indicator of things that could be done.

There are many outstanding books written by the best gardeners of our time about what to plant, how, when and where, but this book has a different remit. It focuses on the maintenance of plants already in the garden: what to do with the annuals, perennials, shrubs and small trees that you would like to care for but perhaps are not quite sure what to do with. The selection includes frequently used garden plants (and a few house plants) which are, by and large, those that I grow, have grown, have failed to grow, or would like to grow given more space and the right soil. Some vegetables are included, but they form only a small part of the book as their care is more to do with timing, rotation and cropping than yearly maintenance. Although many garden trees are included, the book does not extend into the detail of larger trees in arboreta and the wider landscape.

Seasonal vagaries and location have a great impact on plant care, which need to be taken into account when using this book. One friend gardening in the north of Scotland finds that in many years she has only one frost-free month in twelve. If she needed it, she would adapt the advice to suit her environment: the month would change but possibly not the text. Those living in the warm south will have no use whatsoever for the extreme measures I go to in Derbyshire to protect pots and plants

Ceanothus impressus (flowering May–June)

from winter cold and will do things weeks earlier than suggested. The book takes as its reference point a garden which is in the very middle of England, 60 m/200 ft above sea level with uninterrupted views across water that can be whipped by east or west winds. There is a preponderance of plants for the alkaline soil with which I am most familiar, but many others are included which prefer an acidic soil.

On many occasions in the index of plants only the genus is listed, although occasionally species within a genus are given separate entries. While some species (and indeed cultivars) are hardier than others within the same genus, it would be impossible in a book of this size to propose care for every one. If this book were not general in its approach, *The Apprehensive Gardener* would be drowned in caveats. Equally, were there to be an entry for every plant in every month it would become encyclopaedic in size and intolerably repetitious. The presumption throughout is that unless the text refers to the care of a young plant, it has been established for at least two years.

I generally give Latin names except where the English name is in common usage, so, for example, holly is used instead of ilex, lime instead of tilia, box not buxus, snowdrop not galanthus. The English common names for many plants are given in a separate list at the back, so that if the Latin name is unfamiliar, it can be found. Thus, catmint will take you to nepeta, dogwood to cornus. The glossary explains, and where necessary gives examples of, many of the terms which are used in the book. A recommendation to 'mulch', 'feed', 'use a balanced fertilizer' or indeed to 'take a root cutting' or 'prick out' could be irritating if you are not sure what that was calling for.

From time to time more instruction will be needed from a specialist book: this does not set out to be a gardening compendium. Prompted to prune, you may want more detail, for example, in respect of fan-trained fruit trees or the formative pruning of young trees. A good pruning book, one on pests and diseases, another on propagation, one on fruit and vegetables, and a book on basic garden techniques will create an invaluable reference library.

In 'Tradescant's Diary' in *The Garden* magazine of April 2004, Hugh Johnson wrote, 'The aim is for a garden where plants seem happy to have met . . . it sounds like Eden but is just lovely gardening.' These words have been a beacon of light for me since then. Maintenance is important because it contributes to the atmosphere and health of a garden – everyone likes to see plants growing well – but dullness creeps in when maintenance becomes the driving force. Rather than being driven by lists (I do very greatly dislike the word 'task' in relation to a garden), I hope you will find reassurance in *The Apprehensive Gardener* of what could be done to encourage your plants along and will find the journey of gardening a releasing and invigorating one, engendering a sense of joy in the creation of a place, however tiny or big, where plants do indeed seem happy to have met.

The author in her garden under a sweet cherry,
Prunus avium 'Grosvenor Wood' (flowering mid-spring)

ACKNOWLEDGEMENTS

It was 2002 when I first started jotting down what I should be doing to care for the plants in our garden and to make the most of fleeting moments when I was back from Hong Kong. I realized I knew nothing about gardening. My neighbour and friend Robert Vernon of Bluebell Nurseries became my first mentor. There followed two years under Rosemary Alexander's tutelage at the English Gardening School, a year at Broomfield College in Derby and time at Brooksby College in Melton Mowbray – all this while flying in and out of the Far East. There followed lectures at the Gardening School of Coton Manor, courses with Rosemary Campbell Preston at The Plant School, voluntary work at Bluebell Nurseries and study days under Tony Kirkham with the International Dendrology Society. The notes and scraps of paper grew feet high and needed organizing. Basil Postan thought it might be a book and the door to Pimpernel Press was magically opened. To him, to Jo Christian and Gail Lynch, who put their faith in it such a while ago, I shall always be deeply grateful, as I am to Becky Clarke for her calm and assured design. My brother-in-law Andrew Kerr of Bennett and Kerr Books read through it for me. When Nancy Marten became its editor so much good sense was drummed into it.

But there are many people who should be thanked for help given wittingly or unwittingly over the years whose wisdom has formed the backbone of this book. Starting with the particular, I am so grateful to Ian Limmer at Peter Beales Roses and Michael Marriott at David Austin Roses for their many years of support and encouragement on rose care, and to Millais Nurseries for their unstinting help regarding the care of rhododendron and azalea. Sally Gregson at Mill Cottage Plants has for a long time patiently answered questions on the care of hydrangea and epimedium. Christine Skelmersdale, owner of Broadleigh Gardens, Chris Ireland-Jones of Avon Bulbs and Chris Blom of Bloms Bulbs have often pushed me in the right direction, and I live with Anna Pavord's book *Bulb* on my desk. The European Box and Topiary Society has given me guidance concerning box, in particular tracking that new scourge, the box tree caterpillar. Neil Lucas's Knoll Gardens is a paradise for those learning about and selecting grasses – there have been many calls to him over the years, answered always with immense patience and kindness. Philip Bolt wrote with wonderful clarity in *The Plantsman* about cardiocrinum, which helped me to grow the plant much more successfully. Articles by Lia Leendertz and Stephen Lacey have been particularly helpful on brugmansia care. Kelways Plants has answered many questions on peonies, as has Oliver Groom on salvias, Edrom Nurseries on gentians, McBeans on orchids, lockyerfuchsia.co.uk on fuchsias and Pictorial Meadows on the, to me, as yet unexplored territory of planting meadows. Dr Glynn Percival has been here often to help with problems such as honey fungus and phytophthoras affecting woody plants and has become a friend and advisor. The outstanding grape vines at Chatsworth overseen by Faye Tuffrey (described in full by Sarah Raven in the Saturday *Telegraph*) provide a perfect example for growing vines under cover. While few can aspire to such management, their care is relevant to any size of vine and I am extremely grateful to her and Steve Porter at Chatsworth. Clive Simms's *Nutshell Guide to Growing Figs* gave me all the answers I sought in the most digestible form. Having grown sweet peas for many years according to the instruction of Roger Parsons, National Plant Collections Holder for Sweet Peas, I would advise others to do the same. In its planting notes, Thorncroft Clematis makes clear and easy what is often considered the complicated matter of clematis care and pruning. Indeed, the planting notes of nurseries such as Sarah Raven, Ashwood, Crocus, Woottens of Wenhaston, Blackmore and Langdon, Dibleys and many others are an invaluable service to gardeners when purchasing their glorious plants. The *Royal Horticultural Society A–Z Encyclopedia of Garden Plants* is the most useful reference book any gardener can have, while the service provided by the RHS to answer questions on gardening and plant identification is truly extraordinary.

But this book contains the collected wisdom of so many others, most of them household names for anyone even remotely interested in gardening – the late Christopher Lloyd, Roy Lancaster, the late Beth Chatto, Hugh Johnson, Robin Lane Fox – indeed, the list below reads like a litany of great gardeners. Any one of them could write this book standing on their head. In this respect I think particularly of Ursula Buchan, whose gardening articles were my bread and butter for many years. Helen Yemm is another, whose 'Thorny Problems' page in the Saturday *Telegraph* is compulsive reading every week. To all of them I am grateful – the learning goes on until that time when it becomes second nature and gardening is no longer anything to be apprehensive about.

So, in addition to those mentioned above, I would like to acknowledge my debt to the huge number of experts whose advice has been invaluable in compiling this book, including: Louisa Arbuthnott, Claire Austin, Mary Berry, Matthew Biggs, Adrian Bloom, Helen Bostock, Chris Bowers, Val Bourne, Bob Brown, Toby Buckland, Marina Christopher, Phil Clayton, Nigel Colborn, Brian Davis, Tony Dickerson, Helen Dillon, Monty Don, Nigel Dunnett, Bob Flowerdew, Sue France, Fergus Garrett, Pippa Greenwood, Mark Griffiths, John Grimshaw, Bunny Guinness, Rosy Hardy, Mary Keen, Noel Kingsbury, Carol Klein, Arabella Lennox-Boyd, Tony Lord, Dr Ronald Mackenzie, John Massey, Susie Pasley-Tyler, Dan Pearson, Lynsey Pink, Sarah Raven, Graham Rice, Sara Rittershausen, Henry Robinson, Alan Titchmarsh, Jennifer Trehane and Matthew Wilson.

One personal, heartfelt acknowledgement goes to my beloved husband, William, who has proofread, advised and cajoled me to complete this book. The credit for the photographs, all taken in our Derbyshire garden, is his also.

Griselda Kerr
September 2018

JANUARY

What an invigorating month this is, preparing the garden to welcome that unfailingly astonishing new growth nudging out from inhospitable soil. Leaves can be cleared where new bulbs are to emerge, new outlines revealed where brave plants will sparkle; every shot of colour is a miracle.

AREAS TO CONSIDER

Alpines Work over them to remove dead and diseased leaves, checking for slugs. Add new grit around those in the ground and to the surface of those in pots, checking they are not soggy. Take out any that look sickly to check for vine weevil – creamy grubs. These will need to have their roots washed before being replanted or repotted in new compost. A biological vine weevil killer such as Nemasys (available online) only works if the soil is over 5°C so is only useful under glass this early in the year.

Annual meadow In the first year, start preparing the ground. Unlike with a perennial meadow, the soil needs to be fertile, so remove weeds, incorporate humus, rake over to remove stones and lumps. By the time the second year comes round, you can leave the preparation until about the time you sow in April: the less time between ground preparation and sowing, the less time for weed seeds to blow in. Professional advice is worth having. Pictorial Meadows in Sheffield will provide very helpful advice to those planning their first meadow.

Bare-root plants Provided the soil is not frozen, plant bare-root roses, fruit trees, deciduous trees/hedging.

Galanthus plicatus 'Wendy's Gold' (flowering January–February)

Bark Many species of maple, birch and cherry have wonderful bark, especially when cleaned with a pressure hose.

Bulbs Check stored bulbs/tubers/corms, throwing out any with rot. Bulbs in the ground which could provide food for rodents could have a soil drench of a very mild solution of water and paraffin to disguise the scent.

Compost If you are lucky enough to have a greenhouse or shed, bring bags of seed and potting compost into a warmer environment a day before using them. Otherwise, ensure any bags of compost do not get frozen while left outside.

Container and pot plants Even in deep winter do not let the compost dry out completely. Pots of evergreens, and conifers especially, need water throughout winter, though all plants need just enough to keep them going. Keep watch during long cold and dry periods. Placing pots together under a south-facing wall if they cannot be taken under cover maximizes protection and makes their care easier.

Cuttings: root Take root cuttings of perennials with taproots (which are almost impossible to divide) or which have fleshy roots such as acanthus, crambe, dicentra, echinops, eryngium, Japanese anemone, oriental poppy, pulsatilla, verbascum.

Evergreen hedges Newly planted evergreens such as yew lose leaves rapidly in exposed positions. A windbreak will protect young plants. Provided the ground is not frozen, fork into the soil a slow release fertilizer such as Fish, Blood and Bone. None should be pruned.

Frost and wind protection The weather is likely to get colder, so continue and increase protection from wind and deep frost around newly planted trees and shrubs. Wrap outside taps and bring all hosepipes under cover.

Fruit bushes Bullfinches will have a happy time if fruit bushes are not covered with netting.

Fruit trees
- Espaliered and cordon: rejuvenate overgrown espaliered and cordon fruit trees now, removing overlong growth. Stagger this over two years if necessary. Refer to a good book on pruning.
- Free standing with and without stones: complete pruning of apples and pears this month (see December). Check stake ties are firm but not too tight. Feed pruned trees with sulphate of potash, covering all the root area, which should be cleared of competing grass and weeds. Such competition is particularly bad for young trees. Mulch up to the drip line of the tree, leaving space between the mulch and trunk.

Greenhouse and indoor plants
Opening the greenhouse or porch door on warm days improves air circulation, but if housing tender plants the temperature should not drop below 4°C. If it does, keep air circulating with a fan – not to create heat but to keep it just above freezing. Air movement also helps keep botrytis at bay. To avoid waterlogging and root rot, do not water plants more than absolutely necessary, allowing plants to dry out between waterings. To maintain low humidity and reduce opportunities for pests and disease avoid splashing water around.

Hedges Mid-winter is a good time to cut, renovate and plant bare-root hedges like hawthorn, hornbeam, beech, hazel and yew. Leylandii need to be planted later, as they are always sold as containerized plants. If hedges are getting too big they can be root pruned to slow their growth – use a spade to cut their roots back. Do any major surgery like cutting an arch or gap now.

Lawns If possible, avoid walking on the lawn when frosty or covered in snow, though it would spoil so much fun for children to stop them; snowmen do not seem to do any long-lasting damage. On a dry day brush over worm casts, which provide a useful topdressing. Remove molehills (they may be 'fortress building' or nesting) and refirm. Keep the topsoil the moles earthed up as it makes a fabulous soil-based potting compost.

Leaves Collect leaves from areas where the first bulbs appear, attending to places where there are aconites, alpines, cyclamen, hellebores, snowdrops and winter irises. Rake leaves off grass as they do it no good. Remove leaves from the crowns of herbaceous perennials, from under box and around lavender where they shelter slugs and snails and encourage rot. Leaves piled between wire meshing, or held in sacks with drainage holes, eventually produce precious leafmould. Beware of spiking with a fork piles of leaves under shrubs as they may harbour hibernating hedgehogs.

Perennials Ensure the roots of slightly tender perennials (and shrubs) are protected with dry mulches such as bracken, straw or Strulch and wrap those you fear for in horticultural fleece. Do not make the mistake of thinking it is now too late – it is not!

Ponds Keep ponds from freezing over by putting in floats. If it does freeze and there are fish, melt rather than crack the ice as soon as possible using a hot saucepan of water placed on the surface. Net the pond to prevent it getting full of leaves or rake them out.

Pruning On an unbalanced shrub, prune hard down to good buds on the *less* vigorous side to encourage strong growth, cutting just above a bud or side shoot (where there are always strong growth hormones) and slanting the cut so that water runs off. Prune only lightly where growth does not need encouragement (it is almost counterintuitive). Resist random pruning as open wounds do not heal quickly and disease can enter through cuts. It is now considered unhelpful to paint over cuts as it traps moisture behind the seal, but using sharp bypass secateurs prevents the soft tissue around the cut being wounded.

Snow Ursula Buchan once wrote of her determination to get snow off box, yew hedges and a fruit cage even with two broken elbows: there is no more vivid illustration of the importance of this task. The weight of frozen snow on evergreens can do great damage; the netting on fruit cages can be broken. If snow covers the glass of the greenhouse, clear it to allow light penetration as soon as possible as the plants will hate the dark. Leave snow over young plants and pots as it provides a form of protection from searing winds, and knocking it off may kill the plant. I do take snow off pots of lilies when I think the drench of melted snow might leave the compost too soggy.

Topiary If in really cold weather you wrap the stems of topiary in fleece, you will be protecting the top of the root ball, which is where the greatest danger of freezing lies.

Trees: planting and staking Check that ties on tree stakes are not too tight or rubbing, and firm back any young trees rocked and loosened in their planting holes. Ensure the soil and/or mulch is not piled up the trunk above the top of the root ball: a slow but sure death will ensue.

Vegetable beds If the ground is not frozen or waterlogged, dig in heavy organic matter like farmyard manure to improve the soil in empty plots, but do not dig just for looks. Covering some ground with polythene to warm the soil before the first sowings are done can be helpful. Broad beans, cabbages, leeks, onions, radishes, spinach and other early vegetables can be sown under cover now.

Wildlife Prune deciduous hedges before the nesting season gets going; keep bird feeders full, replenish water sources regularly and ensure bird baths are not frozen, scrubbing them out between refills. Beware hedgehogs hibernating in leaf piles under shrubs; erect cat-proof nest boxes (facing north-east is a good angle).

PLANTS

Acanthus (bear's breeches) Cut seed heads back and take root cuttings if more plants are wanted. Protect the plant with a thick layer of dry mulch.

Acer (maple) With the exception of *Acer davidii* and other snakebark maples (see August), any necessary pruning of acers including *A. japonicum*, *A. palmatum* and paperbark maples should be done when dormant between November and early February (never in spring when the sap is rising). Remove any branches that are dead, dying, infected or spoiling the framework. The glowing stems of, for example, *A. palmatum* 'Sango-kaku' and *A. × conspicuum* 'Phoenix' can be lightly pruned to increase their quantity and quality next winter. The colour is always best on one- and two-year-old wood. Long growth can be reduced to lower side branches or to an upward-facing bud to encourage branching. Start this shaping when they are about two years old.

Acer campestre (field maple)
When used as a hedge it needs an annual prune to maintain a good height and shape.

Anemone hupehensis, *A. × hybrida* (Japanese anemone)
Clear up dead leaves and mulch around (not over) the crowns. Take root cuttings if wanted.

Apple and pear: free standing
Before the end of February, apple and pear tree pruning should be finished. See December 'Apple and pear' for notes on pruning. Bin mouldy fruit (do not compost). Give the trees a winter wash when there is no frost or strong wind. Check grease bands are in place to deter winter moths.

Arum italicum subsp. *italicum* 'Marmoratum'
This shady ground cover, with lovely dark green marbled leaves appearing now, produces seedlings whose leaves are unmarked for the first few years. Avoid digging them up as I did thinking they were the plain horribly invasive *Arum maculatum* commonly known as lords-and-ladies. 'Marmoratum' can be just as invasive, however, so keep an eye on it and when the clump is established, cut off the flower spathes before they develop the fruits: mice, moles and birds will otherwise distribute them around the garden. Plant new arum deeper than they are in the pot. (When attempting to dig up *A. maculatum* to get rid of it, which is not easy, ensure no part of it goes into the compost heap or you will be aiding its spread.)

Asparagus When the ground is not frozen, apply a balanced slow release fertilizer and cover with another layer of well-rotted manure (not lumpy), spent mushroom compost or garden compost.

Astilbe Cut down any remaining flower stalks which have provided shape over winter. They can be divided if weather allows; they divide easily and very well, but it may be safer to leave doing so until March.

Bay (*Laurus nobilis*) In very cold winters, bay trees in pots will need wrapping in fleece (the pot, too, if terracotta).

Begonia Inspect tubers to ensure they are not drying out (or rotting – if so remove the culprits to protect the others). If sowing their seed, mix with sand as seeds are so tiny.

Birch (*Betula*) Gather material to use as plant supports later in the year. If branches and twigs are pruned before bud burst, they remain pliable. Sap will bleed if heavily pruned in spring.

Broad bean If they were not planted outside in November, sow them now under cover in root trainers or deep pots for planting out in late February. They like to get their roots established when the ground is cold and wet – this also helps strengthen them against disease.

Canna If overwintering them as rhizomes, check they are not too wet or dry. They need no watering during dormancy but should be stored in a mulch that maintains a degree of damp. If there is rot, find somewhere which is drier; if they look desiccated, move them somewhere with more moisture.

Cardiocrinum giganteum (giant lily)
We are advised against mulching cardiocrinum with organic matter in

winter as the mulch may hold too much water and risks rotting the nose of the bulb. Mature bulbs seem to survive to -10°C. Colder than that and a dry mulch or bracken would be good.

Cordyline It may appear to be completely lost in a cold winter. Wrap well and when spring arrives, cut down to the base. It could reshoot, growing again with a strong root ball and possibly producing much prettier new growth.

Cornus florida, C. kousa, C. nutalii, C. 'Venus' (flowering dogwood) These cornus do not need pruning. If a clear trunk is wanted, take the lower branches off now in the dormant season. Take out any dead wood. For shaping, see June.

Cymbidium (orchid) There are many well-known rules about orchid care: they must not stand in water; water the soil not the plant; avoid sunny windowsills, radiators and TV tops; avoid draughts and proximity to bowls of fruit. Flowering of cymbidium is likely to be between November and May. They like a spell outside between June and September to initiate the production of flower spikes. Water now every couple of weeks, standing the pot in a sink to allow excess water to drain. A tray of moist gravel will provide the humidity they need, but roots must be out of water. A table near a windowsill shaded from hot sun would be an ideal position. They need some feeding: a good regime is a general-purpose liquid feed at half strength for three consecutive waterings, flushing out (so no feed) any remaining minerals on the fourth watering.

Dendrobium (orchid) Water weekly with tepid water (rainwater ideally) including a proprietary feed when in active growth. Remove dying flowers only when they are falling off – do not pull them off. When flowering is over, do not cut back the stem as new shoots will develop into flowers next year. Repot no more often than every two years as they like to be pot-bound. A north facing windowsill is a good place for them.

Eryngium (sea holly) Take root cuttings. They do not like being wet over winter so surround with a dry mulch avoiding the crown. If the dried seed heads are still in place, remove them now.

***Euonymus alatus, E. europaeus, E. phellomanus* (spindle tree)** Shoots of deciduous euonymus can be thinned to maintain the shape. Its winged corky branches are part of the charm of this small tree or large shrub.

Gooseberry Consult a pruning book for new gooseberry bushes. On established plants, choose a dry day to prune. They fruit on older wood at the base of spurs made last year. Cut these spurs back to four buds and cut the main stems back just a little to remove the spores of any sawfly larvae overwintering on the shoot tips. Aim for an open goblet shape with eight to ten main branches: thin out the centre, take out dead, crossing and gnarled unproductive three- to four-year-old wood, low lying branches, straggly stems and any that would touch the soil. Aim for a clear 'leg' of about 7 cm/3 inches at the base of the bush. Mulch and feed monthly with sulphate of potash, avoiding nitrogenous feeds that encourage soft growth. Take hardwood cuttings now. Avoid planting in frost pockets.

Hawthorn (*Crataegus monogyna*) It can be trimmed hard to make an impenetrable barrier or just cut back to size – do so now before nesting begins and after the birds have taken the berries.

Hazel: contorted (*Corylus avellana* 'Contorta') With a mature contorted

hazel, consider whether its decorative effect could be improved with one of the stems removed from the bottom. They can begin to look elephantine when in full leaf. They are easier to prune now when shapes and outlines can be fully appreciated. On the other hand, pruning now encourages the growth of lots of new straight stems which have to be cut out. Done in August when in full leaf, it is much harder to see what to do, but making new growth is not the shrub's priority at that time so it produces little to contend with. Take your choice.

Hippeastrum (amaryllis) As they finish, cut off the dead heads leaving the flower stem and leaves intact, still watering, feeding and keeping in good light. When the stem dies back, cut that off too, leaving any leaves intact. When the leaves finally start to yellow, remove them and let the bulb go into dormancy in the same pot – it likes congestion. Keep dry and dark (under a bench, for example). If the leaves do not die right back, occasionally water and feed, keeping the leaves just going until summer when they will still need their period of dormancy, so then stop watering and move them into some dark. Every few years, repot and divide any offsets when in dormancy.

If a bulb is still waiting to be planted, get it in by the end of January (see October for planting tips). Water well, then leave alone – both bulb and roots hate sitting in wet, so water again only when the leaves start to grow. Put the plant somewhere warm (15–18°C). After it has finished flowering, proceed as in the paragraph above, starting it back into growth again in October.

Hyacinth Hyacinths in the house need pea sticks to stop larger spikes flopping

Iris reticulata 'Katharine Hodgkin' (flowering January–February)

over. Keep them cool. When over, plant the bulbs in the garden with some extra grit, leaving the leaves intact.

Iris
- Bearded iris: if soil has frozen round the rhizomes, they may have risen out of the ground a little. Do not force them back down but wait until it has thawed to apply a layer of gritty mulch around them.
- *Iris unguicularis*: cut away some of their leaves to better expose the flowers of these early gems. Slugs like the flowers so pick them before they do and bring into the house to unfold.

Lemon tree (citrus) Clean its leaves of any undesirables: soft scale insects on the leaves' undersides can be picked off by hand and the excreted honeydew which grows into sooty mould can be washed off with soapy water. Remove any weak shoots, replace the top 5 cm/2 inches of compost with new John Innes No. 3 compost and gently water, still keeping it in a cool light place under cover where the temperature remains between 7 and 10°C. Ensure that the pot is not sitting in water.

Lilac (*Syringa vulgaris*) Winter is a good time to do regenerative pruning, taking out some stems from the bottom, any stems straying from the main clump, suckers and twiggy growth, crossing or crowded stems. To rejuvenate completely, cut as low down as you like but above the graft union if it is grafted. Apply a balanced fertilizer and mulch afterwards. It will sulk for a year or two.

Lily Bulbs can be planted in pots and kept in a cool greenhouse or somewhere sheltered. Use new compost, ensuring that lily beetle or vine weevil is not being rehoused. Check planting depth and pH requirements as lilies vary in their needs.

Mathiasella bupleuroides Take root cuttings if the ground is not frozen. They may be quite thick. Ensure they are placed the right way up in a pot filled with very gritty compost. Put the cuttings in a cold frame or outside under cover to pot up when shoots appear.

Pansy: winter flowering (Viola)
Deadhead and remove weather damaged flowers. What is left will look much brighter.

Phalaenopsis (moth orchid) The light and humidity of a bathroom suit them. When the flowers die, the stems should be cut back, three nodes up from the base, being watered and misted occasionally. When the roots are green they are moist, when they are silver grey they may need a little water, and when they are brown they are dead, probably from overwatering. Roots that stick into the air are fine. See Cymbidium above for orchid dislikes.

Potato In late January in warm areas and February in cooler parts, lay out early potatoes with the 'eye' uppermost, leaving them to chit in a cool, light, frost-free place – egg boxes are useful for this – to get ready for planting in six weeks or so. Leave all shoots on if lots of small potatoes are wanted, but rub off most if bumper size is called for.

Privet (Ligustrum) Provided it is not frozen, this is a good time to cut privet which needs renovation – it can be pruned hard now to encourage new basal growth. Do only one side in a year if the job is dramatic. Its twice yearly trim is done in warmer weather.

***Prunus incisa* 'Kojo-no-mai', *P. serrula*, *P.* × *subhirtella* 'Autumnalis' (ornamental cherry)** Remove crossing branches and ill-placed shoots now, only if the fungal disease silver leaf is not a problem (and you can detect its presence if there is a brown core running through the stem of a cut branch; on the whole, it attacks one branch at a time). If you think silver leaf is present, delay pruning until summer when wounds heal faster. They can have their trunks scrubbed or pressure washed to reveal their ornamental bark.

Rhubarb In early January, on a mature plant, a pot can be put over the top to force it for sweet stems in March. This can only be done every other year as forcing weakens it. We use an old chimney pot, but terracotta forcing pots are available and very attractive.

***Romneya coulteri* (California poppy)** The seed heads are interesting in early winter but now start to look ragged. However, the plant needs top growth for protection so do not cut right down until April. Just trim the top.

Salix (willow) Willow trees can be pruned at any time during the winter, but January is as good a time as any to pollard, coppice or give them an annual prune. If a lot is to be cut out, spread it over a few years to prevent a forest of water shoots. Salix will put on a lot of growth wherever it is cut. These cuttings can be used as plant supports if they are kept for a few months in the dark – used fresh they will root like any hardwood cutting.

Snowdrop (Galanthus) Clear the area around snowdrops of fallen leaves and vegetation so their emergence is exuberant.

***Solanum crispum* 'Glasnevin', *S. laxum* 'Album'** Resist the temptation to tidy up either form until spring – any dead looking leaves will provide essential protection over winter. The white version is infinitely more tender.

Strawberry Spread sulphate of potash around the plants to encourage good flowering and fruits.

Sweet pea Seeds sown in October will have made a lot of gangly growth. For years I thought the top leaves should be pinched out to make sturdier plants, but Roger Parsons, author of *Sweet Peas: An Essential Guide* (2011), encourages us to cut back these early plants by half in late January/early February, having allowed them to grow on until this point (tied to a short cane). He explains that pinching back autumn sown plants as they grow encourages premature side shoot development. Check they are not drying out as they wait in a cool spot (such as a cold frame) to go into the soil. There is still time to sow seeds in deep pots, loo rolls or root-trainers; these late sowings will be helped by some bottom heat but keep them cool after germination. In a heated greenhouse they will become increasingly less hardy.

Tibouchina If it has been indoors all winter, flowering will be over. It can be pruned hard to the desired shape. Nodal cuttings can be taken (reduce the size of the leaves on the cuttings). Repot if need be, but it does not enjoy the experience and sulks.

Weeping pear (*Pyrus salicifolia 'Pendula'*) If pruned well from the start, a weeping pear can be a work of art. It needs a clear trunk up to 1.75 m/6 ft before it starts to weep, so branches up to that height need to be removed and nascent buds rubbed off. Reference to a pruning book when planting will be a great help. I have seen it done so beautifully that every spoke of the 'umbrella' appears to be evident when denuded of leaves, and when in leaf the beautiful white flowers are perfectly set off against the silvery leaves. They can, however, quickly become a tremendous muddle of branches which is difficult to retrieve, as mature trees do not respond well to hard pruning. Even so, the crown will need thinning. Start at the top taking out dead or diseased branches. Then take out any going directly upwards, horizontally outwards or too stridently across other branches. Cut where the upward growth originates provided that is not going to leave an ugly stub, in which case take the cut still further back. Move under the canopy to remove dead, diseased and crossing wood from within. Its habit of growth is zigzag, so pause before too much else is done. Stand back to consider where it is unbalanced, and then, from within, take out a branch where it appears too thick or heavy, selecting one where there is another near it springing outwards that will avoid a hole being made. A gap in a mature tree will probably not be filled. Finally, lift the skirt a few feet from the ground but not too high or it looks silly. The aim is for the look of a waterfall.

Helleborus x *ericsmithii*
Flowering now and into March, its care has a specific reference in December.

FEBRUARY

Gleaming like jewels in sharp light are crocus, *Cyclamen coum*, daphne, hellebore, *Iris reticulata*, *Narcissus* 'Rijnveld's Early Sensation', sarcococca, snowdrops, winter honeysuckle, early white camellia, the berries of skimmia, winter clematis, colourful catkins of alder and hazel and so much else. As days lengthen and cold strengthens, there is much to do to prepare for the explosion of spring. Collapsed perennials that sheltered wildlife and provided winter outline can go, some pruning can be done before bud burst, borders can be tucked under a duvet of mulch. Embrace the chance to work in the garden.

AREAS TO CONSIDER

Borders On wide borders put a plank across to work off or have a piece of wood to step on – anything to prevent compaction underfoot. Beds not mulched earlier because they were full of standing plants can be covered now with compost or leafmould if the soil is not frozen or heavy (heavy soils are best done in March). Cut back herbaceous plants left for winter interest, but leave all top growth on anything even slightly tender to give it extra frost protection (this includes penstemon, salvia, verbena, and anything silver leaved or with a hollow stem).

Climbers Trim and tidy deciduous climbers that flower after June. Seeds of tender climbers can be sown but should be kept warm until they are hardened off when frosts are over. Hardier climbers can be sown and, after germination, put in a cold frame.

Compost heap Hedgehogs and frogs could be overwintering in the compost heap so wait until spring to turn it. Cover if it gets too wet – if there are red worms at the top it is probably too soggy. (The worms are good to have in the heap.)

Alnus incana 'Aurea' (golden alder catkins)

Deciduous trees, shrubs and hedges Finish planting bare-root deciduous trees and shrubs by the end of February. Finish their pruning and moving too.

Ferns Remove any dead/damaged fronds on hardy evergreen ferns, leaving them on those few which are slightly tender (such as *Athyrium niponicum* 'Pictum', *Dryopteris erythrosora*, woodwardia and, of course, tree ferns). Totally hardy deciduous ferns can be cut back to reveal their 'rusty knuckles' (Val Bourne's lovely expression) ready for new growth to unfurl. The Fern Nursery in Lincolnshire has much helpful information.

Fruit trees: free standing with and without stones Young fruit trees with stones should have formative pruning in late February, though mature trees are pruned in summer. See a pruning book for more detail.

Grasses: deciduous In late February and all through March, the most hardy deciduous grasses can be cut to the ground before the new shoots appear. Take account of the weather and specific garden conditions – in some areas, grasses will be cut much earlier than in others. If they have started pushing, try to avoid cutting new growth. These include calamagrostis, chasmanthium, deschampsia, hakonechloa, molinia, panicum and phalaris. Do not divide until they are actively growing.

Hedges Prune or trim deciduous and mixed hedges just before they come out of dormancy to boost their energy and encourage new buds on pruned wood. To renovate existing hedges, cut back the top and do one side per year. Yew can be cut hard into old wood, but for complete renovation spread over two or three years. Feed evergreen hedges with a balanced fertilizer such as Fish, Blood and Bone provided the ground is not frozen or waterlogged.

Lawns Spike areas of lawn worn from use, diverting footfall to allow the area to recover as growth begins. Squelchy patches of mud need decompacting to improve drainage: they will not just go away. Repair edges if not frosty or wet and fork out perennial weeds.

Mulching This is a good time to mulch lighter soils (leave heavier soils until March). Avoid grasses, alpines, Mediterranean plants, eryngium, salvia and others that dislike cold wet conditions. Leafmould is especially good round acidic loving plants. Never mulch when the ground is frozen. Ensure mulch does not build up round the trunks/stems of trees and shrubs.

Plastic plant pots The virtuous will keep pests and diseases at bay by washing pots (and greenhouse) with a disinfectant such as Citrox to reduce bacteria and spores. Pots can be stored horizontally in long snakes supported in guttering to avoid tall wobbly, cluttering piles.

Pollarding With trees' food reserves high, this is a good time to pollard. A pruning book will help. Wait for three years after planting before starting. Angle cuts so water runs off, cutting just above the previous pollarding wound. Many trees are suitable, including alder, catalpa, eucalyptus, lime, London plane, mulberry, paulownia and willow.

Seed sowing Some hardy annuals, such as sweet peas if not yet sown, can be sown this early in trays or modules, under cover with good light (they will become drawn and weak if there insufficient light). Seeds catch up quickly, however, when sown in March or even April, and sowing then will achieve later flowering and helps with succession planting. Hardy annual seeds will not need a propagator to germinate – sunlight rather than warmth is the key (silver foil under the tray also increases the light). A cool greenhouse or cool windowsill will produce tougher plants than those raised in a heated environment. Use tap water, letting it stand for a bit so any chlorine can evaporate. Seedlings respond to attention – as do trees – an occasional sweep of movement through the young leaves makes their roots stronger. (Tony Kirkham can be seen at Kew giving a young tree a friendly shake to strengthen its roots: it is the same principle.) In due course (next month) pinch out the growing tips when seedlings are about 5 cm/2 inches to make them bushier, pricking them out before they get crowded.

Seeds of herbaceous perennials such as delphiniums, hollyhocks, kniphofia and lupins can be started in a propagator at 15°C, then hardened off and grown on in a cold frame. See also 'Vegetables' below. Loo rolls make good short-term root trainers – seedlings can go straight in the soil in them undisturbed. They do not work well for overwintering seedlings as the cardboard collapses before planting time.

Vegetables Seeds of, for example, beetroot, early carrots, lettuce and peas can be sown in modules ready to go out under fleece in March. Early variety peas, started in guttering with drainage holes punched in, can be slid into a trench when the soil warms up. This is a good time to add lime to the soil to increase alkalinity where needed; it helps to reduce club root disease in brassicas. Some crops may need netting against the ravages of pigeons. Applying Sulphur Veg to vegetables after planting out increases their resistance to disease. Sulphur is a key element in their growth, prevents yellowing of leaves and increases f lavour – it is also good for our health – but the dosage on the package must be followed closely.

Watering Newly planted trees and shrubs need watering unless it is really wet. Wind has a very drying effect, and rain seldom makes up for a bucket of water. Plants preferring acidic soil (there are many but examples include camellia, ceanothus, magnolia, pieris and rhododendron) prefer rainwater, particularly when they are still very young, so it is well worth having a water butt or collection point somewhere.

Weeding Weedkillers are unlikely to be effective now – hand weeding is much more reliable. Mulch after weeding to discourage new growth.

Winter bedding In late February give a liquid fertilizer to winter bedding plants such as pansies, pompom daisies, primroses, violas and wallflowers. Deadhead to encourage new flowers and help prevent grey mould. Remove flowers damaged by the weather.

PLANTS

Abeliophyllum distichum **(white forsythia)** Tie in wall-trained plants. Protect flowering stems against a hard frost. Flowers are produced in late winter, so do not on any account prune the leafless stems, which even now can look a bit dead, just before they flower.

Actinidia kolomikta Prune if necessary, removing weak, crossing or overcrowded growth, retaining at least five strong stems at the base on which laterals can be reduced by two-thirds. It responds well to drastic pruning.

Agastache (giant hyssop) Cut back any tall growth left standing over winter, but leave in place some winter protection round the crown.

Amelanchier Feed and mulch with a balanced fertilizer. They enjoy a heavy soil but dislike conditions that are always wet.

Apple and pear: free-standing
Maintain a circle round each young tree (old ones too, if possible) free of competing weeds and grasses. If mulching with wood chippings, do not use a systemic glyphosate-based herbicide such as Roundup to kill grass smothered beneath it – soaked into the chippings, it then reaches the tree roots. The only really safe method is to hand weed the area or carefully weedkill and only then mulch with the chippings. For good flower and fruit formation, fork in sulphate of potash before adding the mulch. Avoid a build-up of mulch around the trunk.

Apricot Late in the month feed with a balanced fertilizer. The blossom is very early, before the leaves, which presents two problems: lack of pollinators and frost. Unless the tree has a wall to protect it, it could need to be covered with fleece and therefore be hand pollinated. If thinking about planting an apricot, discuss its early pruning with the nursery from which it comes.

Arbutus unedo (strawberry tree)
Remove any wayward or crossing shoots to maintain a healthy framework. Do this now when the plant is dormant. It responds well to firm pruning, but do not leave it too late, as the wood carrying last autumn's flowers will now be forming this autumn's fruits. Wind is its only real enemy, so plant where it will have some shelter. Preferring acidic soil, it copes with alkaline. It surprised me to learn that this is one of Britain's native trees.

Aster divaricatus (now called *Eurybia divaricata*) So useful in dry shade, cut the stems back close to ground level from late February through to the end of March and mulch. Divide every four years or so.

Auricula As they come into growth and until flowering, give a half-strength balanced liquid feed every two weeks. In late February pull off any faded leaves and give the plants a soaking from the bottom. Wear gloves as auriculas can induce permanent numbness in the fingers. Thereafter, water regularly but always avoid the surface of the leaves.

Baptisia australis (blue wild indigo)
Cut off the seed pods and stems, having enjoyed their outline over winter, and mulch with leafmould (new plants especially). It prefers acid/neutral soil, and leafmould is more acidic than garden compost. As with all leguminaceae, it fixes nitrogen in the soil so does not need extra feeding.

Beech (*Fagus sylvatica*) During dormancy a beech hedge can be renovated if needed (before the birds start nesting in it). Stagger work over a couple of years, one side and top one year, the

other side the next. Clear out debris from beneath, feed with a balanced fertilizer such as Fish, Blood and Bone and mulch.

Bergenia (elephant's ears) Nip off brown or damaged old foliage so the plant can set off spring bulbs prettily.

Blackcurrant Pruning in the first year needs reference to a pruning book. Prune established bushes before bud burst. Remove crossing or weak stems and any touching the ground to improve air circulation. They fruit best on shoots made the previous summer, so over the years remove the oldest shoots (dark and less smooth) to 2.5 cm/1 inch from the ground, for a gradual renewal of wood and to prevent it getting overcrowded. Avoid hoeing round the bush as it has shallow roots – hand weeding is better. Sprinkle with sulphate of potash or wood ash and a balanced fertilizer.

Blueberry Blueberries need acid soil – ideally pH 5.5 – so if your garden soil is unsuitable plant in containers using an ericaceous soil-based compost. Leave one- and two-year-old plants to get established, but prune mature plants now that the leaf bud (slim) and the fruit bud (plumper) are distinguishable. Fruit is made on last year's side shoots and the tips of this year's growth. The young red stems are pretty, so remove just one or two of the oldest brown stems from the bottom, plus any damaged or wrongly placed stems and any that are horizontal or likely to touch the soil when carrying fruit. Remove the accumulation of twiggy growth that carried fruit last year and the tips of the side shoots they come off (to an upward-facing bud). Cut down any canes too high to manage to a strong outward-facing bud at a reachable height. Feed with a balanced ericaceous fertilizer, then fork in composted bark, pine needles or leafmould. The hardest thing to do is to remove all the fruit buds for the first two years after planting to get a strong plant established. Plant a minimum of two for good pollination even if the label says one plant is enough; it will crop better with two. Use rainwater not tap.

Box Remove debris from under box hedges, cutting out and binning any dead stems. Shake the bushes to remove twigs and leaves lodged within to get air circulating through the plants. Then feed. A dried or liquid seaweed fertilizer is a good one to use as the trace elements and all the key nutrients the plant requires are immediately available. Ring the changes and see which fertilizer you like. Fish, Blood and Bone would also be appropriate. If there is no rain, water or hoe in well, taking care not to damage the roots near the surface.

This is a good time to thin box if some sections have got too large. Lift each plant, split it and replant the division a little deeper than it was before, back in the same hole replenished with compost mixed with leafmould and bone meal. Water well.

Brassica: broccoli, cabbage, cauliflower If the soil is acidic, apply lime to reduce the opportunity for club root. Follow instructions precisely, aiming for a pH of 6.5–7.5, referring if necessary to expert advice.

Broad bean Plant out under a cover or cloche those which germinated in January. They like the cold wet soil.

Calamagrostis Cut this grass down to the ground now. It should be divided every three years or so to maintain its vigour, but do this only when growth begins in spring.

Campsis × tagliabuana 'Madame Galen' This does best on a sunny south-facing wall or pergola so that its new growth ripens fully. It can be pruned back hard now, even to two buds on each lateral, as it makes lots of new growth before flowering in late summer. Take out any weak or damaged stems to the base of the climber, afterwards mulching its roots. It can be cut right back to 30 cm/ 12 inches from the ground to encourage basal growth. In very cold weather protect new growth with a dry mulch.

Cardoon (Cynara cardunculus) The young shoots can be dug up and divided, slicing them apart, each bit with some good roots. Pot them up in a soil-based compost (that is, one that is quite light to handle) and keep above 5°C for six weeks before planting them out and they will get away very fast. Cardoons are slightly more architectural than globe artichokes, their leaves being more elegant and silvery, but their buds are not so good to eat.

Carex (sedge) Do not cut back the evergreen species of carex, but comb through to pull out, with a gloved hand, the debris of last year.

Catalpa This can be made into a small tree or low shrub with considerable impact in its large leaves by pollarding or coppicing now (provided the weather is not freezing). Start when it is three years old with, maybe, five branches as a framework. At Wisley they coppice these branches to two to three buds.

Cercidiphyllum Cut any wayward or crossing stems back to a junction as well as any that are too low.

Cercis canadensis It needs to go in the right place when young as it dislikes being moved. *Cercis canadensis* f. *alba* 'Royal White' and *C.c.* 'Forest Pansy' are two good examples. It does not need annual pruning but can be pruned now to take out crossing branches and to achieve a more accommodating shape. Take care not to take out so much that it loses its natural gracefulness.

Chaenomeles (Japanese quince)

In late February or early March flower buds can be seen forming on the older shoots. These shoots should be cut back to the flower buds. Any shoots without flower buds should be cut back by half to encourage buds next year.

Chasmanthium This grass can be cut down in late winter. It can be divided (every three years) as soon as growth begins. Doing so will maintain is vigour.

Cherry

- Acid (morello): feed with sulphate of potash every year and with superphosphate every third year.
- Sweet: provided the soil is not frozen, feed cherries (and other fruit trees) with a balanced general fertilizer such as Growmore around their rooting area. Follow with a deep mulch, leaving a clear space around the trunk.

Chimonanthus praecox (wintersweet)

Cut branches and bring them into the house to enjoy the fragrance. On established plants, immediately after flowering, thin spindly shoots and shorten older branches by 15–30 cm/6–12 inches. Feed with a balanced fertilizer. The late Christopher Lloyd did not consider regular pruning necessary, but wrote that he cut a forty-year-old specimen to the ground 'and it never looked back'. I wonder if even he was apprehensive when he did so – I suspect not at all.

Chrysanthemum Those taken in as 'stools' over winter can be started back into growth under cover, with a little water and warmth of the sun through glass. Over the next few weeks there will be good cutting material in the basal shoots that will make excellent new plants. Slice off shoots near the base and put them around the outside of a pot of moist compost containing 50 per cent grit, cover with a plastic bag (use sticks to keep the bag from touching the cuttings) and water from below (put into trays or on to capillary matting). When good roots are evident, pot them on individually, keeping them light and frost free until they are planted out in May.

Clematis Clematis fall into three groups depending on their flowering time. Provided its group is known (it will be on the label), it can be pruned correctly. There is pruning to be done for some between February and mid-March depending on the weather. Always cut just above a healthy pair of buds.

- All newly planted clematis, whatever their group, should be pruned down to 15–30 cm/6–12 inches, just above a strong pair of leaf buds, in their first February–March.
- Group 3 need pruning hard now (avoid frosty weather). Cut out all the old growth, clipping to just above healthy buds – knee height or lower. If left unpruned the flowers and seed heads will become out of reach.
- Group 2 can have a light tidy, taking out dead or spindly growth, cutting to strong growth buds in leaf axils but leaving a full framework.
- Group 1 is left alone. If *Clematis rehderiana* needs cutting down from the tree into which it has grown, do this now, but if the size is pleasing, leave it.
- After this pruning or tweaking, apply a slow release fertilizer such as bone meal and mulch with compost or leafmould.

Clerodendrum trichotomum var. *fargesii*

On planting, prune it before the end of the month (before the buds break), cutting back to a healthy bud at the height you wish the branches to start growing: 60 cm/24 inches or more. The next year, as it gets established, leave about six side shoots to create a good form for the tree and take off the rest. Shorten these side shoots to their highest pair of buds. Then let it grow away – I love it – it is a beautiful tree for a small garden. No routine pruning is needed thereafter except to cut off crossing or damaged branches, which is done this month. Take care digging around it as damaged roots encourage suckers, which need excavating and tearing from the parent. Suckers become a menace but are good for propagation.

Cobaea scandens (cup and saucer plant) Sow seeds horizontally, one to a pot, cover thinly with compost, cover with clingfilm and put in a propagator in the light (or give them some bottom heat). After germination provide a stake to twine on to and grow on in a greenhouse that does not fall below freezing, to plant out in May.

Cyclamen This is a good time to plant (or move) cyclamen when they have roots (rather than as dry tubers). *Cyclamen coum* will have flowers and leaves, *C. hederifolium* will have leaves. Plant about 2.5 cm/1 inch deep in well-drained soil which has shade in summer. Mulch but do not feed. House plant cyclamen are seldom hardy in the garden.

Cytisus battandieri (now called Argyrocytisus battandieri) (pineapple broom) Remedial pruning should be done now. To reduce its size, an older stem can be cut back to a younger side shoot and that shoot trained as a leader, but it does not respond well or prettily to hard pruning.

Deschampsia Cut back this grass removing all the ancient flower heads. Left too long, new shoots start coming through, making the job harder. To maintain its vigour, divide it every three years as it starts into growth. Divisions will need to be watered in well. Plants do not last forever. The leaves of *Deschampsia cespitosa* are vicious, so wear gloves.

Edgeworthia (paper bush) Best on acid soil with sun and shelter from wind, sulphur chips scattered around its base any time twice a year will help this ravishing shrub flower better on neutral/alkaline soils. Ensure the plant is not crowded.

Epimedium Early in the month, before the spring growth is in gear, trim over with shears those epimedium that cover the ground in agreeable bulk to remove last years's leaves. Do not leave it any later as it is easy to cut off the nascent flower shoots. I prefer to do a selective cut, removing the older and damaged leaves so that the clump is not so thick. This too will reveal the flowers as they emerge. Though they look more fragile, the numerous Chinese and Japanese species like *Epimedium grandiflorum*, which do not cover the ground in the same way, are in fact bone hardy. Even so, leave their leaves in place; they can look pretty and delicate and will protect flowers being caught by frost (particularly important with the early flowering 'Pink Elf'). Feed with a balanced fertilizer and mulch around the cut stalks with leafmould.

Eucalyptus dalrympleana, E. gunni, E. parvifolia, E. paucifolia, E. pulvurulenta (gum tree) Between February and March (before the plants are in active growth), eucalpytus can be coppiced or pollarded to control its size and to keep the juvenile (round rather than narrow) leaves. It needs to be between two and eight years old before starting. The RHS and Grafton Nursery in Worcestershire are two excellent sources of advice (also on how to prune a eucalyptus to achieve beautiful bark when grown as a unpollarded tree). Left alone it will grow very fast.

Festuca glauca Do not cut this grass back but clean out the dead stems and debris of last year with a gloved hand.

Filipendula rubra (meadowsweet) Cut stems down to the ground ready for new growth. It loves a permanently moist soil and will spread, so site with care.

Fuchsia: tender varieties If a warm shed or greenhouse is available, start to bring tender fuchsias out of dormancy, refreshing some of the compost with new, increasing water and feeding with a balanced fertilizer like Fish, Blood and Bone. If there is no warm place, wait until April.

Galega officinalis 'Alba' (goat's rue) Though it seems to sulk a little after division, it is best divided every three years between January and March. I find the white flowers have much greater impact than the mauve.

Garlic Sulphate of potash will avert lush growth at the expense of the bulb.

Gentian Remove any remaining yellow leaves surrounding the autumn flowering gentians such as *Gentiana × macaulayi* and the willow gentian, *G. asclepiadea*. Put grit around them and around spring flowering gentians native to mountainsides, such as *G. verna* and *G. acaulis*. These earlier flowering gentians tolerate a pH of 6.5+, but almost all autumn flowering ones need more acidic soil. They all like sharp drainage. Edrom Nurseries in Scotland, who are extremely helpful about growing gentians, say that in the north of the UK species can grow in full sun provided they are not too dry. They add that spring flowering gentians (*G. acaulis, G. angustifolia, G. dinarica*) will cope with sun anywhere in the UK, provided they do not dry out.

Hakonechloa Its brown leaves are good in winter but should be cut back late in February to make way for new growth. Divide this grass, if necessary, only when it starts into growth later in the spring.

Halesia (snowdrop tree) Halesia characteristically forms multi-stems from the base. When young, choose one to form a strong leader unless you want it shrub-like. Remove crossing branches and any that spoil the shape now when dormant. It prefers acid soil. The bees love it.

Hamamelis (witch hazel) They do not need pruning, but before the leaves appear they can be reduced in size. Cut back branches to two leaf buds up from the start of last year's growth (leaf buds are longer and thinner than the fat, rounder flower buds). Prune out weak/damaged branches and any that cross and, if necessary, two or three of the longer branches to well-placed side branches. As it flowers on spurs and one-year-old wood, there will be fewer flowers for a few years after significant pruning. Resist doing too much in any one year and nothing until the plant is established. Feed with a balanced fertilizer like Fish, Blood and Bone and mulch with leafmould. When planting, keep the graft union above soil level (unlike with roses) or it may produce suckers.

Hepatica Cut off any tatty leaves with scissors to give space for flowers. Feed with a potash-rich fertilizer to promote flowering or consider calcified seaweed, which is rich in trace elements as well as the essential nutrients and also raises the pH (they like alkaline soil). It is worth checking that the seaweed comes from a sustainable source.

Heptacodium miconioides (seven son flower of Zhejiang) This small tree or large shrub can be pruned hard in winter – down to a framework to get larger leaves and more impressive flowering. Otherwise, remove twiggy growth (it gets very brittle) and shape it a little, taking out badly positioned branches.

Hamamelis x *intermedia* 'Diane' (red witch hazel, flowering January–February)

Holly (Ilex) Late winter, when berries are over, is a good time to do light trimming and shaping of holly and to cut out any diseased branches. Harder clipping – of hedges and topiary – is better done in late summer. Holly can only be shaped well if started as a young plant. Trying to cut arches into ancient holly trees does not work.

Hydrangea
* *Hydrangea arborescens* (including *H.a.* 'Annabelle'): flowering on growth to be made this year, they can be cut down to about 30 cm/12 inches from the ground – too low and they become spindly. Next year prune one bud up from this year's cut to create a low framework. Feed with a liquid seaweed fertilizer or otherwise a general purpose fertilizer, and mulch.

* *H. paniculata*: flowering on this season's growth, it can be pruned any time in winter but *H. paniculata* has excellent dried flower heads so I prune it about now. With a new plant, cut out crossing branches and reduce the stems by half to get a good shape to start the framework. On plants more than two years old, cut down now to a framework of the previous year's wood, leaving two pairs of buds on each stalk. Feed as above and mulch well.

Hypericum (St John's wort) *Hypericum calycinum* (rose of Sharon) can be cut down to a few inches – the more shoots it produces, the more flowers there will be.

***Iris danfordiae, I. histrioides, I. reticulata* (winter flowering iris)**
Mulch around flower stems to prevent rain

spoiling flowers. Slug protection is a good idea. Feed with a potash-rich fertilizer to promote flower development. These iris are happy in some shade and seem impervious to snow though they hate being moved.

Ivy (Hedera) Ivy will not kill a tree unless it brings the canopy down with its weight. It can, however, obscure pretty bark. If it needs reducing, do it before the nesting season, cutting the stems (with a saw probably) at ground level and again a few inches above so the cut cannot join up again. Paint the bottom cut with a tough weedkiller like Vitax SBK Brushwood Killer. Leave it to die *in situ*, as pulling it off does damage. Leave trimming for awhile as the berries are an important food source for birds (as were the autumn flowers).

Lily Pot up any bulbs stored over winter (check planting depth for the species), using leafmould and sharp sand under and above the bulbs; then keep cool and protect the pots from getting too wet (cover with something waterproof or cardboard you can replace). For those already in the ground but not yet showing, a dose of liquid slug deterrent would be good. Next month is the last moment to plant lilies: they need to be settled in before growth begins.

Lime (Tilia) Limes, pleached or otherwise, are easiest to prune in late February when it is possible to see the structure (having had full enjoyment of the red twigged limes). If pollarding, do it yearly, cutting all growth back to just above the previous year's cut. When pleaching, cut shoots going in the wrong direction to base, vertical growth right back to two or three buds and, being ruthless, all but the laterals needed for the form. Do not try to bend stems to your will but cut it to your will. It will respond well though it now looks skeletal.

The limes that do not attract aphids (and therefore do not drop honeydew on cars parked beneath) include *Tilia × euchlora, T. oliveri, T. platyphyllos* and *T. tomentosa. T. cordata*, the small leaved lime, is well regarded for pleaching. When pollarding, ensure the cutting blade of the secateur is beside the edge to be cut. *T. × europaea*, the common lime, usually produces a dense growth of shoots from the base and in the centre of the tree. These can all be taken off, cutting right back to the trunk.

***Limnanthes douglasii* (poached egg plant)** Sow seeds now for planting out in April. Once established, it should self-seed every year.

***Liquidambar styraciflua* (sweet gum)** Stake if it is new to ensure good straight growth as a young tree. Prune gently into shape now, taking off any broken twiggy branches close to the trunk. Do not let it dry out. It prefers neutral to acid soil, so although it will grow perfectly well on alkaline soil, it may not colour quite so dramatically. (On alkaline soil good colouring is helped by the addition of flowers of sulphur or sulphur chips round the base twice annually.) The corky wings on its branches are natural growth.

Mistletoe Rub fresh berries into a crevice on an apple tree branch. After a year or two leaves of a new mistletoe plant may emerge (do not be tempted to try it at Christmas – that is too early).

Molinia Cut down now. It will look like a little hedgehog. Every three years, to maintain its vigour, divide this grass as the soil begins to warm up in spring.

Narcissus bulbocodium, N. cyclamineus These species like acid conditions so in alkaline soils grow them in tubs. Conversely, *N. jonquilla* and *N. tazetta* prefer it slightly alkaline.

Most narcissi like any soil, but it is worth checking.

Nicotiana (tobacco plant) A tray of seeds – *Nicotiana alata, N. langsdorffii, N. mutabilis, N. sylvestris* – sown on the surface of compost now will give such pleasure in autumn. They need to be pricked out and potted on twice, but this effort pays dividends when autumn comes.

Pampas grass (*Cortaderia richardii, C. selloana*) In late February, with thick gloves, goggles and a strong rake, tease out dead foliage and thatch without damaging new growth. Every four to six years prune hard back and new foliage will grow. Some people advocate burning the clump, but the RHS advises against this. Mulch afterwards.

Panicum Cut down before new growth begins. Wait until spring to divide this grass.

Pansy: winter flowering (Viola) Continue to deadhead, cutting back straggly winter growth.

***Parrotia persica* (Persian ironwood)** Look out for its tiny, easily missed scarlet flowers opening from small black flower buds. Take out any crossing or broken branches. It tends to be multi-stemmed. Stake on planting. 'Vanessa' is a columnar cultivar, suitable for a smaller garden.

Passion flower (Passiflora) For plants grown under glass, shorten side shoots to two or three buds from last year's growth.

Paulownia (foxglove tree) It can be coppiced or pollarded annually between January and March to keep the leaves large and juvenile. Start when it is a three years old. The first time take professional advice.

Peach, nectarine and almond Feed with a balanced general fertilizer, mulch and spray against the fungal disease peach leaf curl to reduce spores overwintering on the bark.

Pelargonium As pelargoniums are woken up, repot any that are pot-bound, ideally using a good quality John Innes No. 2 compost and adding 25 per cent extra grit. Terracotta pots are better, not just because they look good but because excess moisture evaporates through the clay. Start cutting back, tidying and lightly watering them. Do not feed until growth begins.

Peony: tree peony Tree peonies are hungry feeders. As buds swell in late February into March, feed with a balanced fertilizer such as Growmore. Do not take off any shoots for their first two years. After that, dead or weak stems can be taken down to a healthy bud. If they have become too large, cut out some of the thickest, oldest stems at the base. They respond well to pruning but not to being snipped.

Plumbago auriculata Cut last year's growth back to two or three buds from the main framework and tie in the laterals you want to keep. It flowers on this year's growth.

Primula: Candelabra and polyanthus If not done in the autumn, gently pull away last year's tired looking leaves. For best results feed with a weak solution of a potash-rich fertilizer like Tomorite every ten days from when the buds start forming to when the first flowers open. Then feed once at the end of flowering but not thereafter (not even if there is a second flowering as feeding then will promote soft growth before winter).

Raspberry: autumn (fruit on current year's wood) Cut all canes to the ground, having left them standing over winter. Feed with sulphate of potash and mulch round their bases, but not over the top of the cut canes in case they rot.

Raspberry: summer (fruit on last year's wood) Prune the weak tips of each cane off at a bud. Training canes along wires increases harvest, but there is often not room to do this. Tips of canes should ideally be about 7 cm/3 inches apart. Take out any weak canes remaining after last year's late summer pruning, leaving about four to six canes on every stool.

Redcurrant and whitecurrant
Prune just before bud burst. Differing from blackcurrants (which grow from lots of shoots below ground), these grow from a single 'leg' of about 5 cm/2 inches. In the first year choose four good branches and remove the rest – difficult but do it – then cut these branches in half. In the second year prune back new growth on all leaders by half to an outward facing bud. Thereafter, remove dead wood and crossing branches, opening up the centre, cutting all leaders by about a third and side shoots to two buds from the previous year's growth. If the leaders are bending down, cut them to an upward facing bud to arrest the trend. Remove any branches touching the ground. They fruit in the axils of spurs off the main branches on two- to three-year-old wood, so if there is congestion start taking out the very oldest shoots at the bottom. To prune cordoned currants consult a pruning book (the process is very similar). It is important now to feed with some potash; you can scatter wood ash around the currants or use sulphate of potash. On poorer soils also apply Fish, Blood and Bone a few weeks later. Mulch with compost or bark to keep roots cool and moist.

Rose There is pruning to be done from now into March. On all roses, the aim is to remove dead and diseased shoots (blotchy purple colour often indicates disease), crossing and congested branches, knuckles of wood where lots of branches start from one point, places where a pair of shoots start from the same junction, and suckers (these need to be torn away from the root, not cut). If the base of the rose is congested, take an old stem or two right out. Weak growth needs to be hit hard or removed. Do not aim for a level prune all over.

Leave alone albas, centifolias, damask roses, gallicas, hybrid musks, moss roses, species roses; they have made the growth that will flower later in the year. Leave floribundas until March and do not touch ramblers now.

Prune:
- Newly planted roses: apart from bare-root roses sent out by rose growers, which are already prepared so can be left as they are, cut any new rose down to 15 cm/6 inches from the ground to establish a good structure.
- Climbing roses: prune climbing roses, tying in long stems into fan shapes, horizontally or round pillars where they can become 'leaders' – pulling them down from the vertical. Tip prune them to encourage branching. Then cut all the side shoots off these 'leaders' to about two buds: a sort of 'stumping' exercise where there is no need to be too precise. If the rose is congested, take out one or two stems from the bottom to encourage new growth. Continue pruning into March; even early April is not too late. Do not put rose clippings on the compost heap but into the green waste. Tying in stems is rather an issue – the stems can go behind the wires only if there is sufficient room – at least 5 cm/2 inches – between the wire and the wall/fence. If there is less than that, air circulation becomes poor and mildew is encouraged; the other thing, of course, is that reshaping a climber that has not been perfectly pruned is much harder if you have to pull a leader

out from behind the wires. Most of us have resorted to this.

- English Roses and repeat flowering shrubs: prune less if they are wanted tall, harder if wanted smaller. Michael Marriott, Senior Rosarian at David Austin Roses, would usually cut the side shoots down to 15–23 cm/6–9 inches.
- Hybrid teas: they benefit greatly from having the old stems cut out to encourage new growth and their relatively few remaining stems cut back to an outward facing bud.
- Patio and ground-cover roses: bring back to size, cutting upright shoots hard back and, if congested, removing old shoots completely from the base.
- Rose hedges: this could be done with a hedge trimmer, but they would still benefit from a hard prune every few years and the removal of some of the oldest stems from the base each year.
- Roses such as *Rosa glauca*, *R. rugosa*, *R. × odorata* 'Mutabilis': although not needing regular annual pruning, they can look very old and woody if left totally alone so give them the occasional hard prune. Take out congested wood, cutting back vigorous new shoots by a third and taking some out of the middle if there is too much growth.
- Standard roses: the variety is budded on to the stem so prune as if it were the variety grown as a normal bush/shrub.

Other care:

- Pick up all leaf litter on the soil to help prevent the spread of black spot.
- Sulphur soil (available online) helps prevent the spread of black spot on neutral to alkaline soils. The soil pH should be 6.5 or above.
- Give roses in pots a slow release fertilizer to go through the season.
- After pruning, a rich organic mulch over moist soil is always a good addition to a rose bed. The soil could also be improved with the addition of Biochar, a charcoal-rich soil amendment.

Rubus biflorus, R. cockburnianus, R. thibetanus At some point before dormancy breaks, most of the white stems should be cut down to the ground. Some could be left for summer interest as, flowering on last year's wood, all the flowers would be lost if the whole clump is cut. Aim for clarity to avoid a muddled bramble.

Sambucus (elder) *Sambucus nigra*, the purple leaved elder, with its many cultivars, needs lots of light to get its roots down and cannot be squeezed in among other shrubs – though when established it likes a little shade. As a new plant gets established, just cut back the previous year's growth by a few buds to get the desired shape. After a couple of years, any time from late February through March, prune hard to create a central framework at the required height, to achieve a vigorous, upright plant producing glorious, often deep purple or lime green leaves. Each subsequent year, cut to within an inch of the previous year's growth. For less dramatic treatment, but achieving lovely flowers and berries and smaller leaves, cut one or two stems from the base, starting with the oldest, as well as any crossing or misplaced stems. Left unpruned it will get thick stemmed and unattractive quite quickly.

Scilla mischtschenkoana **and *Puschkinia scilloides* var. *libanotica*** Scilla flowers emerge in late February and the puschkinia in March, both seeming so pleased to see you that they are already in bloom as they push through the soil; the stalk and leaves then elongate with their growth (puschkinia have two slender leaves while those of the scilla are broader and more numerous). They both spread with ease.

***Sequoia sempervirens* 'Adpressa' (coastal redwood)** If kept in shape now, the tree does not become scrawny and will produce new cream tipped leaves in summer. It is one of the few conifers (yew is another) that can be pruned into old wood.

Shallot When planting – with the tip proud of the soil – dig a proper hole with a fork rather than pushing them in by hand. If just pushed in, the roots will inevitably shove themselves out again as they grow.

***Sorbaria sorbifolia* 'Sem'** If it is getting out of control, the whole shrub can be cut right down as the buds start swelling, or,

less dramatically, one stem in three can be cut out from the base.

Spinach Sow a batch of seeds now and another in a few weeks for a constant supply of young leaves.

Stipa calamagrostis* and *S. tenuissima Cut back to base now, these grasses will flower from June to September. Divide them in April if wanted. *S. tenuissima* is not long lived but will seed itself about. All stipas need very well-drained soil to do well and avoid rotting away.

Styrax If the Japanese snowbell tree (*Styrax japonicus*) and fragrant snowbell (*S. obassia*) need any pruning, do it now. They sometimes have a competing leader; if so, remove it (if large, cut it back by half this year and the remainder next year). Stake for a few years after planting to keep the tree stable.

Sweet pea Those sown last October can be reduced by half their height, still in their pots with a cane. They like light but not the midday sun. Do not keep them in a heated greenhouse as they will get soft. Prepare the ground where the plants are to go – ideally, a trench or hole 60 cm/24 inches deep with a mixture of manure, compost, leafmould and sand at the bottom. I know someone who adds pig's blood to the hole to enrich it. Anyway, add a balanced fertilizer like Fish, Blood and Bone. Fill up the trench with topsoil (the roots would burn if they touched all that richess below) ready to take the young plants next month. When my seedlings were piled high with snow, the only ones to suffer were those I irreparably bruised by knocking the snow off. On the rest, the snow had formed a duvet, and as the snow melted they simply had a good soak. At this stage they can cope with cold but not a really deep freeze or a whipping wind, when it would be better to have them in a cold frame or cold greenhouse.

Trillium (Trinity flower) Sprinkle a light dressing of a balanced fertilizer like Fish, Blood and Bone over the rhizomes before they emerge next month. A light mulch of leafmould would also be good.

Tulip For those left in the ground, a sprinkling of sulphate of potash before any leaves appear will help the bulbs greatly. A dose of slug repellent will also help keep slugs and snails at bay.

Viburnum, evergreen: *Viburnum × burkwoodii, V. davidii, V. × hillieri 'Winton', V. rhytidophyllum, V. tinus* Evergreen viburnums respond well to renovative pruning, which can be done in late winter. The more they are clipped over, the less damage there will be from viburnum beetle (which lives in old wood), but pruning them unnecessarily now removes their flower buds, so it is best to wait until they have flowered. Feed with a balanced fertilizer like Fish, Blood and Bone to get them off to a good start.

Vine: grape (grown under glass) Scatter sulphate of potash and a balanced fertilizer around the base.

Wisteria Prune back to two or three flower buds (about 2.5–5 cm/1–2 inches) all the shoots shortened in the summer. Take care not to cut off flower buds (much plumper than growth buds). Tie in horizontally any young stems that can cover bare patches, and then cut these stems back by as much as a third to encourage them to shoot. If drastic pruning is required, it can be done now. Follow stems back towards a main branch and, using a pruning saw, cut just above a young shoot which can provide the start of new framework. Only do this in mild weather. It is better not to take off more than one big branch a year. Mulch and feed after any pruning.

Wisteria sinensis (from China) flowers before the leaves and, if looked at from above, will be seen to spiral anticlockwise, while *W. floribunda* and hybrids (Japanese) will flower with the leaves and spiral clockwise.

Xanthoceras sorbifolia This small tree or large shrub needs sun and protection from cold winds and gentle pruning before bud burst.

MARCH

Susie Pasley-Tyler, owner of Coton Manor and its beautiful garden in Northamptonshire, wrote in the journal *Hortus*: 'Spring embodies that sense of excitement derived from forgotten plants . . . the eye absorbs every detail of plants . . . because there is relatively little competition for attention and their freshness is breathtaking.' She is so right. This is a wonderful moment, when every new appearance is cause for a lightened step. Weather has everything to do with what should happen when. We may be knocking snow off evergreens or engrossed in the business of an advancing spring.

AREAS TO CONSIDER

Alpine beds Replace or refresh gravel mulch. As growth begins, a half-strength potash-rich liquid feed would be good.

Annuals Hardy annuals still under cover can go outside during the day to harden off (bring them in at night).

Box diseases: control and preventative measures There are three main 'blights' to box: *Cylindrocladium buxicola* (the well-known fungal disease); *Volutella buxi*, which initially looks similar, where the leaves turn yellow then tan in patches but which can be cut out and arrested with nutrition and good growing conditions; third is the box tree moth and caterpillar (*Cydalima perspectalis*), whose caterpillars strip leaves incredibly fast, leaving webbing on the plant and droppings beneath. Box can also get rust: orange pustules on both sides of the leaves, which is dealt with using a fungicide.

   To attempt control of the first, cut out every affected bit, burning it with all the leaf debris underneath. Remove and replace the top layer of soil (about 4 cm/1½ inches) – fiddly around all the

Abeliophyllum distichum (white forsythia, flowering March)

surface roots but essential to destroy active spores in the ground. Clean all tools with disinfectant and spray the area with a fungicide containing tebuconazole and/or trifloxystrobin (such as Bayer Fungus Fighter). This may combat infections when very first identified and will deal with the second of the three blights too. The third blight – the box tree caterpillars, followed by pupae, moth, then eggs – hide themselves and their eggs deep in the foliage sticking to the leaves. They need to be spotted as soon as possible so between March and October set up pheromone traps near the box to catch the male moths (Buxatrap is what you need), and meanwhile watch closely for caterpillars eating leaves and leaving cobwebbing or frass balls (insect larvae excrement). Pick off the caterpillars by hand (putting them in water with a few drops of liquid soap), comb through the plants with a small rake and clear away all the debris. If you are happy to do so, spray with a biological insecticide such as XenTari, which is based on *Bacillus thuringiensis*, effective at killing caterpillars and not detrimental to bees or other beneficial insects and animals. There are also nematodes than can be used, very effective if applied at just the right time, and chemical insecticides that need professional application in order not to harm other insects. Water the plants well at the base; avoid wetting the leaves. Register your trap at www.ebts.org/bmctracker to help monitor and deal with the spread. Follow developments!

Bulbs Deadhead flowers so that energy returns to the bulb. When shoots appear of bulbs planted last autumn, feed them with a potash-rich liquid fertilizer or use a slow release balanced fertilizer such as Vitax Q4 (feeding bulbs in grass is a waste of time as it just benefits the grass). Incorporate a controlled release fertilizer with bulbs planted in containers and also give them a potash-rich liquid feed such as Tomorite.

Conifers Mulch round conifers to maintain moisture levels. Leave a 7 cm/3 inch margin around the trunk.

Containers and pots Renew the top 5 cm/2 inches of compost (John Innes No. 3 would be good). Repot plants every three to five years. Any plant that cannot be repotted can be root pruned, a third of the roots being cut off to get it back into the same pot. Check for vine weevils when doing so (nematodes will eradicate them when the soil warms up from about May but meanwhile you may need to wash roots and replace compost). Water in new compost well. It is easy to forget to water plants in containers when it is cold. Evergreens and conifers, especially, can suffer from winter drought. Pots containing deciduous plants will need to be given more water once they start into growth.

Division Divide late flowering herbaceous perennials like asters, helianthus, persicaria, phlox, rudbeckia and sedum, which have time to recover before flowering. Also divide, once they are growing well, campanulas, geraniums and most deciduous grasses. Most perennials need dividing at least every four years. Vigour after division is remarkable.

Feeding the soil to nourish the plants
Plants can be overfed: getting the soil in good condition with the repeated addition of organic matter – well-rotted farmyard manure, garden compost, leafmould, purchased bags of soil improver or whatever is available – is by far the most important activity in gardening. Plants then take up the nutrients, the soil does not get eroded, good drainage is maintained and mycorrhizal activity increases. Soil condition is far more important than the addition of fertilizers. Plants that produce lots of flowers like dahlias and roses do need extra feeding, but most things get along without endless doses. If the plant looks sickly, then a likely issue is that it is not getting the nutrients it needs. Maintaining soil fertility is helped if, around now (timing, as always, dependent on location), a general purpose fertilizer is sprinkled selectively on soil around bulbs, around trees, along hedges, under shrubs and perennials. Nutra-Allround Plus is a good once a year feed for plants in alkaline soils above pH 6.5. Vitax Q4 HN, Growmore or pelleted chicken manure would also be fine. Avoid feeding newly planted perennials and annuals, all grasses and silver leaved plants that do well in harsh conditions (eryngium would be one such), plants from the Mediterranean (like cistus and rosemary), alpines and a few plants such as heather, hebe and sedum which do not enjoy rich soil. Use a different feed for ericaceous plants – acer, camellia, cercidiphyllum, fritillaria, magnolia, pieris, raspberry, rhododendron and skimmia, amongst others. For them, a once yearly dose of Nutra-Allround Micro Plus is good. Any plant which is looking sick would be helped by a seaweed based liquid fertilizer.

Frost and wind protection Keep fleece to hand. Bitter wind, snow or frost can still stop spring growth in its tracks.

Fruit bushes and canes Apply a general-purpose fertilizer and sulphate of potash to bush and cane fruit and mulch with well-rotted manure or garden compost. Wood ash (not coal ash) provides a small amount of potassium. If the soil is alkaline, provide a sequestrene plant tonic to balance any lack of iron and magnesium.

Fruit trees: free standing with and without stones If frost is forecast, protect blossoms of apricot, peach and nectarine with fleece. Those under cover will need hand pollination using a soft paintbrush or cotton wool on a stick as natural pollinators cannot reach them. Hand weed round young trees so shallow roots are not harmed.

Grasses See February: most deciduous grasses will be cut down this month.

Green manure Phacelia, clover, buckwheat, yellow trefoil or agricultural lupin can be sown in empty vegetable plots as green manures, to be dug in before flowering and setting seed; they greatly improve the nutrient levels in the soil. Meanwhile, they suppress weeds.

Greenhouse – and mice The door or vents can be opened on warm days. Mice will seek newly sown seeds. Soaking seeds in seaweed fertilizer overnight makes them unpalatable (I hate finding mice in traps but I know they love peanut butter.) Seedlings need protection from strong sunlight during the day and to be above 3°C at night.

Hedges Now the bare-root season is ended, prepare ground for planting containerized (mainly conifer and evergreen) hedges next month, removing weeds and incorporating a balanced fertilizer such as Growmore. Avoid too rich a planting hole: roots need to be encouraged to spread out.

Mulch established hedges. Look out for nesting birds.

Herbs The herb garden is best cut back in spring not autumn. Overwintered herbs (including margoram, mint, sage and thyme) can be cut back. Seeds of hardy herbs (chives, coriander, fennel and parsley) can be sown outside, thinning and repositioning when big enough to handle.

Lawns Lightly scarify with a rake to remove moss and debris. If moss has got the upper hand, apply a moss killer and check the drainage. 'MO Bacter' is an organic product that kills moss as well as feeding the grass, disintegrating the moss so it does not have to be collected. If the lawn is 'tined', the holes can be filled with sand to improve drainage. This aeration helps to remove compaction. If time is short, just work on areas of high footfall, topdressing worn out patches with sand, fine soil and grass seed (keep people off it for some weeks). Mow with blades set high – too close and the grass may turn yellow. Clippings can be used in layers on the compost heap with woody material sandwiched between or can be left on the grass. In late March, feed with a proprietary spring lawn feed that is high in nitrogen. Straighten lawn edges if it is dry enough. Mown lines look 'right' on an irregular lawn if you start at the centre, make a bee line for a central focus point and then do all subsequent strips parallel to that line, working outwards. Mowing each cut at 90 degrees to the previous one helps to keep a flat surface.

Layering of shrubs Some shrubs can be layered to propagate them: for example, akebia, cotinus, exochorda, hydrangea, kerria, parrotia and philadelphus. Leave pegs pinning branches down in the soil for a year, cutting them off next March.

Mulching Even more important than feeding is to continue mulching with organic matter (see February). As the soil starts warming up, after feeding layer mulch 5–7 cm/2–3 inches deep on moist soil. If you cannot make compost/ leafmould, procure it from council recycling or buy it locally. Manure must be extremely well rotted, not claggy. Go around, not over, the crowns of herbaceous perennials, avoiding ones that may not like wet. Brown corrugated cardboard has no nutritional value but is often used to warm up bare soil.

Paths Use a residual weedkiller before weeds have a chance to grow and set seed. Pathclear Weedkiller PC + Preventer is good. It must not leach or spray on to shrubs, borders or lawn edges so a still, dry day is essential. Remind people not to walk from path to lawn until the weedkiller has dried.

Ponds A layer of gravel added to aquatic pond baskets stops fish stirring up the compost.

Pruning Now is prime time to prune late summer flowering deciduous shrubs. There is a saying, 'prune by Cheltenham' (the races are in mid-March). Hold back on pruning shrubs that will flower this spring and early summer or you will cut off the nascent flower buds; your targets will be any that flower after midsummer. Consider their shape, reduce their canopy if need be, open up any congestion, remove wayward branches and, of course, anything dead, dying or dangerous.

Seed sowing Half-hardy annuals are good sown under cover now – earlier they may get leggy in their wait to go out – as would seeds of tender perennials which need a heated propagator and warmth to germinate. They need good light too (see February).

Seedlings Watch out for emerging seedlings: it is so easy to whip out something that turns out not to be a weed. An allium, for example, looks just like a blade of grass. Move self-sowers now as the soil is moist and their roots have not yet started to expand (such as foxglove, hollyhock, honesty, sweet rocket, verbascum and verbena).

Staking and supporting plants Getting supports in for plants now when they are still small reminds me of the pleasure of organizing what to wear for an occasion long before it happens, negating the need to think about it any more. Left until later, the plants are hard to reach and flower shoots are snapped off in the effort to stand them up.

For large areas of a single species, 15 cm/6 inch square pea netting stretched over canes at heights suitable for the plant works well. If noticeable at all, it just looks efficient. Leave a way through to other groups of plants – it is exasperating to find stretched netting blocking the route further back. For heavier plants like peonies and phlox, domed supports woven with twiggy lengths of birch, hazel or willow look very attractive. Otherwise, use linked stakes or appropriate sized metal grid rings. Go round the garden getting supports in, ready for everything that could need them – satisfaction levels will be high.

Trees grown for autumn berries Sprinkle wood ash around their bases or feed with sulphate of potash and bone meal, over this month and next.

Vegetables The classic advice is that if soil sticks to boots it is still too early to sow seed outside. Covering soil with polythene/plastic for some weeks helps to warm it. 'No dig' vegetable gardens are helped by adding a layer of cardboard sandwiched between two layers of organic compost to prevent weeds coming through. Cover newly planted vegetables with a cloche or fleece to protect early growth from sudden drops in temperature. A fine mesh (burying the edges) will prevent pests feasting. Use John Innes No. 2 if planting vegetables in containers. If sowing different seeds, a line of fast growing radish between blocks of vegetables gives definition and looks good.

PLANTS

Abelia On established shrubs cut out a few stems to tidy up the shape and improve flowering.

***Abeliophyllum distichum* (white forsythia)** Established wall-trained shrubs can have their stems taken back to three or four buds from a permanent framework, with new stems tied in after flowering is over or, if it is still quite young or free standing, to a newly developing shoot further down. Shoots facing out from or towards the wall and any that are crossing need to be removed. Feed with a balanced fertilizer like Fish, Blood and Bone.

Acanthus (bear's breeches) If it looks a mess, cut it down and it will soon reshoot. Check for snails in the crown. It is difficult to divide because of its taproot, but if necessary now is the time to divide a well-established clump with a spade, cutting it into large sections and replanting immediately. It responds well when given some kind of support it can grow through.

Achillea (yarrow) Most achillea (including 'Moonshine') need regular division to maintain vigour; otherwise they do not live long. It is a good idea to propagate by pulling away some young growth with a little piece of stem (a 'heel'), potting these up in a sandy compost

to use as replacements. Even if it is not being divided this year, it can be helped by lifting it, taking out any dead areas in the centre, improving the soil around and beneath it, and replanting with some bone meal. Some support to grow through will help it present well.

Aconitum (monkshood) Mostly tuberous (a few have fibrous roots), aconitums need occasional division. Tubers push themselves outward from the centre of the clump as they multiply, so that in the end the group has nothing in the middle of it. Every few years, as growth begins in March, dig up and pull apart groups of thick tubers with their emerging leaves to re-form two or three smaller clumps using the best bits. Every part is highly poisonous so do handle carefully.

Agapanthus: tender cultivars in pots Upturn the pot to find dry, shrunken roots. Only if necessary should you divide them, ensuring there are a couple of growing points in each division; they do not like this to be done very often. Repot in 2:1 John Innes No. 3 compost and grit. Water well. They need full sun (or sun for two-thirds of the day minimum).

Agave americana They are probably best grown in a container unless your soil is very well drained. Plant new specimens with gravel round the neck. If leaves get frosted and go soft, leave them until they become brittle and then cut them off. This way the plant seals the leaf before the cut wound spreads rot. Keep as dry as possible in cold and wet conditions. Remove and burn any leaves with black spot. Old basal leaves can be cut off mature plants. Pot up young plants round the base. Beware the spines!

Ajuga (bugle) Dividing it by separating rooted stems will help to maintain its vigour. Cut off damaged leaves.

Alstroemeria (Peruvian lily) Sprinkle bone meal round the roots as shoots emerge. Protect from snails. Put in a support network of twiggy stakes or netting through which they will grow. Established clumps can be divided now, but the roots are brittle so do so carefully. Replant quite deeply (about 20 cm/8 inches).

Ammi majus, A. visgnaga Ammi seedlings (totally hardy) need to be hardened off and moved from a 9 cm/ 3½ inch pot straight into the ground when the soil has warmed up to above 7°C, and planted where they will be naturally supported by surrounding plants.

***Aralia elata* (Japanese angelica tree)** Prune out any badly placed branches, but it produces suckers when cut back so do not overdo it.

Argyranthemum frutescens These lovely daisies, which so many people grow in pots very decoratively, probably need to be treated as summer bedding as they are not hardy. If they have been successfully overwintered in a cool room or greenhouse, bring them out, feed and water them. If they have been in the ground, cut them low if they are still alive: they may regenerate.

Asparagus A native of salty sand dunes, asparagus needs to be very well drained, which is why it is usually planted over a long mound of soil; it also does best with a rich mulch at the bottom of the planting trench. Much is written on spacing and planting methods so consult a specialist when first setting up a bed. When purchasing new crowns, ask for male ones if possible as they produce the tastiest spears. Resist any harvesting for the first two years. On established beds, give the crowns some balanced fertilizer in late March and a mulch of spent mushroom compost or garden compost.

Should you finish with a covering of salt, as many growers do (they are salt-loving plants), you will not have to weed the bed all season. Perennial weeds are almost impossible to remove without damaging the crowns.

Aster (now mostly classified as Symphyotrichum): *Aster amellus, A. × frikartii* 'Mönch' (and others still belonging to the Aster genus), *A. cordifolius, A. diffusus, A. ericoides, A. lateriflorus, A.* 'Little Carlow', *A. novae-angliae, A. novi-belgii, A. pilosum* var. *pringlei* (all now known as Symphyotrichum) and *A. divaricatus* (now known as *Eurybia divaricata*) Feed all with a balanced fertilizer such as Fish, Blood and Bone and mulch around the crowns. Divide now rather than in autumn. Established clumps of the *A. amellus* group should be divided every third year. Every four or five years divide *Eurybia divaricata* just as they begin to grow away, adding lots of grit to the new planting and discarding old bits. This can be done using two forks back to back. *A. novi-belgii* cultivars (daylight dependent, not flowering until there is less than eight hours' daylight – hence 'Michaelmas' Daisy) and *A. novae-angliae* cultivars are the easiest to divide because they spread by subterranean runners. Replant only the vigorous young shoots. Like *A.* 'Little Carlow' (nothing small about it – the 'Little' refers to a place, not its size), *A. cordifolium, A. ericoides* and *A.× frikartii* cultivars, they need dividing more often: about once every two years. It is advisable not to make the divisions too small – chop them in half and use the best bits. At Great Dixter *A. latiflorus* var. *horizontalis* is cut down to the ground early in the month to make way for new growth.

Astrantia A mulch of well-rotted manure is just what they need now as humus-rich, moist soil is key to their long flowering. They can be divided at the end of the month – divisions will take a couple of years to re-establish well.

***Aucuba japonica* (spotted laurel)** They are forgiving, needing no regular pruning but can be clipped or cut back hard in spring. All new plants should be pruned by about a third to establish a good bushy shape from the start.

Azalea See Rhododendron, below

Bamboo: non-invasive, including Chusquea, Fargesia and Phyllostachys Clear away winter debris, cut out dead foliage and remove damaged, spindly culms to their base using loppers or pruning saw, thinning out any that are crowding each other. Make the cuts very low and horizontal, so that you do not leave pointed daggers at ground level to kneel on next year. The cut stems will not grow back. Do not take out more than a third in one year. I have seen Roy Lancaster walk through a great stand of bamboo to illustrate good husbandry. Give a nitrogen-rich fertilizer such as a spring lawn feed. Mulching round the base with a multipurpose compost containing John Innes No. 3 and adding some grit will provide the silica it needs for strength in its culms and help to keep the soil moist in summer and well drained in winter. The roots of many bamboos in pots will quickly outgrow their space so repot every few years. Remove from the pot, prune out dead or weak stems, saw off a good slice of the root ball (5–10 cm/2–4 inches), cut or saw the plant in half (or more), replanting what was the outside edge in the middle in John Innes No. 3 compost with some slow release fertilizer. Water in well. Again, removing some of the leaves and lower branches will show off the stems to much better effect. Thamnocalamus and Himalayacalamus need to have all the previous year's culms cut out, leaving only this year's still leafless stems behind.

Baptisia Flowering in April, this plant would benefit from discreet hazel or birch supports, especially if it is on a free-draining bank. If necessary, large clumps can be divided now, though they may sulk for a while.

Begonia: tuberous Bring overwintered tuberous begonias into growth. Cover the tubers (in a pot not much larger than the tuber) with slightly moist compost and keep at around 18°C. They can also be split if they have got too big. Pot on into 18 cm/7 inch pots as knots of leaves appear so that they can develop a good root system.

Box In mid- to late March, depending on the temperature and amount of sunlight, start to keep an eye out for box tree caterpillers. They will be waking up and starting to feed on the new leaves. The more you can remove at this point, the fewer will go on to become adult moths and lay eggs.

Brugmansia (was called Datura) They can be started back into growth, repotting or replacing the top 10 cm/4 inches of compost. If they were not pruned in autumn – perhaps because they were flowering all winter in a conservatory – they can be cut down to as low as 30 cm/12 inches from the base now to control their size with time enough to make new growth to flower this summer. We are advised not to cut this low every year or they get exhausted. Any cuttings taken last autumn can be moved into larger pots using John Innes No. 2 and lots of grit. The only thing that will hold back these cuttings – or indeed their parent – is too small a pot and lack of water or feed. They will require a liquid fertilizer (ideally seaweed extract) and a good watering once a week throughout the growing season.

Spraying against a host of pests is probably inevitable. When they are moved out, they need good light but will wilt in full sun. They work well as standards: train one stem up a bamboo cane, tying it on as it grows. When it has got to about 1.5–1.75 m/5–6 ft, nip off the top to encourage it to branch – these new shoots will become the weeping flowering shoots. (The advice given here and elsewhere has been gathered from a number of sources, but in particular from research by Stephen Lacey following his interviews with a grower and from articles by Lia Leendertz.)

Buddleia
- *Buddleja alternifolia*: do not touch now as it flowers on the previous year's shoots.
- *B. davidii* and cultivars, *B. fallowiana*, *B. × weyeriana*: as buds begin to swell in late March/early April, prune this group of buddleia (which flower on growth about to be made), cutting back last year's growth to two buds (leaving about 5 cm/2 inches of stem above where last year's growth stopped). This builds the framework to which to cut back every year. Equally, you can cut the whole bush down to about 30 cm/12 inches from the ground or lower the framework to get the height you want. Delaying a few weeks achieves later flowering – probably August rather than July – and the advantage of this is that August coincides with a new generation of emerging butterflies. Feed with something like Vitax Q4. On *B. fallowiana* this pruning encourages silvery foliage and bigger flower size. *B.* 'Lochinch' can be left unpruned or lightly pruned if desired.
- *B. globosa*: this is pruned after flowering in summer, but it can look dreadful after a few years of improper care. If it has become really leggy and tatty, in late March prune it all down to 30 cm/12 inches (expecting no flowers this year), give it a potash-rich feed, mulch and water.

Calycanthus I find that it responds well to being pruned to shape (not too hard) just before it comes into leaf. It can also be tidied up after flowering is over in midsummer.

Camassia They like moist soil. Plant them where the leaves can die back without being seen or where the grass does not need to be mowed. If not grown in grass or amongst other plants, the tall *Camassia leichtlinii* will eventually need support so it is better to have it in place now for the brief but glorious flowering in May.

Camellia Water regularly until late autumn, preferably using rainwater not tap. Deadhead wherever feasible, using secateurs or finger and thumb, carefully removing just the flower head. Mulch with leafmould (or shredded bark for those in pots). Camellias in pots will need repotting every two to three years as growth begins or their roots will curl round and round the pot. Use a John Innes loam-based ericaceous compost. If planting a new camellia, the top of the root ball needs to be level with the surrounding soil or even just above it so that future mulching comes up to the edge of the rootball and no higher. The site needs to be out of the wind and out of the reach of the early morning sun.

Campanula lactiflora Difficult to lift intact, so when the clump is too big and new green stems can be seen emerging, chop off the outer parts of the crown and replant these. The central piece can then be discarded (and will be easier to raise). Be cruel to be kind to the rest of the border, which will enjoy the freed up space. Deter slugs, which love the new growth.

Top: *Pulmonaria* 'Blue Ensign' (lungwort) Flowering now, find reference to its care in May when flowering is over
Bottom: *Camellia* x *williamsii* 'Donation', braving the snow (flowering late winter to early spring)

Canna If the rhizomes were stored dry, they need bottom heat to start bringing them back into growth without rotting. In late March/early April start this with gentle watering and feeding. The tubers expand rapidly so may need splitting and repotting. If they have been overwintered in pots, cut off old growth to allow the new shoots to take over and give a liquid feed every two weeks as they re-establish.

Cardiocrinum giganteum (giant lily)
March is too late to move the offsets – this has to be done when the plant is dormant so any offsets setting out on their first season should now be left where they are. Cardiocrinum do not succeed if they are waterlogged so may not thrive in clay soil. Gently fork in some bone meal around the bulbs, taking care not to damage the tips just below the soil. The 'cheat' extravagance is to buy, in early spring, a plant or three when the mature bulb is available and growth has started. They need setting at the same height as they are in the pot – again taking care not to damage their roots. Should you discover that slug protection is needed, use Neudorff Sluggo or other ferric phosphate based slug killer, which is safe to pets and is totally organic.

Seeds sown sixteen months ago may have started to germinate, in which case pot them up when they have a true leaf. Only water when out of dormancy. These seeds will take another five years or so to flower. They can be planted in pots but (unlike in the ground) may need support when eventually producing a stem; in pots they will need a liquid feed.

Caryopteris clandonensis and cultivars
Cut close to ground level just above a breaking bud or to an existing framework two to four buds above last year's growth. Cut out wispy bits and branches going in the wrong direction. If a much larger shrub is needed for the back of a border (with something in front to cover its then bare stems), create a higher framework each year but always cut back only when new growth is showing. It produces the best show of flowers on wood made this year, so pruning will encourage plenty of new growth for it to flower on. Feed with bone meal, then mulch around the root area.

Ceanothus: deciduous species such as 'Gloire de Versailles' Deciduous ceanothus should be pruned in March to encourage growth of new wood on which to flower this year. Cut the main flowered stems by up to half to improve the shape and weaker side shoots even harder – to about two buds. If there is a lot of unproductive growth in the middle, clear it out. Feed and mulch well, keeping clear of the stems. If the plant is still immature do not do more than trim back a few stems.

Chaenomeles (Japanese quince)
When flowering is over, shorten all shoots that have flowered to strong buds or lower growth to get the desired shape. On old plants take out one or two shoots from the base to encourage new growth. *Chaenomeles × superba* 'Knap Hill Scarlet' is a good variety.

Chrysanthemum The Korean, Rubellum and Japanese semi-pompon varieties (the normal ones for UK gardens) can be divided now as new growth begins and should be done every three years.

Clematis Feed all clematis with a balanced fertilizer. Depending on the weather you can do the pruning outlined in February now (and by no later than early April). To those notes add:
- Group 1: after flowering of *Clematis cirrhosa* is over, do some untangling and thin out some older stems to their base.
- Group 2: if there are any in this group that need renovation, they can be cut right down. *C. florida*, unusually

for this group, can be hard pruned down to approx 30 cm/12 inches. If in a container, where they do very well, provide a fresh topdressing of compost and a slow release fertilizer. They are fast growing.

- Group 3: *C. diversifolia*, *C. heracleifolia*, *C. integrifolia* and *C. recta* can have their dead stems cut just above soil level, taking care not to nip off newly emerging shoots. *C. viticella* cultivars have lovely seed heads used by nesting birds. They could be left a little longer and then, like others in the group, cut down close to the ground. *C. tibetana* subsp. *vernayi* needs a little extra care. Lift what a may be a tangled mass and inspect pencil-thick stems beneath. If there are new green shoots showing, prune them to 45 cm/18 inches above a bud and tie in to a support. Delay pruning if there are no green shoots as water may otherwise penetrate and cause dieback.

Cornus (dogwood)

- Cornus grown primarily for ornamental foliage: if grown for its elegant leaves as much as its coloured stems (such as *Cornus alba* 'Elegantissima'), cut hard in the early spring of every other year to prevent the shrub getting out of hand, taking out one stem in three from the base and reducing the framework to a suitable size for the site. Feed after pruning. *C. alba* 'Spaethii' also has a strong yellow margined leaf and calls for the same treatment.
- Cornus grown primarily for winter coloured stems: to enjoy the vibrancy of winter stems to the full, leave cutting back of *C.a.* 'Kesselringii', *C.a.* 'Sibirica', *C. sericea* 'Flaverimea' and others until late March (this is when it is done at The Savill Garden). Stems grown this year will give the brightest colour next winter so cut them down to 5–10 cm/ 2–4 inches above the ground – eventually a low framework will be

formed, to which the annual cut can be made. Feed with a balanced fertilizer followed by a mulch. The standard advice is not to start cutting back until the plant is two years old unless it is a very vigorous one. Otherwise, let it build up its resources before cutting too hard. See April's entry for slightly less vigorous cornus grown for winter colour.

Correa (Australian fuchsia)

As it finishes flowering, reduce the flowered stems back towards last year's growth to keep it well shaped. Give it a slow release fertilizer and mulch. Correa is an Australian evergreen, flowering on this side of the world from October to March, so in cold areas its flowering often takes place under cover in winter. In mild areas of the UK it could get through winter in a pot (using ericaceous soil) in a warm, sheltered courtyard.

Corydalis They all like well-drained soil but ensure they do not dry out in spring. The longer they keep their leaves after flowering, the better they are next year. As shoots emerge, water with diluted potash-rich liquid fertilizer to strengthen the tubers. A mulch of chipped bark or garden compost round the base will help retain moisture. Mark with grit where *Corydalis flexuosa* and *C. solida* have appeared, to know where they are when dormant in summer. *C.* 'Kingfisher' will be dormant now and can be divided. The ubiquitous evergreen *C. lutea*, which seeds everywhere, does not like being moved, but its seedlings can be transplanted now before it starts flowering again in May. Corydalis can be deadheaded, which helps prolong blooming, but that obviously prevents seeding.

***Cotinus coggygria*, *C. obovatus* (smoke bush)** Cotinus (there are many varieties with stupendous autumn colour) need to be established for two years before any hard pruning. This should be done no later than this month. The choice is for a good small tree/large shrub with smoke flowers or a smaller shrub with intensely coloured larger leaves but no flowers. For the first choice, take, if needed, one stem in three out from the base, removing dead or crossing branches, shortening straggly growth, and removing twiggy growth or multiple shoots from previous pruning cuts to obtain a good shape. Dark buds will be forming on the stems – cut above these in the direction the stems should grow. For even stronger coloured leaves but at the expense of the wonderful smoke bush flowers (produced on last year's wood), cut the whole lot back to a low framework: coppice it, starting in about year two. They put on a remarkable amount of growth very quickly so do not be fearful of controlling them as you would like. Cutting back can be done to an old plant where the trunk is thick but this will produce lax growth as well as very large well-coloured leaves. This is fine if a low mound of powerful colour is acceptable but not if what is needed is a well-behaved shrub. Wear gloves as the sap can irritate. To propagate, take cuttings as soon as new growth begins in a few weeks, placing them in shade under plastic. Alternatively, you can layer a branch, severing the stem next summer when it will have rooted. Mulch well after pruning.

Crocosmia (montbretia) Cut any leaves remaining from last year to ground level. Every two years, dig up the clump and discard the long chains of old corms, replanting the fat new top corms 5 cm/ 2 inches deep, adding plenty of compost or well-rotted manure to the planting hole. This will achieve bigger, better flowers. Pippa Greenwood cleverly suggests squirting a strong jet of water at the base of the clump to divide the tightly knitted together corms more easily.

Crown imperial (*Fritillaria imperialis*) As soon as shoots are seen, feed with

a general purpose fertilizer such as Growmore and start watching out for lily beetle (see April).

Cymbidium (orchid) Unless using a proprietary orchid feed, use a nitrogen-rich fertilizer from now until June at half strength.

Dahlia If they were left in the ground and the leaves were not blackened by early March (anything is possible), cut them right down and dose with liquid slug repellant (particularly necessary in heavy soils). If they were stored, moisten the compost and move to a place in the light to start them back into life. If tubers in storage are found shriveled, try soaking them in warm water to see if they revive before throwing them out.

Daphne bholua* 'Jacqueline Postill', *D. cneorum*, *D. mezereum*, *D. odora*, *D. × transatlantica Daphnes do not move happily and do not respond prettily to hard pruning. If they are getting oversized, the time to remove branches that are spoiling the shape is as flowering finishes (some species will not yet have flowered so await the moment). Bear in mind that a branch made ugly when cut will remain ugly. You can safely trim areas of healthy leaf growth but avoid nascent buds. D. *mezereum* needs to be left alone. When *D. bhuloa* has finished flowering, it drops many leaves even though it is evergreen – this is not a problem. Bayer does a good phostrogen all-purpose plant feed that would be suitable to use as a general fertilizer. Mulch deeply. Daphnes do not have a vigorous root system so can easily dry out if they are not somewhere moist and cool; if they suddenly die, which they are prone to do, dry roots could be the problem. They are best planted now – choose one suitable for the soil's pH.

Delphinium As young shoots emerge, vigorously deter slugs and pile fine grit around the crown. If using a garlic liquid drench, apply it weekly during the growing season, covering a wide circle (recipes available online). Feed with a balanced fertilizer now, and again when the flower spikes form. Late March/April is the best time to divide delphiniums. For new plants, give them a generous hole and place the crown at ground level. They need space to get themselves established so position at least 45 cm/ 18 inches apart – the Elatum Group particularly like a lot of room round their roots. Take basal stem cuttings of Elatum hybrids and the Belladonna Group to propagate in gritty compost in the greenhouse. *D. elatum* can also be propagated by seed now or in the autumn. If sowing seeds, try soaking them between damp towels for a day to aid germination.

Dicentra: including *Dicentra spectabilis* (now called *Lamprocapnos spectabilis*) (bleeding heart) Mulch and feed with a general purpose fertilizer. Divide *D. spectabilis* every few years to keep vigorous, either now or when the leaves have died down around midsummer. Other species of dicentra may not die down until autumn. Divisions need to be quite large and do not want to be crowded.

Dicksonia antarctica A granular feed round the base of the tree fern will be helpful as it starts into growth. Take off any winter protection at the end of March.

***Eccremocarpus scaber* (Chilean glory flower)** In its first spring, cut back all new growth to 15 cm/6 inches to encourage growth from the base. In subsequent years cut back to more like 50 cm/ 20 inches. The new stems will carry the orange/red trumpets.

***Echinacea purpurea* (coneflower)** Needing occasional division (see

September), they resent frequent disturbance. They like an annual mulch and good quantities of compost in their planting holes. They have a tendency to die suddenly – possibly from winter wet. Take root cuttings as a precaution.

Edgeworthia (paper bush) When the beautiful scented flowers produced on bare stems are over, remove wayward, crossing or unproductive growth, but only prune lightly, keeping its nice shape. A monthly liquid feed during the growing season will strengthen its tender tendencies.

Elaeagnus, deciduous: *Elaeagnus angustifolia* (Russian olive), *E. commutata*, *E.* 'Quicksilver', *E. umbellata* Resist tidying the branches now, as flowers will appear in early summer so you should not remove the buds (lovely scent on 'Quicksilver'). Once in a while, cut out one stem in three from the base to encourage new growth. They will tolerate hard pruning after flowering if necessary. Mulch and feed. Take hardwood cuttings or pot up suckers to propagate.

Enkianthus Requiring acid soil, they do not need regular attention, but if there are problems with shape or size they should be dealt with now. A deep mulch of composted pine needles or leafmould will be good for them. If the soil is neutral to alkaline, sulphur chips round the base now and in September would help.

Eremurus (foxtail lily, desert candle) They come into growth early so are easily caught by frost: repeated frost damage will stop them flowering. Give them a dry mulch and watch where you tread! Slugs are a pest so a garlic drench would be good (recipes available online). When planting the fleshy, octopus-like roots, lay them on a bed of grit with the crown nudging the surface and place a cane near the crown so that when a support is needed later, you can insert one in that hole without harming the roots. Sulphate of potash will strengthen them as they start to grow.

Erica arborea and other tree heaths

A new tree heath can be shaped in early spring to get a nice bushy plant. Stems can be cut back by as much two-thirds.

Erigeron karvinskianus (fleabane)

Flowering from June to October, clumps should be cut back and moved if necessary so that this daisy grows where you want it – classically up steps. It spreads agreeably.

Erythronium (dog's tooth violet)

Protect emerging foliage from slugs and snails. Give plants a light application of potash-rich fertilizer. Do not position under shrubs – they need the moisture for themselves.

Eucryphia

These glorious trees really only like acid soil – though *Eucryphia × nymansensis* 'Nymansay' will tolerate alkaline conditions. Early spring is the best time to plant them: roots in the shade, canopy in the sun and where the soil stays moist in summer.

If there are problems like crossing branches or branches broken by bad weather, now is the moment to deal with them but no regular pruning is needed. *E.* 'Dumpling' is small enough to go in a pot where its soil can be regulated, so is the only one I can grow.

Euphorbia (spurge)

Divide plants now. Beware of the very irritating sap on skin or eyes. If basal cuttings are taken, dip the cut surfaces in lukewarm water to stop them bleeding.

Fig (Ficus carica)

Clive Simms's *Nutshell Guide to Growing Figs* is a delight for anyone growing them. Cut out suckers, diseased/damaged wood, any wood that is bent or spoils the shape, overlong branches and any growing straight out. Avoid doing too much in any one year or there will be massive regrowth (and all fruiting wood will be lost). On young trees, take out weak branches leaving the sturdy ones alone. Fruit grows on the tips of last year's growth so do not tip branches unnecessarily.

Foxglove (Digitalis)

Foxglove seeds sown now in modules can be planted out in May to flower next year.

Francoa sonchifolia (bridal wreath)

Cut back the semi-evergreen foliage to encourage fresh growth for its June to August flowering. Water well and feed every month. It can be divided now.

Fremontodendron 'California Glory'

Plant small as they hate root disturbance. These plants are happy in poor soil, where vigorous growth will be restricted but not at the expense of flower production. Frost protection is needed until established.

Fuchsia, hardy: Fuchsia magellanica cultivars

They can be hard pruned now to a few inches above the ground just as new shoots start showing. The best flowers are produced on wood made from spring onwards, and cutting hard will encourage plenty of new growth. If height is wanted, cut back every year to a permanent higher framework. Feed with a slow release fertilizer and mulch with a rich compost. If planting, place the base of the stem 5 cm/2 inches below the soil surface.

Galtonia candicans

Plant bulbs in pots under cover to plant out later in spring when in growth. Slugs adore them.

Garrya elliptica (silk tassel bush)

As soon as the long catkins, like tassels, are over, cut them off to allow new growth to ripen. Pruning, not always necessary, should be done now. Clip gently into shape or, if it is too big, take a stem or two, judiciously chosen, out from the bottom. The male shrub has better catkins than the female (Garrya is dioecious so both plants are needed for the best catkins). Spots on the leaves will have been caused by stress over winter but the new foliage will be free of them. Mulch and water well after clipping/pruning.

Geranium (cranesbill) Divide them now as the young shoots push up. Slice off little groups of shoots with roots attached, plant out and mulch. They will make rapid progress into decent sized plants.

***Geum coccineum*, *G. rivale* and cultivars (avens)** Divide every four years or so when they get too big. My experience of dividing the brilliant *G.* 'Totally Tangerine' was that it led to no increased vigour – indeed, it set it back. I then read that this one can stay undivided for many years. Each division needs good roots with compost and grit added to the planting hole. Water well and surround with mulch.

***Gillenia trifoliata* (Bowman's root)**
Slugs like the young shoots of this excellent perennial; it prefers neutral to acid soil and, though happy in some shade, needs half a day's sun to be at its best. It can be divided now.

Heather: summer flowering
Calluna vulgaris (Scottish heather), *Erica cinerea* (bell heather), *E. ciliaris* and *E. vagans* can be given a light prune. Stay within the green as brown wood does not regenerate, so cut just below the old flowers.

Hebe Most need little or no pruning, but they can be given a light trim in spring to keep them bushy. With shorter varieties remove the top 5 cm/2 inches to maintain

the shape; with taller varieties pruning back a bit more (15 cm/6 inches or so) will have the effect of opening up the centre of the shrub, encouraging new growth. If renovation is needed to correct the symmetry, the stem should be cut to a new side shoot lower down, leaving at least two buds on the stem being cut. If they have been frosted over winter, cut back when there are signs of new growth, to where new shoots have begun to form near the base. They will not like this as a regular occurrence.

Hebe pinguifolia 'Pagei' and other low growing varieties: a way of stopping them becoming too woody is to cut out one stem in three, starting with the oldest and/or weakest branches, and then choosing other stems to open up congested areas.

Helleborus
- *Helleborus argutifolius* and *H. foetidus*: cut off old flower stems at ground level as flowering finishes to make room for new foliage and feed with a balanced fertilizer if they are looking a bit sad. If you want seedlings, leave the flowers on. They do not divide but self-seed easily.
- *H. torquatus* can be divided now – leave other species until September.

Hemerocallis (daylily) In mid-March tidy up the old foliage of the evergreen and semi-evergreen varieties, giving them a potash-rich liquid feed every two to three weeks until the buds begin to form.

Heuchera and heucherella They need some loving care in spring. Cut out completely any small woody stems and cut back any leggy bits to a healthy looking bud. Clear out dead or damaged leaves, mulch and feed with a balanced fertilizer such as Fish, Blood and Bone. If they have lifted out of the ground, replant a bit deeper.

Hippeastrum (amaryllis) When the leaves have more or less died down, it will be apparent whether there are offsets with their own roots. These can be separated and potted up to flower in a couple of years' time. Keep them around 21°C.

Honeysuckle (Lonicera) All honeysuckle will appreciate a good rich mulch as spring begins.

 If a climbing honeysuckle (evergreen or deciduous) needs renovation, cut it down to 60 cm/24 inches off the ground now. Feed with a balanced fertilizer and mulch.

- Deciduous twining honeysuckle (*Lonicera × brownii* 'Dropmore Scarlet', *L. caprifolium, L. etrusca, L. periclymenum, L. sempervirens, L. × tellmanniana*): tie in as necessary on to wires or trellis. New growth will accelerate after flowering so spread it out as much as possible. Flowering is on last year's growth, so avoid any cutting back other than shortening overlong shoots. Tweaking now will result in lots of unsatisfactory twiggy growth (though in due course pinching out the tips of new growth encourages leafiness). Prune only after flowering.
- Evergreen twining honeysuckle (*L. japonica*): remove any woody stems to keep under control. It does not need regular pruning but it can, if desirable, be cut right down to rejuvenate.
- Box-leaved honeysuckle (*L. pileata*): if this ground-cover honeysuckle looks too rampant, cut two-thirds off each new shoot.
- Deciduous/semi-evergreen shrubby honeysuckle (*L. fragrantissima, L. × purpusii* 'Winter Beauty'): resist the temptation to prune later than immediately after flowering is over: doing so dramatically reduces flower power the following winter. It can be reshaped now, cutting back damaged and weak stems, flowered shoots and other badly placed stems to a side

shoot. It is important that every few years a quarter to a third of the shoots are cut back to the base, starting with the oldest and thickest stems, keeping the overall shape pleasing. Feed with a balanced fertilizer such as Growmore or Fish, Blood and Bone to the extent of the roots, water and mulch.

Hydrangea
- *Hydrangea aspera, H.a.* 'Villosa' (rough leaved hydrangea) and *H. involucrata*: no particular pruning is necessary but overlong stems, branches overhanging paths and weaker growth can be cut out now. Up to one stem in three can be cut out to improve the shape: cut either to the ground or to a good side shoot/bud, never leaving a stump. Pruning needs to be done before the end of April to get flowers this year. Do not despair if *H. involucrata* is not yet in leaf – it will be all right.
- *H. petiolaris* (climbing hydrangea): this will tolerate hard pruning now to reduce its size but flowering will be lost this year.
- *H. quercifolia* (oak leaved hydrangea): prune only to shape, removing any flowers from last year and damaged stems. To reduce it in size, take out one stem in three from the bottom.

Hypericum (St John's wort) Cut back last year's growth of the deciduous/semi-evergreen *Hypericum × inordorum* to about 5 cm/2 inches from the ground. Divide if wanted. It is tough and will respond well to radical treatment each year, producing flowers and lovely berries. The evergreen *H.* 'Hidcote' just needs shaping now.

Indigofera ambylantha, I. heterantha, I. pendula Prune out frosted wood now – there almost certainly will be some. They flower on this year's growth and cutting back will encourage new shoots to break, even from the base. In very cold areas, wait until late spring when new growth can be seen and then prune to shape, cutting above fat buds. Louisa Arbuthnott of Stone House Cottage Garden and Nursery, from whom my *I. pendula* originated, sometimes cuts stems to the ground to encourage new growth rather than trimming back regularly, which, she suggests, can make the lovely pink racemes smaller. So she takes the pragmatic approach of any non-apprehensive gardener and removes as much or as little of each variety as necessary to produce a pleasing shape that particular year.

Ipheion These sweet bulbs eventually clump up. Feed when they are flowering well: they do not do so their first year. They are only just frost hardy so a long frost will probably kill them. Protect from snails and slugs. They disappear so mark them and then, with mulch and grit, keep them moist but not soaking in dormancy. If soil is clayey, grow in pots.

Iris
- Bearded iris: sprinkle with a granular balanced feed such as Growmore or Vitax Q4.
- *Iris laevigata, I. versicolor* (blue flag iris): as they come into growth in spring divide these fast spreading water iris. Either plant them in mud (not just gravel) or in plastic buckets with small holes (Finofil make them).
- *I. pseudacorus*: an absolute thug, this water iris is better divided in autumn. It is hard work.
- *I. danfordiae, I. histrioides, I. reticulata* (winter flowering iris): let the leaves die back before doing anything. If you need to move them, do so when the bulbs are dormant but they are much better left undisturbed.
- *I. unguicularis*: tidy up, individually removing old and damaged leaves by raking through the foliage. Once every five years or so you can cut back by

half all the old foliage: half the clump one year, the other half the next. The clump itself should be left undisturbed.

Jacob's ladder (*Polemonium caeruleum*) Divide just as new growth is showing, replanting the basal rosettes to keep it vivacious. Provide support.

Jasminum
- *Jasminum nudiflorum* (winter flowering jasmine): this needs dealing with the moment it has finished flowering. Tie in new shoots if there is more space to fill; cut back flowered shoots to a few inches from the base and any dead stems. If there is still too much growth, shorten side shoots beyond the old wood, cutting to a bud. Feed and mulch. If it is a total mess, cut it down and let it start again – it will be fine.
- *J. officinale* (common jasmine): if the plant is happy, getting lots of sun, it can be pruned gently, possibly removing a few stems at the base. Do not cut the side shoots as these will produce this year's flowers.

Juniper
- Ground-cover juniper: this needs controlling or it gets out of hand. Do a little every year from year two, cutting back overlong shoots to a junction. It will not shoot from old wood so selectively prune out, to the point of origin, the older, slower growth underneath, ensuring cuts slope backwards so are less evident. This will let light in and keep it healthy. Avoid trimming new growth or the shape is lost.
- Shrubby juniper: Robert Vernon of Bluebell Nurseries says to 'fingertip pluck' the tips off the sprays of leaves to achieve prettier, shorter and thicker sprays covering the plant. He adds, 'Do it every time you pass it.'

Laurel: cherry and Portuguese (*Prunus laurocerasus, P. lusitanica*) They can be pruned now that, hopefully, the worst of winter weather is over. Mulching will help retain moisture and reduce the need to weed round their bases. Feed with a balanced fertilizer such as Fish, Blood and Bone. If pruning a standard (*P. lusitanica* is the best) use secateurs not hedge cutters as the cut leaf edge will turn brown and look horrid. It will need pruning again – see June and September. This is a good time to do regenerative pruning down to the main upright stems. Leaves and fruits of both are very poisonous.

Lavatera (tree mallow) Having reduced it in autumn to avoid wind damage, now be more radical. Prune down to about 60 cm/24 inches from the ground if there are no young shoots, or just above them if there are, to encourage new growth, avoid leggy plants and allow time for good new stems on which to flower this year. Do not prune *Lavatera × clementii* 'Barnsley' too hard as it can revert to producing the ordinary small pink flower; cut out one stem in three back to the ground or shorten the shoots of the previous year that come off the main stem to about 23–25 cm/9–10 inches, always cutting above a young shoot.

Firm the roots as they get rocky. Feed, then mulch around the stems. Lavatera do not last forever, grow very fast and are easily replaced.

Lemon tree (citrus) In early March take off overcrowded or crossing branches or any spoiling the shape and shorten any that are too long. If leggy, the leader and any other shoots can be pruned back by as much as half to create a bushier plant. In late March start feeding with a nitrogen-rich fertilizer (or preferably one specifically for citrus), mixing it into a watering can of rainwater (if possible) each watering. Water when the top of the compost feels dry but before the leaves start to wilt.

Continue until October. There is much advice on the RHS website about citrus.

Lemon verbena If it has got through winter alive, cut it back further and keep inside until May.

***Leucanthemella serotina* (autumn ox-eye, giant daisy)** This white ox-eye daisy flowers in October with greater vigour if divided and replanted in improved soil every three years. Planted in gravel it grows much shorter.

***Leycesteria formosa* (pheasant berry)** Wait for signs of regrowth, then prune before the end of March – it flowers on stems grown this year. Cut out the oldest shoots from the bottom, some less old halfway, achieving a pleasing shape, leaving any new growth. If it is a thicket, cut it all down to the bottom. It helps to get a good shape if new shrubs are cut down to 10 cm/4 inches above the ground in the first year.

Liatris spicata Plant in late March, in sun and reliably moist but well-drained soil. If the corms get soggy they will rot. Plant 7–10 cm/3–4 inches apart as a clump; the flat side of the corm is the top. They can be divided at any time in spring.

***Liriodendron tulipifera* (tulip tree)** There is often dieback in winter on young trees. Cut this off now and take out or shorten any unwanted branches. If there are two competing leaders, shorten one by a half to give the other the lead. The soil must be well worked on planting as the roots do not extend far. They need moisture retentive soil to do well. Feed with a balanced fertilizer such as Fish, Blood and Bone. The fastigiate variety is good placed down the edge of a drive.

Lobelia cardinalis Ensure it is planted the same height as it was in the pot. Mature plants divide easily: pull off the rosettes at the base. Sprinkle bone meal into the hole when planting divisions.

Magnolia Feed with Vitax Conifer and Shrub Fertilizer or Fish, Blood and Bone, then mulch up to 7 cm/3 inches from the trunk. Beware of its easily damaged shallow roots if digging round it.

Matthiasella bupleuroides This monospecific woody perennial (with an AGM) is a little unusual. I have much of it and find its management testing. I used to prop up its increasingly brittle and wild stems even while it flowered beautifully, but the plant became leggy and rank each winter. Its hollow stems mean that cutting it back in autumn is not an option, so in late March/early April (as new growth begins) I cut back to where there are good new fan-like leaves appearing, cutting out the stems damaged over winter and reducing other stems as much as possible to a healthy leaf axil. This reduces its bulk and encourages it to shoot from the bottom, avoiding legginess and too much bare stem, achieving a rounded, multi-stemmed plant.

Meconopsis (Himalayan poppy) Provide a deep mulch of leafmould round the crowns and a balanced feed such as Growmore. If necessary, divide as growth begins.

Melianthus major In warm parts of the country, it may start to flower on last year's growth through late spring into summer. If neater bushy foliage is wanted, cut back to two or three buds from the base. In much of the country, however, it will not be hardy even with the best winter protection. If foliage is frosted, it is worth a long wait to see if new growth is apparent: it sometimes surprises. Do not water during the growing season – no more is needed than what it gets naturally. Feed with a balanced fertilizer such as Fish, Blood and Bone and mulch again.

Miscanthus Cut down to the ground. Some years ago, finding I was doing this later than usual and was cutting through new stems, I asked Neil Lucas of Knoll Gardens and Nursery for advice. He told me to cut through the new shoots of this grass and all would be well – and, of course, it was. (Beware of doing this to other grasses.) Hoe and mulch round the plant when the soil is damp.

Nandina (heavenly bamboo) Take some stems out to thin it, keep a good shape and encourage new growth. Then mulch as it likes moisture. If congested, one or two stems can come out from the bottom. Cultivars with amazing red foliage, best in full sun, are usually either male or female, so for berries as well as foliage colour, two plants would be safer. (They have no relationship to bamboo.)

Nectaroscordum siculum Clumps of these large allium-family bulbs can be split now – they self-seed quickly if they are happy. In a pristine border they can look a mess, but their flowers and the shuttlecock seed heads that follow are very beautiful. Staking is essential to keep them standing well and this should be done now.

Olive (*Olea europaea*) A plant damaged by frost over winter should recover slowly but keep it wrapped up. Gently increase watering. Start feeding monthly with a balanced liquid fertilizer such as soluble Vitax Q4 around the outside edge of the root ball to encourage roots to spread. Keep the soil moist during the growing season. Repot every two years to keep the compost fresh, increasing the size if necessary, using John Innes No. 3 plus 20 per cent grit. Good drainage is essential in a pot or in the ground.

***Omphalodes cappadocica* (navelwort)** Divide this lovely clump-forming perennial now, ensuring the divisions are set into well-mulched ground and watered in well.

Onion When planting onion sets (traditionally done on 12 March), do not just push them in the soil but plant them carefully, three-quarters buried. Birds may try to pull them out and they do not replant well. They can be netted as a precaution.

***Osmunda regalis* (royal fern)** The new fronds of this incredibly beautiful fern will just be appearing. Plant now, with the crown at soil level, incorporating lots of rich organic matter if the soil is rather alkaline (they prefer acid). They can be divided now or in autumn. Beside a pond or stream, there is nothing like them for spring green and autumn gold, but moisture and rich soil are essential.

Pachysandra To encourage new growth, cut back last year's growth to a couple of buds. It can, if needed, be divided now.

Parsley To get early seeds going, wash them in warm water the day before sowing and dry on kitchen paper overnight.

Pea Towards the end of March sow the first batch of peas in zigzag rows, four seeds per hole. Cover with chicken wire (anti-mice) held down by 1.25 m/4 ft birch branches through which the peas can grow. As they grow, pinch back the main stem and shorten laterals until a strong root system is in place and then let them go (just like sweet peas).

Peach At bud burst, peach leaf curl starts to become apparent – pick off every single leaf and bin. New leaves will grow. This does not bother a peach in the greenhouse (it is thought rain carries the spores), but when in blossom a greenhouse peach/nectarine will need pollinating. Touch all the stamens with a piece of cotton wool on the end of a stick.

Pelargonium From the first sight of buds, give a potash-rich feed fortnightly until October (though once a month is enough for the species such as *Pelargonium tomentosum* (brilliant in shade) and *P. sidoides* (glorious in sun). Cut back spindly growth vigorously and with increasing circumspection as time goes on. Water regularly. If cuttings were made last summer, pot them on into John Innes No. 2 plus vermiculite, keeping under cover until June.

Peony: herbaceous Most herbaceous peonies need hazel cages or metal hoops to stop the heavy heads falling forwards. Feed with a balanced fertilizer.

***Perovskia atriplicifolia* (Russian sage)** Left to stand over winter, in year one it will do best if cut back to two or three buds from the base. In following years, cut back when young shoots are seen pushing out from old wood, creating a framework to which you can cut back each year between March and April. Add a generous layer of mulch. Perovskia seem to prefer standing alone with sun and air all around them.

***Persicaria amplexicaulis* (red bistort)** Cut right back if it is still standing.

Phalaenopsis (moth orchid) After a long rest – perhaps a year – repot using moistened proprietary orchid compost if it has overfilled its pot with roots (though it likes compaction). It will need supports for any new growth. A transparent pot allows one to check the roots are happy, but it does not otherwise seem to matter. Start watering weekly using tepid water, feeding each time with a tiny amount of orchid feed. In about six months look out for a new stem or two nudging out from the stalk between the leaves, then perhaps another. It needs light, indirect warmth and humidity. Occasional sunlight is good but not where it will get baked.

Phlomis fruticosa, P. russeliana, P. tuberosa Cut off stems that were left over winter when new growth can be seen pushing (see May). Remove damaged and dead wood; to deal with lopsidedness, cut to a bud further down.

Phlox Feed with a balanced fertilizer and mulch well. They are greedy and thirsty plants, disliking competition from other plants round their roots. They benefit from discreet support.

Photinia × fraseri 'Red Robin' If renovation is needed, cut hard to a low framework. Mulch and spray with fungicide to prevent leaf problems. Cut out any winter damage now. Otherwise, leave pruning until after flowering.

Pieris If needed, renovation pruning can be done this month – they will look unattractive for a year or two but will grow back. Otherwise they need very little attention. Feed and water well after pruning. Pieris does best on acid soil.

Poppy
- *Papaver commutatum* (ladybird), *P. rhoeas* (Shirley poppies), *P. somniferum* (opium) (all annual): sow directly where they are to flower. They hate disturbance so do not work well sown in trays. If germination is slow, gently fork over the ground to bring them to the surface.
- *P.* Oriental and Goliath Groups (perennial): feed with a potash-rich fertilizer such as Tomorite and mulch in early spring – they thrive in rich, well-drained soil.

Potato 'Earlies' (new potatoes) are traditionally planted outside anytime from 17 March (St Patrick's Day), four to six weeks after being chitted. Cover with fleece if frost is forecast. They will be ready by the middle of June.

Potentilla They seem to tolerate neglect but need lots of sun, not minding much about soil or requiring much feeding. To improve the shape and flowering of the shrubby *Potentilla fruticosa* and its many cultivars, cut out one or two stems (cutting out entirely, not into old wood) and small twiggy growths. Shorten the stronger young stems by half but do not cut into old wood that forms part of the framework. A light trim could be enough. They are long flowerers: *P. fruticosa* 'Abbotswood' with white flowers is so good. Trim potentilla grown as hedges.

If any stems of the herbaceous clump-forming potentilla (such as *P. astrosanguineus* and *P. nepalensis*) remain standing from last year, cut them down to the ground ready to start again. They can be divided now if necessary.

Pulsatilla (pasque flower, Easter flower) Feed with bone meal. They will almost certainly die if, once established, they are moved. They also dislike being hemmed in by other plants, so give these utterly beautiful plants as open a site as possible. Remember where they are as they disappear when their glorious seed heads are over.

Pyracantha On free-standing bushes, cut out misplaced shoots. On wall-trained bushes, tie in those wanted, removing any looking wrong. As they flower on old wood, the more that is cut, the fewer the flowers. Prune off the remains of old berry clusters to make room for new growth. Apply sulphate of potash or comfrey pellets around the plant and its root spread. Mulch. Wear gloves as, being a member of the Rosaceae family, a thorn can lead to infection.

Quince (*Cydonia oblonga*) Feed with bone meal, raking it into the soil, and then mulch well. This is a good time to plant: 'Meech's Prolific' (see page 182) and 'Vranja' are two lovely cultivars.

Raspberry Feed with Fish, Blood and Bone, adding chicken manure pellets for extra nitrogen if growth was weak last year. Mulch well again: spent mushroom compost, garden compost or well-rotted manure would be good. Early March is a good time to plant them but ensure they are no deeper than they were in the pot. If summer and autumn raspberries are both wanted, plant well apart or their underground runners will spread between the two, they will entwine and fruit less well. Replant disease is a problem if positioning where raspberries have been before, so change the soil to a depth of at least 35 cm/15 inches before doing so.

Rheum palmatum Divide in early spring. Apply a thick organic mulch. Give it space!

Rhododendron and Azalea Azalea, deciduous or evergreen, is a group within the largely evergreen Rhododendron genus. Azaleas have five stamens, Rhododendrons ten or more.
Feed now, before flowering (and again in June), with a slow release ericaceous fertilizer (specialist grower Millais Nurseries in Surrey provides an excellent one) but avoid forking over the soil, which is where surface-level small feeder roots grow – they are easily damaged. Avoid using bone meal (too calcareous) and do not use weed suppressant mulches like mats or gravel, which stop aeration and are heavy on the roots. Mulching (with leafmould ideally) around the outside edge of the plant where the roots want to reach is fine.

It may be necessary to remove dead wood. Follow growth back into the shrub and prune out at a side shoot. *R. ponticum* (and other rough-barked rhododendrons) can be hard pruned now, with less severe pruning after flowering, unlike others which are just pruned after flowering.

Rose Finish the pruning of shrub roses by early March – end of February ideally –
including roses left unpruned for their hips or winter stem colour. At bud burst feed roses with a proprietary rose fertilizer. Hoe in around the base of each plant and then mulch if not done already. Do not use any old fertilizer or 'chuck in extra' – they will become soft and floppy or worse, poison the soil and inhibit nutrient uptake, causing deficiencies. Do not generally feed rugosa roses. However . . .

- Floribundas (clusters of flowers) can be pruned now. Cut side shoots from the main stems back to two to three buds above last year's cut to keep a branching framework and maintain the characteristic mass of flowers.
- Rugosa roses (also including *Rosa moyesii*, *R. roxburghii* and *R. spinosissima*): all species roses and their near hybrids can benefit from a feed if growth is poor but do not generally feed them. The small-ribbed leaf is a useful identification feature of rugosa cultivars.

Salix (willow)

- *Salix alba* var. *vitellina* 'Britzensis' and many other excellent cultivars: willows grown for winter coloured stems should be pruned by early March, cutting back last year's growth to a few inches off the ground. Alternatively, pollard them having allowed the trunk to grow cleanly to the required height – perhaps 1.5 m/5 ft. Cutting the stems down to the same high framework on the trunk every year gives a goblet shaped crown of golden young stems looking like a flaming torch in winter. *S. alba* var. *vitellina* 'Yelverton' does excellently treated like this.
- *S. caprea* (goat willow), *S. gracilistyla* 'Mount Aso' and 'Melanostachys', and others grown for catkins: to achieve long straight stems of pussy willow catkins for decoration – 'Mount Aso' is so beautiful – cut hard to just above the ground as the catkins are fading but before active growth begins. Catkins

are produced on this new growth, so next year's display should have new straight stems perfect for flower arrangements.

- *S. caprea* 'Kilmarnock' (pendulous goat willow): leave for the first few years; then, as it starts to become congested, take out stems from under the umbrella of stems, starting with the oldest. Always cut to a junction, not leaving any stubs behind as branches are reduced.
- *S. exigua*: a beautiful 4.5 m/15 ft willow with silvery-grey leaves, it produces vigorous arching stems from wherever it is cut back in spring: 30 cm/12 inches off the ground, 1.25 m/4 ft off the ground, at selective branches or left to grow naturally. Prune to whatever suits the situation best. After a few years you will find suckers that need to be removed unless used as a replacement for a tree that has got out of hand.
- *S. fragilis* (crack willow) and other willows used in the wider landscape can be pollarded now with last season's branches cut off just above low, permanent stumps.
- *S. integra* 'Hakuro-nishiki': prune robustly as new shoots are forming to maintain a thick head of leaves. Take out old or damaged stems at the bottom. Then by cutting off old growth across the plant, shaping rather than too much thinning, it will maintain its colourful effect. Grown as a standard, all side shoots need to be removed and it will need staking.

Sanguisorba (burnet) The seed heads, mostly worth keeping over winter provided it is not becoming invasive, need cutting down now. If it is seeding everywhere, ensure you take out the seedlings when very young. See also September.

Sedum (now called Hylotelephium) (stonecrop) When they become too big,

divide when still low but pushing, using a spade to cut through the crown. Discard the oldest piece, replanting divisions just deeper than previously. Planting the divisions more deeply will also help prevent the stems falling outwards (a collapse of stems that is also helped by staking or doing a Chelsea chop – see May).

Sidalcea (false mallow) Divide using a spade if tough and take healthy pieces from the outside of the clump. Add grit to the planting hole as they hate bogginess.

Snowdrop (Galanthus) Divide clumps into smaller divisions and replant immediately where they are wanted, a small handful at a time. They prefer alkaline soil and, while needing good drainage, do not mind the sun or shade so spread them about in groups to create new colonies. Dividing them 'in the green' when flowering is more or less over is the simplest way of multiplying their number. Dig some leafmould or compost into the new ground first, incorporating a slow release fertilizer such as Vitax Q4 (or feed with a weak high-potash liquid fertilizer after they have gone in and before the foliage starts to go yellow). Plant a little deeper than they were before – at least 15 cm/6 inches deep. Water in well and, if showing signs of stress, reduce their foliage. Mulching their area with spent mushroom compost when they have disappeared would be excellent. Experts divide them in early June when they are dormant or August when the bulbs are beginning to root, but this requires knowledge of exactly where and which they are.

Val Bourne, one of the country's great galanthophiles, provides lovely advice as to which snowdrops are the easiest ones with which to start a collection – refer to the Hartley Botanic magazine online.

Solomon's seal (*Polygonatum × hybridum*) Divide the rhizomes now as they are starting to grow. Dig up a clump and ease apart, replanting them shallowly in cool damp shade (it can be done in October if too cold now).

Spiraea japonica and most of its many cultivars (including S.j. 'Shirobana'), S. canescens These spiraea can be cut back hard, to two or three buds or a low permanent framework, as they flower on this year's wood. Let young ones get established for a few years first. Mulch well after pruning. *S.j.* 'Firelight' and 'Candlelight' are diminutive and have pretty spring foliage – although these are *S. japonica* cultivars, trim them very gently. Do not prune spiraea that will flower later this spring and early summer: *S.* 'Arguta', *S. cantoniensis*, *S. × cinerea*, *S. douglasii*, *S. prunifolia*, *S.* 'Snow White', *S. thunbergii*, *S. × vanhouttei* – see July.

Stachys byzantina (lamb's ears) As growth begins in late March, propagate by division, which will improve them greatly. This is a plant so useful in well-drained, dry conditions.

Stipa gigantea Take out the once golden stems as low into the main clump as possible. Give the foliage a moderate haircut at least as far as getting the grass off the ground. With a gloved hand, comb through the plant taking out as much dead foliage and old stems as possible. Leaving this cutting back and tidying up too late leads to cutting out some of the new stems which, unlike miscanthus – see above – it seems to mind. It can be divided every three to four years. Delay a few weeks for the weather to warm up before doing so. (Divided, it will sulk.)

Strawberry Move them to a new site every three or four years: rotation is important. When planting, mulch the ground first and make a wide planting hole so that the roots can spread easily, setting the crowns level with the soil surface.

Remove any flowers in the first year to allow the roots to strengthen, starting to crop only in year two. Water well, feeding fortnightly with a potash-rich fertilizer like Tomorite as they start to put on growth. If not moving or planting, remove old leaves and old runners, tidying up the bed.

Streptocarpus (Cape primrose) Wake it up by repotting into a slightly bigger shallow pot (they like filling the pot) and gently watering.

Sweet pea On any recently germinated seeds, pinch back the tips when the seedlings are about 10cm/4 inches high to encourage side shoots. Keep them in a cool greenhouse, not in the heat. Late frosts are not the enemy of sweet peas but icy winds are. In late March, provided the weather is reasonable, those sown in October can go out into the ground prepared last month. Have some fleece near by to use if the weather turns vile. The more time they have to put on growth before flowering starts in June, the better and stronger they will be. Plant 15 cm/6 inches apart, 6 cm/2½ inches from their support and slightly lower than they were in the pot. Mulch and protect from slugs after planting. Keep the soil moist when planting and then water well. Seeds sown now will produce later flowers with shorter stalks.

Tomato For plants to be grown under cover, sow seeds in deep pots or root-trainers in a propagator at 21°C, or in a plastic bag. After germination move into good light, slightly cooler – then prick out and keep cooler still (12–15°C). Wait a month before sowing plants destined for outside and also delay sowing seeds where tomatoes are to grow on a windowsill – they will become too leggy in what is a relatively low light.

Trillium (Trinity flower) If you want to pamper them, provide a foliar feed of seaweed extract as the leaves emerge.

They are tough and were already fed last month.

Uvularia grandiflora* var. *pallida Divide these wonderful acid-loving, shade-happy, slowly spreading woodlanders now. Though not edible, their new shoots look like asparagus and slugs really love them.

Verbascum (mullein) The big overwintering rosettes of the yellow self-seeding verbascum can, amazingly, be moved if needed – but do it carefully. Take root cuttings, which is the best way of propagating them.

Veronica When planting make sure the root ball is level with the top of the soil. They love full sun and not too moist soil (too little sun and too moist soil and the tall species will need staking). Nonetheless, a spring mulch would be good.

Viburnum* × *bodnantense* and cultivars, *V. farreri These two viburnum flower between last winter and this spring. When flowering is over – ideally within the month of doing so – take out some of the old stems from the base; they make new ones easily. Prune side stems down to a developing shoot to keep the shape in control. Let it get established for two to three years first and do not attack hard every year. The RHS recommends *V.* × *bodnantense* 'Charles Lamont', flowering slightly later than other × *bodnantense*, as the best one for frost-prone gardens.

Vine: grape (grown under glass) Thin out growth if necessary and tie the laterals down so they do not touch the greenhouse glass – otherwise they will scorch in summer sun. At Chatsworth, the heating is turned on, vents are closed, and the floors are damped down twice a day to maintain humidity. Warmth and humidity are key.

Yew Although an annual trim is usually done in August, formative and renovative pruning can be done now (keep an eye out for nesting birds). To renovate, cut back to 15 cm/6 inches from the main stems, one side first, the other a year or two later when the growth has started to recover. Weed, then feed with a balanced fertilizer such as Fish, Blood and Bone, hoeing it in lightly.

Anemone blanda – in flower March and April. They can be spread by division of the tubers – see May

APRIL

Life in the garden is still just about containable: new growth abounds, the heart soars as bluebells colour the woodland floor, pollinators are hard at work, the hours of daylight lengthen. Dividing, feeding, planting, staking, mulching, weeding – it sounds like a mantra for the manic gardener, yet if little was done, the garden would still be a joy next year.

AREAS TO CONSIDER

Annual meadow Choose a site in full sun with rich fertile soil. Cultivate to 10 cm/ 4 inches, rake to a tilth, leave for weeds to reappear, hoe off, seed with an annual mix (adding some sand helps with even distribution), adding soil conditioner if necessary (Westland does a good one). Lay canes across the soil to make a square metre grid for each handful of the mix. Cover with 1 cm/½ inch of sand and press down lightly. Wait for it to rain. Take out weeds as they appear. Expert advice can be had from Pictorial Meadows in Sheffield (and other sources).

Annuals: hardy As the ground warms, hardy seeds can be sown directly outside – calendula, centaurea, larkspur, snapdragon – there are so many choices. If weeds are growing happily, annuals will too. April and May are the classic times to sow outside (in the north probably May/ June). Sown too early, the seeds may rot. Annuals grown hardy over winter can also be planted out. Seedlings in the greenhouse will need hardening off before being planted out next month.

Annuals: half hardy Half-hardy annuals like amaranthus, cosmos, nasturtium, nicotiana, statice, *Tithonia rotundifolia*

Underplanting *Magnolia* 'Susan' in the shrubbery

(a brilliant addition to early autumn) and zinnia should be started mid- to late April.

Black spot and mildew Black spot and mildew indicate dry roots. Wet ground keeps both in check, but then high humidity and poor air circulation bring both to the fore again. Black spot spores overwinter on stem injuries, dormant buds, infected leaves and leaf litter beneath shrubs. Rain splashing spores from the soil up on to leaves and secateurs moving uncleaned between plants both spread it. Recipes to prevent mildew can be found online.

Bulbs Plant summer and autumn flowering bulbs: acidanthera, cautelya, crinum, gladioli, nerine, tree lilies, tulbaghia. Give them a balanced fertilizer such as Growmore on planting.

Climbers To arrest apical dominance and achieve flowers the full length of the shoots, wall-trained climbers and rambling plants should have new shoots tied as horizontally as possible. Help climbers such as honeysuckle and clematis do their twining if necessary.

Compost heap Now that hibernating insects, mammals and frogs are awake, it is safe to turn the compost heap.

Conifers Feed with a nitrogenous fertilizer like Dried Blood to improve foliage colour. Pine, fir and spruce can be pruned if necessary late this month or early May. They have shoots that break from the bud in spring, grow to midsummer, stop extending and form next year's buds by autumn. Yew, cedar, cypress, swamp cypress, thuja and juniper can be pruned any time from now until late summer. When pruning, do not cut into old wood (though yew, taxodium and juniper will usually regenerate). If it has to be done, cut a branch off altogether or at a strong side shoot. Take conifer cuttings – it is not difficult and is very satisfying – refer to a book on propagation.

Containers and pots Begin planting up summer containers using a loam-based compost (John Innes No. 3), incorporating some water-retaining granules and a controlled release fertilizer such as Osmocote. As containers are brought back into life, trim leggy growth, placing smaller pots outside on warm days, and bringing them in at night. Gradually increase watering and begin feeding. Wait until late May to move them into their permanent summer positions. After Plant by Rootgrow is an organic balanced fertilizer that contains beneficial mycorrhizal fungi and other nutrients to kick-start plants which may need a boost.

Cutting garden Stretch netting tightly over canes placed at 30 cm/12 inch intervals for plants to grow through – the netting will soon disappear from sight.

Deadheading and cutting back
All spring flowers and shrubs that are deadheaded will perform better next spring.

Evergreen hedges, trees and shrubs Plant or move evergreens now (September may be better in the south). There is time for them to establish before the soil becomes warm and dry. Evergreen shrubs that have become leggy may need some stems cut out from the base to promote new growth: their renovation is best done after flowering from late April to August. Evergreen trees do not generally need pruning, but if they do this is a good time (see above for conifers). Formative pruning of newly planted evergreens needs doing now – refer to a pruning book. Leave evergreen magnolia pruning to the summer. A dose of Epsom salts will give all evergreens a good start to the growing season.

Ferns Divide by cutting through the caudex at the base of the fronds. This is easily done before they have got going.

Flowers of sulphur/sulphur chips
On alkaline soil, sprinkle round the base of acid loving plants to gradually lower the soil pH, improving autumn colour. Avoid heavy-handedness with sulphur: it remains in the soil and overuse cannot be undone.

Grasses: evergreen and semi-evergreen They can be planted now and, if need be, reduced in size as the weather warms up – any time from mid-April until July. Do not cut down when still dormant and do not cut down hard unless really necessary. Most just need a tidy up. There are some semi-evergreen grasses that should be treated like evergreen unless they are looking tired, in which case cut them right down to the ground: elymus, helictotrichon, hordeum, leymus, poa and sesleria fall into this group.

House plants Repot or topdress with fresh compost, taking the top 5 cm/ 2 inches off last year's compost. Do not overdo the size of a new pot as roots may rot if surrounded by too much soggy soil.

Perennial meadow For a newly establishing meadow in its first year, watering is critical now and all through the summer. Hand remove as many perennial weeds as possible. For the sowing of a perennial meadow, see August and September.

Perennials This is a good time to divide almost all perennials, but in particular late flowering ones such as aster, bergenia, chrysanthemum, hemerocallis, penstemon, sanguisorba and those that dislike cold and wet so would struggle with division in autumn: kniphofia is one such example. Avoid the temptation to crowd divisions back into a small space – they are vigorous, needing room to expand. Spares can be used as infillers later in the season or given away – or best of all sold in aid of the National Gardens Scheme on opening days. Aim to finish moving plants by late April, starting again in September.

Pests Aphids get going now, especially on new shoots of roses. Squash them between fingers or spray with watery washing up liquid and a pinch of cayenne – do not spray with an insecticide which kills their natural predators – in fact, don't fuss about them too greatly. If you must spray, do it only in the evening. Yellow sticky traps in the greenhouse will trap whitefly; watch out for red spider mite (greeny-yellow at this time of year); keep the greenhouse well ventilated; pick off the worst rose leaves with black spot. Lily beetle could appear on fritillaries (see below and lilies in May). Scrub off (with more washing up liquid) the white 'woolly aphid' that may appear on fruit trees, particularly round old pruning cuts.

Phytophthora: turning on tree defences against disease
Dealing with tree disease is an increasing concern to everyone. I follow keenly the research done by Dr Glynn Percival at the University of Reading into the benefits of sugar feeds on trees under stress. He recommends 30–50 g per litre of water per square metre of ground from trunk to canopy drip line. He also advocates the use of pure willow mulches over the area of root spread (always keeping the tree buttresses clear). This is because the willow mulch contains cellulose in its cell walls, and to break down a mulch soil funghi and bacteria produce the enzyme cellul*ase* that also attacks Phytophthora. He also stresses the importance of the removal of competing grasses and weeds and the decompaction of the soil surrounding the tree. The incorporation of a biochar/potassium phosphite mix available commercially as 'Carbon Gold' into the topsoil is another recommendation that has shown remarkably positive results.

Planting This is a prime planting time for shrubs. Determine the plants you want to see flowering in the autumn and procure them now so that they can get their roots well established. Do not feed new plants but always water and mulch well. Neither cold weather nor rain replaces the need to water new plants thoroughly.

Pruning Early April (in most of the UK) is the last opportunity to hard prune shrubs that are going to flower after midsummer on wood to be made this year – giving them enough time to make that necessary growth (many people would say mid-March is the latest). Some shrubs will need less 'hard pruning' but 'shaping' to where new growth is emerging. Take every care not to prune shrubs which have already made their new wood and are shortly to flower. Poor shrubs which are old and miserable – I can think of some philadelphus and syringa – may just revive if cut hard now, either completely to the ground or leaving a few young shoots. Feed, water and mulch.

Seeds Seeds of hardy herbaceous perennials that you may have collected last autumn and stored over winter (at 5°C) can be sown in trays or modules and grown on outside to flower next year. Keep cool, in the light but not direct sunlight and with some protection from rain; a cold frame is ideal.

Shrubs This is a good time to plant shrubs, particularly any slightly tender ones: salvia, for example. Dose any shrubs that were not brilliant last year with sulphate of potash.

Slugs and snails For slugs try beer traps, coffee grounds, Christmas tree needles, sheep wool, garlic or shredded yucca leaf drench recipes, which are easily found online. So unkind but they love beer: set jars in the soil leaving a rim so beetles do not fall in. Part cover the top to make it dark. Clear out regularly as the smell is horrid. Try also half-grapefruit skins placed, cut side down, on the soil. They cannot deal with coffee – even a dilute solution takes them out. There are copper rings to protect plants. My garden is full of toads; they help with control. Hedgehogs also eat them. Where slug pellets must be used, Neudorff Sluggo is a good organic one which, as well as being highly effective, does not poison pets or anyone else inquisitive. The pellets are biodegradable and unconsumed pellets convert into iron and phosphate in the soil.

Succulents Start watering with tepid rainwater, allowing excess water to run away and the compost to dry out between watering. Start a monthly liquid feed of a balanced fertilizer like Miracle-Gro.

Trees Keep watch on young trees, tying the leading shoot to a stake. If there is a lateral competing to become another leader, now is the time to cut it by a third to a bud or out entirely. If there are branches where a clean trunk is wanted, cut them back by half now and take them back completely in autumn (this last from year two).

Turf Laid now, it benefits from a pre-turfing fertilizer (then rain). Keep off it for a month.

Vegetables Sprinkling wood ash would be good (but not while applying other fertilizers). Sowing begins in earnest once the soil is warm – beetroot, carrots, peas (repeated at regular intervals) with the start of successions of lettuce, parsley, rocket, spinach . . . steel yourself against sowing *all* the seeds in the packet at once. Long seeds (such as pumpkins) are better sown vertically so water runs off them. Tomatoes, courgettes and squash can be started under cover but not chard, which bolts if planted too early.

Weeding Do not turn the soil unnecessarily as that just propagates weeds; instead, pick weeds out by hand without disturbing the soil, or use a hoe, which reduces unintentional digging out of bulbs and disturbing young shoots still underground. Nascent growth of ground elder and bindweed can have a glyphosate-based weedkiller such as Roundup applied to the leaves.

PLANTS

Abutilon Remove wind and frost damaged leaves and any that are diseased (do not compost). Abutilon need lots of organic matter and regular feeding from the end of the month. When there is new growth and the first buds appear (this may be April or May) each stem on mature plants can be cut back to the strongest bud – this may be halfway down the stem, which is fine. They put on lots of growth if cut back just as these first buds appear. Winter moth caterpiller seems to be a pest on *Abutilon vitifolium* now and it may need spraying.

   A. megapotamicum and its hybrids like 'Kentish Belle' and 'Yellow Trumpet' are more lax in habit. As new growth begins, now or in May, cut out frost damage and all the stems down by about a third. It is possible to cut right down to a stubby framework near the base (I keep a bit of height). The stems need supports at various heights to enable them to arch over like a waterfall. Left to go on growing upwards with higher and higher support they begin look a bit sparse. Feed with a potash-rich fertilizer such as Tomorite or a proprietary rose feed and mulch.

***Acer japonicum, A. palmatum* (Japanese maple)** Acers like a cool root run, so mulch with leafmould and, if the soil is alkaline, sprinkle flowers of sulphur twice yearly around their base. They need regular watering from when the first leaves appear until they fall in autumn. Avoid liquid fertilizers, which burn the roots, particularly of young trees.

Acers in containers Every three to four years, they need root pruning and repotting as they begin to push new shoots. The roots may need unspiraling and a bigger pot may be needed – avoid using pots with a 'belly' as repotting then becomes difficult. Use John Innes ericaceous compost and extra grit plus slow release fertilizer. The root ball should only just be covered. Mulch the surface with chipped bark or gravel. Keep the pot moist but not soaking wet. Young leaves about to appear may need protection from late frosts. Place the pot out of wind and direct sun. For acers not being repotted, replace the top few inches of the compost, provide a liquid ericaceous feed and water.

Achimenes (hot water plant) Get hanging baskets ready and awaken these plants from their winter in dry compost; water and feed them fortnightly with a potash-rich fertilizer.

Aeonium After winter they may look gaunt. Cut off the tallest rosette with a few inches of stem, allow the cut surface to dry off for a day or two, and then pot into some very gritty compost.

Agapanthus in pots and in the ground Remove old tatty foliage and tidy up after winter. If winter damage is considerable, all the leaves of hardy evergreen agapanthus can be removed (I wait awhile until I am confident there is not going to be another freeze). Deciduous and evergreen agapanthus will benefit from a potash-rich liquid feed every two to three weeks from now until October or a twice yearly feed of rose fertilizer, now and in July. (Hoyland Plant Centre in South Yorkshire, which holds a National Collection, has a proprietary potash-rich feed.) If they start to decline, divide them now rather than in autumn, replanting divisions, if in pots, in compost with John Innes No. 3, adding some grit. In the ground they need to be in well-drained soil and full sun.

Alstroemeria (Peruvian lily) If bought as small plants (easier than tubers, which should be planted in late summer) they should be potted on into larger pots and grown on under cover before being planted out in May. They need lots of space as they do not like disturbance. Feed established plants weekly with a potash-rich liquid fertilizer to improve flowering.

***Amaryllis belladonna* (Jersey lily) (This is a different genus to the hollow stemmed Hippeastrum known as Amaryllis.)** Remove any extra mulch given to the bulbs in winter so they get all the sunshine needed to ripen. Give them a potash-rich liquid feed. Plant new bulbs outside, somewhere sunny, sheltered and in free-draining soil. Soak the roots (just the roots) of the bulb before planting. Place the bulbs so that their neck is level with the soil and water very sparingly. They should flower in October.

Anemone hupehensis, A. hupehensis var. japonica, A. × hybrida, A. 'Wild Swan' If, as leaves appear in spring, they seem to be covered in a mosaic, Helen Yemm suggests in her Saturday *Telegraph* 'Thorny Problems' page that hot water poured over the top of the plant may kill the nematode causing the problem. If they need to be divided, do it now as by autumn their roots are deep. These anemones have offshoots which can be potted up to plant out in summer. If the aim is to move or remove, dig carefully in order not to chop a root in half. Do not cut back the leaves to make more space as this will reduce the flower power of those that you are cutting back.

Argyranthemum frutescens If grown as a standard these decorative daisies can be sheared over to form a neat head. Start deadheading as soon as they come into flower. Constantly pinch out growing tips to keep them dense.

Artemisia: perennial and shrubby
Perennial artemisia, such as *Artemisia ludoviciana* 'Valerie Finnis', divide more happily in spring than autumn. Shrubby, woody based perennials should be cut down now. *A.* 'Powis Castle' does not always get through winter. Provided it has done so, look for new growth and cut all stems back to it or, if there is already a woody framework, cut to a few inches of that. If pruning has been left too late and the plant is already old and leggy, it is more risky, so just shorten the stems to the previous year's growth unless shoots are still developing lower down, in which case cut above them. It is much easier if pruning is started when the plant is young. Pinch out shoot tips to encourage bushiness.

Arundo donax This strong, tall grass, hardy in the south, can become invasive if it is too happy. This is the time to split the rootstock if necessary.

Asparagus The asparagus season traditionally starts on St George's Day, 23 April (and finishes on the solstice, 21 June). Harvest, cutting spears 2.5 cm/ 1 inch below the soil when they are about 18 cm/7 inches tall, from mid-April for the next six weeks. It can take eight weeks of harvesting from year four onwards. Resist harvesting at all until year three. If frost is forecast, cover with a double layer of fleece.

Astilbe Divide every three years. They thrive on moisture so a deep mulch would be good for them.

Astrantia major If new astrantia leaves look patchy, spray with a bug killer: it will be a specific fly that likes young astrantia. Mulch them as they will love the moisture.

Ballota pseudodictamnus An endlessly pretty green, so good in well-drained, poor soils, cut and shape this plant as the weather begins to warm up (not in the middle of a cold spell). It is best divided now – it tends to rot if this is done in October.

Banana If plants have been covered (see October), uncover them in late April.

Bay (*Laurus nobilis*) Give them (and all evergreen trees and shrubs) a dose of Epsom salts. Now is the time to repot bay trees, ideally renewing the compost every two years. At the very least, lift the plant as much out of the pot as possible and push fresh compost around the exposed roots, replacing the top 5 cm/2 inches of compost all round. While this is a good time to trim or raise the skirts of bay grown as shrubs or trees, leave topiary bay until later in the summer. Leaf tips damaged by winter may need removing.

Beetroot Table salt (68 grams per square metre/2 oz per square yard) sprinkled over light sandy soil helps the roots absorb phosphorus and grow better while a nitrogen-rich fertilizer helps on heavier soils.

Begonia rex Cultorum Group Start feeding with a potash-rich fertilizer. Pinch off newly appearing flower buds to promote foliage growth, and on young plants pinch out some stem tips to encourage more branching and bushiness. Allow to almost dry out before watering with lukewarm water. Plants standing in trays of water will rot. Ideally they like a humid, steady temperature of about 21°C out of direct sun.

Bergenia (elephant's ears) Remove old stems and leaves to tidy them up. Mulch and feed or split and replant 15 cm/6 inch lengths of rhizome, each with a rosette of leaves. Plant more deeply than before, spaced 30 cm/12 inches apart.

Bluebell, English (*Hyacinthoides non-scripta*) To contain them in clumps only where you want them, cut the stems right down as soon as the flowers fade. Conversely, if you want them to spread, divide them in late April when still 'in the green' (you have to dig very deep) or leave them to drop their seed before cutting the flowers and spent foliage. They are almost impossible to eradicate so have them only where they will be welcome in spring. Stems held in boiling water for fifteen seconds will stay upright in a vase.

On the English bluebell the flowers all fall on one side of the stem, which bends over at the top. On the invasive Spanish bluebell flowers hang both sides of the stem, which is much more erect; unlike English bluebells, they have no scent.

Blueberry Provide an ericaceous liquid feed monthly from now, watering regularly with rainwater. Keep the mulch refreshed. Flowers may need fleece as protection from a late frost.

Box Feed with a balanced fertilizer like Fish, Blood and Bone. If cuttings were taken last summer, pot them on, move them to a sunny spot outdoors and give them a monthly liquid feed, pinching out young shoots from time to time to make them bushier. When the plants are about 25 cm/10 inches tall they can be planted out as a new hedge.

See May for preventative measures against box blight.

Brachyglottis (was called Senecio) Starting when the plant is young, cut back very low or to a low framework as growth begins in spring. With older bushes just cut back last year's growth unless good shoots can be seen developing further down. No feed is needed.

Brassica: broccoli, cabbage, cauliflower Netting is needed over all brassicas from now on to prevent caterpillers hatched from the cabbage white butterfly having a feast.

Brunnera The crown needs to be 2–3 cm/¾–1¼ inch below the surface of well-fertilized soil in shade.

Bupleurum fruticosum At Coton Manor Gardens in Northamptonshire a wonderful specimen is cut right back every year, probably extending its life as they tend to be short-lived. The normal procedure is to trim lightly.

Callicarpa bodinieri (beauty bush) To encourage new growth, cut out up to one stem in three before growth begins. To maintain a smaller size just prune out problems.

Caltha (king cup/marsh marigold) When flowering is finished, cut the foliage back as it often gets mildew. By removing these leaves, the plant will grow fresh ones and possibly provide a second flush of flowers.

Camellia When flowering is over, feed with an ericaceous fertilizer (not bone meal) monthly until August and then stop – or use the Millais Nurseries slow release feed you may have for rhododendrons. (Later feeding and a shortage of water in late summer both cause bud drop.) The moment to tidy up or hard prune is just after flowering. Gentle shaping is good; reduce last year's growth to a few buds to achieve a bushier plant. They do take harsh pruning after flowering but at the cost of next year's flowers.

Ceanothus: autumn flowering evergreen, such as 'Autumnal Blue', C. 'Burkwoodii' Gentle pruning only: remove damaged stems and cut back last year's growth to two to four buds from the previous year's growth. If the plant has got far too big, take out one or two complete stems from the base, but do not cut into old wood as it will not regenerate.

Ceratostigma
- *Ceratostigma plumbaginoides*: cut back flowered shoots to 1 cm/½ inch beyond last year's growth to shape this woody perennial and then mulch, tidying up under and round its base.
- *C. willmottianum*: this beautiful plant can be cut back in early April provided it is not still very cold – the extent depends how it fared in winter. Just prune out a few stems if it is young, or if there is concern for its hardiness simply neaten last year's growth, taking out damaged stems. If it is growing happily in a sheltered south-facing corner, cut it back to about 15–23 cm/6–9 inches from the ground when you can see new shoots breaking. Feed, then mulch.

Cercidiphyllum Sprinkle flowers of sulphur or sulphur chips around the base if the soil is alkaline. Then mulch and water well.

Chamaecyparis lawsoniana (Lawson's cypress) Shaped varieties such as 'Minima Glauca' and 'Stardust' will need trimming now and again in August to keep in good shape. You cannot cut into old wood.

Cherry: formative pruning Mature ornamental cherries and sweet and acid cherries are pruned in summer, but formative pruning of young trees is done at bud burst. Refer to a pruning book. The acid morello cherry could be fed again with sulphate of ammonia or other nitrogen-rich fertilizer now.

Chive Planted round the base of a rose they will probably keep the rose aphid-free (until you decide to move the chives elsewhere). They make good companion plants for tomatoes, sunflowers, chrysanthemums and much else. When cutting, take a handful to the ground rather than a few inches off the top.

Clematis and clematis planting
Give all clematis a handful of sulphate of potash or bone meal and a mulch of garden compost. April is a good time to plant (as is September). Rootballs must be out of direct sun, mulched and watered. If surrounding plants are still not high enough to shade the base of the plant, I have found that an upturned black plastic pot with the bottom removed, placed over emerging clematis, provides good protection. Always release clematis from their nursery ties and spread them, however small. A clematis destined to grow up a tree should go on the north side near the drip line, so roots are not in the sun. For one against a wall, leave a space of about 50 cm/20 inches: too close and it will not thrive.

Group 1 *Clematis armandii*: this evergreen needs its browned leathery leaves removed. Just trim to fit the space. It will die given a chance.

Group 2 clematis should be planted 5–7 cm/2–3 inches deeper than they were in the pot, in a generous hole with the first set of leaves buried beneath the surface.

Clerodendrum Tear suckers from the parent as they start back into active growth (they sucker badly) and pot up a good one or two in case you need a replacement.

Colchicum (autumn crocus/naked ladies) and autumn flowering crocus (Colchicum and crocus that flower in autumn are two different genus.) Give the corms a foliar feed such as liquid seaweed extract.

Convolvulus cneorum To keep the plant compact, before bud burst cut back any overlong shoot to a well placed side shoot, or remove the shoot completely if it spoils the shape.

Cornus (dogwood)
- Cornus grown for showy bracts: *Cornus alternifolia*, *C. controversa*, *C.* 'Eddie's White Wonder', *C. florida*, *C. kousa*, *C.* 'Norman Hadden', *C. nuttallii*, *C.* Venus and others: give these cornus a sequestered iron feed every two weeks from early April until mid-May.
- Cornus grown as ground-cover: *C. canadensis* (creeping dogwood): this beautiful ground-cover cornus will only grow well (in sun or part shade) on neutral to acid soil. I have nurtured it to no avail. It can be divided now, the divisions planted with lots of leafmould or composted pine needles.
- Cornus grown for winter stem colour: *C. alba* 'Sibirica', *C.a.* 'Kesselringii', *C. sericea* 'Flaverimea' and others: it is usual to cut these back hard in late March but if they are still looking good now, wait until just before bud break. Some are thought less robust, in particular *C. sanguinea* 'Midwinter Fire' and *C.s.* 'Anny's Winter Orange'.

These rather smaller coral and flame coloured dogwood may require lighter pruning than their *C. alba* and *C. sericea* cousins. Start their pruning in year two and judge how they respond to being cut right down every year. Be prepared to be less drastic than with 'Sibirica', 'Kesselringii' and 'Flaverimea'. Feed with a balanced fertilizer like Vitax Q4 and mulch after cutting.

Cosmos Either sow *in situ* from mid-April or harden off those grown inside and plant out towards the end of the month/early May.

Cotoneaster: evergreen or semi-evergreen If necessary, be fairly brutal now, thinning out, restricting long growth or hard pruning. Always cut to a bud facing in the right direction. Leave *C. horizontalis* until May.

Crambe cordifolia Add grit and lots of mulch around the emerging shoot. It likes very well-drained soil. A large hoop around the plant helps to keep the leaves looking good as, with a little encouragement, they grow over it. When planting, add copious quantities of grit and a handful of Fish, Blood and Bone to the hole. They do not move, so place them well first time.

Crinum × powellii (swamp lily)
Plant in deep fertile ground, the tip of the bulb at soil level, its long neck above the soil. Add grit if in pots (they like root restriction). They do not like being disturbed once established. Having very big leaves, they are hard to mix with other flowers. Anna Pavord, in her book *Bulb*, suggests a narrow south-facing border or the base of a greenhouse wall. Wherever they go, give the clump its own space, planting bulbs about 60 cm/24 inches apart in moist, deep, fertile soil.
They will need a lot of watering as they get established.

Crocus: spring flowering Covering the soil above the bulbs with grit deters mice and is a reminder as to where they grow. Do not cut the leaves until they have died down; then they can be divided.

Crown imperial (*Fritillaria imperialis*) Feed with a potash-rich fertilizer such as Tomorite every week until the foliage begins to turn yellow and the bulbs re-enter dormancy. If after two or three years they have not flowered well, leave them until early autumn and then replant: they need to be at least 30 cm/12 inches deep and on their side. Watch for lily beetle (see below).

Cymbidium (orchid) Every couple of years, repot using a bark-based orchid compost. Do not pot on too large as they like to be pot-bound. If it is difficult to remove from the pot, soak it for half an hour. Shake off old compost, trim dead roots (live roots are white and firm). Push new orchid compost round the roots and start feeding with a proprietary orchid fertilizer. Water (tepid) from above, not letting the plant sit in water. Let the compost dry out between waterings.

Dahlia Pinch out the tips of the main stems as they grow, down to the top pair of leaves, using these for propagation – they take very easily. Stock can also be increased by cutting tubers in half, each with a piece of root and good new shoot, potting them up separately and watering in. Another recommendation is to cut out the centre stem when new growth is about 45 cm/18 inches high to achieve a stronger plant. Meanwhile, prepare the ground for their return (presuming they have been under cover over winter) by digging in lots of manure or leafmould and a balanced fertilizer such as Fish, Blood and Bone.

Diascia Cut back in late April if straggly. Do not feed as it makes them leggy.

Dicentra spectabilis (now called *Lamprocapnos spectabilis*) (bleeding heart) When planting, the roots need space to spread out. The crown should be 3–4 cm/1¼–1½ inches below the soil surface.

Dierama pulcherrimum (angel's fishing rods) Plant now. Using sharp scissors cut to the base any dead leaves or winter damage in the clump – avoid overzealous pulling or the growing shoot will come out. Cutting the leaves right down stops them flowering for a year or two. Mulch with leafmould and feed with a balanced fertilizer like Fish, Blood and Bone or Growmore. They need regular watering in summer but hate being waterlogged. They take ages to recover from division, but if the clump is very big (a lovely problem to have) do it now – their roots are very brittle so divide with great circumspection. They are most happy given sun on all sides.

Doronicum (leopard's bane) Deadhead this early blooming yellow daisy regularly. It can be cut back hard to prevent self-seeding and acquire new foliage if it becomes untidy. It sometimes goes dormant in a hot summer. Some taller varieties will need support. It needs some slug protection.

Dryopteris erythrosora (buckler fern) Resist cutting off last year's fronds too early in the growing season as they provide some protection for the unfurling fronds. They can be divided now or in the autumn.

Elaeagnus, evergreen: *Elaeagnus × ebbingei* (now called *E. × sub-macrophylla*), *E. pungens* 'Maculata', *E. × reflexa* To control size, take out up to 50 per cent of old growth, prune to side branches or cut older stems from the base, encouraging attractive new foliage. Use secateurs, as leaves cut in half are not pretty. If it is growing as a hedge and autumn flowers are not important, it can be trimmed. Left unpruned, it flowers on last year's growth. The variegated varieties are less tough than the all-green species. Cut out reversions. Their shallow roots need protection so mulch after feeding with Fish, Blood and Bone.

Eranthis hyemalis (winter aconite)
Do not remove leaves: they must die naturally or they will not flower next year. Collect seed when they turn black in the dying foliage. Throw seed under deciduous shrubs and trees (and under horse chestnuts and sycamores where, Noel Kingsbury writes, they grow well). They will take three to four years to flower. Clumps can be divided now, needing good drainage and no competition from dense roots nearby. If buying dry tubers soak for two hours first. Note their position as they disappear as it is too easy to dig up the colony to plant something over them.

Eryngium (sea holly)
Remove any remnants of last year's foliage and ensure it has room around it to grow out. A low metal grid ring which foliage will disguise is often really helpful to support the flower stems. They do not like wet (so avoid mulching) and do best on poor soil (so avoid them in the general feeding too).

Escallonia
In the first spring after planting, a much bushier shape will be achieved by tipping back the main branches. Its annual prune is in September.

Eucomis (pineapple lily)
If they have overwintered in a shed, bring them into a cool greenhouse to start them back into growth, cleaning them and watering them with rainwater. If they have been left in the ground, every three or four years in early April dig up and replant (and their offsets separately) with their tops 7 cm/3 inches below the soil surface and with lots of grit below, backfilled with a mixture of soil, composted bark and a sprinkling of Fish, Blood and Bone. Feed every year with a diluted potash-rich fertilizer. They do well in pots so long as they have lots of room: bulbs will need to be about 35 cm/ 14 inches apart to allow for leaf expansion. Here each bulb should be just beneath the soil level. They will need watering and feeding regularly until October and need full sun to sparkle. *Eucomis comosa* 'Sparkling Burgundy' is a show stopper in big pots.

× Fatshedera (false castor oil plant)
If it needs reducing, cut out about a third of the stems to their base to encourage new foliage. Avoid cutting bits off branches; take off the whole stem or the graceful shape is lost.

Fennel
The perennial fennel does not transplant so sow where it is to grow. If a stand of fennel is getting too big, chop it back a bit. It will not be hindered. Florence fennel, producing the bulb crop, has to be planted each year (but not until June).

Festuca glauca
Trim brown tips, cutting back dead leaves to the base. Divide this grass every three years to maintain vigour.

Fig
Tip the branches just above the top developing fig. Minimal feeding is needed, but if the leaves are too close together or start to look yellow, give the plant a potash-rich feed such as Tomorite.

Forsythia
Prune hard after flowering – flowered shoots need cutting back to new growth and a developing bud: cut out floppy growth to an upright shoot. Keep the shrub sprightly by cutting out one in five of the shoots from the base. Leave new plants unpruned for two years.

Freesia Buy prepared corms which have had a period of dormancy, planting them anytime from late April to July. Sarah Raven's advice – see her excellent website for information in greater detail – is to plant them pointy end upwards (six in a 12 cm/5 inch pot of 3:1 compost and grit) with support in place from the start, to water them and keep in the shade until the corms start to sprout, and then to move into full sunlight, continuing to water. When the buds show colour they can come inside. Grown in pots they do not need feeding, though in the soil (in light shade 5 cm/2 inches deep, 5–8 cm/2–3 inches apart) a feed of potash-rich fertilizer such as Tomorite would help as they are growing. Flowers appear 100–120 days after planting.

Fritillary Keep an eagle eye out for red lily beetle, which will appear about now on fritillaries. See lily beetle below for how to deal with them.

Fuchsia: tender and standard
Bring out of dormancy any that have been kept in a cold greenhouse (see February). For those that are already growing well, start a weekly feed with a potash-rich fertilizer such as Tomorite and continue pinching out to make the best bushy shape for later. The advice of Lockyer Fuchsias in Bristol is that earlier blooms will be achieved on a smaller plant if pinching out is stopped at this stage.

Gardenia augusta, G. jasminoides
Prune out any wrongly placed shoots. Move pots in and out as the weather dictates. They like acid soil that is kept moist but not too wet. In the ground they like partial shade. Water pots with rainwater and mist when not in flower (July to September probably). Start feeding now with a fertilizer suitable for acid plants – do not overdo but continue monthly until about September. Indoors, they need bright light and high humidity: damp but not wet pebbles underneath the pot would be good.

Gaura lindheimeri Cut down last year's stems as new shoots emerge. They are slow to get going, looking like dead sticks for ages. New plants need to be about 2.5 cm/1 inch deeper than in the pot, 5 cm/2 inches lower if planting in gravel. Their deep taproot (they do not move happily once established) appreciates lots

Fritillaria meleagris (snake's head fritillary, flowering April–May)

of organic matter in the planting hole but thereafter sharp drainage is desirable.

Gentiana asclepiadea (willow gentian) Established clumps (growing in dappled shade and neutral to acid humus-rich soil) can be divided or rooted offsets taken now before flowering in July.

Gladiolus murielae (was called Acidanthera bicolor and G. callicanthus) Separate the numerous cormlets when still dormant and, with any newly purchased corms, plant now, generously, 7 cm/3 inches apart, 12 cm/ 5 inches deep in compost with added John Innes No. 3 in pots or in well-mulched soil. Those from last year which are bigger than about 2.5 cm/1 inch in diameter should do even better this year. Little cormlets can be planted in pots or in spare ground to grow on. They are not entirely hardy so they may not get through next winter outside unless very sheltered, but they do look wonderful cast amongst plants that will give them support during their flowering in August. I think it is worth losing a few in the ground even if they then get caught by cold or dug up by mistake. Others can be planted in the safety of pots to be brought in over winter.

Grisellinia Not requiring regular pruning, it can be clipped or cut back hard now – it recovers well.

Hazel (Corylus maxima 'Purpurea' and C. × 'Red Zellernus') Having enjoyed the wonderful red catkins, cut out one stem in three to improve leaf colour or cut it all right down to a few inches from the ground for regrowth.

Hebe They prefer neutral to acidic soil so water, if needed, with rainwater. They must be well drained so incorporate grit on planting. Never give a nitrogenous fertilizer but fork in a scattering of a balanced feed like Fish, Blood and Bone now to help them along.

Helenium A good time to divide them (every three years) is just as they start to reappear, trimming their roots if necessary and removing old material. Feed with Fish, Blood and Bone and mulch. They enjoy open, reliably moist soil: if too congested they will get mildew. The taller ones will need staking; twiggy supports or pea netting would be good to grow through.

Helianthus, including Helianthus 'Lemon Queen' (perennial sunflower) Spring division is easiest using a sharp spade around the edges. Dispose of the central piece of the crown – it flowers much better from younger growth. Mulch generously with a rich compost. A netting support across the clump would be beneficial later on.

Helichrysum italicum (curry plant) To stop it getting leggy, thus losing much of its charm, cut it back now to where it was last year; starting early in the plant's life is key to its good appearance.

Helictotrichon sempervirens Using gloves, remove old leaves and dead flower stems, tidying up this steely blue grass. Cut right down only if it is looking sad. It is happiest in sun and poorish alkaline soil.

Heliopsis helianthoides Every few years, divide as new shoots emerge, providing support for the taller cultivars like 'Sommersonne'. Feed with a balanced fertilizer like Fish, Blood and Bone, mulch and water the divisions well.

Helleborus × hybridus Deadhead to keep colours pure; otherwise, collect the seed or let them self-seed naturally for lots of mixed colour offspring. (Seeds need to be sown fresh so do not store them.) Cutting off the flower stems at the base before the seed pods split open does help to bulk up the clumps, as would a few fortnightly feeds of Vitax Q4HN (which contains added nitrogen). In any case, remove any leaves that look past their best, mulching with leafmould or mushroom compost before leaves block the soil from sight. They can be divided when flowering is over but they do sulk after division (see also September). *H. argutifolius* and *H. foetidus* can be deadheaded too (but not divided).

Hepatica Watch out for seeds in late April – they need to be sown very fresh. Thinly cover with 5 mm of grit, water well, protect from slugs and leave outside. They will germinate in six to eight weeks and can be potted on in September. I always miss my chance to collect seeds. Divide now.

Hesperantha coccinea (syn. Schizostylis coccinea) (kaffir lily)
Moisture and rich soil is key so a thick mulch of manure and a covering of grit now will keep the moisture in. They take quite a while to bulk up but will get there so long as they do not dry out. They can be divided now if congested – each new clump should have at least five to six leaves.

Hippophae rhamnoides (sea buckthorn)
I had one which did nothing for years and eventually I pulled it out, disappointed it had not produced the wonderful berries I was expecting. I did not know then that it was dioecious so I needed a female with a male close by. Pity. To stop legginess, cut out one stem in three from the base as it begins to establish.

Hosta As tips emerge, mix a nitrogen-rich feed like chicken pellets with some garden compost and spread it around the plants. Then put some fine grit on top to start the slug war which will need to be maintained. Protect new shoots from slugs – pellets, coffee grounds, an organic liquid slug killer (see online) or a mulch of sharp gravel all help. They seem more fond of the thinner leaved varieties that have less ridging. Plants can be divided now their pointy new shoots are just poking through the soil and before their leaves develop. Chop through the clump and divide into smaller bits, each with at least three to four shoots, repotting or replanting immediately. They can be divided in early autumn too, but it is easier to do now without leaves.

Hydrangea
• *Hydrangea macrophylla*: there are two forms – mopheads and lacecaps – and they are treated in very much in the same way. These hydrangeas flower on shoots from the previous year's growth. The dead flowers will have been left on over winter for frost protection. Before the leaves start expanding, take off the dead flowers (unless more frost is forecast), cutting above the first fat pair of buds at the second pair of leaves just below the flower head – it will be obvious now (the nascent flower bud is fat, the leaf buds are slim and pointed). Christopher Lloyd apparently never pruned hydrangeas wearing sleeves as he knew he might unwittingly knock off these buds. Then remove to the ground any very old stems, wandering or weak-flowered, thin stems and dead wood. To shape or rejuvenate the plant cut further back – all will be fine but no flowers this year. Feed and mulch. Now denuded of its winter protection, if a frost descends, throw some fleece over it. Mulch but do not fertilize now or there will be lush growth at the expense of flowers. (For growing blue hydrangea see December.)
• *H. serrata*: these delicate hydrangeas – like *H. serrata* 'Kiyosumi' with its inner mass of small fertile florets and pretty, petal-like sterile flowers in the outer ring – have noticeably more

twiggy growth than their more robust macrophylla cousins. So just clean up the delicate *H. serrata* and cut back to the next fat healthy looking pair of buds on the previous season's shoots as above for macrophylla. Again mulch, but do not feed at this stage. Some cultivars of *H. serrata* are more robust – 'Grayswood', for example, can be pruned by taking out old growth from the base if there is a need to ease congestion.

Hyssopus officinalis Cut back to 2.5–5 cm/1–2 inches of the previous year's growth to stop it becoming leggy and charmless and to produce lovely flowers from midsummer to autumn. Divide now if necessary.

Imperata cylindrica 'Rubra' (red baron grass) The stems and dead leaves of this grass can be cut out in mid-spring, ideally as the first new growth begins. Leave division until actively growing in early summer. It needs warmth in summer to do well.

Iochroma australis Bought out of a cool greenhouse now into a warm sheltered courtyard, what it needs is a gentle prune to shape, the replacement of its topdressing and the start of a monthly feed of a balanced liquid fertilizer.

Itea ilicifolia Trim back to tidy, staking or tying back if necessary. Grow it, ideally, against a warm wall.

Ivy (Hedera) Trim in spring, not in October/November when flowers provide pollen for bees. The ability of ivy to absorb pollutants from the atmosphere makes it an invaluable plant in towns and in the house, but what it absorbs slowly destroys older growth. So in these situations, the more new growth is encouraged, the better it will be. A balanced liquid feed may be appropriate now.

Knautia macedonica Get support in early or it will fall over its neighbours.

Lathyrus vernus (spring bitter vetch) Feed with a potash-rich fertilizer like Tomorite (the pea family do not need nitrogen). Keep picking to get more flowers. Check for slugs as new shoots emerge. Divide as soon as flowering is over.

Lavender When frosts are over, most of the growth left on last year can be removed to encourage bushiness but do not cut into old wood. On one-year-old plants, if small neat specimens are wanted, all the stems can be cut back to within 7–10 cm/3–4 inches of the ground as new growth begins. This hard pruning can only happen if done from the start.

Lemon tree (citrus) Increase watering and feeding, continuing this care until they go outside in June. Start misting as their environment gets warmer. Always use rainwater, not tap. If roots are not congested replace the top 5 cm/2 inches of compost. Otherwise repot now, into 75:25 John Innes No. 3 compost and alpine grit (which is lime free).

Leucanthemum × superbum (shasta daisy), L. vulgare (marguerite, ox-eye daisy) Both these daisies need splitting every three years or so. Improve the soil when doing so. They may splay open later in the year if not supported by surrounding plants/grasses. Pinching out the new growth will help to keep them from becoming too leggy.

Leucojum vernum (spring snowflake) Divide after flowering when clumps are big enough.

Libertia chilensis Formosa Group (formerly called L. formosa) There may be seedlings (if not unwittingly disposed of as weeds), which can replace the parent as foliage gets less attractive with age. Comb through to remove tired leaves or, if really congested, cut back foliage (by no more than half) to make way for new. They can be divided now. (Mine sulked.)

Ligularia When planting (out of direct sun) give each plant in the clump space to establish happily.

Lily – and lily beetle From their first appearance, feed lilies every month with sulphate of potash. A liquid slug deterrent would be good now.

Lily beetles emerge from the soil in late March and lay their eggs on the underside of plants from April to midsummer. The eggs hatch as larvae, protected with a horrid black excreta. Unless picked off, the larvae feed on the leaves doing a great deal of damage. When feasted, the larvae return to the ground to pupate, leaving what Chris Blom of Blom Bulbs describes as something looking like bird droppings on the soil surface. He suggests covering the soil sparingly with cooking oil to prevent the new adult lily beetles emerging – it works. This is something to look out for keenly from now until midsummer. If they escape this treatment, they will pupate and emerge as red adult lily beetles. When these are seen on the leaf, they can be picked off by hand. Use two hands: one to squash, one to catch. The moment they sense movement the beetles drop to the soil and are gone, so lay a large white handkerchief under the plant to extend your chance to catch them. They, and the next generation of excreta covered larvae, will continue to feed on the leaves and stems of lilies and fritillaries until they return to the soil to overwinter. Spraying with a systemic insecticide is the only other alternative, which must be done after sunset.

Limnanthes douglasii (poached egg plant) This annual, so loved by bees and hoverflies, is pretty round an urn or along a path. Sown in February and planted out now in shallow, well-prepared soil, it will flower in June and, once established, should self-seed satisfactorily. It can also be used as a green manure.

Liriope (lilyturf) Cut back by half anytime until July. Protect from slugs and snails. They are acid loving plants so use ericaceous compost if planting in pots.

Lithodora diffusa 'Heavenly Blue' One of my favourite plants, it needs to be well drained and prefers neutral/acid soil. It grows fairly well on my slightly alkaline rockery but not as sumptuously as it would in more acid conditions. Clip over the first flush of flowers and more will come.

Lonicera nitida Clip or cut out woody stems if they are spoiling the shape. If renovation is needed, prune hard. It generally needs three clippings to keep trim: now, early summer and late August.

Lotus hirsutus (now called Dorycnium hirsutum) Cut all last year's growth back to prevent it becoming woody and to maintain its prettiness. Shaped now, it will flower from June for months and be followed by very attractive seed heads. The seeds germinate easily.

Lupin: perennial Sometimes they rot if they are very close and so need spreading out. They can also become less productive after about five years, so it is well worth propagating new stock from seed later in the year. Do not overwater – they find their own. Clear away last year's foliage as new shoots appear. Beware slugs and snails.

Luzula nivea Cut back by half any time from now until July (avoid cutting it back in winter).

Mahonia: upright shrubs, among them _Mahonia eurybracteata_ (including 'Soft Caress'), _M. japonica_, _M. × media_, _M. oiwakensis_ subsp. _lomariifolia_ and _M. × wagerni_ (see June for ground-cover mahonia) Remove the rosette of flowers when over. If the stem has not flowered, still remove the end rosette of leaves to encourage more side growth. This means missing out on berries, but it stops the shrub becoming leggy. When planting a new mahonia, remove its flower head to encourage it to branch out from year one. Add a handful of a balanced fertilizer like Fish, Blood and Bone, avoiding nitrogen-rich feed. Do not overwater.

Marigold (Tagetes) Sow seed under cover, bedding out _before_ flowering. If buying nursery stock, purchase before they are in flower.

Morning glory (_Ipomoea tricolor_) Nick the seed, soak briefly in warm water and then sow in multipurpose compost to germinate under a plastic bag or in a propagator at 20–25°C. Prick out and grow on in good light, keeping moist. Pot on regularly; being fussy they resent checks like becoming pot-bound, drying out or a sudden change of temperature. Tie the young plant to a cane, harden off, protect from slugs and, in warmer parts of the UK, plant out in late May. Most will put on rapid growth.

Mulberry (Morus) Best planted now, taking care of their brittle roots. Young trees always need staking. For bounty in the long term, water and feed monthly for the first few years. Mulch deeply.

Muscari (grape hyacinth) I spend hours trying to rid some soil of _Muscari armeniacum_: a menace in the wrong place, producing hundreds of bulblets. Let the foliage die down naturally to increase flower power next year but deadhead to prevent their spread. Do not feed as that produces too much lush growth. Cultivars like _M. armeniacum_ 'Valerie Finnis' and other species like _M. botryoides_ f. _album_ are beautifully behaved.

Myrtle (_Myrtus communis_) If frost has knocked it hard, a trim will help it rejuvenate. If it needs to be reduced, trim it every other year in April; some of the flowers will be lost so do not be harsh.

Narcissus (daffodil) Snapping off old flower heads strengthens the bulb for better flowering next year. For really top flowers, apply a liquid fertilizer when flowering is over and repeat weekly until the foliage has died down. I cannot imagine getting round to doing this. However, the foliage must be left uncut for at least six weeks, never tying it up – doing so stops nutrients going back to the bulb. So, no mowing until the bulbs have died down naturally. The sap is toxic: freshly mixed with other flowers in a vase, they will do their companions no good.

Nasturtium (_Tropaeolum majus_) and _T. speciosum_ Soak nasturtium seeds overnight and plant individually in small pots to help get them established outside; the fleshy seedlings are very easily caught by frost. Use them sacrificially in the vegetable beds (where they will be devoured by caterpillars and blackfly) or use them as wonderful mounds of colour (in particular, the Alaska series) to cover the dying leaves of spring bulbs.

The perennial climber _T. speciosum_ can be cut back now before its regrowth begins. It is difficult to establish and is called the 'Scottish Flame Thrower' because, as well as acid soil, it seems to like the hot – but not generally speaking too hot – sun of Scotland.

Olearia × haastii, _O. macrodonata_ and other late flowering olearia (daisy bush) In the first year, these olearia can be cut back to encourage side shoots and make a bushy plant. From year two onwards, cut out all the obviously wrong bits, then just trim to keep the symmetry. Spread renovation of older bushes over two years; they can be cut hard or have one stem in three cut from the base if needed. Cutting out the lower branches of *O. macrodonata* shows its attractive bark. See June for *O. phlogopappa* and other earlier flowering olearia.

Olive There is a natural leaf fall in April so do not fret.

***Ophiopogon planiscapus* 'Nigrescens' (black grass)** This black 'grass' (in fact, not a grass but a member of the lily family) with swollen roots can be divided now as growth gets going. A balanced liquid fertilizer every month helps it thrive.

Pelargonium Deadhead, pinching out growing tips to get bushy growth. Take cuttings of the succulent stemmed 'zonal' pelargoniums (round, wavy, often two-coloured leaves) used extensively for bedding.

Penstemon In late April when new shoots are visible at the base, cut down to this new growth; on some there will be a framework to cut to. If there are *no* shoots showing, just cut the old growth down to the second set of healthy leaves. Penstemons do not like being moved or split, so take cuttings – see August. Some taller varieties will benefit from hazel supports put in now for later.

Phormium Cut out tattered leaves and, in variegated plants, any leaves that have reverted. Use a sharp knife, not secateurs. This is a good time to divide if it has got too big; either pull away offshoots, each with some root, or take a saw to the plant, soaking the divisions well before replanting. They are greedy feeders so an occasional dose of a balanced fertilizer

like Growmore would be good, particularly for those in pots.

***Phygelius aequalis* 'Yellow Trumpet', *P. × rectus* 'African Queen' and other cultivars** My *P. × rectus* 'African Queen' became a thug grown against a sheltered wall. It was cut back hard like a herbaceous perennial every spring. Its surface roots made it easy to propagate but were a nuisance as they wove their way through other plants (so it is no more). Grown as a rather wonderful shrub, it just needs cutting back into shape now and given an occasional balanced feed. Figwort weevil can be a nuisance and will need spraying, but this must not be done when its flowers are out or pollinating insects will be killed.

***Physalis alkekengi*, now called *Alkekengi physalis* (Chinese lanterns)** Divide now, feed and water well. Watch out for caterpillars.

Physocarpus opulifolius If leaf colour is more important than flowers, cut some shoots to the base if they are old, others to a strong bud, getting the desired shape. If its pretty flowers are more important, leave most shoots to bear flowers, just cutting out one or two older ones at the base for regeneration, leaving pruning until July. It needs to be kept moist in dry spells or it will turn up its toes. Hoe in a granular feed.

Pittosporum If a vigorous species needs cutting back it can be done from late this month when any frost damage can also be removed. In its first year, cutting back by a third will encourage side shoots. Pittosporum hedges can be trimmed now. All green reverted shoots must be cut out of variegated species.

Plum Give young plums a formative prune now, as the leaves unfold. Consult a pruning book for advice. Adult trees are pruned in summer so at the moment leave alone.

Polystichum (soft shield fern)
Cut back the dead foliage of this lovely fern.

Pontederia cordata (pickerel weed)
Two to three years after planting, divide this marginal pond plant.

Primula
- Polyanthus: picking flowers of double primroses keeps them going as they continue to produce new blooms in their futile effort to set seed, which as doubles they are unable to do (rather sad little tale really).
- *Primula beesiana, P. bulleyana, P. denticulata* (drumstick primula), *P. florindae, P.* 'Inverewe' (and other Candelabra primulas), *P. pulverulenta, P. vialii* and others: deadhead all through the season to get new flower heads, taking off dead leaves to keep them neat. They must have moisture. Check for slugs.

Privet (Ligustrum) Prune two or three times a year, starting now, to keep in shape. Mulch, feed and water. Treat gently when young.

Protea Those planted in the soil are sensitive to phosphorus (contained in most fertilizers) so do not feed. Potted plants can be fed with a slow release nitrogen fertilizer three times during the year. Avoid using water from butts (the stagnant water could contain fungal pathogens). Use ericaceous compost when repotting.

Rhamnus alaternus (Italian buckthorn)
Prune now (and again midsummer) to keep compact or topiarized.

Rhus typhina (sumach) To get the largest leaves cut back last year's growth to a low framework. Otherwise leave it and prune in late winter. Keep on top of suckers.

Rodgersia Divide and replant the slowly spreading rhizomes in early April. Each piece needs roots.

Romneya coulteri (California tree poppy) Cut back last year's growth to 5–10 cm/2–4 inches from the base. Clear fallen leaves/weeds from around the crown. Mulch. There may be suckers: dig up taking lots of soil with it, hoping it does not notice it is being moved. Romneya dislikes root disturbance of any kind. An all-purpose seaweed fertilizer would help growth now.

Rose
- Where you can, pick off any leaves showing early signs of black spot. (Never denude the plant of all its ability to photosynthethize by removing too many leaves at one time.)
- Rub aphids off with finger and thumb or knock them off with a blast of water. This is preferable to spraying as they are an important food source for beneficial insects. If using a spray, SB Plant Invigorator is organic and as well as helping to control aphids is also a foliar feed.
- Water the soil not the leaves (preferably at dusk).
- Lots of heavy organic mulch is especially important for roses against the walls of houses where soil is dry.
- As the leaves start unfurling and the shoots extend, spray against rust and black spot (if happy to do so). Spray in evening – not just to avoid harming bees but because the plant's stomata shut in hot sun when some sprays will not work. Having slightly alkaline soil, I use Sulphur Rose (as well as Sulphur Soil in February) on both sides of the leaves, aiming to reduce pH and black spot. There are a huge variety of products to choose from: Rose Clear Ultra, Multirose, Maxicrop plus iron. Ring the changes and see what works. Spraying rugosa roses can scorch

their leaves and they do not need it. If using Sulphur Rose or Sulphur Veg, it is important not to exceed the stated application rate and to apply it only on alkaline soil.

- Container roses: provide a controlled release fertilizer and keep well watered.
- Climbers: tie in new growth and finish outstanding pruning by early April.
- Ramblers: they should not be pruned now but they may have become an enormous bird's nest tangle over an arch or pergola. If so, cut out what has to go but leave enough to cover the support with existing growth, tying in as much as possible, horizontally or around supports, to have a good flowering this year.

Rudbeckia (black-eyed Susan)
The moment to divide a clump is just as the new growth begins to show; feed it afterwards with a balanced fertilizer like Fish, Blood and Bone and mulch gently.

Rue (*Ruta graveolens*)
Beware of rue – it can cause skin reactions so wear gloves. Prune as it starts into growth in spring. It can be cut down to 5 cm/2 inches off the ground for a smaller plant; if a bigger plant is wanted, create a framework down to which you can cut each year. It does not rejuvenate from old wood so do not cut further back than this framework.

Russian vine (*Fallopia baldschuanica*)
Pinch out growing tips to make lateral growth. Provide support until it starts to self-cling. It is incredibly vigorous.

Sage: culinary (*Salvia officinalis*)
As new growth starts, trim it back by about a third. Start this while the plant is young so that it does not get leggy. It does not do well cut into brown wood. The leaves are at their culinary best just before flowering.

Salvia
Mulch around the base but never over the crowns, which hate being wet.

Generally, they do not need feeding though I give tender salvias a little fertilizer in summer (see July) and I read that Lynsey Pink, National Collection holder, sprinkles a little pelleted chicken manure round their base in spring. While doing this, avoid the shrubby *Salvia microphylla* and *S. greggii*, as it makes them too leggy.

Hardy perennial salvias left out over winter like *S. nemorosa*, *S. sylvestris* and *S. uliginosa* (this last, despite being considered not entirely hardy, seems to survive here left standing over winter) can be cut down to just above ground level in early April. Half-hardy salvias such as *S. guaranitica* and *S. 'Amistad'*, which are likely to be under cover, can, with the truly tender salvias like *S. 'Wendy's Wish'* and *S. splendens* 'Van-Houttei', be cut back or potted on and lightly fed and watered to start them into growth.

Hardy shrubby salvias including *S. darcyi*, *S. greggii*, *S. × jamensis* 'Hot Lips', *S. microphylla*, *S. 'Silas Dyson'* – and those borderline hardy shrubs that may just have got through winter outside like *S. involucrata* or *S. fulgens* – can be pruned lightly into shape in late April/ early May, shortening stems by as much as one-third to newly developing buds. There are surprising resurrections as the weather gets warmer so do not dig up any that look dead (yet). As soon as salvias come into flower the deadheading should start, to ensure they continue flowering. Tuberous *S. patens* will be just emerging. Slugs love their new growth.

Sansevieria (mother-in-law's tongue)
While perfectly happy above radiators and in the dry atmosphere of a house, they do not thrive in the strong light of a greenhouse. They like being pot-bound but if the rhizomes are pushing the plant out of its pot, they can be repotted now. Use a proprietary compost for succulents

and cactus with John Innes No. 3 compost added. Water (using rainwater) only when dried out and then only a little, avoiding the leaves.

Santolina (cotton lavender) It flowers on last year's growth, so – unless you want the flowers – cut back all last year's growth to keep it from falling apart and to maintain its vibrancy. Start this as a young plant: when old and leggy, cutting into old wood kills it. Santolina hedges can be trimmed now. They do not need feeding.

Scabious Divide and replant in fresh soil every three years or so to maintain good shape.

Schizophragma This climbing plant (like a lacecap hydrangea) takes ages to get going but when it does it is lovely. If needed, prune to encourage branching to fill the space well and remove from gutters, taking off any overlong shoots to a good bud, removing any broken growth. Tie in, not too tightly as ultimately it will self-cling. Feed, mulch and water.

***Solanum crispsum* 'Glasnevin'**
Prune last year's flowering shoots back to two or three buds from the main stem to keep it in order, cutting out any dead material. If overcrowded, thin by taking some shoots down to a lower side shoot. To get new growth from the base, take one or two major shoots out, but cutting it right down may kill it. Tie up carefully and feed with a potash-rich fertilizer. Mulch. Leave *S. laxum* 'Album' alone until May.

Stachyurus praecox On established plants, one or two of the flowered stems can be cut back if new growth is lacking but regular pruning is not needed. Mulch well. Regularly water young plants.

Stipa Divide these grasses when they are in active growth.

Streptocarpus (Cape primrose)
Give it a potash-rich feed to be repeated monthly until it starts to falter about September. Dibleys Nurseries in North Wales, who hold the National Collection, have a proprietary potash-rich feed for them.

Sweetcorn Seeds need to be sown in deep pots and kept at 15–20°C for at least a month before planting.

Sweet pea (*Lathyrus odoratus*)
Harden off seedlings sown in January/February; if not done yet, pinch out these growing tips to encourage bushiness when 10 cm/4 inches high. For those now planted out, taking off all the side shoots from the main growing stem up to about 18 cm/7 inches will concentrate the energy into producing a good stout stem and make all the difference to the ultimate height of the plant.

Sweet william (*Dianthus barbatus*)
They will go on into the summer if deadheaded (though keep some seed). If they get leggy, cut them in half to grow stouter.

Tamarix ramosissima This autumn flowering tamarisk flowers on the current year's growth so can be cut hard back now to new growth showing at the base. Leave alone the spring flowering tamarisk, *T. tetranda* and *T. parviflora*. They need good drainage on moist but never waterlogged soil; a mulch of garden compost would be helpful.

Tanacetum corymbosum This mound of daisy will repeat flower several times if cut back after each flowering.

***Teucrium fruticans* (shrubby germander)** Having left the top growth on over winter, cut back to near the ground and lightly mulch.

Thalictrum (meadow rue) To propagate named cultivars, divide just before they come into growth. Grow the divisions on in pots, planting out only when they have good roots.

Tiarella (foam flower) So pretty in shade, tidy leaves now. It needs occasional division now to keep vigorous. Watch out for vine weevil.

Tomato Do not let the leaves of your seedlings touch each other; that, and poor light, encourage legginess.

***Trachelospermum asiaticum,
T. jasminoides* (star jasmine)** Water well during the growing period. Thin out congested areas and cut out weak or straggly shoots, trimming to fit the available space. If it needs renovation, cut all shoots down to a third of its height to a good shoot or spur. Young growths will need tying in until they get back to clinging on their own. If it looks sickly, it may be that, growing at the base of a wall as most are, it needs an iron tonic: it prefers a low pH and the base of walls is usually quite alkaline. A feed this month and next of Maxicrop Seaweed plus Sequestered Iron (it comes all in one) will probably perk it up. Mine suffers badly from sooty mould at this time of year so I dose it now with a systemic insecticide as well as feeding it. *T. asiaticum* is the hardier of these two and very slightly less vigorous.

***Tricyrtis formosana* (toad lily)** They love moist shade, so a deep mulch would be good.

Trollius (globeflower) They are easiest divided now before they flower. Mulch well to retain moisture.

Tulbaghia violacea Every two or three years, disentangle and divide the thick fleshy roots with two or three growing points on each division. Left on the gravel for half an hour, they disentangle more easily. They need a sunny, reasonably sheltered position and lots of grit. For those in the ground, water well on planting but sparingly thereafter. Potted plants need water until flowering is finished in about October; then they can start to dry out for their winter dormancy.

Tulip Deadhead as the flowers go over, cutting the stem low, leaving the foliage.

Verbascum (mullein) Most grow tall and the more fragile-looking benefit from twiggy support before the flowers appear. Watch out for caterpillars, which appear from late spring, and pick them off by hand while they are still small.

Verbena bonariensis Cut down last year's shoots as new growth appears at the base.

Veronicastrum (culver's root) Divide now if they need spreading out. Mulch well.

***Vinca major* (greater periwinkle),
V. minor (lesser periwinkle)** Cut back last year's growth to get better, thicker foliage and good flowers. It can otherwise start looking very wispy on the ground.

Vine: grape (grown under glass) When the tiny flowers appear, tap the rods to ensure every truss gets pollen on it: flowers are hardly noticeable. Do this on a dry midday when the pollen will float off. Damp down the floor to provide good pollination conditions.

Wallflower: short-lived perennial (Erysimum, such as *Erysimum* 'Bowles's Mauve', *E.* 'Moonlight') They can cope with the poorest soils. Pinch out the growing tips of young plants to stop legginess. Deadhead vigorously, even chopping plants in half if necessary.

The double *Tulipa* 'Angélique' (flowering in early May)

Continue deadheading into the summer and take cuttings as they are short-lived.

Waterlily (Nymphaea) Divide large clumps now; they need dividing when leaves start rising vertically above the water.

Weigela When new, cut back the main stems to encourage bushy growth from the start.

Yew Feed newly planted yew with a nitrogen-rich fertilizer like Dried Blood to help them establish and give their sides a very light trim. Established yew can be sprayed with a seaweed mixture to give it a boost of nutrients.

Zantedeschia
- *Zantedeschia aethiopica* (arum lily, hardy): divide clumps before the leaves have grown too much and before they start flowering in late spring. Bravely chop through the roots. Ensure they are in permanently moist soil. Feed fortnightly with a balanced liquid fertilizer.
- *Z. rehmannii* or Elliottiana hybrids such as 'Garnet Glow' (calla lily, tender): plant out into containers, in compost with John Innes No. 2, the rhizome just below the surface (eyes upwards). Water well, keep moist and feed with a nitrogen-rich fertilizer monthly until flowering starts in the summer, then stop.

MAY

In this magical month, gardeners are teased by having not enough hours in the day. The greenhouse becomes increasingly full of plants waiting to get out and weeds grow at full tilt, indicating that this must be a perfect time to plant. Nonetheless, the French expression not to plant until 'the passing of the Saints de Glaces' (11–13 May) and the well-known English version 'ne'er cast a clout till May be out' are both age-old warnings not to be beguiled by the late spring sun. May can still be cold enough to check plant growth in its tracks.

AREAS TO CONSIDER

Annual meadow It sounds obvious but gentle watering is really necessary now if it has not rained; just ensure you do not wash all the seeds together.

Annuals: half hardy When large enough, harden off to go out at the end of May. Water well before planting. When established, pinch out non-flowering tips.

Bedding Compost any spring bedding now over. Fork in some organic fertilizer such as Fish, Blood and Bone to refresh the ground before summer bedding goes in. Harden off summer bedding plants like marigolds and petunias. I love petunias in window boxes – their tumbling forms are redolent of summer exuberance.

Biennials In late May sow biennials to flower next year, such as foxgloves, hollyhocks, honesty, icelandic poppies, night scented stock, sweet rocket, sweet william and wallflowers.

Box diseases and preventative measures To help control the spread of box blight the following preventative measures will help:

Geranium phaeum 'Samobor' (flowering May–June)

- Clean secateurs or shears frequently when clipping, with a disinfectant such as diluted Jeyes fluid; the blight is sticky and will stick to shears.
- Remove *all* clippings (place a strip of sheet either side to gather them in).
- Clip when overcast but not when rain is forecast (box blight thrives in high humidity).
- Keep the base of the hedge clear of leaf litter for good air circulation.
- Water the bottom, never from above – avoid sprinklers.
- Remove taller plants which drip over box.
- Comprehensively cut out any infection immediately and burn.
- Quarantine new box for six weeks before planting. Buy from reputable growers.
- Topbuxus Health-Mix – a leaf fertilizer, sprayed on four to five times a year, particularly just after clipping – will help prevent blight taking hold.
- Grow Fertilizer, a proprietary feed for box also by Topbuxus, applied mid-April, mid-June and mid-August, is a good alternative to Fish, Blood and Bone, seaweed or bone meal.
- A spray made up of about six old lemons and limes soaked overnight in a bucket of water is an organic mix I have never tried but often read about, used to fend off box blight. It can be applied in May.

Bulbs Deadhead the flowers before they turn to seed (unless, likely in the case of fritillaries, the seed is wanted). Bulbs left in the ground would appreciate a regular foliar feed after flowering until the foliage has died down. Every few years, they need spreading about or their offsets just crowd together, so, excepting tulips, lift a clump with all its leaves – probably still green – and pull apart, replanting with leafmould or compost. When bulbs in containers have finished flowering, they can be lifted and replanted in the garden where their foliage can die down. They will be smaller and more informal. Tulips in pots are seldom worth planting out – they mostly just do one year.

Chelsea chop, Chelsea heave, Chelsea thin (the Chelsea Flower Show being in mid-May) For late flowering herbaceous perennials some control can be helpful. As well as the Chelsea chop (when a plant is cut down by a third to half of its size to achieve later, sturdier flowering), there is the Chelsea heave – a spade is put under a plant's crown and lifted until the roots crack, having the desired effect of delaying growth while the plant re-establishes itself (sedum is a good subject though a chop works as well) – and the Chelsea thin, where high percentages of stems on, say, Michaelmas daisies and phlox are cut out, allowing those that are left to grow finer, bigger flowers. All these should be done when rain is forecast; otherwise the plants may sulk.

Cold frame Open up cold frames to harden off plants, shutting them at night as weather dictates.

Containers and hanging baskets Plant up with summer bedding, including water retaining granules and a slow release fertilizer in the compost. Feed with a liquid fertilizer once a fortnight throughout the summer for the best results.

Cuttings In the early morning, collect softwood cuttings of perennials, herbs and shrubs, putting them straight into a plastic bag to keep them turgid after picking. There are dozens of candidates: artemisia, lavender, santolina to name just a few. Plant out cuttings taken last year.

Deadheading and cutting back
Most perennials flowering before midsummer day need cutting down as soon as they look jaded to give them time to develop new growth (and often more flowers this year). A balanced liquid feed such as Maxicrop Plus gets nutrients to them quickly for regrowth. Left uncut, by August the garden looks exhausted. Allowing flowers to wither, holding on to those last dregs of colour, greatly shortens chances of regrowth – and as soon as seed is set that is it for the year – so cut back happily. The garden will look better for it.

Fruit trees: fan trained or espaliered
During the growing season (up to midsummer) give all fruit trees a balanced fertilizer such as Growmore in their first year and, from the second year onwards, a phosphate- and potassium-rich feed. Mulch after feeding.

May is a good time to prune fan-trained fruit. Remove shoots growing in the wrong direction and reduce old spurs down to a strong side branch. It is essential to refer to a pruning book; the notes below are just pointers.

Peaches, nectarines and acid (morello) cherries need 'replacement pruning' as they produce fruit almost entirely on one-year-old wood. Choose a 'replacement' shoot above and another below a flowering branch. One of these will be next year's fruiting shoot, the other a 'reserve' when this year's flowered shoot is pruned out. Tie these two in beside the fruiting branch, pinching their tips when 45 cm/ 18 inches long. Then thin the remaining shoots on the fan so that air can circulate.

Apricots, sweet cherries and plums do not need 'replacement' pruning, but tie in well-positioned shoots to fill gaps or extend the framework. Cut the top of mature fans back to the desired height, taking side shoots back by about six leaves. Remove any badly placed side shoots, any that stick out too far or are growing towards the wall. If a cordon has grown off balance, cut a notch above a dormant bud, removing a sliver of bark no more than 1 mm into the wood. This heals over and encourages a new branch to grow.

Fruit trees: free standing with or without stones Plum and cherry trees are best pruned on a hot day from late May to July as they are vulnerable to the fungal disease silver leaf. Give them a potash-rich liquid feed, then water and mulch.

Place codling moth traps on apple and pear trees from early May – see Apple below.

Grasses Divide, if need be, now they are in active growth – see individual species below.

Greenhouse Put up shading if it gets above 25°C but do not exclude too much light.

Hardening off When all risk of frost has passed, tender plants can be planted out but need hardening off first. Take them outside during the day, returning them back under cover at night.

Hedges On a new hedge, lightly trim all the laterals to encourage the formation of more side shoots to thicken it up. Only lightly clip the top until it reaches the desired height. Hedges should be widest at the bottom; if the other way round, the bottom is shaded by the top both from sun and, more importantly, rain.

Lawns Perennial weeds need to be forked out as they will not be mown out. Seed over bare patches. If moles are a problem, Sork Anti-Mole Bulbs appear to work in some soils; otherwise, professional help will control them with minimal disturbance.

Perennials: tender Towards the end of the month, tender chrysanthemum, salvia, osteospermum and others can be planted out.

Planting: timely purchases Now is the time to plant asters, salvias and other autumn flowering glories, not when seen flowering in garden centres in August when they will have no time to get good roots down before winter. Order online if necessary.

Ponds This is a good time to add aquatic plants and to divide them if overcrowded. There is a strong recommendation to restrict plants on pond margins to native species only. Never dispose of bits of water plants into the wild. There are many different kinds of algae and pondweed that create difficulties in spring and summer. Changing the water only exacerbates the problem; when topping it up, use rainwater not tap. Options include:
- in moving water, submerging and securing a mesh bag filled with barley straw (50 grams per square metre of water surface), removing when it disintegrates (about six months);
- in smaller areas scooping it off with a rake and adding liquid barley straw extract (produces hydrogen peroxide which kills it). If sinking whole barley bales in large areas, wrap them in netting first to prevent the bale breaking up and becoming flotsam (tubular netting put round Christmas trees works well). Then tie the bale with cord attached to a post rammed in the ground.

- reducing the number of fish (they increase the amount of organic debris);
- adding oxygenating plants like hornwort or willow moss (both native);
- growing waterlilies, enough to cover half the surface area;
- increasing oxygenation with a fountain;
- ensuring there is no fertilizer run-off into the water;
- using ultraviolet clarifiers and pond filters;
- taking off the duckweed and throwing in a bunch of watercress, elastic band and all. I have tried it and it works; watercress feeds on the nutrients that duckweed needs.

Seeds Sow this year's winter bedding plants such as pansies and primroses and next spring's biennials anytime in May or June.

Staking and supporting plants By early May all staking must be in place around perennials that are likely to flop. As well as the metal options, hazel, birch and willow can be used to make attractive domes for plants to grow through that look good until they disappear from sight.

Trees Voles love the sanctuary provided by tree mats, their nearest source of food then being the bark of the young tree, so keep a ring of clear soil around trees. Hand weed or otherwise spray with a glysophate based weedkiller such as Roundup to kill off a margin of grass and weeds. Glysophate is not residual in the soil, so treatment should not affect the roots of the tree, but keep it well away from the stem. Mulch only when the weedkiller has completed its work and the ground is cleared of dead grass (and only mulch when the soil is moist).

Viburnum beetle The viburnum beetle larvae may be feasting on *Viburnum opulus* and *V. tinus* (look for lace-like holes in the leaves). Spraying with

Provado Ultimate Bug Killer will help. *V. carlesii* and *V. × juddii* are both resilient to the beetle.

Winter damage As shrubs start to shoot, trim any stems killed by frost back to a new leaf. On those feared dead, scratch off a sliver of bark to see if there is green cadmium beneath indicating living tissue. Watch for new growth, possibly from soil level. Keep moist.

PLANTS

Abutilon megapotamicum* and *A. vitifolium This is a good time to plant out abutilons, ideally three years old, in soil enriched with organic matter. If planting in pots, the roots need lots of room and water. When established, take cuttings as an insurance against loss. Give a spring feed of a slow release fertilizer (or a liquid feed fortnightly), pinching out the growing tips of young plants to make them bushier. If *A. vitifolium* gets out of hand, shorten new shoots.

***Acacia dealbata* (mimosa)** Prune lightly after flowering, cutting back shoots that spoil its shape. To make it more compact, prune side shoots on the main stem to two or three buds straight after flowering but avoid hard pruning.

Achillea (yarrow) It can be cut back before it blooms to give a later, more compact flowering (a Chelsea chop). Without a chop it benefits from support: hazel or pea netting.

Aconitum (monkshood) To achieve later flowering on more compact plants, the stems can be cut by a third now. Every part of this plant is extremely poisonous.

***Akebia quinata* (chocolate vine)** Cut out old tangles and wayward whips to reduce this climber to a manageable framework as it finishes flowering. In the coming months as it produces more shoots, either cut them back or keep the strongest, trimming the tips to promote branching. It should not face east.

Allium Anna Pavord, in her book *Bulb*, says that despite the tatty leaves turning brown even before the flower is out, do *not* be tempted to cut them off as they feed the bulb for next season. It leads to a considerable reduction in flower power. The only answer is to have lots of other foliage plants around their base to cover up the leaves. For this reason they look very good among grasses.

Aloe Separate offsets now. Grow on in cactus potting compost until they are big enough to go out.

Amelanchier These wonderful trees have so many good seasons and do not need regular attention, but it is still best to prune out crossing branches and any others needing removal, directly after flowering. Remove suckering growth from the rootstock of grafted plants.

***Anemanthele lessoniana* (pheasant's tail grass)** Early May when in growth is a good time to get this grass into shape, raking out the dead leaves (though it does not let go of much). It can be trimmed by half if really necessary, but no more as it will be killed if cut any harder. Do not dream of cutting it back in winter. Divide it every two or three years and replant divisions or use seedlings, which are easily found around the plants.

***Anemone blanda, A. coronaria, A. × fulgens, A. nemorosa, A. ranunculoides* and others** They can all be divided as they go into dormancy late in the month or whenever the leaves are vanishing; gently break up their rhizomes/tubers/roots into chunks and replant. They

will repay the trouble with increased performance. Topdress afterwards with leafmould mixed with grit to mark where they are.

***Anthemis tinctoria* (golden marguerite)** Given the Chelsea chop in mid-May, cutting it back to about 15 cm/6 inches, it will flower in July rather than June and be slightly stockier.

***Anthriscus sylvestris* 'Ravenswing' (Queen Anne's lace)** This lovely purple cow parsley may need some brushwood support. It will look good until July and will self-seed merrily if allowed to. It is better to select plants with really dark foliage to self-seed, to maintain good colour in the next generation, so cut back the less good flower stalks as the flowers lose their freshness.

Antirrhinum (snapdragon) Deadhead as often as you can. Pinch out 2.5 cm/1 inch of the growing tips of seedlings when 5–10 cm/ 2–4 inches high to encourage bushiness.

Apple and Pear: free-standing
Keep the circle of soil round young trees free of grass. Codling moth is a menace, as I discover when pressing apples. Hang pheromone traps in trees to attract the male codling moth (the traps exude the same smell as the female – he approaches the trap, gets stuck and, voilà, no offspring possible.) One trap will be enough for about four to five trees growing in orchard proximity. There is a slightly different trap for plums. An alternative I read of: a piece of corrugated cardboard tied round the trunk of the tree will provide the perfect place – if rather peculiar looking – for codling moths to spin their cocoons. Then you burn it. I have never done this but it sounds effective. It is unlikely that the trap alone will be 100 per cent successful, and the trees may need spraying to combat the

problem at caterpillar stage, which is mid-June. The timing of the spray is guided by instruction on the traps.

Aquilegia May flowering aquilegia should be cut back to encourage a second flowering. Planted with tulips, the aquilegia leaves will cover drooping tulip foliage. This is the best time to divide them if division is necessary, but they do not like root disturbance.

***Armeria maritima* (thrift/sea pink)** This sea thrift will flower from now until September if deadheaded regularly – shears will do. Do not feed as it will not appreciate it.

Aubrieta If, while still flowering, it has become bare and tatty in places, cut those parts back hard now to encourage denser growth in the middle of the plant. When the flowers have finally faded but before it looks exhausted, shear it back hard and it will develop a new cushion of foliage. Doing this can keep it going for years.

Auricula They like to be cool and fresh outdoors in semi-shade from summer until autumn. Deadhead regularly. When watering, avoid the foliage, especially the central rosette. A small dose of Epsom salts with the continuing feed would be beneficial.

Azalea See Rhododendron, below

Bamboo Water is essential throughout the growing season. It will fail if it dries out. Pots are particularly vulnerable.

Basil Plant out basil grown from seed if it is not cold at night. If sowing now, do so on the surface of well-watered compost, protecting it from midday sun. Avoid watering again until after germination and then only water in the mornings.

Beech Lightly prune hedges if desirable and clear beneath them.

Beetroot Mulch the tops of any beetroot that protrude from the soil as they grow, to help prevent them becoming woody, keep them cool and fuel their growth.

Berberis: shrubs and hedges, evergreen and deciduous All berberis, evergreen and deciduous, can be pruned after they have finished flowering, usually around now (a few are summer flowering). They make their flower buds the previous year, so pruning should not be delayed too long to allow them time to produce new growth for next year. On the other hand, if berries are wanted (and on many they are very beautiful), prune now with circumspection. Removal of stems from the bottom is the best method to control size and health. On deciduous berberis, the flowering stems can be cut back to strong buds to get replacement growth and up to a quarter of the stems can be taken out at the base. Evergreen berberis just need minimal trimming back. Mulch afterwards to limit unwanted seedlings. Most berberis will regenerate if cut right down, though we are advised to do it gradually, a third at a time, waiting for new growth each time before proceeding. Hedges are good trimmed now, and again in autumn.

Deciduous berberis grown for colourful growth colour such as *Berberis thunbergii* 'Rose Glow' can be cut low so that the whole plant – in my case a hedge – retains its good colour. *B.* × *lologensis* and dwarf berberis such as *B. thunbergii* 'Atropurpurea Nana' are not as tough as some others, so just prune out problems as they arise. The winter colour of *B. dictophylla* will be improved by pruning after flowering. To get long wands of foliage, *B. temolaica* is best pruned hard now. *B. darwinii* often has another flowering in autumn. The one thing all berberis hate is waterlogging.

Bergenia (elephant's ears) Tidy up old stems and leaves. When they have got huge, lift the clump and divide (using back to back forks if necessary). Cut the rhizomes into pieces about 15 cm/6 inches long, keeping each bit that has leaves attached (chuck out the rest), replanting them deeper than they were previously, 30 cm/12 inches apart. Feed and mulch.

Box Increasingly, I cut my box towards the end of May rather than early June because of the concern that the sun may scorch it after clipping. Traditionally, box is clipped around Derby Day, 4 June. The end of May is also a good time to renovate box. It usually responds to being cut down as low as 15 cm/6 inches provided it has healthy top growth. Give a potash-rich liquid feed two or three times during the growing season and mulch. Seaweed extract works well. For a hedge that needs bushier growth at the base, remove the upper third of the leading shoots. Do this at the end of the month as well. When clipping or planting box, the measures given above (see Box diseases and preventative measures) will help prevent blight.

Broad bean Water vigorously at the base of the plant when in flower (avoid overhead watering). At the first sight of blackfly, spray with a washing up liquid mixture and tip the tops. Even if there is no blackfly, pinch out the growing tips a bit later, when the lowest pods are about 5 cm/2 inches long, to direct energy into making beans. In hot weather, misting the flowers with tepid water in the evening helps the pods to form (a tip from Mr Fothergills Seeds). Provide support for the beans: they look lovely now but not when collapsing under their own weight of crop. Summer savory planted with the rows helps to keep the aphids away, as does planting the beans close to potatoes. Mr Fothergills stresses not to leave the pods on too long: small young beans are far better flavoured than tough old ones. Picking young, before the scar begins to darken (it should be pale green or white), also helps to lengthen the harvest and makes a glut less likely.

Campanula (bellflower) A Chelsea chop early in the month is a means of encouraging upright species such as *Campanula lactiflora* to become bushier. It also responds to its growing tips being pinched out in late May so it flowers on side shoots rather than on top-heavy flower heads that will collapse over other plants. It, and all tall campanulas, need staking. Cultivars of *C. persicifolia* ('Telham Beauty' is wonderful) will mostly support themselves, but like the even smaller ones such as *C. takesimana* 'Elizabeth', all these upright campanulas will be improved if they have some twiggy support to grow through unless they are supported by other plants. A mulch around the base of all campanulas would be good.

Carex (sedge) Divide this evergreen grass sometime now (after its flower spikes have finished flowering). It can be cut back by as much as half any time between April and July – just gather it up like a ponytail and cut – but never do this in autumn or winter.

Carpenteria californica No pruning is needed but late spring is a good time to remove stems that are damaged or badly placed. If it was cut down by frost, it will almost certainly recover.

Cephalaria The foliage of *Cephalaria gigantea* is bulky so I put a support around it to contain what will become quite coarse leaves. More delicate varieties can be found: for example, *C. litvinovii* at Phoenix Perennial Plants in Hampshire.

Cercis canadensis 'Forest Pansy'
Large, luscious dark red foliage can be
achieved on a young plant. Cut all the
stems down to two or three buds from the
base when it has started putting on new
growth. This is not something to try on
an established plant as it would probably
kill it. I prefer it left as an expansive shrub
giving good colour from late spring to late
autumn, but there is this choice.

**Cherry: ornamental (*Prunus glandulosa*
and *P. triloba*)** These ornamental
cherries are great for a small space:
growing to about 1.5 m/5 ft, old flowering
shoots can be pruned back immediately
after flowering or thinned to shape. See
also 'Prunus' below for *P. serrula* and
other cherries with ornamental bark.

**Chionodoxa (now reclassified as
Scilla)** Do not remove the foliage until
it has completely died back; if necessary,
clumps can be divided now and replanted
immediately.

Chrysanthemum Cuttings can be
planted out from mid-May (avoid soil that
gets boggy). When they are settled in,
nip the growing tips and provide some
support for new growth. Mulch around
the plants.

Clematis: Group 1 Give a potash-rich
liquid fertilizer monthly until October.
Some clematis may need tying in – they
grow so fast but are easy to deal with
now. This is the only time to do any major
pruning on this group (with still a year to
regrow). Woody growth or overcrowding
can be removed to let in some light
and bring it back in hand (such as on
Clematis cirrhosa).

Clematis 'Wedding Day' (group 2, flowering May–
June) with *Eremurus himalaicus* (foxtail lily/desert
candle) and Allium 'Purple Sensation'

If *C. montana* needs pruning, do it now,
immediately after flowering, but resist any
further pruning for the rest of the year.
Cut it to a framework of old growth or
thin it, cutting out one stem in three or,
if it is really out of control, cut it down to
the ground. Using shears and denuding it
of leaves is fine. Give a potash-rich feed,
water and mulch.

Cleome (spider flower) This is one
of the best half-hardy annuals for late
summer/autumn colour. Sow seeds quite
late – early May – in deep trays or loo
rolls as they dislike root disturbance.
Germinate uncovered with lots of bottom
heat and water from below. Pinch out
top growth to get a plant with lateral bud
development. When planting add organic
matter as they are hungry plants.

**Cobaea scandens (cup and saucer
plant)** When all threat of frost is over,
harden off and plant out. Water well and
tie in to a trellis, wall or fence straight
away. It has a tendency to swamp other
climbers so is best alone.

Comfrey juice for fertilizer
Symphytum uplandicum 'Bocking 14' is
a good one to plant, not being invasive.
Remove flowers regularly to keep the
foliage fresh. Pick the leaves, throwing
away tough stalks, and put in a bucket to
make a great potash-rich feed suitable
for most plants. Weigh down the leaves
with a brick, topping up with fresh leaves,
adding 10 litres of water to every kilo of
leaves – stir occasionally and leave until
it has broken down into a liquid (which
stinks). Strain, bottle, keep cool and dark.
Dilute again 1:10 to use; it should be the
colour of weak tea. Put used leaves on the
compost heap. For a nitrogenous feed see
'Nettles' in June.

Cordyline Remove dead leaves and
winter damage. It can be cut down to
ground level if it looks dreadful; it will

either grow again looking better (fine) or be lost (also fine, if it was dreadful).

Coreopsis (tickseed) This reponds well to a Chelsea chop for later, more stocky flowering. The taller ones like 'Badengold' will benefit from staking. Deadhead when possible to prolong flowering.

***Coronilla valentina* subsp. *glauca* 'Citrina'** Although it does not need regular pruning, it can be pruned lightly after its spring flowering, taking out damaged or straggly bits or stems overreaching themselves; cut back to a side shoot, leaving no snags. As a legume it does not want feeding but it will flower from November to May (with the occasional check in cold weather). It does not live forever so take cuttings – see July. It can live in a large pot but must have winter sun for its scent.

Corylopsis pauciflora On a mature plant, crossing branches and overcrowded stems can be cut out immediately flowering is over. Mulch with leafmould or composted pine needles. A sprinkling of flowers of sulphur or sulphur chips twice a year, every year, now and in autumn, will help lower the pH if the soil is above neutral.

Cosmos Pinch out non-flowering tips to promote bushiness. Regular watering is especially important when they are first planted out (this applies to all annuals).

***Cotoneaster horizontalis* (fishbone cotoneaster)** This is the moment to cut out one stem in three at the base to keep it in bounds and do other pruning to keep it where you want it or to lead it where you want it to go.

Crown imperial (*Fritillaria imperialis*) These bulbs appreciate additional nourishment so, after flowering, feed with a potash-rich liquid fertilizer such as Tomorite.

***Cunninghamia lanceolata* (Chinese fir)** This conifer does regenerate from old wood, so strong upright shoots can be removed to maintain a bushy habit if it is wanted as a shrub.

***Cupressus sempervirens* (Italian cypress)** Clip it annually from the start to keep it neat, tight and healthy. Clipping the top flat will stop it at the desired height. If it starts to splay out, use Flexi-Tie round it at critical places.

Cymbidium (orchid) Put plants outside in dappled sunlight until September (the flower spikes need a temperature difference between day and night to be initiated). Water weekly with rainwater if dry but do not feed now while they are resting. Restart feeding in September.

Dahlia Harden off dahlias to plant out when there is no danger of frost. Plant new tubers 15 cm/6 inches deep in rich soil incorporating sharp sand. Mark their position with another ring of sand.

Delphinium Early in the month and as the flower spikes get going, feed with a balanced fertilizer such as Fish, Blood and Bone and get stakes in place. Tall delphiniums need canes 1.75 m/6 ft long, while twiggy brushwood support will work around small ones. Avoid tying the stem directly to a cane as it may break as it grows – rather, make a figure of eight between cane and stalk to give some leeway. Tie in again when they have grown another 60 cm/24 inches. Too often delphiniums are staked with too short canes and the flowers then look like ten-year-olds in six-year-olds' trousers. Never tie delphiniums together on to the same cane; they will look like two people stuck together at a party who do not want to talk to each other. In a big clump it is easier to put the tall canes around and inside the clump and make a grid of string or Flexi-Tie (now available in a good muted green) in and out of the stems to give them a support which does not strangle them. Another grid will be needed as they grow further up the supports. At Waterperry Gardens in Oxfordshire, delphiniums are staked every foot of growth so that by the time they reach maturity they have been tied at least three times. Bunny Guinness, fount of so much knowledge, advises us to leave only seven stems in a mature clump to make a better plant – but no need to do this for the first few years. How tough good gardeners are.

Deutzia On young plants, tip prune the soft new growth to encourage bushiness.

Dianthus (old-fashioned and modern pinks) If newly purchased pinks flower without making any side shoots, break off the top of the main shoot above a joint to get bushier plants. Do this in the early morning when they snap easily. Feed with liquid rose or tomato fertilizer after they have first flowered and deadhead regularly for more blooms (kitchen scissors work well).

Dicentra (including *Dicentra spectabilis*, now called *Lamprocapnos spectabilis*) If you have different varieties of dicentra, remove seed heads as they hybridize easily.

Dicksonia antarctica On planting, insert just enough of the trunk to keep it upright. Water the trunk every day until fronds appear from the crown. Do not feed in the first year. In subsequent years give a dilute liquid feed once a month to the fronds and trunk during the growing season or, in May, fork in a slow release fertilizer round the base. Mulch well. Spray new fronds with water when they appear but avoid spraying into the crown. The trunk will like to be sprayed frequently in hot weather.

Doronicum (leopard's bane) If not done already, cut stems right back for a possible second flowering, which happens in a cool summer.

Echeveria To divide, gently turn out the pot and put all rosettes into individual pots of gritty compost.

Echinacea They can be divided now (or in September) and can have a Chelsea chop if desirable.

Edelweiss (*Leontopodium alpinum*) I love it and lose it: it does not live for long. It needs very well-drained, gritty soil, and if it clumps up it can be divided gently now. It is drought tolerant once established and, predictably, likes it cool, hating winter sogginess.

Epimedium Cut off any leaves that are obscuring the flowers of the more fragile (normally Chinese) species. In an article by Sally Gregson of Mill Cottage Plants in Somerset, she strongly recommends that as epimedium are self-sterile – they have to be pollinated by another variety to set seed – all seedpods are cut off to prevent mixed seedlings arising in the crown of the mother plant. This will keep them growing strongly. Some like 'Pink Elf' may well reflower later in the summer. Mature plants can be divided after flowering has finished (see also October), replanting with lots of leafmould. Check for any sign of disease in the soil or on the leaves when doing so and remove promptly if there is.

Eremurus (foxtail lily, desert candle) A discreet single stake before the flowers get to full height is worthwhile. Slugs are a menace to properly formed flowers so check regularly. It does not like any sogginess in the soil.

Erythronium (dog's tooth violet) Removing the flowers before they set seed speeds up the expansion of plants.

Let the foliage die down naturally and mulch over their planting area when they have disappeared (marking them well). Dividing them is a little difficult – they like being in clumps – but eventually it has to be done, so do so as the leaves begin to die back. The roots are very brittle and they will have gone deeper than when they were first planted, so be sure to dig deep enough. Dig the area where the divisions are to go first, add organic matter including a lot of leafmould and sharp sand, then tease apart and gently replant about 10 cm/4 inches deep (not as deep as they have got themselves).

Euonymus fortunei, E. japonicus
The many varieties of evergreen euonymus can be pruned or cut back now if necessary – any time until the end of July. If denser ground cover is wanted, cut back all the previous year's growth so that about two buds remain. If height is wanted but it has overshot its space, cut out some stems from the base. Otherwise just trim it. It is important to cut out reversions on variegated cultivars. In the first year of planting reduce the size of the shrub by about one-third to promote growth around the bottom and prevent legginess. They are very forgiving.

Exochorda (pearl bush)
On established shrubs, as soon as flowering has finished, cut out a number of stems to ground level ('one in three' is the normal cry but do it by eye), also removing anything spindly. Reduce other stems which have flowered to keep the shrub a good shape. Choose very old or weak branches first and then take out others in crowded areas.

Exochorda × *macrantha* 'The Bride' has a tendency to produce many crossing branches. Its habit is to fall down a bank or over a wall like a fountain. Another pearlbush, the upright *E. racemosa* (given to us by our children for our Pearl wedding anniversary), needs the same treatment to keep in shape.

Fatsia japonica Prune now that the frosts are over, cutting out any winter damage, and if it is too big or tall, remove one stem in three from the base to allow more air in the centre and to encourage new foliage. Cut other stems back by half to a good bud to shape it satisfactorily.

Fritillary When the flowers are over, let the leaves die back completely, not removing them until they are totally brown. This allows them to set seed. If in grass, avoid mowing over the area until late July/August. Collect some seed as well, to broadcast in September when the ground is cooler and moist.

Gaillardia Mulch plants well with garden compost or a rich compost with good nutrient value purchased online or at a nursery. Divide congested plants now. *G. × grandiflora* need deadheading frequently to encourage more flowering.

Galtonia candicans Plant out now, to flower in the autumn, any that were started off in pots. Anna Pavord suggests that there should be at least five in a group to have an impact in a mixed border. They need to be well watered when in growth, and, predictably, slugs simply love their leaves. Plant 10 cm/ 4 inches deep and the same apart.

Garlic This is a critical time for watering: if allowed to dry out in April or May the bulbs will be small.

Geranium (cranesbill) If geraniums look floppy, give them discreet, probably twiggy, support as soon as possible. Feed all geraniums monthly during the season with a balanced fertilizer such as Growmore.

Gerbera Pick regularly to encourage fresh growth. Twist and fold the stem to separate it from the base instead of cutting it. Take basal cuttings towards the end of this month or next.

Gladiolus Now the danger of frost is past, plant out from early to mid-May, using lots of organic matter and extra grit in the planting holes, staggering the planting for a longer flowering season. The foliage will be ugly as it dies so surround it with other plants. Sarah Raven recommends planting the corms a spade's depth – deeper than normally prescribed – minimizing the need for canes, which still could be necessary on the tall cultivars of the Grandiflorus Group and, for example, the wonderful *Gladiolus cardinalis*. The shorter ones, the Nanus Group, look good through a support of birch twigs. In pots (*G. × colvillii* 'The Bride' is lovely) stake as you plant to avoid spiking the bulb later. In cold areas keep pots inside until they have put on some growth. Whether they are in pots or the ground they are good planted densely: pack them in. When flower spikes are 15 cm/6 inches high (ground or pot), feed with a potash-rich fertilizer such as Tomorite every two weeks until at least three weeks after flowering is finished.

   G. communis subsp. *byzantinus*, which is totally hardy and spreads and flowers about now, will be better if it is discreetly staked, and has plants around to hide the leaves.

Gunnera Keep covered until early May in case of late frosts and then provide a fresh mulch.

Gypsophila (baby's breath) The stems are brittle so early on provide support for the plant to grow through.

Hakonechloa Add lots of compost to this brilliant (40 cm/16 inch high) grass when planting and mulch afterwards. Feed it annually with a slow release fertilizer. It will not thrive where it is too dry.

Heather: late winter/spring flowering (*E. carnea, E. × darleyensis, E. erigena*)

Early flowering heather will go on until about now. As soon as it is finished, shear off the old flowers to keep the plant together and dense and to promote good flowering next winter, but never cut into brown wood as it does not regenerate. Left until midsummer to trim, next year's flowers will be cut off. *E. carnea*, less vigorous, will probably need be trimmed only every other year.

When planting, do not tease out the fine roots and take care not to pull at the neck where it is quite fragile. Plant so that the lowest foliage rests on the soil surface. If it has become leggy, dig it up and drop it into a new hole, leaving just the top few inches showing and backfilling with gritty compost. Within a year, new roots will have formed. Water regularly, preferably with rainwater, to stop foliage turning yellow and do not feed, though mulching helps retain moisture.

Helenium Pinch out the growing shoots to make a bushier plant.

Heliotropium arborescens If young plants are tipped, they will stay bushy and if older, leggy plants are cut in half they will stay compact. Feed once a month with a potash-rich fertilizer such as Tomorite when they start flowering next month, continuing until August. Their scent is wonderful so have them near a door.

Hibiscus syriacus Prune this month (from two to three years old) to keep in shape and to encourage new growth that will produce flowers for this year. Take out crossing branches and any going off in the wrong direction. Then cut back side branches off the main framework to above a node and new shoots will be produced. They can be incredibly late into leaf so if still leafless do not despair; take a tiny sliver of the bark off and check for the reassuring green cadmium beneath. An annual dose of potash-rich rose fertilizer now will be good for it, as will plenty of mulch worked into the surrounding soil.

Honeysuckle As deciduous honeysuckle comes into leaf, keep a sharp eye out for aphids and blackfly, which are so disfiguring, and spray if necessary.

Hosta Hoeing round them brings slug eggs to the surface, providing bird food. They like copious water in May and June. A wet mulch would be excellent.

Hydrangea Hydrangeas are easy to propagate any time during the growing season. May (if the new growth is ripe enough) and June are a good time to take softwood cuttings of deciduous species while semi-ripe cuttings of evergreen species work well in midsummer. Hardwood cuttings can also be taken in winter.

Iberis (candytuft) Pinch out growing tips to promote bushy growth.

Impatiens (busy lizzie) The perennial *Impatiens walleriana*, treated as an annual, ideally likes morning sun and afternoon shade. It needs frequent watering or it will lose its leaves.

Iris: Pacific coast Tidy up just before flowering, which they will do shortly. Take off old leaves and clean around them – 'they spruce up quite well,' says Christine Skelmersdale of Broadleigh Gardens in Somerset, from whom I have had so much advice – 'but take care not to pull off the edges, which are the very best bits of the plant' (they tend to die back in the middle).

***Jasminum officinale* (common jasmine)**
Water pots of jasmine well when in growth. For those in pots, feed monthly with a potash-rich liquid feed such as Tomorite. For those in borders, fork in a balanced fertilizer such as Growmore around the plant now.

Kalimeris incisa Flowering June to September, pinch out the growing tips of these soft blue or white daisy-like flowers. The runners can be dug up for propagation.

Kerria japonica Cut out one in three stems at the base of this shade tolerant plant now that flowering is finished and cut back other stems to wherever makes a good shape. Take suckers out and mulch.

Kirengeshoma palmata This beautiful woodland plant likes deep, cool, rich, moist, acidic soil and shelter from wind. It likes to be watered often and given a potash-rich liquid feed from time to time to improve flowering. If need be, divide in spring; lift the clump, knock off the soil, pull apart so that each bit has at least three buds, trim the roots to 15 cm/ 6 inches and replant with lots of leafmould in the planting hole. Never use manure for woodland plants.

Kniphofia (red hot poker) Early in May tidy old foliage (it can be trimmed quite hard) and rummage through the remaining leaves to seek out snails still lurking in the evergreen species. This will help prevent the emerging flower heads being eaten. Dividing established plants can be done either by digging up the whole plant or by slicing off bits from the crown but leaving them *in situ* to develop good roots before being moved to a new site.

Lavender Early May is good lavender planting time – ensure the neck is not buried. As a hedge, plant 35–45 cm/ 15–18 inches apart. Water in well but do not feed (now or ever). It likes poor soil, full sun and good air circulation; roots rot if they sit in wet soil. Lavender does not grow easily from old wood but if, in the centre of the plant, there are little shoots now pushing, prune to them. Hopefully, though not certainly, a cushion of young shoots will emerge.

Lemon tree (citrus) In late May plants can go outside in part shade so roots do not bake and leaves do not scorch. Exposure to full sun needs to be done gradually as they dislike great fluctuations in temperature. It is important that the roots do not stand in water and can dry out between waterings (see March). Once every three months use plain water to clean the soil of any residual fertilizer salts.

Lemon verbena It is easiest to buy a small plant or get a cutting and grow in a container. It likes sun and some afternoon shade. Water well on planting and then once a week. Pinch out to encourage bushy growth. Start harvesting leaves in late June. A fortnightly balanced liquid feed would help it thrive until autumn.

***Lespedeza thunbergii* (bush clover)**
Cut it back to a low framework a few inches from the ground as it moves out of its long dormancy. In mild climates when it does not die right back, it can be pruned more lightly to encourage it to branch and stand up straighter, though I love its fountain effect and have it tumbling over a wall. Hardy's Cottage Garden Plants in Hampshire advises that there is only a two-week window to propagate this glorious plant: as new growth appears in early May, take young tip cuttings early in the morning after a wet night; the cuttings then are turgid and may take.

Lewisia Plant on their sides where there is sharp drainage. Water each plant individually until established, avoiding the leaf rosettes. Deciduous species need full sun, evergreens part shade.

Leyland cypress (× *Cuprocyparis leylandii*) Trim hedges and trees (do not cut into old wood). Do not prune the top until it is about 15 cm/ 6 inches below the desired height. Leaving it with a few inches still to grow ensures final growth is thick, so can be neatly trimmed.

Lilac (Syringa) Deadhead if possible; using secateurs, cut just below the flower head. It may well flower again with smaller, fewer flowers. Avoid heavy pruning now.

Lily If plunged in their pot into the border they will need attentive watering. Continue feeding (with a potash-rich liquid fertilizer such as Tomorite) and watering – essential for real success. Check daily for lily beetle; they destroy the plant very quickly (see April). Green aphids can be rubbed off gently. An anti-slug soil drench would be worthwhile.

Lily of the valley Do not remove the leaves when flowering is over as they are needed until they die back naturally in about October. Should you have pink lily of the valley, do not, as I did, expect them to bulk up like their white sisters: however happy they may be, they do not do so.

Lobelia cardinalis, L. × speciosa (perennial lobelia) They can have the Chelsea chop if shorter plants are wanted. Keep an eye out for slugs. They must not be allowed to dry out in summer.

Lobularia maritima (sweet alyssum) If a bit bare in places, cut back hard now to encourage denser growth in the middle of the plant. Otherwise, trim back after flowering to encourage a new flush.

Macleaya This can be cut by a third now to grow stouter and less vigorously.

Magnolia: evergreen Preferably do not prune evergreen magnolias but some, like *Magnolia grandiflora*, outgrow their allotted space. Prune as little as possible either just before growth starts in spring or, with those that flower in spring, just after flowering – about now.

Malva moschata f. alba A beautiful, useful perennial, it will flower from June until September and self-seed where it is happy, but do not feed as this will produce leaves at the expense of flowers. Put in supports now for its flowering next month.

Mint Pinch off the growing tips to encourage busy growth. If congested, divide.

Miscanthus This grass needs occasional division now – using a sharp spade, axe or saw, discard weak parts from the centre, replant and water. If divisions sulk, pot up and keep cool until they re-establish.

Monarda (bergamot) Feed with a nitrogen-rich fertilizer such as pelleted chicken manure as new shoots appear. Avoid mulching as it slows down growth (and harbours slugs). Divide when clumps lose vigour, slicing off the edges, chucking the centre and replanting each piece with bone meal. They must be kept moist.

Narcissus (daffodil) Continue to deadhead until they are over, allowing the foliage to die down naturally. Overcrowded clumps can be divided now. Replant immediately 10–12 cm/4–5 inches deep. Some offsets can be left on the bulb to develop naturally. Others can be planted in their own space or in pots. For those in containers, use a potash-rich feed such as Tomorite for six weeks after flowering.

Nemisia It will go on flowering the whole summer and autumn if new growth is pinched out, and it is deadheaded, watered (it loves water) and fed regularly. It will spread too and behave well.

Nerine bowdenii In late May remove any winter mulch still covering the bulbs, which now need the sun. Clean up old leaves and stems. They need to be warm and dry during this dormant period.

Olive If needed, remove anything dead or diseased and thin out branches to allow light into the centre, shortening (or removing) any branches that spoil the shape (if it does fruit – unlikely in most of the UK – it does so on the tips of last year's growth). Avoid hard pruning, which just encourages lots of watershoots. I read somewhere that a swift should be able to fly in, around and out again. Shaking any branches in flower would increase chances of pollination.

Ornithogalum
- *Ornithogalum thyrsoides* (chincherinchee): plant with extra grit in full sun 10 cm/4 inches deep, starting off in a greenhouse in cold areas, and move out when shoots appear. They need lots of water but good drainage. Cut flowers last for ages.
- *O. umbellatum* (star of Bethlehem): fully hardy and needing to be in the sun to flower, they will do so from April to May. They spread easily.

Osteospermum Take softwood cuttings and put in a cool greenhouse/windowsill until rooted. Most are not reliably hardy so propagate and treat as annuals. Deadhead all season.

Pampas grass (Cortaderia) It can be divided every four or five years. If a sharp spade fails to do the job, an axe or saw may be needed. Discard weak parts in the centre, replant and water well.

Panicum About every four years this grass can be divided now as the soil

warms up. Discard any weak parts from the centre of the clump, replant and water well. A sharp knife will split the clumps.

Parsley Warm the soil by pouring boiling water along the drill. Folklore but it works. Then sow the seeds, covering with compost containing John Innes No. 2.

Passion flower (Passiflora) If it is outside and is out of hand, prune as the weather warms up and new growth has started. Do not cut too hard into main stems, concentrating mostly on side shoots, cutting any Medusa-like serpents of growth back to a good bud. Feed with a potash-rich fertilizer such as Tomorite. Mulch well with leafmould or mushroom compost. It can be cut down to 60–90 cm/ 24–36 inches from the ground if needed.

Pea Unless it is very dry, do not water until the flowers appear and then give them a good soaking, watering regularly thereafter.

Peach, nectarine and almond Watering is vital – hosepipe is best – with a monthly liquid feed of diluted potash-rich fertilizer until August. They do well as trees in containers, but as fan shapes in containers they do not work: against a wall the pots get too hot, so fan shapes have to be in set in the ground.

Pennisetum As the soil warms up, cut out dead growth and old flower stems which will have been protecting the crown. When planting, add grit to the base of the planting hole. Warm, sunny and dry is good; soggy ground is hopeless. It divides best (maybe every four years) when actively growing. Discard weak parts from the centre of the clump, replant and water well.

Penstemon Plant rooted cuttings taken last summer. Softwood cuttings taken now from vigorous cultivars and given

A pink flowered seedling of *Paeonia rockii* (tree peony, flowering May–June)

bottom heat to get going can be planted out later this year.

Peony

- *Paeonia emodi, P. lactiflora* and cultivars, *P. officinalis* and others (herbaceous): peonies will bloom better next year if deadheaded so pinch off the faded flowers. If picking the flowers cut in the early morning, plunge the stems into boiling water for thirty seconds, and then the flowers will last longer. Never cut more than half the stems as it reduces the strength of the plant too much.
- *P. delavayi* and cultivars, *P. suffruticosa* and *P. rockii* (tree): remove peony flowers as they fade. After the main flush of flowers is over, flowered stems can be cut back by up to a third. These will hopefully produce side shoots which will flower on their tips next year (see February for main pruning time). *P. suffruticosa* and *P. rockii* are less dense than others so seldom need attention, though wayward stems can be removed.

- In wet weather check for peony wilt; if evident, dead growth should be removed and a fungicide applied round the base of the plant. If suckers (less finely divided leaves) appear from below the graft, cut these out. Newly planted peonies sometimes do nothing their first year. Do not give up, but put a cage over them so they do not get trodden on.

Perovskia (Russian sage) If they are flopping in rich soil, cut them back by half at the end of May (or do the same, less sternly, in June).

Phalaris (gardener's garters) It can be divided as it comes into growth. It is invasive so should be done more regularly than for most grasses. To keep its pretty variation, cut back all but the young growth.

Phlomis They can be divided if necessary. Being Mediterranean, they like sun and an open site; the leaves like to dry out quickly after rain. It is advisable to cut back the flowers of young plants for a few years to get a strong structure at the base before letting them go.

  Phlomis fruticosa (Jerusalem sage): this evergreen subshrub can be damaged by hard winters and late frosts so only cut back weather-affected shoots now.

Phlox Thin out weaker and older stems from the clump to get good air circulation. They can have a Chelsea chop around the last week of May; cut them to half their height to get sturdier plants flowering slightly later. Cutting half the clump would give an extended flowering season. Stake any not chopped as in August they will need this support.

Photinia × fraseri 'Red Robin' For best foliage colour, clip as soon as the small white flowers have finished, cutting some side branches to encourage new growth. Regular pruning until midsummer will keep it compact. In year one cut by half to promote bushiness.

Physostegia (obedient plant)
This can be chopped by a third to give a sturdier, later flowering plant.

Pieris After flowering, take off faded flower heads and any frost damage. Avoid hard pruning but a gentle cutting back encourages regeneration, better colouring and helps keep it a good shape. Always cut back to a suitable side branch. Sprinkle around its base with flowers of sulphur or sulphur chips on neutral to alkaline soil.

Pine (Pinus), such as *Pinus mugo*, *P. parviflora* 'Bonnie Bergman'
Dwarf pines can be pruned to keep a manageable size with a shrubby habit. The 'candles' – new upright growth – can be halved each year from year one. Avoid pruning the needles, which will turn brown if mistakenly cut. It can also be kept small

without compromising the shape too much by shortening growths to a branch junction.

Plectranthus argentatus Invaluable as a grey leaved container plant for shade but tender so overwintered inside, it can now be cut back hard to form new stainless-steel coloured leaves from the base. Take cuttings. I first saw it at Coton Manor in Northamptonshire where wonderful lessons can be learnt in container planting.

Poppy: oriental (*Papaver orientale*)
Oriental poppies need discreet staking just as much as delphiniums. I always forget and fondly imagine they will stand up like the annual *P. rhoeas* (the 'Flanders Field' poppy and the cultivars of its Shirley Group). When planting poppies, dig in lots of organic matter first.

Potato Should a late frost be forecast, throw fleece over the shoots of earlies that have already emerged. If they are producing foliage, earth up; stop only up when the foliage of individual plants meets in the middle of the ridge. Never water in full sun. Maincrop potatoes should be planted by the end of May.

Primula (primrose) Their seed can be harvested and sown in seed trays. Keep cool and well watered, even when they appear to take an age to germinate – it could be months.

  Primula beesiana, P. bulleyana, P. denticulata, P. japonica, P. pulverulenta, P. vialii: do not plant too close to little neighbours whom they will swamp; they bulk up considerably. Deadhead as often as possible, especially *P. vialii*.

Prunus serrula (ornamental cherry)
Rub off unwanted new growth on the trunks rather than allowing them to develop into shoots. This will minimize blemishes on the ornamental bark.

Pulmonaria (lungwort) Shear back just above ground level after flowering (they are very promiscuous). This also prevents them getting mildew, to which they are prone. Feed with a slow release fertilizer, water well and in a few weeks there will be new growth. Divide now (or in September). If planting now, firm in very well taking care not to damage their roots.

Pyracantha As it flowers on old wood, the easiest time to prune a pyracantha hedge is as flowers start to go over; then it is clear what to take off and what to leave to have good berries. Cut off a few wayward shoots and shorten side shoots to a few buds (which will make the berries sit well). Pruning it now, on a hot day, will help to prevent fireblight. Wear gloves.

Redcurrant and whitecurrant The larvae of gooseberry sawfly start their defoliation of currants about now. See 'Gooseberry' in June.

Rhododendron and Azalea They need another feed this month with a slow release ericaceous plant fertilizer (Millais Nurseries do a very good one). After flowering finishes (more about this in June), deadhead as much as feasible, snapping off (using thumb and forefinger) the single flower or truss, taking great care not to snap off the new leaf growth just beneath the flower. This conserves energy for next year's flowers and makes for better, bushier growth. It is critical that they do not dry out now; use rainwater in preference to tap. Curling leaves is a sign of stress from lack of water. After flowering, height can be reduced if necessary – they will rejuvenate over time even if cuts are made into thick old wood. Small leaved rhododendrons and azaleas can be pruned anywhere along their stems as their buds will be forming in a couple of months.

Rhubarb Resist harvesting in its first year. After that, pull (do not cut) the stems when they are about 30 cm/12 inches long for maximum sweetness, harvesting no more than half the stems of an established crop over the season. Remove any flowers that appear as they weaken the plant. Spring is traditionally the time to harvest rhubarb, stopping in May (when forcing covers are removed) and allowing it to grow freely for the rest of the year. (The cultivar 'Timperley Early' can be harvested until August.) A topdressing of nitrogen-rich nitro-chalk would be good now from year two onwards.

Ribes sanguineum and ribes hedges (flowering currant) Advice from the RHS trials is that the less pruning, the better the flower/leaf ratio will be. As soon as flowering is over, therefore, cut out crossing and damaged branches, taking out flowered shoots only where there is a need for strong new growth low down. Removing a few old stems from time to time will encourage growth but let it get established first.
   R.s. 'White Icicle' (white flowering currant) and *R.* × *gordonianum*: do not prune either too hard; just cut back slightly.

Rosemary It can be pruned to shape when it starts taking up too much space. The stems of older plants which have got straggly can be reduced by half. It is quite resilient but be wary of going too hard into very old wood. A regular light prune is best. A good time to do this is after flowering, but it can be done anytime as new growth appears and as often as needed until August. Check for and pick off any rosemary beetle larvae if seen.

Ruscus aculeatus (butcher's broom) When its 'leaves' (actually 'cladodes') turn brown, they can be removed at the base – new stems will be replacing them. Ruscus is dioecious so to be sure of berries (the key attraction of this plant) both male and female plants are needed. There are some hermaphrodite forms, of which 'John Redmond' is the most readily available.

Sanguisorba (burnet) The taller ones like *Sanguisorba officinalis* 'Arnhem' will probably need staking unless the plants around them provide support.

Sarcococca (sweet box, Christmas box) These wonderful shrubs do not need regular pruning but they can be clipped or reduced now. *Sarcococca confusa* is the most bullet-proof against drought and neglect and self-seeds very easily.

Saxifrage
- Evergreen, perennial, rosette forming, such as *Saxifraga* 'Southside', *S. × urbium* (London pride): the big family of saxifrage has many different cultivation techniques and much specialization. The rosettes on established plants can be divided now or in September. If the mother rosette has died (many are monocarpic so this can happen), take off and replant the children round the edge. They need a soil mixed with well-rotted compost or leafmould and grit – well-drained soil that will nonetheless retain moisture. Like other alpines, they also need to avoid long bouts of direct sunshine; they are often therefore planted in pots, so they can be moved about. London pride can be divided now or the rosettes removed individually and replanted. Some saxifrage may look a bit dismal in the middle; if there are no young rosettes to plant, sift new soil over the plant, then lift, reorganize and replant, gathering it together. Remove the flower spikes when they are over. Add some coarse grit around the rosettes whether divided or not.
- Autumn flowering *S. fortunei*: these clump forming saxifrage will flower beautifully in September if they have lots of humus in the soil and are not in a frost pocket.

Sedum (now called Hylotelephium) (stonecrop) If the strong varieties are cut back by half in late May, slightly shorter, sturdy plants will result that do not flop out at the sides. They do not want rich soil, so do not feed or mulch.

Sisyrinchium They die very easily as they are so shallow rooted, but respond well to division and firming in.

***Solanum laxum* 'Album'** The leaves of this pretty half-hardy climber usually get frost damage. Wait until now to tidy and cut off poor growth to where new shoots can be seen.

Solomon's seal (*Polygonatum × hybridum*) Check the underside of leaves for caterpillers (sawfly) and spray the moment they are spotted – or pick them off by hand – it is depressing to find these lovely plants shredded to bits.

Spiraea Prune those spiraea (for example, 'Arguta') which have now finished flowering; take out up to one stem in three from the base and, to get a good shape, remove flowered growth down to a strong side shoot.

Spruce (Picea species and cultivars) They can, if necessary, be sheared now to get a more conical shape, or can be thinned by pruning back to a lateral or a bud. The new growth of the blue spruce (*Picea pungens*) can be pinched back to help manage its size. It is very slow growing.

Stephanotis floribunda This heavenly scented conservatory plant will flower on and off until October if fed with a half strength liquid fertilizer every month from now until then, misting occasionally to maintain humidity. Avoid positioning in full sun as it flowers best in semi-shade. Keep potbound but if repotting use 2:1 of John Innes No. 3 and grit.

Sternbergia lutea (autumn daffodil)
These bulbs need to be kept as dry as possible during their dormant period from now until late August so do not water them inadvertently (even put some netting over as a reminder).

Strawberry Should a frost be forecast, throw a fleece over the flowers or the crop may be lost. Feed with a potash-rich fertilizer such as Tomorite to encourage more flowers. As the fruits develop, spread straw as a dry mulch under the leaves – it will deter slugs and keep the fruit clean. Net the strawberries in preparation for the crop. Any runners that have been potted up for propagation can be planted out now. If there is no room for a strawberry bed, grow some in a pot (minimum 30 cm/12 inches deep) filled with John Innes No. 2 and slow release fertilizer.

Streptocarpus (Cape primrose) Keep light but out of direct sunlight, always frost free. Let it dry out between (about weekly) waterings, only watering into its saucer. Deadheaded frequently, it should flower until autumn. Its leaves will wilt if overwatered, just as much as if underwatered.

Sweet pea Plant out later sown seedlings 5–7 cm/2–3 inches from their supports; tie in, feed with a balanced fertilizer such as Growmore, water, mulch and protect from slugs. As the young plants get going, cut off each side shoot on the main stem for the first 30 cm/12 inches to get a thick, sturdy stem support for the plant throughout its long season. Keep tying in. The only benefit of cutting off the curly tendrils (kitchen scissors work well) is that this stops the stems being pulled over so more straight stems are obtained. I find it very time consuming and it means even more tying, which becomes a frequent occupation from now on. As soon as the first flowers appear, start picking. Sow some extra seeds directly into the ground for late colour and shorter plants.

Sweet woodruff (*Galium odoratum*)
Cut right back when flowering is finished; shears are fine. Then gently rake off the cut foliage.

Thalictrum (meadow rue) Divide as new growth begins. *Thalictrum delavayi* 'Hewitt's Double' will need dividing every two years to maintain its vigour. Most thalictrums need staking, though the yellow *T. lucidum* is fine without it. Mulch them well.

Thuja Hedges and trees can be trimmed now to keep in good shape. There are buds in the crotches of branches where more serious cuts can be made, but it is best not to cut into old wood.

Tomato Wait until the first flowers show colour before planting into growbags or wherever is their destination, in or out. If potting into growbags, warm the bags in the sun or in the house first and consider making small extra slits in the bottom of the bags to prevent waterlogging. If setting them in a greenhouse, allow for good air circulation between fully grown plants (60 cm/24 inches would be good) and incorporate lots of organic matter and a balanced fertilizer such as Growmore. Plant up to their lowest leaves – they will put out roots from the stem and become much stronger plants (nip off the leaves going into the soil). In a growbag this cannot be done but the plant can be lain sideways and it will produce roots along its stem before turning up towards the light (take care not to push the cane through the stem). Of course, you could cut the bags in half, upend each half and plant in the cut end to get a much deeper planting medium. Canes or strings from a baton above the plants will be needed. We grow tomatoes in 25 cm/10 inch plastic pots, their bottoms removed and set into the greenhouse soil. Watering the soil sends the roots deep. Avoid blocking their light with other greenhouse plants. The soil will have to be changed or at least very much refreshed if tomatoes are grown in the same spot two years running.

Trollius (globeflower) Cut back hard after the first flowering for more flowers and feed with a liquid fertilizer (provided, if they are near water, there is no danger of the fertilizer seeping into the water).

Tulip There are four choices: leave them in the ground (in which case deadhead and give them a foliar feed of a balanced fertilizer such as phostrogen, keeping the leaves intact until they have died right down – they will then flower better next year); if the space is needed but the bulbs are wanted, dig up with foliage intact and replant out of sight to die down elsewhere, still deadheading and feeding; deadhead, then dig up with leaves on, knock the soil off, dry on newspaper and, when the leaves have perished, clean the bulbs of rough skin to store dry, mouse-proof, dark and airy until next year; or chuck them out. With very few exceptions (I have a wonderful one called 'Weisse Berliner' which goes on from year to year in a pot), those in pots plus their compost should be discarded after a year. Species tulips reflower and some cultivars repeat flower better than others (see November).

Uvularia grandiflora When flowering is over, feed with a nitrogen-rich fertilizer such as chicken pellets and mulch. They will not love you if they dry out.

Viburnum, evergreen: *Viburnum × burkwoodii, V. davidii, V. × hillieri 'Winton', V. rhytidophyllum, V. tinus* When pruning viburnum – after flowering – it is better to use secateurs rather than shears, as leaves cut in half look hideous. *V. tinus* and its cultivars like 'Eve Price' will have finished flowering and the flowers of *V. × burkwoodii, V. davidii* and *V. rhytidophyllum* will soon be over. Those

that do not have particularly good berries can be clipped over to keep neat as soon as the flowers are over. If they need a harder prune, cut well back into the plant's profile to mask the cuts. *V. davidii*, however, has beautiful metallic coloured berries (two shrubs are needed for this) so delay its pruning until the fruits are over. *V. × hillieri* will flower in summer so needs to be left for now. *V. tinus* is often beset by viburnum beetle (see above). Frequent clipping will reduce the amount of old wood on which the beetle can lay its eggs, but as new wood is wanted for next year's flowers frequent bouts of tidying it up after the middle of the year will cut off the buds for next year. Feed and mulch after pruning.

Vine (grape) (grown under glass) At Chatsworth, once berries are the size of peas, at least half the total number of bunches are removed to prevent the vine becoming exhausted, while the remainder are thinned, taking out half of every bunch with scissors to allow those remaining to develop.

Wisteria If a wisteria is looking thin, it may need feeding – when up against a wall and therefore in rather inhospitable soil, it can get tired. Growmore followed by a mulch to prevent the soil drying out would help. If the soil is sandy, sprinkle some sulphate of potash around the base of the plant.

Yucca Remove dead leaves and rooted suckers.

Zinnia These annuals hate any root disturbance so sow seeds in loo rolls, coir or newspaper pots which biodegrade in the ground, planting out when they have two tiny leaves. Seeds will germinate on a warm windowsill or in a propagator at 20–25°C. Late May is the earliest they can go out. They will need support so stake individually or stretch pea netting over low stakes for them to grow through. They need sun.

JUNE

The exuberance of June is glorious; the change of pace as plants surge upwards in luscious growth is palpable. Planting seems less urgent now – though any gaps in the borders are a welcomed home for the plants being emptied out of the greenhouse. Anything amiss in the garden is wonderfully camouflaged (at least to everyone else) by the effulgence of planting. One can be breezily optimistic that gardens will be fun to visit.

AREAS TO CONSIDER

Annuals Thin direct sowings of annuals. Half-hardy annuals kept in the greenhouse or on the windowsill can be planted out.

Borders Fill gaps with annuals grown from seed. When planting pot-grown plants, always soak them in a bucket of water until the bubbles have stopped. Thereafter, they all need vigilant watering.

Bulbs Foliage of spring bulbs can be cut back or mown over now that it is six weeks after flowering. Split clumps of spring flowering bulbs if they have become congested.

Containers and pots Take a leaf out of Glyndebourne's book: they select one day a week to liquid feed all their containers, and with that routine they are not forgotten. Unless there is a slow release fertilizer in the compost, containers do need feeding every week from at least six weeks after planting up.

Cuttings Harden off cuttings that were taken over winter, moving them out of the greenhouse/cold frame during the day.

Lewisia cotyledon (flowering May–August)

Deadheading Every day go around the garden deadheading. Nothing prolongs the flowering more.

Evergreen hedges They can be clipped now frost is no longer a threat.

Feeding If plants are well watered but still seem lacklustre, an individual tonic may be helpful: seaweed tonics, Miracle-Gro or Biochar incorporated into the topsoil around the plant could all do the trick. Yellowing leaves on ericaceous plants suggest a lack of iron – Librel SP Iron is a good one to use. If pests are the cause of ill health, try SB Invigorator, also a plant tonic.

Fruit canes Tie in new canes as they are being produced. Water generously, then apply mulch to moist soil.

Fruit trees: free standing Small trees can be sprayed to clear the remaining codling moth. On wall-trained trees, cut out badly placed or weak shoots and cut back to six leaves any shoots that are too vigorous.

Hedges Some hedges may need two clips during the summer: box, hawthorn, Lawson's cypress, Leyland cypress, *Lonicera nitida*, privet and *Prunus*

Laurocerasus almost certainly will and can be done this month. (Thuja is better clipped spring and autumn, beech, holly and hornbeam once in late summer.) Clearing out weeds and debris from under the base of a hedge is good practice after pruning to improve air circulation. All plants appreciate a mulch (on to wet soil) after pruning, but this may be impracticable with extensive hedging.

Herbs Early in the month cut back those leaves you want to harvest so that they reshoot with fresh growth into summer and autumn.

Lawns They could be given a proprietary nitrogen-rich summer lawn feed, mixed with some sandy soil to help distribution and prevent scorching. Allow grass to get longer in hot weather.

Perennial meadow Both an established meadow and one planted last autumn/winter will need its first cut of the year by the end of June – by the time it is 15 cm/6 inches high – be brave and do it.

Perennials Removing fading flowers strengthens the plant, improves its looks and increases the likelihood of more flowers, so resist hanging on to the end of colour. After a good soaking, mulch around any that are standing free of other plants.

Pests If plants are being destroyed (small brown-edged holes) it may be the capsid bug: a fast moving pale green pest. Cut off the damaged stems and spray with a systemic insecticide. The plant still has time to put on new growth. (See below: red spider mite and vine weevil.)

Red spider mite The presence of these leaf-sap-sucking tiny mites – browny/yellow now, red only in winter – can be identified by speckling over leaves and, ultimately, webbing across leaves and stalks. They thrive in hot and dry greenhouses so raising humidity helps, but the most effective treatment is the use of a predatory mite called *Phytoseiulus persimilis* sold online as 'Red Spider Mite Control'. For a small infestation, caught early, a pest control spray gun which encompasses red spider mite will probably suffice. For a broader scale application in the garden another predatory mite called *Amblyseius andersoni* is recommended.

Seeds Some fast growing annuals can still be sown for this year's flowering (calendula, California poppy, clarkia, godetia, larkspur, marigold): many grow to flowering in six weeks.

Vegetables French beans and winter brassicas can go in, intercropping with spinach, carrots to eat as baby veg and new salad crops sown every two to three weeks. Net the beds to protect against insects. Provide a potash-rich feed to tomatoes and peppers. Hoe regularly leaving the weeds on the soil to shrivel. Sulphur Veg is a useful means of reducing pH and improving the resilience of vegetables to disease. It can be applied regularly during the season but never to apricots, or to courgettes, cucumbers or any other cucurbits.

Viburnum beetle They will have dropped to the ground to pupate, so gently digging around in the top layer of soil beneath the shrub, changing as much as you can, may help to get rid of them. In July they crawl back into the shrub, so spraying again with a bug killer may be needed. Water and mulch.

Vine weevil The tell-tale square notches on the margins of leaves give their presence away. BugClear Ultra Vine Weevil Killer can be used in pots as a soil drench. The very easy to use nematode, Nemasys Vine Weevil Killer, applied when the soil is warm, is effective in the ground and in pots. Purchase it online – being alive, it has a short shelf-life.

Watering Watering of new trees and shrubs is vital now: do it well and occasionally, not little and often. They need two or three cans of water per plant per week so it is worth getting a hose on to them. Overhead watering encourages grey mould – strawberries and sweet peas are particularly susceptible to this. Lawns do not need watering at all as they will recover. When planting in dry conditions, dig the hole, insert the plant, fill the hole with water and then immediately backfill with the dug out soil so that the soil is dragged down with the draining water.

Weedkilling Most weedkillers work best about now when leaves and roots are big. Ground should not be dug over before or after the application as the weeds need to be whole for a weedkiller to be really effective. (See July: bindweed.)

PLANTS

Acanthus (bear's breeches)
Discreet staking of flower heads may be necessary. If flowering is poor – it can be erratic, good one year and bad the next – apply a balanced fertilizer now to encourage growth. There could be slug damage on young flower shoots, in which case apply a deterrent.

Acers in containers
They will benefit from another liquid ericaceous feed now, but do not be over-enthusiastic as too much will burn the roots. Prune gently to keep a good shape and desired size.

Ageratina altissima 'Chocolate' (was called Eupatorium)
The wonderful chocolate coloured foliage of this self-supporting, shade tolerant (but better in the sun), late flowering perennial can be kept looking vivacious by trimming

it back to 15 cm/6 inches and again in August. It does mean no flowers. If flowers are wanted, a Chelsea chop now will give a shorter, sturdier plant flowering into October.

Anchusa Deadhead after the first flush is over and further flowers will follow. Once established, these plants will not survive if moved.

Anthemis Snip off flower heads as they fade as low as possible to avoid unsightly stems, being careful not to take off new buds nearby. This will extend the flowering period considerably.

Apricot Thin out the crop only if it is very heavy, then mulch widely over watered soil.

Aquilegia Cut down before they set seed to avoid a prodigious number of unidentifiable children. This also guards against mildew and they will clump up better next year.

Argyranthemum frutescens (marguerite)
Pinch out growing tips and take softwood cuttings as an insurance policy. Take them early in the morning and pot up quickly. Trim the 7–10 cm/3–4 inch cuttings just below a leaf joint, remove the lower leaves, dip into hormone rooting powder and dib around the edge of a small pot. Firm in, water and put in a plastic bag or propagator. Continue deadheading garden plants until early autumn.

Artemisia, perennial Clip off the yellow flowers of the lovely grey foliage artemisias as they appear (they start like tiny silver balls) to achieve a pleasing, more compact shape all season. Of course, you may like yellow and grey . . .

Artichoke, globe Pick the globes (with an inch of stem) before they open, the top one first, then the side buds as they swell in turn. When the whole stem is finished cut it down to the bottom. Feed and water. There may be new growth but not a second harvest. If growing from seed, do not harvest in the first year.

Asparagus When harvesting is finished in mid-June, weed and give established beds a balanced fertilizer. Allow the spears to grow into fronds and leave them (propping them up if necessary) until they have turned yellow in autumn.

Aster (mostly now reclassified as Symphyotrichum or Eurybia)
When asters are still small, pinch out their side shoots to produce stockier plants. Tall cultivars can be reduced by half their height for shorter and stouter plants when flowering. Cutting the front half down gives a tiered effect. Personally I like their full height, though *Aster* 'Andenken an Alma Pötschke' is a good candidate for this chop.

   Those given their full height are going to need support – twiggy support works well. At Waterperry Gardens in Oxfordshire, asters are staked when they are about two-thirds their expected height so do not leave it too long. *A. novi-angliae* varieties need support as otherwise their heavy heads flop over neighbours. *A.* 'Little Carlow' will certainly look better with support. Spray *A. novi-belgii* against mildew (*A. novae-angliae* is more resistant to it). *Aster × frikartii* 'Mönch', less than 1 m/39 inches high, is good near the front, as are the Amellus Group, *Symphyotrichum lateriflorus* 'Horizontalis' and *S. ericoides*, none of which will need staking.

Auricula If the weather is cool, this is a good time to repot (but see September if the weather is hot). Knock off old compost to see the roots, remove any little offsets and set aside, shorten the taproot to a healthy looking point, trimming other fibrous roots a little, then dust them with sulphur or charcoal to protect from infection. Repot using clay pots and John Innes No. 2 compost with lots of grit. Treat offsets similarly. Water and leave in the shade for a couple of days before moving to a north or east facing position in open shade, ideal for their display. A huge amount of expertise on this subject is available at plant fairs, in books and online.

Azalea see Rhododendron below

Basil When harvesting, cut to a pair of leaves lower down the stem to encourage immediate regrowth. Just nipping odd leaves off the stalk weakens it.

Bay (*Laurus nobilis*) Bay is a foreigner, not a native evergreen. It grows strongly until late summer when it suddenly slows down; this late slow growth will not toughen up before the frosts catch it. So prune any time from now until August at the latest. Use secateurs to avoid cutting the leaves in half (which looks ugly).

Begonia, tuberous Plant out in early June. Remove the first flower buds to get bigger flowers later on.

Blackcurrant To help fruiting and to control aphids which may colonize the tips, shorten this year's growth to about five leaves beyond last year's cut, taking out any weak growth at the base. Puddle in lots of water and mulch – they need so much water.

Blueberry Do not let them dry out: to be plump they require water. I read that they like fifty litres of water every fourteen days – and rainwater, not tap. Continue the monthly ericaceous liquid feed but do not ever feed them with a non-ericaceous fertilizer.

Box Traditionally trimmed around Derby Day (early June) when danger of frost is past, I find myself doing it a bit earlier now, to avoid weather that could scorch newly cut leaves (see May). If it is only going to have one clip in the year, leave it until August. Many professionals now clip during winter, partly to spread the workload but also because there is a growing feeling that susceptibility to spreading blight is reduced in cooler weather, and leaf scorch is much reduced; however, frosty periods need to be avoided. Whatever the season, it is best done on a shady day but not if rain is forecast as box blight thrives in humid conditions. If there is dew on the leaves that is fine; just never do it in bright sunshine. So if clipping now, get the first cut of box hedges and topiary done by early June, and see May for some preventative measures.

Broom

- Cytisus: it can be stopped becoming straggly and bare at the base by cutting back all the green shoots – all the new growth – by half now to encourage branching. Start this on a young plant and it will have a much longer life. Do not cut into brown stems as this will almost certainly kill it, but cut out at the base one or two stems if there is conjestion.
- Genista: a very light trim after flowering will stop it becoming straggly and bare at the base. Start this on a young plant and it will have a longer life. Cutting into brown stems is fatal.

Brugmansia (was called Datura) It

can go outside for summer but not in full sun. Stephen Lacey's research revealed that perhaps what pleased them more than any fertilizer was six drops of lemon concentrate every day during the growing season: he guessed they like the acidity. He also suggested putting a tray of water under the pot, which would help to keep up the humidity levels. All parts are extremely poisonous.

Brunnera Cut back as the flowers fade. On *Brunnera* 'Jack Frost' cut out any leaves that have lost their white variation. They need dividing about every three years.

Camellia japonica, C. × williamsii Give camellias in pots an ericaceous liquid feed. Remove any remaining fading flowers so effort is concentrated on next year's bud production and not on producing seed. Take care not to damage new shoots below the flower heads. From now until the end of August, water well, preferably using rainwater. Cuttings taken now need warm bottoms, cold tops and lots of misting. Pot these on next March. If leaves are yellowing, give an iron tonic.

Campanula (bellflower) Deadhead regularly all forms – trailing, clump forming, spreading and upright – as the flowers fade. More flowers will follow.

Canna Few cannas are frost hardy so unless the weather is clearly set fair for a hot summer, wait until early June to plant out those which were overwintered under cover. Add as much richness to the soil as possible, then feed, water well and mulch. A ring of sand around the plant helps to keep slugs and snails off new growing points. Cannas respond extremely well to regular feeding and watering throughout their growing season. Use a balanced fertilizer and stop feeding in about August.

Caryopteris Take softwood cuttings. Spray against capsid bugs as this is one of their favourite foods.

Ceanothus: late spring/early summer flowering evergreens (*Ceanothus arboreus* 'Trewithen Blue', *C.* 'Cascade', *C. concha, C. impressus, C. repens, C.* 'Yankee Point') Prune lightly after flowering, probably June but some will be July, avoiding making any cuts into wood older than one year – it is evident where that is by the change of colour. On wall trained plants, prune the previous season's growth by about half and cut back shoots growing into the wall or too much outwards. It will not regenerate if cut into old wood. On young plants, pinch out the soft growth to make bushier specimens. Water well and mulch with leafmould after pruning. If it looks sparse, it may have come to the end of its life; they do not live more than about ten years. Leave autumn flowering ceanothus such as 'Autumnal Blue' and 'Burkwoodii' alone.

Cephalaria gigantea Like scabious, deadhead for more flowers to keep it going until September.

***Cerinthe major* 'Purpurascens' (honeywort)** Pick it at a node and it will flower again even better. Keep picking.

***Chamaecyparis lawsoniana* (Lawson's cypress)** Hedges and shaped varieties of chamaecyparis should be given a trim now. Cut lightly, not into old wood.

Cherry
• Ornamental: if a flowering cherry has to be reduced, do so after it has finished flowering, restricting pruning to what is essential and keeping wounds as small as possible. Vigorous growth can be cut back to a bud or side shoot. Remove at the base any shoots growing straight up. Cherries can be infected through pruning wounds with the fungal disease silver leaf, so do the work on a hot sunny day when infection becomes less likely.
• Sweet: thin out the crop if it is very heavy. Now is a good time to prune mature cherry trees: take out crossing wood and anything that is damaged. It may be necessary to shorten the leader to restrict its growth. They fruit on last year's and older wood so keep a balance between young and old branches; it is often better to take a

whole branch off at its point of origin to open up the canopy. It will, however, throw out watershoots in response to heavy pruning. A book on pruning fruit trees is invaluable to provide a great deal more detail.

Chive Cut the plant down to 5 cm/ 2 inches before the faded flowers set seed. It will quickly regrow if given a potash-rich feed such as comfrey.

Choisya Prune *Choisya ternata* after its spring flowering, either just reducing shoot length or, having inspected it within, down to the new growth pushing near the base. It can be reshaped as hard as you like down to these shoots – however awful it looks, it will recover. Then feed and mulch well.
  C. × *dewitteana* 'Aztec Pearl' and *C.* 'Sundance' (both slightly less hardy, 'Sundance' flowers less prolifically) need more gentle treatment: more haircut, less amputation.

Chrysanthemum Woottens of Wenhaston advises in the excellent planting notes that accompany purchases to cut back in early June (like a Chelsea chop) late flowering chrysanthemums – the Korean and Rubellum Groups and the Japanese semi-pompons – removing any spindly stems. These will still flower in October and November, the taller ones almost certainly still needing support, so get that in place. On other forms, pinch out leading shoots to encourage bushy growth. Apply a slow release fertilizer but do not feed again while buds are being formed and water only very occasionally as too much of either brings on the horrid white rust fungus.

Cirsium rivulare It dislikes having its leaves shaded out by other plants so ensure it has space and moisture.

Cistus Plant out cistus cuttings taken last August. Spent flower sprays could be removed if time allows, but it is probably easier to take the shears to them when finished in early August.

Clematis Water all clematis really well and if the soil around their base looks dry (as it so often does under a wall), give them a mulch of garden compost (watering first).

Group 2: lightly prune this month those whose first flush of flowering is finishing to get a possible second flush. If it is a tangle or very top-heavy, it can be cut back hard but there will then be no chance of a second flush this year – which there could be with gentle treatment now, cutting to large buds or a strong side shoot just below the fading blooms.

Colchichum (autumn crocus)
Take care when mowing. Do not trim the foliage, which needs to die right down for the bulbs to receive all the goodness from the leaves.

Cornus grown for showy bracts Just after these cornus have finished flowering they can be very gently pruned if they have got too big for their space. I sought this information for *Cornus* Venus, which had become leggy and needed reshaping. My neighbour, mentor and friend, Robert Vernon of Bluebell Nurseries, from whom so many of my plants have come, told me to do it now, to allow the new shoots time to develop the necessary flowering buds initiated by midsummer weather, before the autumn sets in.

Courgette They can be planted out now 90 cm/36 inches apart in very rich, water retentive soil over which a balanced fertilizer has been sprinkled. A short pipe could be sunk beside each plant to water the roots without rotting the neck. They do well in growbags if space is short. Planted on the edge of a raised bed, the leaves will fall over the sides and do less swamping.

Cytisus battandieri (now called Argyrocytisus battandieri) (pineapple broom) Best trained against a wall, it should be pruned gently after flowering, cutting back flowered stems to young side shoots, removing damaged and wayward stems back to the main framework. Being a leguminaceae it should not be fed. See February for hard pruning.

Dahlia Dahlias that have been taken in over winter are not safely planted out before June, despite the occasional beguiling warmth of May. They never catch up again if caught by a late frost. Shoots should be 'stopped' by pinching out the growing points of the top two pairs of leaves to encourage stronger, bushier growth. When planting, cover the base of the hole with compost or manure and sharp sand, watering the hole well. Place more sharp sand round the top of the planting hole to deter slugs from eating the new shoots (though you might resort to slug pellets). A slight indentation in the soil round the plant will also help with watering. Place a square of stakes around the plant (hazel or willow will show less than bamboo) with a cat's cradle of Flexi-Tie to provide the support that will be needed. After about a week in the ground feed with Fish, Blood and Bone and give them a good soak. Thereafter feed once a fortnight with a balanced liquid feed; there is a good one called Liquinure. In dry weather, water well at their base once a week. If dahlia cuttings have been taken, when they are about 15 cm/6 inches, harden off for a couple of weeks and then plant out in good rich soil.

Delosperma Such a brilliant rockery plant, feed it during its seemingly continual flowering from June to autumn. Add grit around it to keep the crown dry.

Delphinium Support all the tallest delphiniums; without it, a strong wind will wreak havoc. As the first wonderful flowers go over, before the heads are looking totally tired, cut back to flowering side shoots, feed with a balanced fertilizer such as Growmore and water well.

Dianthus (old-fashioned and modern pinks)

Pinks do not live forever so take cuttings between now and July. Hold the main stem and pull the shoot away; remove lower leaves and trim to a leaf joint 7–10 cm/3–4 inches long. Dib them in round the edge of a pot of seed or cutting compost (or 50:50 perlite and multipurpose compost). Keep out of direct sunlight and do not overwater. Being silver leaved plants they do not lose water quickly, so should not need a plastic bag over their heads or a propagator. Pot on when they have rooted (about three to four weeks).

Diascia

Cut back after each flush of flowering to encourage more.

Dichelostemma ida-maia

This cormous perennial will flower brilliantly and then need a three-month dry, warm dormancy in the soil, so it is important that it is placed somewhere very well draining and in full sun (as always, good advice from Avon Bulbs in Somerset).

Dipelta floribunda

By late May dipelta flowers will be over. By cutting back badly placed shoots and flowered stems to strong buds and by taking out one or two stems to the base, a well-shaped shrub with more flowers will be achieved.

Eremurus (foxtail lily, desert candle)

Cut away the dead flower heads unless seeds are wanted: it self-seeds well. Keep the leaves and crowns clear of other plants.

Erica arborea (tree heath)

Unlike other heathers, an established tree heath will respond to hard pruning in late spring/early summer, but spread the renovation over a few years.

Euphorbia: early spring to early summer flowering (spurge)

Most euphorbias found in UK gardens have yellow/green, sometimes red, sometimes brownish 'flowers' (technically cyathia cupped by involucres). Having looked so good and fresh in spring, they are in many cases now going over. Flowered stems should be cut down to the ground when they are past their best, leaving a much better looking plant. Take care not to cut out the stems which are to flower next year. They flower on one-year-old shoots and are both there together. The sap is an irritant so take care not to get it on your skin. Liquid feed after pruning. Depending on the flowering time this will include the following species.

- *Euphorbia amydaloides* needs to have its flowers removed immediately after flowering to get good further basal growth.
- *E. characias* subsp. *wulfenii* should have its flowered stems cut out right at the bottom as they go past their best. Do not cut just halfway down because it is difficult to get to the bottom. Leave all unflowered shoots alone. If one discreet flowered stem is left, it will produce seedlings to be nurtured on.
- *E. × martinii* may have a few weeks more to flower, but the same principle applies as for *E. characias*.
- Remove the flowers of *E. myrsinites* as they start to go over and continue to do this over the next few months to allow the long blue-green stems space to look fresh.
- *E. polychroma* (now called *E. epithymoides*), whose involucres have looked so good, will want to shut down for the hot summer. It will be better for it next year if the whole plant is cut down to the ground now.

Many of these border plants (especially characias cultivars) tend not to live long so take cuttings now or allow them to self-seed.

As an aside, in flower arrangements euphorbias need to be placed in a separate bucket to other flowers as their fresh sap burns companions if mixed straightaway.

Fennel: bronze (*Foeniculum vulgare* 'Purpureum') Unless the seeds are wanted, cut off the flower heads and a bit extra, to stop it self-seeding everywhere and to promote bushier growth.

Fig Cut any side shoots made as a result of April's tip pruning, back to four leaves. These side shoots will produce embryo fruits next year and doing this will help to keep the tree compact. Pots should be watered but not overwatered. If there is too much growth remove the weaker. Too much lush growth can be controlled by incorporating fresh sawdust into the surrounding soil: it will draw the nitrogen from the soil (this idea taken, with his permission, straight from Clive Simms's *Nutshell Guide to Growing Figs*). If there are areas of bare stem where a branch would be good, make a notch above a dormant bud to stimulate growth.

Foxglove (Digitalis) If special ones are planted, white for example, ensure any purple foxgloves are pulled out before the flowers open and bees mix up the colours. They come true from seed if not cross-pollinated. Determine a purple from a white by looking at the midrib of a basal leaf. If it is pale greeny white at this time of year, it is white; if it is tinged purple, it is purple.

***Fremontodendron* 'California Glory'** Wait until well established and then, to control size, cut two-thirds off each new shoot; this will encourage more shoots and more flowering next year. If trained against a wall, take just the side shoots back to two or three buds after flowering (and take out any dead wood). Do not feed or hack at it too hard. Wear gauntlets as it has fiendish hairs like slivers of glass.

Fuchsia Take cuttings of tender ones now.

Gentian A liquid feed now of Tomorite (particularly for those in pots) will help promote good flowering. Gentians are almost impossible to overwater.

Geranium (cranesbill) The huge variety of hardy geraniums have varied flowering times and habits: some want their spreading growth kept in check, some need cutting harder than others – trial and error – but all need cutting to a degree and none would be killed by too hard a cut; they just might not flower again so promptly. So, as the majority of flowers fade, cut back to about 10 cm/4 inches (or even lower) for fresh foliage, new flowers and a neater plant. As they are not all equally responsive to being cut back hard, try a patch and watch for speedy regrowth. Helen Yemm gave interesting advice about *Geranium* 'Johnson's Blue', which she says is too shocked by a hard haircut to produce more flowers so proposes a sharp tug of the flower stalks that are over. *G.* 'Rozanne', which goes on and on flowering, does not need more than an occasional tidy and cutting back to fit its designated space. *G.* 'Patricia' is a wonderful and vigorous magenta one for a pot needing no support. The flowered stems and old leaves of *G. phaeum* 'Samobor' and other shade tolerant geraniums will need cutting back to encourage fresh growth. 'Samobor' is excellent in moist shade, *G. nodosum* in deep dry shade. Soak well and give those cut back a potash-rich feed like Tomorite. (This will be instead of the monthly feed of Growmore – see May.)

Geum (avens) Patches of geum die out if they are not kept watered. If they look miserable cut them right back, keep moist and they may produce nice new foliage. Some geum flowers have now started to go over so, as deadheading starts, cut down to lower flowers and when the stem is finished pull it out from the base so it can regrow. The seed heads are pretty so do not feel every one must be removed.

Gladiolus murielae (previously called Acidanthera bicolor or G. callicanthus)
Keep soil moist and continue feeding monthly with a liquid seaweed fertilizer or Tomorite. The leaves of those in pots will finally look much better if grown through metal or twiggy supports.

Goldenrod (Solidago)
Cut back by half in June, it will flower more sturdily in September rather than July. Its particularly harsh yellow possibly fits that season better.

Gooseberry
The green caterpillar gooseberry sawfly will be on the rampage. Squash, spray or use nematodes to prevent defoliation. As fruit is carried on older wood, shorten this year's growth back to five leaves unless an increase in size is wanted. Keep watering: this is a critical time for the soil not to dry out. It is a job for a hosepipe not a watering can.

Gorse (Ulex europaeus)
Now is the time to trim or cut back hard any gorse which has got out of hand.

Ground elder
It is said that a way to eradicate ground elder is to plant lamium, the common deadnettle, amongst it: it outruns and eradicates the ground elder while not being quite so hard to get out. I have not tried it. I also read that *Tagetes minuta*, the Mexican marigold, will beat it.

Hawthorn
Trim hawthorn hedges after flowering to keep neat. It can be done again in late autumn.

Helenium
Start deadheading, snipping off to a side shoot with a bud.

Helianthus (perennial sunflower)
Helianthus can be cut down to 30 cm/ 12 inches in early June to make shorter, bushier plants that will flower slightly later than usual. Personally, I love their towering height.

Heliopsis
Emerging flower stems need slug protection and may need staking. Water new plants frequently.

Hemerocallis (daylily)
As the buds develop, stop feeding but ensure they are kept well watered. They do need sun and moisture to flower well. If the buds are being eaten, spray against thrip, using a systemic insecticide (or grow thrip resistant species).

Hesperis matronalis (sweet rocket)
These biennials will flower again if cut back, but leave some seed heads for collection or self-seeding if that is what is wanted.

Hibiscus syriacus
One might think hibiscus would not mind it dry given its origins, but as they break into bud keep them well watered.

Hippeastrum (amaryllis)
Bulbs will have been kept just watered and occasionally fed. They now need to experience a temperature drop at night to flower again; this could happen if the greenhouse is cool enough, but otherwise put them outside for a month. Remove any old flower stems but not the leaves. Pots can even be put on their side.

Holly
It can be trimmed anytime and doing it now means that regrowth will be well hardened off before winter. Really hard cutting back should be done in winter (see February).

Hollyhock (Alcea) Deadhead down to a lateral bud to prevent it going to seed too early. Remove any rusty leaves at the bottom and spray with a fungicide if bad.

***Houttuynia cordata* (variegated orange peel plant)** I first met houttuynia weeding the vicar's garden and wondered if it was special. The next time I looked it was everywhere, and I realized it was a thug loving the wet soil of his poolside garden. Trim its roots regularly to keep within bounds. It will keep algae away by using up surplus nutrients in the pool but then may become invasive.

***Imperata cylindrica* 'Rubra' (red baron grass)** This grass can be divided every four or five years as it comes into growth. Discard weak parts from the centre of the clump, replant and water well.

Iris
- Bearded iris: some, like the lovely blue 'Jane Phillips', will need unobtrusive individual staking, as will any others that may be bent by wind. Some reflower and these varieties need to have their faded flowers removed promptly. In any case, remove spent flowers daily as they are not pretty. Cut off the flower spikes as flowering finishes. Only remove brown tipped or dying leaves (scissors work well). There is an excellent alternative method of splitting bearded irises in June where the part of the rhizome to be retained is left undisturbed in the soil. Devised by Anthony Jarvis of Doddington Hall in Lincolnshire, where most beautiful iris have been grown for years and called the Doddington system, it is well worth considering as an alternative to the traditional August division. Details can be found online.
- Dutch iris (*Iris* × *hollandica*): remove deadheads but leave the leaves so the bulb can build up strength.

Jacob's ladder (*Polemonium caeruleum*) Deadhead frequently, then cut the stems right down and it may reflower in September. Even if it does not, the new foliage will look better than a tatty plant. Give it a foliar feed to encourage regrowth.

Kalmia latifolia If I had moist, rich, partially shaded, acid soil I would grow so much kalmia and provide a mulch of composted pine needles or leafmould now while deadheading the small, pretty flowers, which make me think of a Beatrix Potter painting of tiny dinner plates.

Kniphofia (red hot poker) Whenever the selected species comes into flower, deadhead when about two-thirds of the spike is finished, cutting the stem right down into the foliage to encourage more flowers. Allowing the flowers to set seed weakens the plant.

Laburnum A few weeks into June, flowering will be over. If possible, remove all fading flowers with secateurs as its seeds are highly poisonous to humans, animals and fish (never plant over water). But unless it is a ravishing arch like *Laburnum* × *watereri* 'Vossii', practically seedless, perfectly tied in, deadheaded and fed annually, this is often an impossibility: the subject may be a large tree after all. Deadheading, however, directs energy into producing even more glorious flowers next year. When feeding, do not use nitrogenous fertilizer (it is a legume so does not need it). Water only in drought.

Laurel: cherry and Portuguese (*Prunus laurocerasus*, *P. lusitanica*) Evergreen prunus can be pruned to keep their shape anytime after flowering until early September. If there is a hole to fill, cut back a branch in that section to a few leaves and a new side shoot will appear. If possible, use secateurs so leaves are not cut in half. Renovation pruning is better done in late winter. All parts are poisonous.

Lavender Take softwood cuttings from non-flowering stems. Prune early lavenders like *Lavandula stoechas* immediately after flowering to get a second show.

Lemon tree (citrus) Moving citrus into their summer position should be done gradually: avoid giving them a shock. Choose somewhere sheltered from wind and not a suntrap which would bake the roots. An energetic misting of the leaves early in the morning, preferably using rainwater, is helpful. Continue feeding with a nitrogen-rich or proprietary citrus feed. As stems produce new growth, pinch off the tips to encourage dense shorter growth. If watershoots appear at the base cut them out; if near the top, provided they do not spoil the shape, just shorten them. A tray of gravel under the tree will help maintain humidity, but ensure the bottom of the pot is above the water level as it will die if the roots sit in water.

Early June is a good time for an occasional repot – once every four to five years – using a proprietary citrus compost with the correct low to neutral pH or a peat-free potting compost with lots of grit and garden compost. The water should run through easily. If it has reached its ultimate size, remove 5 cm/2 inches off the circumference of the root ball, then repot in the same pot, reducing some of the top growth and lightly reshaping to get good air circulation.

Leucojum aestivum (summer snowflake) Divide after flowering when the clumps are large enough.

Liatris Deadhead as much and as often as possible to keep the plant flowering the whole summer. Beware, mice love the roots and snails love the leaves. *Liatris spicata* likes reliably moist soil.

Lilac (Syringa) As it finishes flowering, take off old flowers (if reachable) back to the first leaf below the flower cluster. The more this is done, the better it will flower next year. If there are just one or two over-tall shoots, take them down to (probably a pair of) side shoots, but do not prune back branches generally to reduce overall size; it will react badly, throwing up vigorous new shoots and sulking for years. Sprinkle round the bottom with a potash-rich feed.

Lily – and lily beetle Continue feeding every month with sulphate of potash. Search for lily beetle and pick off by hand (see April).

Lonicera nitida Clip as topiary or hedge; it will need two trims a year to keep neat. While the species is happy in shade, 'Baggesen's Gold' needs full sun to sparkle.

Lovage Cut halfway down in early June to prevent it flowering: this will provide a fresh supply of new leaves.

Lupin: perennial When flowers are two-thirds finished, cut them off. Allowing them to set seed reduces their vigour and shortens their life. There may well be a second flush on shorter stems. If they seed naturally any special colour will be lost as they do not come true; vegetative propagation is the only method of continuing a colour. Snails and aphids are their worst enemies.

Mahonia: ground cover *Mahonia aquifolium*, *M. nervosa* and *M. repens* can be helped to stay neat and compact by shearing them back every two years, taking out some older stems at the base. In the intervening years remove unwanted suckers from the edge, leaving younger stems unpruned.

Marigold: annual French (*Tagetes patula*) Better, bushier, larger plants are achieved if planted out before they are in flower. Do not water flowers from above and let them dry out a little between waterings. Deadhead often.

Marjoram (Origanum) Cut back to about half its height to reshoot, producing good fresh leaves.

Mathiasella bupleuroides In bloom from April to June, flowered stems can be cut right down to new growth near the base, leaving non-flowering stems standing but giving enough room for new growth to come through. However, some of the flowers continue to look attractive long into the season – until September – and are often a talking point for visitors, so I cut the most wayward that have flowered hard back as soon as they are over their peak (late June) while keeping the strongest and most upright flowered stems for interest.

Meconopsis (Himalayan poppy) Deadhead to get new flowers. Water regularly. Use birch twigs to provide support.

Monarda (Bergamot) It can be cut in half to make a bushier, later flowering plant.

Nasturtium (*Tropaeolum majus*) Plant out early this month, sowing in a depression, then drawing soil around the developing plant to keep it firm. If used around beans, brassicas, squash and cabbages, they will become shredded by cabbage white caterpillars and covered by blackfly – but that is the point. Some cultivars (those with an AGM) may keep flowering until November if deadheaded regularly and planted where not under attack, but still keep a watchful eye out for pests and spray in the evening if necessary. They like acidic, not very fertile soil, so do not feed.

Nettle, stinging (*Urtica dioica*) If I have time, I cut the roots and seed heads off nettles and put the rest in the compost heap – it is a great composting power boost. Nettles can also be stewed like comfrey to produce nettle juice: a nitrogen-rich (plus iron, calcium and magnesium) feed for leafy plants (1 oz nettles can be boiled in 1 cup of water for thirty minutes, strained and used diluted 1:10 parts rainwater). Comfrey is perhaps easier to use than this highly nitrogenous solution, which is good for leafy growth but not for all plants.

Nicotiana (tobacco plant) If they have started to produce flowers, they are in pots that are too small and are short of nutrients. Pot them on again into John Innes No. 2 compost.

***Nigella damascena* (love-in-a-mist)** Deadhead regularly to keep the flowers going until September and support with twiggy brushwood if necessary.

Olearia (daisy bush) Early flowering species such as *Olearia phlogopappa* and, a little later, *O. nummulariifolia* should have a haircut after flowering to keep them compact. At the same time remove any unwanted branches spoiling the symmetry.

Olive Take it outside if it is in a pot. It is programmed to survive very dry conditions so let the soil dry out between each watering.

***Osmanthus × burkwoodii, O. decorus, O. delavayi* (spring flowering) and *O. × fortunei, O. heterophyllus* (late flowering)** These species can be trimmed back into shape now – the spring flowering ones will have finished and the late flowering *O. × fortunei* and wonderful *O. heterophyllus* 'Goshiki' can also be trimmed if necessary. 'Goshiki' does well with a haircut. Done every year this stops it becoming thin at the bottom. If looking ragged, take two-thirds off all the shoots to encourage more side shoots (cut where buds are going in the direction needed).

Peach and nectarine Mature peach trees can be pruned now, taking out any branches that cross or are damaged, aiming for a goblet shape. One or two very old branches can be lopped off if rejuvenation is needed, but preferably avoid making the cuts in the crown as this produces lots of watershoots. After the 'June drop', fruit can be further thinned by taking out every other one to get bigger fruit.

Petunia Pinch out the growing tips when the plants are about 10 cm/4 inches high to make them bushier. Remove the sticky flower heads as they go over to prolong the flowering.

***Pimpinella major* 'Rosea'** Like a pink cow parsley, it needs to be cut right down to flower again – do this well before it has finished the first time round, leaves and all. I find it does better with support.

Pittosporum Many species will have finished flowering; give any that need tidying up (*Pittosporum tenuifolium* for one) a haircut.

Plum If all the plums are left on the tree, the branches may break under the weight, the plums may not taste as good as those from a less densely fruiting tree and the tree may become exhausted from fruiting, failing to produce sufficient flowers next spring for a good crop (eventually becoming a biennial fruiter). So, in early June when plums are nut sized, be stout of heart and remove enough to leave one every 7 cm/3 inches. Take care not to bruise those left behind.

Potato Early potatoes will be ready to harvest. Do not put potato plants on the compost heap as they are poisonous.

A view down the bank towards the rose tunnel.

Privet (*Ligustrum delavayanum, L. ovalifolium*) While tree renovation pruning is done in winter, privet grown as hedges or topiary need to be pruned two or three times in the summer to stay neat. Vine weevil and red spider mite can be a problem and late June/early July is a good time to deal with both, using nematodes for the first and a predatory mite for the second. See above, and the glossary, for both.

Raspberry Take out the thinnest/weakest autumn canes if overcrowded and pull out suckers appearing between the rows. Mulch again with organic matter to retain moisture during the summer. Water now is very important: the more they have the better, but avoid wetting the fruit.

Redcurrant and whitecurrant Like raspberries above, they too need a great deal of water.

Rhododendron and Azalea Feed again with a slow release ericaceous fertilizer. Ensure they have lots of rainwater as it is important they do not dry out. Where practical, pick off carefully any remaining flowers, still taking care not to damage the new and brittle leaf growth just beneath. Allowing the development of seed capsules weakens growth, especially in the first few years after planting, and deadheading withered flowers will help gather strength for next year's performance. When they have grown to their ultimate size, perhaps after fifteen years, they can be pruned every year if need be by removing one stem in three or by shaping them with hard pruning. They will reshoot but you may lose a year of flowers.

Rose
- Deadhead very frequently, snipping off with finger and thumb. As stems get tougher and whole clusters need removing, cut back to a full set of five outward-facing leaves.

- Roses in pots need watering every day unless there is a downpour.
- Do not think you have to spray aphids – wiping them off with fingers or a jet of water may suffice.
- If a shrub rose puts up 'blind shoots' (with no bud) cut them in half.
- Water the soil, never overhead on to the leaves unless it is warm and windy (when the leaves will dry out quickly).
- Some species roses (so only flowering once) such as *Rosa cantabrigiensis* will now have finished their flowering. They may not need any attention: their natural growth is open and graceful but this is a good moment to reduce them in size if need be. As they flower on wood made last year, the new wood made this coming season will bear the flowers next year and there is time for them to make that growth. Take out what is needed to rejuvenate them, removing one or two old stems from the bottom, removing stems from areas of congested growth and cutting back stems that make the rose too high or wide.
- Banksia roses will now be over. Take out flowered branches completely to make room for new growth, leaving unflowered stems unpruned, not tipped but tied in. It flowers on two-year-old wood. Feed with a potash-rich rose fertilizer.
- Rose suckers: Michael Marriott, Senior Rosarian at David Austin Roses, has a keen warning about suckers; he says it is tempting to think that a watershoot coming from the base which looks very different from older stems is a sucker when in fact its removal could spoil the rose. The best way to tell the difference, he says, is to look at the very youngest unfurling leaves and if there is any hint of red in them then they are *not* suckers. The only exceptions are the alba roses and some species roses. He goes on to say that because of the rootstock that David Austin and other UK growers use, suckers are now less usual.

Salvia Some salvias could still push out new growth from what appears to be a dead stump so do not despair (yet). Plant out tender salvias from the greenhouse and cuttings taken last year. Hardy salvias like *Salvia greggii* and *S. nemorosa* 'Caradonna' will need selective cutting back for repeat flowering. They will be much better for it. The annual *S. viridis* grown for the colourful bracts rather than the flowers will do best watered only when dry rather than frequent small amounts.

Saxifrage Cut the stems of London pride (*Saxifraga × urbium*) right down when the flowers are over.

Senecio (dusty miller) Cut back to half its size as it will bush out again producing fresh foliage. You may want to remove its rather dull yellow flowers, doing it nothing but good. Senecio is a perennial – though it is often grown as an annual – and it is a useful plant for really dry soils. It does not need feeding.

Skimmia Most skimmias are male or female though a few are hermaphrodite. Both sexes are needed for berries. The majority are female (such as *Skimmia japonica* 'Nymans'). *S. × confusa* 'Kew Green' is male, as is *S.j.* 'Rubella'. A few, like *S. reevesiana*, are both. Hermaphrodite skimmias apparently flower better with a male nearby nonetheless. They can be pruned after flowering, about now, but do not need to be. If removing unwanted stems or lopsided growth, cut into the canopy to obscure the cut. Pruning a female variety obviously means no berries this year. If old leaves are yellowing, the soil may be too alkaline; flowers of sulphur and an ericaceous feed would help (some people suggest teabags or, prettier, tea leaves too – also good around camellias). If pH is not the problem, feed with a dose of Epsom salts to restore any magnesium deficiency. Mulch well with leafmould.

Sorbus (mountain ash, rowan)
Greenwood cuttings can be taken of all sorbus in early summer. The lovely *Sorbus vilmorinii* can be very gently tidied up now flowering is over, wayward branches removed and shape improved.

Strawberry Allow the soil to dry to out between waterings – ripening fruit will rot if long in soggy conditions. When runners are produced, pin them down to root either in the soil or into an adjacent pot of compost (ready for transfer to another bed in August when cut free from the mother plant). Do not allow more than four runners per plant.

Sweet cicely (*Myrrhis odorata*)
Cut down the flowers to base when finished, removing flower heads before seeding to control its spread. Seeds need to be sown in autumn (when it can also be also divided). To increase the flavour of the aniseed-flowered leaves, remove the flower stems as they develop.

Sweetcorn Those planted under cover in pots can go outside once their roots have filled the pots.

Sweet pea Continue to tie in to achieve straight stemmed flowers. As soon as flowering starts, pick (and deadhead) daily. Give a diluted liquid seaweed feed every two weeks and water regularly at soil level, not from above.

Tamarix parviflora, T. tetranda This spring flowering tamarisk can be pruned gently after flowering to encourage new growth, cutting stems back by about half of the previous season's growth. If more growth is not wanted, wait until winter to improve its shape.

Tarragon Pinch or prune back to maintain a good shape and get fresh leaves. The less nutrient rich the soil the more intense the flavour, so do not feed. A mulch around the plants now will keep them moist without rotting the roots, which could happen with overwatering.

Tiarella (foam flower) Deadhead as flowering finishes. *Tiarella* 'Spring Symphony' is very pretty and is not invasive, unlike the much coarser, bigger *T. cordifolia*.

Tibouchina urvilleana It can go outside as the weather warms up, but out of direct sunlight. Prune to keep the desired shape: be severe if necessary. Take cuttings from the prunings.

***Tithonia rotundifolia* (Mexican sunflower)** Plant out these brilliant coloured annuals with lots of organic matter. They will look best with twiggy support to grow through.

Tomato Indoors, aid pollination by gently tapping the stems. Remove the side shoots that grow between leaf and main stem (except on beef tomatoes, which usually grow lots of side shoots, many of which produce trusses; even here, if there is too much growth, carefully reduce the number). Any competing leaders should be taken out. Support new growth as necessary. Mist with water if the air is dry and hot. If tomatoes are grown inside and whitefly is about, grow tagetes or nicotiana nearby (or use yellow sticky traps). Tomatoes in garden soil will benefit from a general fertilizer such as Miracle Gro every two weeks until the fruits appear, when the change is made to high potassium: Tomorite. Growbags and multipurpose compost usually have enough feed in them for at least six weeks – thereafter the same would help.

Trollius (globeflower) Cut hard back after its repeat flowering is over so it can build up its strength for next year.

Tulip Remove leaves of tulips left in the ground as they become dry and papery. Do not leave them to disintegrate into the ground.

Tulipa sprengeri: this self-seeding tulip is the last to flower, in early June. The seed heads can be left to self-seed or be picked to distribute elsewhere. It takes up to six years to make a bulb big enough to flower, so their glorious red may burst upon you when you have forgotten about them. I hand weed the still small area to avoid pulling out or disturbing the tiny bulblets and their minute grass-like blades of leaf.

Veratrum The soil must be kept moist for them to survive. Young growth is ambrosia to snails. I use pellets remorselessly here.

Veronica gentianoides, V. longifolia, V. 'Shirley Blue', V. spicata Deadhead throughout the season until September to get more flowers. Regular deadheading of the sweet *V. gentianoides* makes it flower much better next year. An application of superphosphate would be excellent for root development.

Viburnum
- Deciduous spring/summer flowering (*Viburnum betulifolium, V. × carlcephalum, V. carlesii, V. × juddii, V. odoratissimum, V. opulus*): these deciduous viburnums flowering from early spring to early summer can be pruned after their flowering to make them less congested, with some stems coming out from the base and with side shoots shortened to a developing bud. (*V. betulifolium* and *V. opulus* will be next month.) *V. carlesii, V. odoratissimum* and in particular *V. opulus* all produce good berries so prune judiciously, only doing what you have to. *V. opulus* 'Roseum', very pretty, will not berry. (Next year's flowers will be on the ends of growth made this year, so pruning, if needed, cannot be left until the berries are over.) Feed with a balanced fertilizer such as Growmore if not already done in spring. When *V. lantana* (wayfaring tree) is very well established (after about five years), it may gradually be reduced by cutting out one stem in three every two or three years. It too may need spraying against the viburnum beetle.
- Evergreen (including *V. × hillieri* 'Winton'): evergreen viburnums all have berries (less impressive than the deciduous species). To enjoy them, pruning after flowering needs to be kept to a minimum. *V. × hillieri* will have flowered. Its leaves in autumn are a lovely bronzy colour so when pruning, shape it to give it good form.

Vine (grape) (grown under glass)
Pinch out shoot tips to two leaves beyond the flower cluster and remove any little shoots coming into the axils below and opposite the bunch, so that all the goodness goes into the one bunch per spur. Good leaf cover over the bunches is important to prevent sun scorch on the fruit. Ensure good ventilation. If leaves start yellowing between veins, feed with Epsom salts. Watch like a hawk for mildew, red spider mite or mealy bug. Keep wasps at bay; the old trick of jam and water in a jar will do. Start ventilation if necessary.

Viola cornuta They need a mid-season haircut, a midsummer break from flowering and a potash-rich tomato feed to keep them going, so trim back to 5 cm/2 inches. They will look ugly for a few weeks but will soon flower again. Moisture with good drainage is important, so ensure they have plenty of humus-rich soil as they get established. They are then incredibly good value.

Wallflower: biennial (*Erysimum cheiri*)
Sow the biennial seeds now to plant out in October to flower next April. If there is no

space for seeds, buy plug plants in August or bare root plants in October. You will now probably want to throw out those biennials that flowered from last year's planting.

Weigela For those that have finished flowering (a few species flower later in the year), cut below the spent flowers as soon as they fade to a strong shoot lower down. If the shrub needs bringing back into order, take out up to a fifth of the oldest stems at the base to let more light into the centre and improve its form. Start by taking out stems that cross and the oldest wood and then stand back to review its shape. *Weigela florida* 'Foliis Purpureis' does well cut down to a framework as soon as the flowers are over. A neat ball shape can be achieved if pruning is left until August, after which there will be little additional new growth. It will flower next year on shorter stems and look more formal.

Yew Lightly prune. Cancer research organizations will collect any large quantities of yew clippings between July and September.

Zaluzianskya ovata **(night scented phlox)** This half-hardy perennial, delightful on a sunny rockery or in a pot of rich, moist but sharply drained soil, should be close by a door for its wonderful scent to be appreciated. Keep deadheading, do not let the plants dry out and it will go into autumn. The little flowers with their knotched edges are indescribably pretty as well. Take cuttings from the tips of non-flowering shoots as it is short-lived and more plants will be wanted since its little evergreen dome is so small. Put the cuttings into a 50:50 mix of multipurpose compost and grit or vermiculite, cover with a plastic bag and keep in the shade.
  Z. capensis 'Midnight Candy' is the annual species of this wonderfully

scented plant. Its seeds can be sown in the autumn and potted out now – it gets leggier as the season progresses but is also wonderfully scented.

Zantedeschia (arum lily and calla lily)
They like to be kept moist so provide a good watering occasionally from now until August.

Zaluzianskya ovata (night scented phlox, flowering June–August)

JULY

Helen Dillon described a time and motion study for a gardener this month and it made me laugh – here was I: a job begun, I need another tool; en route to get it, I am sidetracked by a rampant weed; my eye is caught by a rose in dire need of deadheading, and hours later – having been distracted by realigning a lawn – I am back to the first job; and so it always is this month, gardening on one's toes. It is an exhilarating journey where neither the route nor the stops are prescribed.

AREAS TO CONSIDER

Annuals Pinch them back to encourage bushy growth.

Bindweed and black bryony
A glyphosate-based weedkiller works best when its target is in flower. A transparent plastic cup in the ground with a dash of weedkiller and the bindweed stem is one way of dealing with it. Helen Yemm in her Saturday *Telegraph* 'Thorny Problems' column also addresses the bindweed problem: in 2005 I learnt from her to gather together, while wearing *two* layers of the thinnest 'throw-away' plastic gloves, as many strands of bindweed as possible without pulling them from the soil, then spraying the gathered weed with glyphosate in the palm of the gloved hand. Next, peel the *outside* glove off, encasing the bindweed/black briony, and bury the lot out of sight. The old glove can be binned when that area is dug next, by which time the systemic weedkiller will have reached the roots.

Borders Make notes of successes and failures, to recall them when summer colours are no more and the bed looks quite different. Cut back faded flowers,

The bog garden: Primula, astilbe, *Lythrum salicaria* 'Fire Candle' (flowering June–August)

hoe weeds to shrivel on the soil surface, water only in the early morning or evening.

Compost heaps Turn them to aerate – covered, they get too dry in summer; occasional watering helps.

Containers and pots Check daily to see if they need water. If a controlled release fertilizer was not used in April, give containers a general purpose liquid feed monthly until the end of August. Do not delay pulling out tatty or finished plants – just do it.

Cuttings Take semi-ripe cuttings of evergreens and perennials from this season's growth – as plant stems harden, the tip will still be soft. Try anything that is precious or you would like more of. With large leaved plants, cut leaves in half to reduce water loss. For difficult to root shrubs like magnolia, cut a sliver off the base of the stem. (A propagation book is invaluable here.) If space is at a premium, these (unlike softwood or greenwood cuttings) can go straight outside for the season, ready to plant out early next summer.

Deadheading Do not delay deadheading. Everything benefits from it.

Feeding A potash-rich feed would be good for hanging baskets, bedding plants, box, roses, shrubs, sweet peas, summer pots. The feeding of containers of summer flowers will tail off as the month ends. At Coton Manor, borders get a dose of Growmore in conjunction with a thorough watering as a boost as the first flush of flowering comes to an end.

Fruit trees Ensure trees have enough water – they need lots now to develop fruit. After the 'June drop', further thinning will almost certainly be necessary and should be done by mid-July. As a rough guide, cooking apples need about 15 cm/6 inches between them and dessert apples no less than 10 cm/4 inches, the rest of the cluster being removed. Pears should have no more than two per cluster, about 10 cm/ 4 inches apart. Peaches by this time will need to be thinned to one every 20 cm/ 8 inches (if you are lucky enough to have that many), and plums, vital to thin or the branches could break, need reducing to one fruit every 7 cm/3 inches or one pair every 15 cm/6 inches. It all sounds brutal, but if a tree overproduces, it starts only fruiting biennially.

Greenhouse Keep cool and humid, swooshing water on the floor in the morning to be dry by night. Humidity helps to keep red spider mite away and dryness in the evening helps to prevent botrytis. Keep the greenhouse door and vents open. Sticky yellow traps help to reduce whitefly. It may be necessary to clean the greenhouse with a contact insecticide to control whitefly and red spider mite or to use a biological control (see June: red spider mite).

Hedges Trim fast-growing evergreen and conifer hedges, checking first that there are no nesting birds.

Herbs Take cuttings of non-flowering shoots of herbs such as mint, oregano, rosemary, sage and thyme and push into sandy compost, cover with a plastic bag and keep in the shade.

Lawns Mow shaded lawns less often than those in full sunlight. Delay mowing if the soil is soft after rain to prevent an uneven sward. Keep the blades high (above 1 cm/½ inch) or the lawn may be scalped and weeds encouraged. Resist watering even if it turns brown – it will recover. Spiking helps rain penetration when it comes.

Mulching Mulch vegetable beds after rain to suppress new weeds and help maintain moisture.

Pests Lily beetle is a menace; see April: lily – and lily beetle.

Ponds If ponds start to dry out put in a ramp so amphibians can escape; otherwise they have a miserable death. Fish too need enough water and oxygenation if levels drop: a fountain helps. When clearing pondweed, leave it by the side for a while so pond life can return to the water before it (and they) are composted.

Pruning Trees that are best pruned in midsummer or early autumn (if at all) include cherry, chestnut, hornbeam, magnolia, maple, walnut. Shrubs whose flowering has finished can be pruned. Reversions need cutting out where green shoots replace variegation.

Seeds Biennials can be still be sown now to go out in September where they are to flower next year; anchusa, foxglove, sweet rocket, sweet william, *Salvia sclarea* var. *turkestanica*, wallflower are examples. If collecting seeds, do so on a dry day – they are completely spoilt if wet. Seeds from cultivars do not come true.

Staking and supporting plants As early summer perennials are being cut down and space is made for the expansion of late flowering perennials such as asters, hardy chrysanthemums, dahlias, helianthus and tall sanguisorbas, ensure you have good stakes in place for them. They need to look as natural as possible: if they are bunched up they will look awful and get mildew.

Topiary This is a good time to clip topiary for a dense, balanced shape.

Watering Create a circular gully a foot or so out from new shrubs and trees to help water reach the roots rather than soaking the crown.

PLANTS

Abutilon Deadheading and gentle cutting back encourages more flowering.

Achillea (yarrow) Deadheading flowers as they fade, down to the next bud, keeps them going until September.

Actaea simplex (was called Cimicifuga) (bugbane) The tall stems of *Actaea simplex* may need support when they emerge in September. It is worth getting in discreet hazel or birch branches now through which they can grow.

Agapanthus In dry weather give them extra water; it is needed now through to October for good flowering next year.

Akebia quinata (chocolate vine) In July finish tying everything in, then leave alone to allow it to make next year's flowers. Its habit is to be leggy so plant something at its base.

Alchemilla (lady's mantle) As soon as the major flush of flowers of *Alchemilla mollis* loses its gilt, cut off all flowers and old leaves and new fresh pretty growth

will soon appear. It will otherwise become a dismal flop, seeding everywhere. *A. erythropoda* is a pretty, very well-behaved smaller species whose spread is much easier to control.

Alkanet (*Pentaglottis sempervirens*) A thuggish cousin of borage with blue flowers, prickly hairy leaves and very deep taproot, flowers of this weed must be cut before they seed. Seedlings look like little foxgloves but have leaves that are already rough (foxglove seedlings are silky to the touch).

Allium If heads are removed as they go over now and during the coming months, rather than allowing them go to seed, the dying stems feed the bulb. On the other hand, the heads are decorative in their dried state.

Alstroemeria Remove old flower stems to encourage new ones. Pull the whole stem firmly rather than deadheading or picking the flowers – when the stem comes away from below ground it encourages a new flowering shoot. In the first year only, cut, rather than pull, the stems.

Amsonia tabernaemontana When flowering is finished, unless it is leggy, do not cut back as it has lovely autumn colour. If it is leggy, cut back by a third to encourage bushier growth.

Antirrhinum (snapdragon) Cut down to 15 cm/6 inches if they look spindly. They will rebound to flower well.

Apple and pear: espalier, cordon, fan, stepover, pleached, dwarf pyramid In mid-July start with formally trained pears, moving on to apples and crab apples: cut back to about 20 cm/8 inches (length of a pair of secateurs) lateral stems off the main branches – this may be to about three leaves from the basal cluster. Shoots off these should be taken back even further – stumped to about one leaf from the basal cluster. Then take off completely any vigorous upright shoots that look wrong. The purpose is to expose young fruit to the sun. When purchasing, always choose spur fruiting not tip bearing varieties and, of course, dwarfing rootstock. Leaves with pear rust (orange spots on the upper surface) need to be picked off and destroyed.

Artemisia *Artemisia* 'Powis Castle' may need a light trim in midsummer to keep an attractive rounded form.

Trim back *A. ludoviciana* ('Valerie Finnis' is the best) to get a good carpet of silver leaf for the rest of the summer.

Asparagus Set up canes and twine either side of rows to support growing ferns. Remove any seedlings. Keep an eye out for asparagus beetle.

Aster (mostly now classified as Symphyotrichtum or Eurybia) It is important to deadhead the first flowers as they fade – *Aster × frikartii* cultivars may well start to flower towards the end of July, and if deadheaded at the start (it would be relentless to go on longer than the first flush) they will perform for much longer. There will be a secondary bud further down the stem which will be lost if it goes to seed (and they self-seed very easily, producing much less pretty progeny). They need moisture to support their long flowering season, and as they are so good, make sure they get it.

Astrantia major Cut back hard after first flowering is over to get a fresh crop of new leaves and a second flush of flowers in autumn. Keeping them well watered (and fed) is a vital part of this routine.

Azalea See Rhododendron, below

Baptisia australis (blue wild indigo) If cut back by at least a third after flowering has finished, the foliage will not flop. However, its seed pods and stems can look good in winter if some clever staking is done.

Bay (Laurus nobilis) On bay trees grown as standards, cut off any new shoots on the stems. Odd lanky shoots can be cut further back in – they will grow out to match the rest. Use secateurs, not shears. Thick curled leaves may suggest leaf suckers: pick them off and destroy. If in a container, turn occasionally to achieve regular growth.

Beetroot A last sowing can be done now – perhaps mix the available colours.

Box Orange leaves indicate dry roots that are unable to draw up the potash needed for good growth and healthy colour. Sprinkle the correct dosage of a potash-rich feed such as sulphate of potash at the roots and water in well. This will probably be the last feed of the year (but see October). All being well, now is a good time to take semi-ripe cuttings, all from a single plant so they are uniform, cutting them 10–15 cm/4–6 inches long. They will be ready to pot on next April. Box rejuvenates from old wood so old or neglected plants can be cut back to 15–30 cm/6–12 inches from the ground – or cut back just to improve the shape.

Brassica: broccoli, cabbage, cauliflower Cabbage white caterpillars will still be on the rampage so ensure brassicas remain netted. One lot will be under the leaf surface, more will be hidden in the crown. Pick off and leave for the birds (or spray).

Broad bean When over, cut to ground level but leave the roots to dig in, as they fix nitrogen in the soil.

Buddleja alternifolia Grown as a shrub or standard, having finished flowering, it needs pruning. If training a new plant as a standard, seek advice – correct pruning needs to be done from the start. When established, cut out about one in four of the flowered shoots from where they break to keep it elegant and to encourage replacement growth, cutting other flowered stems back to a strong bud going in the right direction. Grown as a shrub, cut flowered stems back to strong buds and, when established, take out one or two stems completely. If it has been pruned hard, feed with Fish, Blood and Bone and mulch, but fed or not, make sure it is well watered and mulched.

Camellia in pots Give them a potash-rich feed (such as liquid tomato fertilizer). Continue to water well until September (important to prevent bud drop next year).

Campanula (bellflower) Whether upright, trailing, clump forming or mat forming, all need a firm hand with the deadheading (some continuing past midsummer depending on the species). In particular, take a pair of shears to the bellflowers trailing over walls and spreading along paths. Be brave. Apply a diluted liquid feed and fresh foliage and more flowers will appear. All campanulas need dividing regularly to maintain vigour. None like soggy soil.
- *Campanula lactiflora* will be flowering in July; cut off the spent upper flowers as more will appear lower down. Take cuttings every spring to replace the mother plant.
- *C. persicifolia* ('Hampstead White' is a lovely one): cut back these wire stemmed campanulas after flowering to produce a second, less profuse set of flowers. When they are finally over, cut them down to the ground. All campanulas are unruly seeders.
- *C. takesimana* 'Elizabeth' is really pretty but a great spreader so cut back after flowering – a second smaller flush may follow.

Canna Every two weeks give a potash-rich feed such as tomato fertilizer.

Carpenteria californica When flowering is over lightly cut back any shoots that spoil the symmetry. Mature plants can, if desirable, have one or two old stems cut from the base to keep it in good shape.

Centaurea (knapweed) Cut back as soon as the flowers start to fade. New growth will soon reappear with new flower stems. It may get mildew, in which case cut it down again.

Ceratostigma willmotianum The blue of this ceratostigma's flowers is ethereally beautiful when it appears in September. Take cuttings now, below a node, and put in 50:50 sand and compost.

Chaenomeles (Japanese quince) Spur prune hard in July – that is, cut back all the laterals to ensure good flowers next year and to keep it from being too 'branchy'. If it is grown against a wall, tie in extended branches.

Cherry: ornamental
- *Prunus avium* (wild cherry), *P. cerasifera* (cherry plum), *P. padus* (bird cherry) and others (ornamental): all trees in the prunus family should only be trimmed if needed and then on a hot dry day in summer to avoid silver leaf infection. (If silver leaf is not a problem, see January: prunus.) Net the trees if the fruit is wanted or it may well be lost to the birds.
- *P. × cistena*: the threat of silver leaf infection means it too should be pruned, if necessary, on a hot day. Stems can be taken out from the bottom to thin it or selected branches that spoil the shape can be cut back, cleanly, above a node.
- *P. × subhirtella* 'Autumnalis': if pruning at all, do so now on a hot day in midsummer.

- *P. incisa* 'Kojo-No-Mai: if required, prune lightly after flowering to retain the shape, taking out crossing branches. It can be kept to 90 cm/36 inches high – unpruned it will slowly grow to about 1.75 m/6 ft.

Cirsium rivulare Deadheading is essential to keep them looking good, removing dishevelled thistle flowers with finger and thumb if necessary, taking care not to remove the next bud. Remove leaves that become tatty.

Clematis Group 2 clematis flowering will be coming to an end. As some may have a second flush just tidy them up. On well-established plants take some old stems from the base to get new growth lower down.

Normally group 3 clematis will be flowering well into late summer, so leave alone as there will not be another flowering and cutting will lose the good seed heads. If, however, there is a group 3 specimen (such as *Clematis recta*) which has finished flowering by as early as the end of July, it can be cut back by no more than a third, leaving enough leaf for it to recover quickly and produce more new flowers by late summer.

Colchicum autumnale (autumn crocus) and *Crocus speciosus* (autumn flowering crocus) These are two different families – lily and iris respectively. Colchicum have six stamens and crocus three and the corms look different. The leaves of last year's colchicum will be dying down – when they have turned yellow, they can be shorn off at ground level ready for the flowers in a couple of months. Colchicum should be planted at the end of July. It is worth remembering that, if in grass, it is going to have to remain unmown from the time the flowers appear in late August until the foliage has died down next year (late June). Plant the corms immediately on arrival 15 cm/6 inches deep, pointy end upwards. Those clumps being divided (every four years or so) should also be replanted immediately. Autumn flowering crocus are similar and many species also have flowers emerging before the leaves. They too should be planted now, 7–10 cm/3–4 inches deep.

Coreopsis grandiflora and C. verticillata Deadhead to side shoots to keep flowering into autumn. If they fall over cut down to the base rosette to start again. 'Moonbeam' is a lovely cultivar. The taller clump-forming *C. grandiflora*, which likes more moist soil than *C. verticillata*, will need support now.

Coronilla valentina subsp. glauca 'Citrina' Take non-flowering supple stems 10 cm/4 inches long and put them into a very gritty compost. Plant these cuttings out next year after the frosts are over – important as this winter flowering plant does not live very long. It needs a winter-sunny, sheltered, well-drained spot in only moderately fertile soil.

Corydalis *Corydalis flexuosa, C. malkensis, C. solida* and cultivars flower in spring and early summer so can be divided now. For *C.* 'Kingfisher' and the ubiquitous *C. lutea* see March.

Cosmos Deadhead and water regularly all through the season until October for continued flowering. *Cosmos bipinnatus* 'Purity' sometimes needs staking, depending on how exposed the plants are, and this could be done now. The more flowers are picked, the more flowers will appear.

Courgette Water regularly but if you have a glut, stop watering and the plant will go dormant for a while, starting again when the soil is watered. In containers they need regular feeding with an organic fertilizer such as chicken pellets.

In beds they will only need feeding – Growmore would be suitable – if growth is slow or the soil was not well fertilized before they were planted. Bicarbonate of soda is good for powdery mildew, a common problem.

Crab apple As fruit develops over the summer, new leaf growth extends from the ends of each shoot and from side shoots so there is much foliage around the fruit. Cutting back the new growth to within two or three buds of where this year's growth started maintains the shape of the tree and exposes the fruit to the sun. If pruning is done now, this year's growth is clear to see as the wood is still pale – it will darken soon and become harder to see where to cut. This is not a big prune but it neatens the tree's outline and keeps size in check.

A pleached crab apple needs to be tied in, trained and pruned now (during its early years it will need pruning in winter as well – resort to a pruning book).

Crambe cordifolia Cut down the flower stems as low as possible when the flowers are finally over. Do this before the huge flower stem starts to look rather drunken.

Crinodendron hookerianum (lantern tree) Those of us not living on a wet, warm, west coast can only dream of having a crinodendron that needs pruning – this would be the moment to cut one stem in three out of it from the base if it would be improved by doing so and to encourage new growth.

Cyclamen Mulch around the disappearing leaves, marking their position with grit. Watch for seeds developing on their springy coils, normally transported by ants and wasps, but which can be collected (either when they are ripe or when they are still sticky and taken indoors to ripen from white to orangy/brown) and then scattered, with some grit and mulch to aid distribution, where they would be happy – perhaps under deciduous shrubs or on a shady bank. Seed can also be sown into pots – see online for instructions. Cyclamen tubers do not split – they just get bigger; the old name for cyclamen is sowbread as pigs feasted on them.

Dahlia Growth will be taking off and they will need to be staked to keep standing well – ideally in a way that additional support – more Flexi-Tie perhaps – can be given to them as they grow. Feed every two weeks with a potash-rich fertilizer such as Tomorite. Disbud if bigger blooms are wanted but, more important, start deadheading as soon as they come into flower. Earwigs love dahlias: the traditional control is to put pots filled with straw, upside down raised on canes, through the dahlia patch. Another ruse is to fill loo rolls with paper and secrete them under the plants. The earwigs crawl into both during the day and can be disposed of in the evening.

Delphinium Having cut the glorious first flower stalk down to secondary flower stems below and these now over too, cut the stems down to the bottom – one or two nice looking leaves can be left to fill the gap but everything can go. There is a high probability it will flower again in late August/September given a feed (such as Growmore), water and mulch. Use a slug deterrent of some kind.

Deutzia It flowers on the previous year's shoots; now the flowers are over, cut back the recently flowered stems to the lowest two or three buds. This will encourage new growth for next year's flowers and keep it bushy. If it is a mature bush needing to be brought back into order, cut out from the base up to three of the older shoots which have flowered this year, opening up the shrub into a better shape.

Dianthus (old-fashioned and modern pinks) Old flower heads can be sheared off with about a third of the foliage to stay compact and make cuttings – this is about the last moment they can be taken (see June). This is also a good time to layer pinks and carnations: peg down a shoot half cut through, and it will root at the peg. They like sharply drained, not rich, alkaline soil. A potash-rich feed once or twice during the summer is beneficial.

Dicentra spectabilis (now called Lamprocapnos spectabilis) (bleeding heart) This species of dicentra will be dying down now. When all the leaves are yellow (not before), cut it down to a few inches above the ground (so marking where it is). There are glorious species of dicentra which flower in summer, others in autumn, all liking a mulch of leafmould now.

Doronicum (leopard's bane) Cut right down after flowering is finished. Feed and add a gritty mulch.

Eccremocarpus scaber (Chilean glory flower) Deadhead regularly so that seed heads do not form – well tended, it can go on until October.

Elaeagnus angustifolia 'Quicksilver' This deciduous elaeagnus can be shaped after it has finished flowering towards the end of July. It particularly repays shaping in its early years.

Enkianthus Now that its flowering is over, take out any dead, diseased or crossing branches. That is all that is needed, though another ericaceous mulch would be beneficial.

Erigeron (fleabane) All daisies benefit from regular deadheading. The tall ones will need staking. If *Erigeron karvinskianus* (Mexican daisy) is losing its charm, cut it back to base and it will bounce back to flower until late autumn.

Eryngium (sea holly) Deadhead to keep them looking good to the end of the season (the last seed heads are good left over winter). If not deadheaded now they go brown too early.

Eucomis (pineapple lily) *Eucomis comosa* 'Sparkling Burgundy' is glorious, dramatic and not difficult in containers. Water in some weak tomato feed from this month and consider discreet stakes for the soon to emerge flower spikes.

Felicia amelloides This sweet blue daisy flourishes if regularly deadheaded and occasionally given extra water.

Foxglove (Digitalis) Remove the central flower spike when it is three-quarters faded to encourage side shoots to flower (unless seedlings are wanted, in which case leave it intact). Water round the base but not the plant itself.

Francoa sonchifolia (bridal wreath) Deadhead the first blooms to encourage a second flush.

Galega officinalis (goat's rue) Deadheaded painstakingly it will reflower satisfactorily on side shoots. I think the white variety is much the prettiest.

Gardenia augusta, G. jasminoides Deadhead regularly. Keep humidity high. If in a pot it needs warmth, but not sun at the hottest time of day. In the garden it likes partial shade.

Garlic Harvest autumn planted garlic as soon as the leaves turn yellow, probably early July. Hang bulbs out to dry.

Garrya elliptica (silk tassel bush) Feed in midsummer with a potash-rich fertilizer as it starts to make buds for next year.

Gaultheria (pernettya) After flowering, it can be gently trimmed but the best part of this plant is its glorious mid-winter berries – and for them a male and female plant are required as it is dioecious. Good in shade, some sun will improve the berry quality. It has to have acid soil.

Gaura lindheimeri Mary Keen wisely advises growing this late summer flowerer in pots until July when, as other plants have been cut back, there will be space for them in what was until then a crowded border. A well-established plant can, if desirable, be cut back now, in the middle of its flowering season, to regrow looking fresh and avoid floppiness. Now is also a good time to take cuttings or to pot up seedlings – it does not last for years. Pinch out stems of new plants.

Gypsophila (baby's breath) Take softwood cuttings – it needs sharp drainage and with its taproot does not move well (and does not divide). The flowers will dry out naturally on the plant if they are not cut.

Hebe Some hebe will be in flower until November or even later but many flower in July. Scatter and fork in some Fish, Blood and Bone and deadhead as flowers fade to prolong its season.

Helenium There may be a lull in flowering. It can be cut back now to flower well later in the season. 'Moerheim Beauty' is wonderful and will go on until October.

Helianthemum (sun rose/rock rose) As soon as flowering is finished, pull the now leggy flower stems to see their length and cut off where the leaves begin so the plant ends up as a neat mound. Take cuttings at the same time. Feed with liquid seaweed and resist any more tidying up this year.

Helianthus (perennial sunflower) Stake discreetly if not already done – they will be so much happier.

Helleborus Look on the underside of the leaves – if there is a happy throng of aphids, spray with Provado or something similar. Remove unsightly foliage and give a potash-rich feed. Mulch over moist soil (spent mushroom compost is ideal) as new buds are forming, still out of sight.

Hemerocallis (daylily) Daylilies need deadheading regularly – each flower lasts a day, another then opening on the 'scape' (stalk). Doing this keeps the plant in good shape. Do the essential division after flowering – see September.

Hesperis matronalis **(sweet rocket)** It self-seeds as easily as it is controllable and will soon be going over. Pick a stalk and shake the seeds over a new area of ground to colonize it: it is that easy.

Heuchera and × Heucherella They need dividing every few years or they become woody and dismal. Take off little plantlets from the edge with good growing shoots and pot into 50:50 compost and sandy grit until big enough to plant out next spring. They also lift themselves out of the ground so, even if not dividing, check they do not need replanting just below the soil level. When out of the soil check for vine weevil. You will know they are there from limp looking leaves and large gaps in the eaten roots. Remove any dead leaves and flower spikes to the base, water and mulch.

Hoheria sexstylosa **'Stardust',** ***H.*** **'Glory of Amlwch'** The evergreen/semi-evergreen hoheria does not need much pruning, but shaping after flowering is fine. Any major work should be done in winter.

Hollyhock (Alcea) Hollyhocks normally come true from seed so collect the seeds of good colours now and next month, as they ripen and split. Sow in deep pots and put in a cold frame for next year.

If reduced to the lowest pair of leaves before any seed is set, the plant may return next year.

Honeysuckle (Lonicera) *Lonicera periclymenum* **(common honeysuckle),** *L. × brownii, L. × italica, L. × tellmanniana, L. tragophylla* **(these two like the shade) and others.** Whenever flowering is finished (it might be now or as late as August/September: *L.p.* 'Belgica' is early, *L.p.* 'Graham Thomas' later, *L. × brownii* 'Dropmore Scarlet later still), cut back the long extension growths to a few leaves from where they join the main stem and, if necessary, reduce all the height back to strong, young growth. This could be by about a third (it does mean no berries – perhaps leave some). Like many plants, honeysuckle is susceptible to powdery mildew and aphids, particularly when in full sun, so water well and feed with a balanced liquid fertilizer across the root zone. Mulch richly after pruning. Honeysuckle likes its feet in the shade (like so many climbing plants).

Hypericum **'Hidcote'** This semi-evergreen may begin to lose its charm. Cut right down after flowering, to within a few inches of the ground, and fresh new foliage will soon emerge.

Iberis (candytuft) Keep removing dead flowers throughout the summer. When flowering has finished, trim it all over to keep compact, particularly where it tumbles over a raised bed or rock garden.

Iris Bearded iris will need dividing after three years. Start after they have finished flowering, towards the end of the month and into August (division is normally done during the six weeks after flowering). See August for detail.

Kalimeris incisa Flowering can be prolonged from May into August/September if these blue aster-like flowers are deadheaded and the mound of foliage kept neat.

Kalmia latifolia Deadhead as much as possible, trimming back very lightly after flowering is over.

Knautia macedonica **(red scabious)** It is prone to mildew so must have air circulation. Stake well and avoid bunching it up to keep it standing. Deadhead as much as time allows – though this will become more cavalier as time goes on (see August).

Lamium (dead nettle) When the clump has flowered, cut back to keep compact and encourage fresh foliage; otherwise it will lose its charm. If it spreads too far dig out the rhizomes now.

Lavender Lavender is best picked on a dry day just as the flowers are about to bloom. Hung up as bundles in a dark, warm place, they retain much scent and colour.

Leptospermum scoparium **and cultivars (such as 'Kiwi' and 'Red Damask') (tea tree)** To keep in shape once established, give it a haircut as flowering finishes.

Leucanthemum vulgare **(marguerite, ox-eye daisy)** To control them, deadhead like any other plant. After flowering they can be mown right down to the ground. Next year they will come back as strong as ever.

Leyland cypress (× *Cuprocyparis leylandii***)** If hedges are clipped once a year, now is a good time – though they can sustain up to three clips a year. Every year from the start, the sides need pruning to thicken up until Leylandii reach the desired depth. Leave a minimum of 2.5 cm/1 inch of green foliage as they will never reshoot when clipped into brown wood. Upward growth can be left uncut until a few inches below the final height (see page 104). While the top can be reduced by up to a third of the overall height, the sides never can be reduced significantly. Cutting more than half off will almost certainly lead to dieback and big brown patches. They can grow to 36 m/120 ft so really do need regular attention.

Lily Give lilies a liquid feed of a potash-rich fertilizer such as Tomorite every fortnight. Remove faded flowers as they go over. If cut for flower arrangements, take only half the stem so that the bottom half with leaves can go on feeding the bulb – otherwise it may not do very well next year (Anna Pavord's advice from her book *Bulb*). Tall lilies still to flower will almost certainly need discreet staking. Check for the bright red lily beetle and remove by hand – see April.

Lime (Tilia) Established pollarded lime hedges should be trimmed in summer, training and tying in at the same time. Clip all growth from the stem up to the pleached section.

***Limonium platyphyllum* (statice)** Pinch out the first flowers as they appear in July, to get a more bushy and floriferous plant.

***Lithodora diffusa* 'Heavenly Blue'** Trim over this prostrate shrub now, cutting new growth back by half to keep it bushy.

Lupin A garden visitor, Robert Hill, showed me how to collect seeds: when black, the flower heads should be put in a tray with a lid over them: the lid catches the seeds as they pop – they can travel a long way! Collect when popped and store until spring. Lupins prefer slightly acid soil and need to be planted young to get good roots down. Never feed them. Snails love them.

***Luzula nivea* Cut only the flower heads off when flowering is over to prevent it seeding everywhere.

Lychnis
- *Lychnis chaledonica* (Jerusalem cross): this bright red perennial is wonderful provided it is deadheaded as soon as it starts looking less than perfect – it will then reflower well into August. It is one I always stake.
- *Lychnis coronaria* (rose campion, dusty miller): regular deadheading keeps it going and stops it getting leggy. It needs water but good drainage. Take basal cuttings or find its silver-leaved seedlings – after a few years it starts looking battered and fungus ridden and the young should be allowed to take over.

***Lythrum salicaria* cultivars such as 'Fire Cracker'** Cut it back a little to extend its flowering on smaller side shoots.

Magnolia Formative pruning of magnolia should be done between now and September on a hot summer day. Crossing/rubbing branches can be cut out, the wounds healing more quickly in the warmth. If a mature deciduous magnolia needs reduction, it can also be done now – never remove more than 25 per cent of the canopy in one year. If leaves look rather yellow it may be a magnesium deficiency. Epsom salts (to the soil or in a foliar spray) would help, as would an iron tonic. Feed with sulphate of potash whether or not it has been pruned, then water and mulch.

Marigold: African (*Tagetes erecta*), French (*T. patula*), Mexican (*T. limmonii*, *T. minuta*) Single flowered marigolds are the best for bees. It is safer to grow plants from seed as those bought in garden centres are often sprayed with insecticide, which is bad for pollinators.
Cultivating tagetes for bedding is one thing – when in flower they must be vigorously deadheaded – but the use of French marigold as a companion plant to control pests is widely known.

On tomatoes it keeps whitefly away; onions, broccoli, beans, potatoes, kale and squash – I am sure there are others – are all happier with it nearby. Sarah Raven's 'Companion planting: friends with benefits' on her website provides excellent reading. *T. minuta* planted in a patch of bindweed, couch grass or ground elder will, I read, clear the ground around it.

Meconopsis (Himalayan poppy) The key ingredients for successful cultivation are deep organic soil in a little shade, and a site which is cool in summer with constant moisture but where there is no sogginess or cold drying winds in winter. This all matters more than the pH, though they prefer neutral to acid soil. Should you wish to gather seed, do it now and store in the fridge until January. The RHS website is very good on growing meconopsis from seed.

***Milium effusum* 'Aureum' (Bowles's golden grass)** Cut back clumps after flowering so that they reshoot to form neat clumps.

Mint Cut some to the ground and water well for a new flush of leaves. Oregano, sage and thyme can be given the same treatment.

Monarda (bergamot) If not cut back last month, deadhead for extended flowering. If they dry out they get powdery mildew – in which case cut right back to basal growth – or grow mildew resistant varieties.

***Morina longifolia* (whorlflower)** Needing sharply drained soil, this perennial smells of tangerines when caressed. Its white/pink flowers turn darker when they have been pollinated and they set seed easily so leave them to colonize a patch. Seedlings look like young thistles.

Mulberry (Morus) Water well as the fruit swells and feed with a balanced fertilizer such as Growmore.

Muscari (grape hyacinth) Clumps of well-behaved muscari should be divided now, in dormancy, to retain their vigour.

Nepeta (catmint) As soon as flowering finishes, cut stems right back. New foliage will quickly appear and instead of a sprawling mass, a neat reflowering in autumn is achieved.

Nerine Bud formation needs heat (not baking) and warmth. Give a half strength tomato feed monthly from now until the leaves have died down into dormancy. They can be repotted now if extremely overcrowded but they like a crowd (of themselves, not others!).

Nicotiana (tobacco plant) Plant out now, pinching the tips for stocky plants. Beware of slugs. Avoid planting in dry beds – they need moisture in the soil. *Nicotiana sylvestris* is surprisingly good in shade.

Onion When the leaf tips yellow and the neck topples, it is ready to harvest. Lift on a dry day, shake off the soil and dry on a rack until the outer skin is brown. Store cool and dry.

Parahebe Clip into shape or cut hard if it is becoming untidy. Removing finished flower stems will encourage another flush.

Parthenocissus Both Boston ivy (*Parthenocissus tricuspidata*) and Virginia creeper (*P. quinquefolia*) can be tidied up now. Trim to bring back to the desired size, cutting off any too long growth.

Pelargonium If looking leggy, cut back hard – new foliage and new flowers should appear. Take cuttings below a joint 7–10 cm/3–4 inches long.

Persicaria (bistort) If some of the earlier flowering ones such as *Persicaria bistorta* already look exhausted, shear them down. They may return with fresh leaves and more flowers until October/November.

Philadelphus (mock orange) On plants more than three years old, cut back the now-faded flowered stems to strong shoots or buds lower down. It is much easier to do this before the flowers have vanished. For vigorous philadelphus, removing about one in four of the oldest stems from the base lets more light into the centre and improves the shape. Do not wreck the plant by tugging long cut branches out from the centre. Cut them up *in situ* first. For small, compact varieties, a similar but much lighter prune is needed. After a hard prune I always feed with a balanced fertilizer, but after any prune, water and mulch.

Phlox: perennial Deadhead perennial phlox, angling the cut to mask it.

Cut out, at the base, any reversions on variegated phlox.

Phlox subulata (creeping phlox) will probably be over – tidy up, cut out any bits that have not flowered well and replant the good bits, on the surface of the soil, not burying the stems. Water in well and feed with a balanced fertilizer such as Fish, Blood and Bone.

Physocarpus opulifolius If you resisted pruning earlier (see April), cut back the flowered shoots to a strong bud to achieve the shape wanted. Old stems can be taken back to the base – up to a quarter of them if need be. Then mulch well with leafmould or mushroom compost. It does best on acid soil but soil fertility is more important than pH.

Plum Prune around the fruit, preferably on a hot day. Take out dead/dying/crossing branches aiming for an open goblet-like structure. Do not take off too much or it will produce a lot of unwanted new growth. Having cleared competing grass from under the tree, cut any suckers away, water it well and mulch over the root area with wood chippings or homemade compost on to damp soil.

Poppy (Papaver Oriental and Goliath Groups) Each plant will produce a number of flowers – cut out the whole stem as each flower fades, back to 5 cm/ 2 inches from the ground (unless they are wanted to self-seed), and give a potash-rich feed for strength. There could be a second flush. When finally they are all cut down, they will go dormant and, as the weather cools, will start putting on new growth to form a mound of fresh leaves. These mounds will stay through winter. Mulch, as they like rich, damp but free draining conditions. If you can bear to stop them flowering in their first season, their roots will strengthen.

Potato Maincrop potatoes will start to be ready but can be left in the soil until needed.

Potentilla: clump-forming species and cultivars such as 'Gibson's Scarlet', 'Gloire de Nancy', *Potentilla alba*, *P. nepalensis* On these perennial potentillas, cut out to the ground any flower stems now finished to encourage continued flowering into late summer.

Primula: Candelabra (*P. x beesiana*, *P. bulleyana*, *P. pulverulenta*), drumstick (*P. denticulata*), giant cowslip (*P. florindae*) and others, including *P. vialii* Collect seeds if desirable and store in an airtight jar in the fridge (not in the freezer) until needed. Otherwise, cut back when flowering has finished.

Redcurrant and whitecurrant Early in July get light and air into the bush to ripen the fruit: prune out some non-fruiting side shoots to three or four buds and any other unwanted growth going into the

middle. If the bush needs to be reduced, take back all new growth to two or three buds.

***Rhamnus alaternus* 'Argenteovariegata' (variegated Italian buckthorn)** This evergreen buckthorn can be cut closely again (no berries) or it can have wayward/crossing branches taken off now, losing only some berries. It also needs reversions cut out. It is not totally hardy so pruning now allows wounds to seal over before winter. If the garden is warm or coastal, then midwinter pruning would be better.

Rheum palmatum Cut off flower stems as they fade. So architectural, its mound of leaves cannot be confined.

Rhododendron and Azalea Key to good flowering is to keep rhododendrons and azaleas moist at the roots until September while next year's flower buds are being formed so, in pots or in the ground, keep them mulched and well watered (with rainwater). Do not feed after June – overfeeding can also cause bud drop next year. Remove any unhealthy growth.

Rose After the first flush of flowers has ended around early July, feed all but species roses with a rose fertilizer. (David Austin Roses does a very good granular one. Toprose is also good.) Anything high in nitrogen should be avoided.

- Rambling roses can start to be pruned now. Henry Robinson, holder of the National Collection of Rambling Roses, starts pruning straight after flowering has ended to get the maximum time for new wood to be made on which they will flower next year. He finds he is still doing it in October so take heart. Ideally, take out all the flowered stems to make them less crowded. All the side shoots off the main stems can be shortened by at least two-thirds or back to a couple of buds. Where possible, tie in long strands to flower next year, shortening them by a few buds. Hard pruning of ramblers late in the year can encourage leafy growth in spring at the expense of the flowers, so renovation pruning can be done now, though it is usually done in winter when the somewhat battered look of the hard pruned rose does not matter so much.

- Shrub roses that only flower once can be pruned when flowering has finished to produce new wood for next year. Dead/dying/diseased stems, unproductive wood and overlong branches can be cut back to encourage this fresh growth. Equally, you can leave them until the February prune if that is preferable for the look of the rose now.
- Repeat flowering hybrid musks (like 'Buff Beauty' and 'Prosperity') can be pruned by at least 30 cm/12 inches to get strong growth for a late flush of flowers in September and October.
- Spray again with something like Rose Clear Ultra against pests and diseases if necessary (avoiding rugosa roses).
- Sulphur Rose: having too alkaline a soil for completely happy roses, I use Sulphur Rose again in July. It helps to reduce the pH and blackspot.
- If leaves are yellow, a dose of Epsom salts or sequestrene tonic may help.
- Continue to tie in shoots of climbers – there may be more flowers to come.
- Do not deadhead roses which will have ornamental hips.

Rosemary Propagate by inserting semi-ripe cuttings round the edge of a pot filled with gritty compost. Cover with a plastic bag, out of direct sunlight (open the bag occasionally to let moisture escape).

Rubus cockburnianus, R. thibetanus Cut down to the ground those stems which were left in January to flower and which now have done so. The young non-flowering stems left standing will have good winter colour and they will flower next year. If there are long arching stems which touch the ground, shorten them so they do not root.

Rudbeckia (black-eyed Susan) Hungry plants, they like good compost on planting and a sprinkling of Fish, Blood and Bone now.

Salix integra 'Hakuro-Nishiki' (willow) Having been pruned in March, it could have another haircut now, thinning it a little.

Salvia Deadhead perennial salvias to keep them flowering. Shrubby cultivars like *Salvia darcyi* can be cut back by a third in early July for later, bushier flowering. Take soft-tip cuttings of all salvias and pot them up in moistened 50:50 compost and grit or perlite (really well draining). Clear plastic bags, a half-bottle used as a propagator or any high dome set over the cuttings will keep humidity high and prevent wilting. Misting may also be more successful than watering.

S. confertiflora, S. guarantica, S. involucrata and other tender salvias that will eventually come in over winter need to be well watered during the summer; mixing in a half-strength potassium-rich feed every couple of weeks with the watering would be very beneficial to them.

Santolina (cotton lavender) Though mainly pruned in spring, it should be cut back to just below the base of the flower stems as they fade, to promote new growth and keep the shrub compact. Take cuttings at the same time. The dryer and tougher the conditions, the better it will be – no feeding, no watering.

Scabious Deadheading, though tedious, will extend the flowering time into September.

Schizophragma Once over, the flowers of these lovely plants (like climbing hydrangeas but less vigorous) can be removed, though I enjoy them in their dead state for much of winter.

Shallot Harvest when the leaves turn yellow, leaving them on the ground or on racks to dry.

Sidalcea, such as *Sidalcea* 'Elsie Heugh' As flowers fade, cut down the stems to 25 cm/10 inches above ground to encourage lateral flowering shoots. They prefer slightly acid soil, love the sun and hate waterlogging. Strong stemmed, they do not require support.

Sophora Remove flowers (produced on the current year's growth) when finished, cutting back all damaged or wayward stems. The sap is less likely to bleed if this is done now.

Spinach Remove the outer leaves, taking the heart out only when it starts to bolt.

Spiraea* 'Arguta' (bridal wreath), *S. cantoniensis, S. × cinerea, S. douglasii, S. prunifolia, S.* 'Snow White', *S. thunbergii, S. × vanhouttei All these spiraea flower on wood made last year, so whenever these mature plants have finished flowering (some will have already done so) cut from the base a few old flowered stems to make room for new growth. Having winkled these out, cut the other flowered stems back to a strong bud to give the height and shape wanted. They are not pruned as hard as late flowering spiraea (see March). On *S. × vanhouttei* cut only the oldest stems, treating it gently. See August for *S. nipponica* 'Snowmound' and *S. canescens* yet to flower. Do not prune new spiraea plants for a couple of years so that they can get established first.

Stephandra incisa Some stems can be cut back to ground level to encourage new shoots – or just shaped – or cut right down if out of control. It makes good ground cover.

Stokesia laevis With some twiggy support and deadheaded regularly, it will flower happily into September. It prefers acid soil and really dislikes sogginess.

Strawberry Strawberries must be planted by the end of July – planted any later, they will not fruit next year.

Sweet pea (*Lathyrus odoratus*) Pick and tie in regularly (not too tight). Florist's tape is very handy. Water and mulch the soil to prolong flowering and to stave off mildew. To last well, pick the very first thing in the morning and keep cool until needed.

Tanacetum Feverfew is a well-known tanacetum which must be deadheaded to prevent lots of seedlings. All types (*Tanacetum niveum* 'Jackpot' is a prolific flowerer) are best cut back after flowering to keep tidy and encourage possible further blooms.

Thalictrum (meadow rue) Deadhead those which are over unless seedlings are wanted. They can be cut right back as flowering finishes, possibly getting a small second flush by doing so. Seed has to be used as soon as it is ripe as it is viable only for a very short time.

Thyme Shear off flower heads after flowering to promote denser growth.

Tomato For greenhouse tomatoes, when there are six or seven trusses of flowers, cut off the stem two leaves above the highest truss and remove all the leaves below the bottom truss. For outdoor tomatoes, do the same when there are four trusses. Feed with a proprietary tomato fertilizer such as Tomorite or Chempak Tomato Food when the first small fruits appear and then weekly (many experts say that half a dose twice a week is better). Do not overfeed. Overwatered and overfed plants have less taste than those slightly deprived of both, so once the fruits are ripening continue to water regularly but less often. If the soil dries out, the skin thickens, cracking when it has moisture again.

Tradescantia They will continue flowering until early autumn if flower stems are cut down as they go over. This also prevents them seeding and makes a much better looking plant.

Trillium (Trinity flower) As they start dying down between July and October, mulch with leafmould where they are planted – or after division (see August). The deeper, more humus rich, free draining, moisture retentive the soil, the better. Mark where they are.

Valerian (Centranthus) If self-seeding is a problem (its fleshy roots can damage walls), deadhead vigorously as its first flowering goes over. At the same time, cut any collapsed stems to keep it sprightly. It will flower again until early autumn if deadheaded frequently. The white form can be rather less thuggish.

Verbena bonariensis Pinch out the leading shoot of each plant to encourage better growth. When it is flowering away, either leave it to self-seed or, to get additional plants, peg down lateral shoots in the soil as they grow. A liquid feed will help if you want to encourage its vivacity.

Veronicastrum The flower spikes have a long vase life if picked. I love the spikes in winter so I leave them.

***Viburnum plicatum* f. *plicatum* and its many lovely cultivars** After flowering, cut back to a junction with another branch anything (such as vertical shoots) that spoils the symmetry. Then feed, water and mulch. Allow it space to spread.

Wallflower: short-lived perennial (Erysimum) Mulch well to prevent them drying out and take cuttings. By late July they may need trimming to keep compact and vigorous – they tend otherwise to fizzle out.

Waterlily (Nymphaea) Remove yellowing leaves and deadhead if possible.

Weeping pear (*Pyrus salicifolia* 'Pendula') Prune over lightly to keep the shape, taking out any dead/crossing branches.

White rosebay willowherb (was called Epilobium) (*Chamaenerion angustifolium* 'Album') Cut back spent flower heads so it flowers on side shoots. The seeds are infertile. Its roots spread but it is easily contained.

Wisteria As wisteria often grows against a wall, it can become short of water and nutrients. A potash-rich feed now and regular watering until September will help a not very floriferous plant form next year's flower buds.

Zantedeschia
- *Zantedeschia aethiopica* (arum lily): as its flowers roll up into a tube and droop, they are better cut off. Cut the stem leaving only a small stub at the bottom. The energy will then be diverted into strengthening the rhizome.
- *Z. rehmannii* and other tender zantedeschia (calla lily): do not feed while in flower but give a potash-rich feed fortnightly as the foliage dies down.

Zenobia pulverulenta It will have finished flowering this month so prune all the stems back to strong buds, even taking it quite low. It likes acid soil and does not want to dry out, so if in a pot keep in partial shade.

AUGUST

The *Garden* magazine once gave a wonderful summary of what *not* to do in August: do not cut grass too short or lay turf, do not mulch hot dry borders or feed randomly, do not plant large specimens or water wastefully. Instead, consider what should be moved, reduced or cut out in the coming months, where colour or shape could be made more interesting, where soil could be improved or where the design is weak.

AREAS TO CONSIDER

Annuals Feed their roots with diluted Miracle Gro or other balanced liquid fertilizer to encourage late summer colour. Bin those which look sad.

Bulbs Start planting spring bulbs; daffodils and fritillaries are the first call, while amaryllis, autumn flowering crocus, colchicum, crown imperial, ipheion, leucojum and winter flowering iris are all candidates. When watering, avoid soaking where dormant snowdrops lurk (they like a dry summer).

Containers and pots Feed plants with a potash-rich fertilizer, moving them into the shade if going away, standing them on trays of wet gravel if practicable. Treat containers using nematodes if vine weevil is evident (square nibbles on leaf edges).

Deadheading Deadhead all late flowering summer plants: annuals, dahlias, penstemons, roses and so much more.

Feeding Perennials and shrubs mostly have high levels of nitrogen by midsummer and do not absorb fertilizer well in dry weather. Nor do they need encouragement to put on leafy growth

Rosa 'Pegasus' (flowering June–September)

which could be caught by winter weather. However, a liquid feed of Tomorite or rose fertilizer with directed watering could improve late summer colour and help woody growth next year on any plants that specifically look in need of help.

Flowers of sulphur/sulphur chips On alkaline soil, sprinkle this in a mulch around the bases of acid-loving plants, to improve autumn colour. This is a gradual process – it takes a decade to make any visible difference.

Fruit trees: espalier/cordon/fan
Pruning of espaliers and cordons should be finished this month. See 'Apple' below. Apricots, nectarines, peaches, plums and sour cherries all have slightly different pruning requirements so find the necessary detail in a pruning book or an online search.

Fruit trees: free standing Remove spurs bearing mummified and fallen fruit with brown rot, binning (not composting) everything. Perhaps leave a little fallen fruit for the birds.

Greenhouse Keep humidity high, wetting floors in the morning to be dry by night.

Hedges Late August is the classic time to trim evergreen hedges. They will still put on a small amount more growth which has time to harden off before the frost. For new hedges, trim the sides to promote thickness, not cutting the top until it is growing well – then trim that too.

Herbs Harvest herbs, hanging them up before they flower and before all their essential oils have been released. Pick mid-morning so any dew has dried. Tough ones like mint, oregano and thyme can be dried in bunches; others like chives and tarragon are better chopped and frozen with water in ice cubes. Put some into pots for indoor use in winter.

Perennial meadow Start preparing the ground where a new meadow is to be established, so that it is totally clear of weeds. The ground should not be enriched in any way. Pictorial Meadows in Sheffield will help with advice if needed. If an existing meadow is looking a bit sad, a second cut (the first having been made in June) can be done about now when there is a 'down moment' in the flowering – much new growth will appear. If, however, it is looking wonderful, leave it. It can go on as long as it looks good.

Pests Scab on apples and pears, clematis wilt, potato and tomato blights, powdery mildew, capsid bugs on dahlias and fuchsia, vine weevil . . . Pippa Greenwood and Andrew Halstead have again updated the *RHS Pests and Diseases* first published in 1997. Another twenty-five pests and diseases were added to the list in 2017 since the previous edition in 2007. Do not turn a blind eye to their control: they just multiply.

Seeds and seed storage On a dry day, collect ripe seeds of hardy annuals and perennials and store in the dark, in paper bags or jam jars, not in plastic.

Shrubs Prune any that have finished flowering this summer which have escaped notice. Cut out reverted foliage (including

anything incorrectly white or pale yellow). After pruning, all shrubs will benefit from a good watering and a mulch. A feed with a potash-rich fertilizer could be helpful to a young shrub, but otherwise hold off feeding at this time of year.

Slugs So appalling at this time of year, they come up for surface moisture in the evenings. Biological controls work well now in the warm soil. See April for other suggestions.

Watering Do not flood plants or just wet the surface, which encourages rust and powdery mildew. Slow, thorough watering is better than little and often, with the exception of pots and containers where little and often is desirable. Established plants will not normally need watering (limp leaves will indicate that need), but those to flower through the coming autumn months and producing their buds now, such as agapanthus and dahlias, do need regular watering, as indeed do azaleas, camellias and rhododendrons, which are also producing their buds for next year.

Weeds and weeding Before the soil gets wetter again, hoe borders and leave weeds on the soil to shrivel.

PLANTS

Acer davidii **(and all snakebark maples)** *A. davidii* and all other snakebark maples are better pruned in late summer when cuts are faster to heal. Reversions should be taken out and badly placed branches removed, but not much else is needed.

Aconitum (monkshood) Ensure they have enough water as they suffer during dry periods. *Aconitum carmichaelii* is wonderful, needing no staking even in full flower in September.

Aeonium Cut off rosettes with a 5 cm/ 2 inch stem, removing any dead bits. Allow the stem to dry in the shade for a couple of days, leaving it on its side; then plant into a 50:50 mix of compost and sharp grit, water well from the base to get thoroughly moist, and then do not water again for six weeks. Repot the parent if necessary.

Agastache (giant hyssop) Trim the flowers lightly as they fade to keep the plant shapely and to encourage reflowering.

***Ageratina altissima* 'Chocolate' (was called Eupatorium)** Adrian Bloom in *Bloom's Best Perennials and Grasses* recommends chopping off the top 15–25 cm/6–10 inches in early August (see June as well) to prolong its wonderful foliage colour into October. Otherwise, cut flower stems to the ground when they have finished flowering (probably September).

***Anemanthele lessoniana* (pheasant's tail grass)** Remove handfuls of seed panicles before they drop everywhere unless that is what you want.

Anemone hupehensis* and *A. × hybrida Resist the temptation to cut back leaves as they take up room in the border. The leaves and flower stalks grow together: cutting back the leaves greatly reduces flower power.

Anemopsis californica This bog plant with its honey fragrance likes its toes in the water. When flowering has finished, cut back spent flowers and any dead leaves. Look out for long brown, slightly dead-looking runners attached to the parent (I pulled one out the first time thinking it was a pernicious weed). When a new plant is rooted, separate it and plant it out or pot up in an aquatic basket.

***Anthriscus sylvestris* 'Ravenswing' (Queen Anne's lace)** Cut down to the ground. It is short-lived but you should

enjoy its offspring if you have left the best, darkest-coloured stems to seed, and pulled out any white cow parsley around it before that seeded.

Apple and pear: free standing The removal of this year's growth around the fruit will let light in and get the tree into ripening mode. From David Rington of Derby Allotments I remember learning that if, in the first week of August, the spurs are pruned down to three or four leaves above where they meet the main branch, the crop will ripen well while encouraging better growth next year. On tip bearers, if about a quarter of the new shoots are taken out to lighten the load of the tree, again there will be better fruiting next year. When pruning, always cut to an outward facing bud or branches will grow in the wrong direction. Woolly aphid should be scrubbed off.

Thin dessert apples to two to three fruits per cluster and all but one or two in a cluster of pears, removing diseased/ damaged fruit at the same time. With cooking apples, remove the largest and smallest fruit in the cluster. This thinning achieves a better-tasting crop every year as the tree is not exhausted by its efforts.

Although apple and pear pruning is traditionally done in winter, if the crop is poor or the tree is growing too big, rejuvenation pruning can be done now. Remove dead/dying/diseased/crossing branches, any going in the wrong direction and any unproductive vertical stems (watersprouts).

Apricot: free standing When fruiting is over, prune mature apricots immediately, choosing a hot day to reduce the risk of silver leaf. Take out dead/dying/ dangerous wood and any branches that cross, aiming for an open structure like a goblet. One or two very old branches can be lopped off if the tree needs rejuvenating, but preferably not from within the crown as these cuts will produce lots of new growth. Finish pruning by the end of the month. The fruit does not keep for long, which is lucky for neighbours of those who have bountiful trees. If it was a poor fruiting year, there may be a lot of leafy growth which needs controlling to prevent overcrowding.

Argyranthemum frutescens
Deadheading keeps these decorative daisies going on until early autumn.

Aster (now mostly classified as Symphyotrichum and Eurybia) Provide a foliar feed such as liquid seaweed as they begin to bulk up.

Azalea see Rhododendron below

Beech (*Fagus sylvatica*) and copper beech (*F. s.* Atropurpurea Group) If a beech hedge has its last clip of the year in August, it will hold its leaves all winter and look neat. This is probably the most important cut of the year. Clean out the base of the hedge. If time allowed, a mulch underneath, after a good soaking, would suppress weed growth and help it maintain moisture. For the first few years, just cut off the shoots which are too long and tip back shorter ones to encourage branching. After three years, trim all of the sides achieving a wedge shape, the top narrower than the bottom; otherwise a wide top puts the bottom in shadow and prevents it getting enough water.

Birch Birch trees are best pruned in late summer to avoid bleeding sap.

Blueberry Pinch out (to encourage bushiness) those fast growing young shoots that turn into the lovely red canes producing fruit next year. Do not let them dry out. Continue the monthly ericaceous feed. If they look as though they need help retaining moisture, so crucial to blueberries, a mulch of leafmould or pine needles would help. Never mulch blueberries with manure or mushroom compost.

Box If box is to be clipped only once a year, do it in August. Ideally, finish box topiary clipping by early September as the last clip of the year. Water and mulch around the roots after clipping. Work on a dull day.

Broom
- Mount Etna broom (*Genista aetnensis*): if it has got a bit straggly, half the new growth can be taken off but avoid cutting into old wood. The sooner in its life this is started, the better the plant will be.
- Spanish broom (*Spartium junceum*): unlike Mount Etna broom, the old wood of Spanish broom can be cut into, so it can be renovated by cutting back hard now.

Buddleia
- *Buddleja colvilei*, *B. crispa* var. *farreri*, *B. globosa*: when flowering has finished, cut back shoots to a strong bud or to young growth lower down, taking out a few stems from the bottom if really necessary. Be more gentle than with the *B. alternifolia* pruning that was done last month. See also note in March about *B. globosa* renovation pruning. As always, water and mulch after pruning; take semi-ripe cuttings if wanted. If any look as though they need help, then a potash-rich feed would be suitable as soon as autumn appears.
- *B. davidii*: if you cut off faded flower heads, new smaller flowers will come from just beneath them, prolonging the flowering period; it also prevents unwanted seedlings.

Camellia Ensure camellias do not dry out. Use rainwater in preference to tap water. Lack of water now leads to bud drop next year. Stop feeding after August and start again in March.

A teaspoonful of Epsom salts round the base once or twice a year helps the leaves stay bright and will compensate now for any mineral deficiency (it is helpful to all evergreens).

Canna Do not deadhead a canna! Apply a potash-rich liquid fertilizer. Keep well watered. New flowers will come out of the same shoot as the dying flower, so just pick off dead petals. When a spike has no more buds, prune it down to the next side shoot to get a smaller secondary flower spike.

***Cardiocrinum giganteum* (giant lily)** Once flowered, the 'mother' bulb dies – the plant is monocarpic – but the bulb produces good strong offsets. Leave these where they are for now, safely underground (until November). The stem with seed pods is a work of art in itself, so leave the flowers to form seed heads which open to look like a carnivorous plant, eventually drying on what becomes a decorative sturdy stem.

Cardoon (*Cynara cardunculus*) If the leaves begin to look messy and call for staking, cut them right down instead. There may be regrowth. Otherwise leave the flowers to dry attractively on the stem; they also look nice picked and dried as decorations (globe artichokes, which look almost identical to cardoons, are better to eat – cardoons are more decorative).

***Cautleya spicata* 'Robusta'** From afar, their leaves and seed heads create an interesting profile as they emerge through my hellebore leaves, so I leave them standing after the orange and yellow flowers are over.

Ceanothus: early summer flowering evergreens (*Ceanothus arboreus* 'Trewithen Blue', *C.* 'Cascade', *C. concha*, *C. impressus*, *C. repens*, *C.* 'Yankee Point' and others) To increase the bushiness of the plant, lightly trim it again now.

***Chamaecyparis lawsoniana* (Lawson's cypress)** Shaped varieties and hedges should be given their last trim now so that any new growth has hardened off before the first frosts.

Cherry: acid (morello) Prune fan-trained acid cherries cutting out wood that has fruited but leaving as much young wood as possible. I recommend reference to a pruning manual first time round.

Chrysanthemum Stake the side shoots so that none of the flowers touch the ground. Pea sticks from coppiced hazel or birch might fit the bill. A soaking of half-strength Tomorite – rich in potash – will bring on the flower buds. The same applies to dahlias.

Cistus When the flowers are finally (or almost) finished, cut back as far as possible without going into old wood. Treat larger cistus with even more circumspection – they just need a haircut. Shears do the job well. If desirable, use the cuttings as semi-ripe propagation material. Never feed cistus, as that produces weak growth.

Cleome (spider flower) This will flower until the first frosts if it is deadheaded (or cut for flower arrangements) down to lateral buds.

Convolvulus cneorum It flowers on side shoots produced the previous year, so cut off two-thirds of all the side shoots when it has finished flowering. This will encourage new side shoots and, next year, more flowers and a denser, more compact plant.

Correa This Australian fuchsia seems programmed to flower in the UK winter, so needs to be tended now. Cut out wayward branches, refresh the topsoil with some mulch, and feed this month (before it flowers in October) with a

balanced liquid fertilizer such as Gro-Sure Ericaceous Plant Food.

Cotinus (smoke bush) When the sprays of 'smokey flowers' formed on last year's growth are over, take them off to keep the bush under control. It will probably produce more growth and will need its proper prune in March.

Courgette Take off some leaves so maximum sunshine reaches the fruits.

Cymbidium (orchid) Provide a potassium-rich proprietary orchid feed. Chempak does one but there are several others.

Dahlia Continue feeding every two weeks with tomato fertilizer and keep the soil moist. If blooms are becoming smaller and stems floppy, remove some buds below the central shoot between the leaves and the stem to strengthen the main stem. Deadheads masquerade as flower buds but do not be conned – buds are bun shaped, deadheads are pointy and soggy – and there will be another bud just further down the stem, so cut to that.

Delphinium If wanted, collect seed once ripened, sow into pots and place in a cold frame out of direct sunlight to plant out next spring. If that is difficult, put the seed in the deep freeze and sow next March in seed trays under cover to plant out in summer. Cultivars will not come true from seed, but you will get the same type of delphinium (an elatum, a belladonna, etc.) and a good strong plant. It is well worth doing if blocks of specific colours are not essential.

Dianthus (pinks and carnations) Trim the plants, removing flowered shoots

Cardiocrinum giganteum
(giant lily, flowering July–August)

completely to keep the clump neat. Do not mulch – it will lead to stem rot.

Diascia When finally finished, cut them right back to base.

Echinacea purpurea **(coneflower)**
There are several flowers on each stem; deadheading will neaten up the plant but nothing more. I read that it was a fussy plant, not liking competition, but Bob Brown of Cotswold Garden Flowers, whose catalogues make wonderful reading, says no one quite knows: they just do not last forever and hate winter wet. The seed heads are worth leaving on as they will be good over winter.

Echinops bannicatus **'Blue Globe',** *E. ritro* **'Veitch's Blue' (globe thistle)**
Ecinops like poor soil so do not feed or mulch. These two particularly good ones may reflower if the stems are cut down to the ground just as the blue globes lose their first sparkle. By cutting down their leaves, which will be starting to look tired, they will anyway be refreshed.

Eremurus (foxtail lily, desert candle)
When weeding be careful not to damage inadvertently their octopus-like, fleshy root systems, which are very near the surface. Should they need moving – they do not like it, enjoying congestion – do so after the leaves have died down and before September. If the roots are tangled, leave them to dry out on the ground; they will separate more easily but will snap given half a chance so need gentle treatment. When all top growth has disappeared completely, avoid watering however dry the soil becomes. As Mark Griffiths wrote in *Country Life*, 'It doesn't do to douse a Desert Candle.' There should be no carpeting plants or shading perennials around them as they need as much sun as possible.

Fennel: bronze (*Foeniculum vulgare* 'Purpureum') Collect the seeds and then cut back to about 30 cm/12 inches. It cannot be moved happily.

Fig Stop any feeding so that there is no tender new growth to be bitten by frost.

Filipendula rubra 'Venusta' (meadowsweet) Remove the sugar candy flower heads when finished.

Foxglove (Digitalis) When the seed has finished developing, cut off the flower head and collect the seed to distribute round the garden where foxgloves are desirable. If seeds are not needed, cut the plants down to the basal rosette. Bin rather than compost its debris of dead leaves, which almost always get mildew.

Fremontodendron 'California Glory' It is worth getting a ladder out to do some deadheading – it will flower much longer.

Fritillary This is the time to sow seed and put into a cold frame. If they are growing in long grass, when you mow let the hay sit for a while for the seed to settle. If planting bulbs, they should be handled gently as, Anna Pavord reminds us in her book *Bulb*, having no tunic they bruise easily.

Gaillardia Cut back perennials (*Gaillardia x grandiflora*) to 15 cm/6 inches during late summer to stimulate new, winter-hardy growth. Cut back the annual *G. aristata* as flowers fade so that those remaining can fill out and look buoyant.

Gladiolus Feed every two weeks from the start of flowering with a potash-rich liquid fertilizer such as Tomorite, until at least three weeks after flowering is finished. This will produce strong good corms for next year. Pinch off fading blooms to encourage the remaining buds to open. Leave a bit of stem and all the foliage to die back.

Gladiolus murielae (was called *Acidanthera bicolor* and *G. callicanthus*) Continue to feed and water during their growing period. Move those in pots near to a door to enjoy their scent when the flowers emerge.

Goldenrod (Solidago) Remove all seed heads to prevent it spreading seed where it is not wanted.

Hazel: contorted (*Corylus avellana* 'Contorta') Pruning now (rather than in January) means that it will not produce a mass of new straight growth, which will then need to be cut out. It is, however, harder now to see the form and where to improve it.

Heather: summer flowering (*Calluna vulgaris*) In late August trim the spring foliage of summer flowering heathers to improve their appearance and encourage new foliage and flowers. Keep within the green as brown wood does not regenerate.

Hebe There are hebe species flowering at different times from late spring to early winter. None appreciate great pruning, but when flowering is over, a gentle haircut helps to keep them in shape. Avoid going in deep. They are easy to propagate from semi-ripe cuttings. When rooted, pinch out the growing tips to promote bushiness.

Hippophae rhamnoides (sea buckthorn) Trim branches now or leave it to grow wild – it will get huge. Both male and female plants are needed for the wonderful berries; I gather it is impossible to identify the sex as saplings so plant a number to take your chance.

Holly (ilex) Late summer, when leaves are firm and glossy, is an excellent time to clip holly hedges and carry out topiary clipping. Bare stems only reshoot (very slowly) from a bud, so do not leave a hole.

Gaillardia arisata 'Firewheels' (an annual, flowering June–October)

Hosta Removing leaf litter exposes any slugs. A scattering of Growing Success slug killer, harmless to other animals, is a good deterrent. (They do not fancy the thicker, ribbed hosta leaf as much as more delicate leaves.) After flowering is finished, remove the flower stalks immediately. A balanced liquid feed could be given to promote good root growth in autumn if they seem to need it. Ensure the soil is really damp before doing so.

***Hydrangea anomala* subsp. *petiolaris* (climbing hydrangea)** As soon as flowering finishes, cut back long shoots to a bud or leaf joint (or its point of origin for harder pruning). If pruning is delayed, next year's flower buds get cut off. The fat shoot tips indicate which ones will carry next year's flowers so do not prune too harshly.

Indigofera *Indigofera amblyantha*, *I. heterantha* and *I. pendula* go on flowering right into autumn (*I. pendula* until the first frosts). Two-thirds can be cut off each new non-flowering shoot to encourage more bushiness if it looks a bit sparse.

Ipheion Having marked their position in April, dig up, divide and replant established clumps.

Iris
- Bearded iris: to set the maximum amount of flowers their rhizomes need sun between August and October so must not have competition. Cut leaves down to a neat V shape only to make them easier to handle – there is no need to do so – but to keep them in good condition, remove dead leaves

when they pull away easily from the rhizomes, cutting back tired leaves and those with brown tips. Lift the clumps every three to five years (when they look congested), prize the rhizomes apart and cut them into two or three bits, each with good roots, discarding any rotten or ancient sections. Chuck them into a bucket of water as they await replanting. Plant these new sections in broad shallow holes, spreading out the roots, pressing them into moist, well-mulched soil but leaving the rhizome level with the surface. A scattering of bone meal will help the roots establish.

- *Iris danfordiae, I. histrioides, I. reticulata*: plant 5–7 cm/2–3 inches apart, from late August to early October, 15 cm/6 inches deep: planting this deep stops them producing lots of tiny bulblets and then not flowering so well after their first year. Sprinkle in some slow release fertilizer mixed with sharp sand. Lay some grit around them to improve drainage and help identify their position so they are not covered by later planting.
- *I. graminea*: feed this clump-forming, fragrant beardless iris with a potash-rich liquid fertilizer such as Tomorite at the end of August and it may bloom again in September (having flowered in early summer).
- *I. pseudacorus*: remove dead flower heads before seeds are formed, and also any dying foliage. This iris is invasive (and beastly to dig out).
- Pacific Coast irises: this is a good time to take sections off the edges of large plants to spread them out and refresh them.

Jasminum officinale (common jasmine)
Prune gently immediately flowering has finished so new growth made this autumn has time to mature before the first flowering next year. Cut back flowered stems to a lower strong side shoot, remove weak and spindly stems and thin out any stems crossing with lots of others, crowding the space.

Kolkwitzia amabilis 'Pink Cloud'
When established as a good clump and flowering has finished, it is important to cut flowered stems back to a non-flowering side shoot or good bud and take out some stems from the base, starting with the oldest. Without this annual attention it becomes untidy and flowers less well. Remove suckers. If cut right down to base it will start again.

Knautia macedonica (red scabious)
Deadheading takes hours and is terribly fiddly: there are always new buds nearby which get cut off mistakenly and the dead flower heads are quite pretty anyway. An article by Carol Klein proposed a good way to deal with its time consuming pruning: cut down whole big stems when they get too exuberant to make room for new growth rather than fiddling about with the waving pincushions – an editing process from now until autumn that will keep it in good shape. It made such a difference when I tried this instead of deadheading for hours. It also ensures better air circulation and thus less tendency to mildew.

Lavender Living in the East Midlands, I lightly trim the flowers as they go over, leaving about 2.5 cm/1 inch of the old flower spikes (doing this always reminds me of the end of the summer holidays). This will not look as neat as a close haircut, but the extra growth will provide protection over winter. In mild areas it can be pruned much harder to induce a flush of new growth that will harden off before winter, producing more compact plants. Lavender thrives in poor, dry, sunny, alkaline soil – never feed and keep soggy leaf litter off the plants.

Leyland cypress (× *Cuprocyparis leylandii*) It is better not to trim after August. Research suggests it leads to brown patches and dieback.

Ligularia The plants must not dry out. Protect from slugs and snails for whom it is ambrosia. Remove fading flowers back to the foliage to extend flowering. When clumps get too big, divide them when flowering finishes.

Lily – including *Lilium candidum*
Resist cutting whole stems down too short: it can divide the bulb into two as it dies back.

This is the month to plant *Lilium candidum* bulbs – earlier than most. Unlike others, they form rosettes in autumn that are visible throughout winter. They have a very short dormant season so if they need moving, now is the time to do it. Happy in a little shade, the tip of the bulb should be planted just below the surface of alkaline soil about 20 cm/8 inches apart with a shallow layer of gravel over the top of the soil. Leave well alone to multiply.

Lobelia erinus (trailing and clump-forming annual) It will keep flowering until the first frost if fading flowers and tired straggly stems are trimmed regularly. Give plants a regular high-potash liquid feed throughout the growing season and do not allow them to dry out.

Lonicera nitida Whether hedge or bush this evergreen will need a trim.

Lythrum salicaria cultivars such as 'Fire Cracker' Bold and colourful, they must be deadheaded before seeding everywhere.

Mahonia: upright Mahonias are good left unpruned but sometimes need care if they are bare at the bottom and have long unwieldy branches. On established plants, shorten over-long stems by as much as a a half, always pruning to a shoot or bud. Thick old wood can be reduced and will reshoot, although it may take a few years to recover; there just needs to be at least one side shoot below the cut. If there is not even one shoot, cut the branch out completely. New growth will be encouraged by taking out some branches totally to let more light into the centre. A mulch is always worthwhile after pruning.

Mahonia eurybracteata subsp. *ganpinensis* 'Soft Caress' will flower from late this month so do not cut off its flower buds. If it is getting too big, it can be cut back hard after flowering, mulching well round its base afterwards.

Metasequoia glyptostroboides (dawn redwood) Do any corrective pruning in August when the weather is hot. Try to maintain the habit of the tree, which is for the lower stems to sway down to the ground – not always possible if it is near a path. The cultivar *Metasequoia glyptostroboides* 'Gold Rush' is lovely in a smallish garden, growing only to about 9 m/30 ft.

Myrtle (*Myrtis communis*) A potash-rich liquid feed will strengthen hardiness before the cold weather kicks in. Administer the same to other slightly tender plants.

Narcissus (daffodil) It is not too soon to plant the bulbs in late August – they like to get their roots down early.

Nerine As they move out of dormancy, give them a soaking to initiate growth. Water every ten days or so until they have stopped growing, allowing pots to dry out between watering.

Nicotiana (tobacco plant) When deadheading the flowers, pick or cut just above a node to encourage it to branch out and keep flowering. Tall varieties will need staking unless they are supported by surrounding plants. Monthly feeding will benefit them all, but especially *Nicotiana langsdorffii* and *N. mutabilis.*

Parsley Soak lots of seeds for thirty-six hours and then sow in warm, well-moistened compost. Cover with clingfilm to germinate as a winter crop.

Penstemon Penstemons tolerate dry soil and do not need to be fed; deadhead energetically to get continuous flowering, cutting at the bottom of the flower head. Flower power is lost when they are allowed to go to seed. Take semi-ripe cuttings from non-flowering side shoots. Trim off the lower leaves, cut the stalk below a node and dib into gritty compost up to the second node. We are told to pack them in: sixteen in a 10 cm/4 inch square pot. Cover the pot in a plastic bag ensuring the sides do not touch the leaves. When rooted (two to three weeks), pot on separately, overwintering somewhere frost free, to plant out next April/May. As penstemons are not totally hardy, cuttings could well be needed.

Petunia Petunias have to be deadheaded relentlessly to keep them going until October. Seeds can be collected off the removed sticky deadheads as they wither away.

Phalaris (gardener's garters) Check there is no reversion to plain green of the pretty variation – if there is, cut it out.

Phlomis Leave cutting down those phlomis whose flower heads provide excellent winter interest. *Phlomis italica* seems to benefit from being cut back gently after flowering (but do not cut the stems right down to the ground). *P. fruticosa* needs to have any weak and muddled stems removed to maintain its shape, but its flower heads can then look wonderful over winter. *P. tuberosa* will look good in late autumn and tall robust *P. russeliana*, which may still be flowering, certainly needs to be left as long as possible into the winter months.

Phlox paniculata Keep deadheading (it may flower again) and renew the mulch around its base to preserve moisture: it is a very thirsty plant. If it is crowded, consider cutting back surrounding plants or dividing clumps later this autumn. Enabling air to circulate will help prevent mildew. When watering, avoid splashing the leaves, and if it is collapsing, make a note to stake it next spring.

Photinia × fraseri To keep it neat – for example, if growing as a hedge – prune it for the last time this month. New growth is very tender and may get caught by frosts.

Phygelius aequalis 'Yellow Trumpet', P. × rectus 'African Queen' and other cultivars Cutting – or just deadheading – will keep it fresh. It may get figwort weevil, identified by black tips on the flowers. Pick off the beetles or spray after sunset when there are no pollinators around.

Pittosporum To keep the shape, prune little and often, starting when young, and avoid hard pruning. The current season's growth can be given a haircut as the last prune of the year.

Primula (primrose) Towards the end of the month, lift polyanthus primulas, soak in a bucket of water and then pull apart, planting in clumps under deciduous trees or shrubs, on banks or in rough grass. This division can be done in May, but they then risk drying out in summer. With *Primula sieboldii* divide the rhizome – any bits with some shoot and root should grow. Divide *P. vialii*, too, which will only cope with sun if it is kept moist all the time.

Quince Chris Bowers of Whispering Tree Nurseries in Norfolk advises the removal of strong upright leaders by about a third now while removing completely badly placed branches, watershoots and lower branches touching the ground, aiming for a fairly open centre and pleasing shape. Harvesting of fruit will begin in autumn so this will guide some of the pruning.

Raspberry When summer raspberries are over, cut down to the ground all canes that fruited this year. Leave no stubs. The sooner this is done, the easier it is to identify which to cut. Yellowing, weak, spindly, damaged or brittle canes also need to be cut out even if they have not borne fruit (bin them, do not compost). Tug out by their roots all canes that are growing away from their proper stool. Tie in the remaining canes, about 10 cm/ 4 inches apart, six to eight canes to a plant (reduce the number of canes if too many). A string tied to a post at one end, looped round the wire and around each stem, saves tying them individually. If remaining leaves are yellow give them and the roots a foliar spray of 20 grams of Epsom salts per litre of water plus a drop of washing up liquid to make it stick. Pull out, also by the roots, any wandering autumn flowering raspberry suckers.

Redcurrant and whitecurrant After picking the fruit, shorten new shoots back to five leaves.

Red orache (*Atriplex hortensis* var. *rubra*) Grown as an annual for a border, cut it down the moment it is past its best, unless you want it to self-seed, which it will do with ease.

Rhododendron and Azalea Ensure all azaleas and rhododendrons (and camellias) are well watered as they now make next year's flower buds.

Rose
- Remove leaves on the ground and as many leaves with black spot as you have time for from the roses themselves, but do not denude the shrub entirely: it still needs to photosynthesize.
- Deadhead as often as possible, cutting back to an outward facing leaf.
- Leave watershoots (though they can be reduced in height) – these are the shoots that will flower next year. So long as they have leaves on, they will be making a positive contribution to the plant's strength.
- On damask roses, a very old stem or two could be taken out to open up the shrub.
- Albas, centifolias, gallicas, hybrid musks, rugosas, moss roses, Scottish roses, sweet briar and species roses should be left alone so that their natural shape is not spoilt. If they are really too big where they are, cut out now, from the base, the stems you do not want and ease any areas of congestion. Ideally leave them to achieve their full size.

Rue (*Ruta graveoleus*) The yellow flowers go on all summer so it should be cut into shape when they are over. Do so wearing gloves. If you do not care for the flowers, cut it into shape in spring.

Salvia I am seduced by salvias at this time of year and put them in expecting miracles – they really need to be planted in early summer so they can put down roots and be pinched out to make bushier plants. Provide slug protection around new growth. *Salvia guaranitica* (which can get quite large) does not like being crowded. *S. microphylla* may need a little gentle shaping now but does not want heavy autumn pruning. All salvias need deadheading to prolong flowering. Those that are borderline hardy will, even now, appreciate a planting position that is protected from cold drying winds and one that is not going to get too wet in the coming months.

Sempervivum (houseleek) Incorporate a slow release fertilizer and extra grit when planting. Only water if they start to look shrivelled.

Snowdrop If snowdrops were not divided in spring when green, established clumps can be expertly divided now if you know exactly where they are and can do so without disturbing other plants: a good time as they start to root.

***Solanum crispum* 'Glasnevin'** Deadhead and it will continue flowering with no dying brown flower heads to spoil it.

Sorbaria sorbifolia After flowering it can be thoroughly tidied up with wayward shoots cut out. It has such good leaf colour it is a pity to cut out too much.

***Spiraea canescens, S. nipponica* 'Snowmound'** These midsummer flowering varieties do not need regular pruning, but to keep mature plants in good shape cut back flowered shoots to strong buds. If needed, cut a stem or two from the base. Semi-ripe cuttings can be taken at this time of year.

***Stachys byzantina* (lamb's ears)** Cut off all the flower stems as they finish in the approach to autumn, removing any tatty or dead leaves. This will keep growth more compact – otherwise it tends to wander a bit.

***Sternbergia lutea* (autumn daffodil)** They are easiest planted when about to flower, in light, sharply drained soil which will not get too wet in winter and where they can be baked by summer sun while dormant. To build up a beautiful autumn flowering colony, they must not be disturbed.

Strawberry Plant rooted runners into new beds forked over with a sprinkling of a balanced fertilizer such as Fish, Blood and Bone and incorporating some leafmould if you have it. (Leafmould is more acidic than garden compost and they need acidic soil to flourish. If growing them in pots, use ericaceous compost.) Keep plants well watered now, into autumn, as next year's buds are forming. Avoid watering from above, which encourages grey mould. They need full sun, preferably out of the wind.

Sweetcorn When the hairs turn amber brown, press into a corn kernel. If milky liquid comes out it needs longer – a creamy liquid and it is ready for the pot.

Sweet pea Keep watering, tying in and picking. Collect any seeds now as by September they get too damp. Even so, dry the seed and store in tightly sealed packages or jars. When they have finally finished flowering, cut to ground level but leave the roots as, like all legumes, the roots fix nitrogen into the soil and can be dug in. Also see July.

Symphoricarpos (snowberry) As it finishes flowering, this bullet-proof plant can be cut back to strong buds, some stems being taken out at the base to keep it in shape.

Thuja plicata Thuja needs its final trim this month to prevent dieback and brown patches.

Tomato Remove any leaves that stop the sun reaching the ripening fruit. Feed once a week with Tomorite or similar. Steady regular but not overly generous watering is best. With greenhouse tomatoes, it may be necessary to top up the soil over roots that have been exposed by watering.

***Trachelospermum jasminoides, T. asiaticum* (star jasmine)** As flowering finishes, trim back some of the older shoots to keep it in good shape and tie in some new ones. It flowers on the short laterals of older wood so this will direct the pruning. A feed of a potash-rich fertilizer, a good water and mulch will help deter the sooty mould that, as growth slows down, gathers on the lower leaves again.

Trillium (Trinity flower) They need time and patience to bulk up; division, if really necessary, is done as the foliage dies back but when the leaves are still attached. Each piece of rhizome needs at least one bud and some roots. It is worth getting advice from an expert. Plant the rhizomes (7–10 cm/3–4 inches deep) so they get their roots well settled before emerging in March/April. Moist soil is essential but they will not survive if the roots are drowned. Acid conditions are ideal but rich soil with lots of organic matter is the key ingredient. From seed it is about a five-year wait. Slugs and snails enjoy them too.

Tulbaghia violacea Christine Skelmersdale at Broadleigh Bulbs in Somerset grows these lovely bulbs at the edge of a sheltered sunny path. If deadheaded all season, they flower continuously from midsummer to autumn.

Veratrum Cut down the flower spike when finished to let the plant build up strength. Mark where it is as it comes up so late each year. Wear gloves as it is very poisonous.

Verbascum Removing fading flower spikes to the ground well before they are really over extends the life of the plant. *Verbascum chaixii* 'Album' lasts longer than others. To collect seed, on a hot day cut the long flower spikes into manageable lengths and store cool and dry. The seed of hybrids is usually sterile so the only way of propagating these is by taking root cuttings in early spring.

V. *bombyciferum*: the flower spikes will be about over; if possible, leave them in place to look good over winter, which also enables this biennial to self-seed.

Vine (grape) (grown under glass) Keep the vine watered and well ventilated all month. At Chatsworth the well-watered soil is covered with white polythene to maintain moisture levels while preventing botrytis from rising damp. Plants are then not watered again until after harvest. This process of covering the soil would be a bit impracticable for most places but it could be done.

Vitis coignetiae This amazingly coloured climber will romp away up a deciduous tree, a wall or trellis but needs netting to cling to its first year (and lots of watering). If already established, cut back the young shoots now to restrain its size. A good cultivar is 'Claret Cloak'.

Wisteria Wear old clothes when pruning as its sap stains. First, tie in the still flexible new shoots needed to extend the framework or fill in gaps. Then shorten all the current season's growth – the long tentacles – to about 30 cm/12 inches or five or six leaves. This allows sun to ripen stems and promote flower bud formation, and of course it controls its size. Remove stems from behind or around gutters or roof tiles: it is very much easier to keep them out than to get them out.

Yew Traditionally given its last prune, with other evergreens, in August, yew is sometimes left until September because of pressure on time and its ability to regenerate from brown wood.

Zaluzianskya ovata (night scented phlox) When this long flowering, half-hardy, short-lived, small and sweet smelling night scented phlox has finished flowering, cut it back hard. Protection from too much wet (and frost) will help carry it through the winter so surrounding it with some grit would help.

Zantedeschia rehmanii and its many cultivars (calla lily) When the leaves of the tender calla lily have died down, stop feeding it and allow it to dry out as the bulbs need a period of dormancy. Take them under cover until next April.

SEPTEMBER

The changing seasons were something I missed greatly during the many years we spent in Hong Kong. You could not look out of the window and 'feel' September all around you: feel its change of tempo, rejoice in its colours, appreciate its softer light as the sun fell lower in the sky, or relish its sunsets knowing that dew and cooler mornings would balance the warmth of the evening. No Hong Kong poet, as far as I know, has ever waxed lyrical about the coming of autumn.

AREAS TO CONSIDER

Biennials Plant out biennials grown from seed where they are to flower next year: Canterbury bell, foxglove, honesty, sweet william, wallflower. Do not crowd them as they will be pretty interspersed with bulbs, added over the next few months.

Bulbs Plant spring/summer flowering bulbs – allium, anemone, camassia, chinodoxa, crocus, daffodil, erythronium, lily, muscari, narcissus, puskhinia – a wide choice (not tulips yet). Open bags of bulbs on arrival, keeping them cool and airy if they cannot go in immediately. If there is blue mould on the bulbs, it is superficial – wipe it off; if they have any rot or show any signs of mildew, throw them out. If bulbs are soaked in a mild mixture of water and paraffin for ten to fifteen minutes before planting, it deters squirrels and mice. Add grit to the bottom of holes, and as a rule of thumb plant at least two and a half times the depth of the bulb. Newly planted bulbs do not need feeding but add some bone meal into the holes of those being replanted. To avoid them looking regimented, throw bulbs on to the ground and plant where they land. If

Dahlia 'Waltzing Mathilda'
(flowering August–October)

planting in turf, score the underside of the turf with a hand fork before laying it back down to help the bulbs get through.

Bulbs for Christmas Dwarf tulips are lovely for Christmas. Unless they have been pre-chilled, they need six weeks in the fridge (away from any fruit) before planting in a clay pot with drainage holes, their tips just proud of the compost. See also October.

Conifers Do not clip after early September as new growth will get caught by frost – a frequent cause of brown conifer hedges.

Division Perennials past their best, too bulky or weak in the middle can be divided from now until the frosts set in. This is the optimum moment to divide those which flower up to midsummer but, in general, divide autumn flowering perennials or plants in heavy soils in spring so they have plenty of time to establish before flowering again. Cut down to about 7 cm/3 inches from the ground, dig up the clump and pull apart by hand, prize apart with two back to back garden forks, or slice off pieces with a sharp spade or knife. Add good compost or leafmould and bone meal to the soil when replanting the best bits, watering them in well. Pot up spare pieces and keep them in the shade, watering occasionally.

Evergreens Lower branches of evergreens can be removed to achieve a longer view. Clip or move evergreen hedges before mid-September. This is the ideal time to plant evergreens in warmer parts of the country – the soil is warm but not dry as in early summer or as cold and waterlogged as in winter and they are still in growth. Spring is probably the best time for this in the north.

Green manure Green manure can be sown in fallow vegetable beds. Phacelia can be sown any time until the end of September; it suppresses weeds, improves the soil and provides flowers very attractive to bees.

Greenhouse Begin to reduce watering as temperatures start to fall. Tender fruit growing in containers outside, for example tomatoes, must come in before any frost.

Hedges Give fast growing hedges their last trim of the year and a mulch (on damp soil) around their roots.

House plants During the course of the month bring in those that have had a season outside.

Lawns After a hot summer the lawn may need some care. The latter half of September is an excellent time to scarify while the ground is still hard; this may need to be done every three years or so, particularly if prone to waterlogging or compaction during the summer. Having scarified, ideally spike it and brush in a topdressing containing an autumn feed; it will be one that is rich in phosphates, low in nitrogen. Repair turf edges: cut a square round the damaged turf, take it out and turn it round with the damaged

side inwards, filling up any holes with soil – it soon becomes unnoticeable.

Perennial meadow New perennial meadows can be sown anytime from about September, even until as late as April. Cold weather will help break the dormancy of some seeds. Seeds need to be spread thinly on top of unfertilized, unmulched soil (the poorer the better). Added sand aids distribution; rake over it, walk over it to press in the seed and wait for rain. The inclusion of yellow rattle seed in your mix is something to consider. It keeps stronger grasses at bay, but this may not be necessary unless you are planting into established grassland. Take advice for your particular project.

Perennials As the month moves on, start taking in any that are tender and have finished flowering, cutting off nothing more than the flowered stems as they are potted up to bring under cover.

Planting Plant shrubs and perennials now while the soil is still warm, watering them in well. Continue to water new plants if there is a lack of rain; even during the winter months they will still need watering if there is a long dry spell.

Ponds Remove leaves so they do not rot, depriving fish of oxygen (netting a small pond during leaf fall, and regularly emptying it, could save hours of time). Avoid clearing the pond in full sunshine as the occupants will be near the top. Cut back soft foliage and stems from plants in or near the pond edge so they do not collapse, decomposing in the water. Thin out oxygenating plants while the water is still quite warm; remove blanket weed, duckweed and dying water lilies.

Seedlings Watch out for self-sown seedlings to cherish, such as box, foxglove, hellebore, hollyhock, honesty, sarcococca: pot them up ready to plant where they are wanted in spring, by which time they will have established stronger roots. Honesty can be moved now.

Succulents Before they get sodden and start rotting, move them under cover where they will not get rained on but where they still have good ventilation. Stop feeding and reduce watering.

Turf Early autumn is an ideal time to lay turf and to renovate old lawns.

Vegetables There is still time before the middle of the month to sow herbs such as parsley and coriander and more spinach. Carrot fly is at its most active now.

PLANTS

Acanthus (bear's breeches) If mildew is a problem, cut it out – however, leaves are needed to protect the crown in winter so only cut down to the base if gardening in a warm enough area to get lovely bright green regrowth. Otherwise, just cut out mildewed or tatty leaves, clearing the slugs' retreat underneath the plant to get air circulating more freely. If it looks suspect, spray with a fungus fighter or bicarbonate of soda before mildew gets a grip. Support flower stems if needed – they will provide wonderful winter outline if they are still strong.

***Acer japonicum, A. palmatum* (Japanese maple)** Now (and in early March) is a good time to plant acers: when they are still in leaf and temperatures are cool but not low. Although a low pH is preferable, shade from scorching sun, shelter from wind and avoidance of wet roots in winter matter more to them. On alkaline soil, a sprinkling of flowers of sulphur or sulphur chips round all acers now (indeed, around all ericaceous plants) and again every spring will gradually lower the pH. Ideally, a new tree should

have a can of water about three times a week, early morning or early evening, into the root area.

Achillea (yarrow) They can be cut down to a few inches from the ground as flowering finishes to allow for some healthy regrowth before winter, though tall *A. filipendula* looks lovely left standing.

Achimenes (hot water plant, cupid's bower) When flowering has finished, stop watering, letting it dry out completely. Remove dead growth and prepare to overwinter in dry compost.

Aconitum (monkshood) Cutting back the old flower stems will encourage a further, sporadic flush of flowers. Always use gloves as all parts are extremely poisonous.

***Actaea simplex* (was called Cimicifuga)** Provide twiggy support to give a more natural appearance to waving stems. When flowers finish next month they provide a good winter outline for a while. Mulch to retain moisture.

Allium Leave undisturbed until overcrowded. If necessary divide bulbs now, not enriching the soil. Plant at four times the diameter of the bulb with extra grit. If set amongst other plants with lots of June foliage, their leaves (which turn yellow just as they are about to flower) will be successfully hidden. Alliums in pots need a discreet stake as the shoot comes up from the side, not top, of the bulb, so they are inclined to lean.

Alstroemeria (Peruvian lily) They resent root disturbance so ensure they are planted where they will be happy: fertile, well-drained soil with at least half a day's sun. They take two years to establish as a clump.

Ammi majus and **A. visnaga** Ammi seeds can be sown now and overwintered under cover, to flower from June (though if there is space for them to be sown directly where they are to flower that would be even better).

Anchusa When flowering is finished, cut back to encourage the development of basal rosettes. They dislike winter wet so choose a site carefully when planting.

Anemone blanda, A. coronaria, A. × fulgens, A. nemorosa, A. ranunculoides and others Planting is easier if one is sure what their characteristics and needs are. *A. blanda* is a good ground cover in spring, *A. coronaria* (including the De Caen and St Brigid groups) erect and pickable, *A. nemorosa* less vigorous. All require different conditions: *A. nemorosa* and *A. ranunculoides* like moist rich soil in shade; *A. blanda* prefers alkaline humus-rich soil in sun or partial shade, while *A. coronaria* and *A. × fulgens* like light sandy soil in full sun.

   A. blanda: if planting dry corms, soak before planting. Robin Lane Fox reassures us that the corms are so hard they will break a squirrel's front tooth if it tries to dig them up. (I suspect this was in his regular column in the Saturday *Financial Times*; in his wonderful book *Thoughtful Gardening* there is an excellent tirade against squirrels and much advice generally.) He throws them over well-raked soil and covers them with a scattering of soil. This is particularly helpful as they are lovely under deciduous trees where roots would make digging difficult.

   A. coronaria: tubers can be planted now for March flowering, or in spring for summer flowering, in light sandy soil with good drainage, 5 cm/2 inches deep, where they are going to get lots of sun (they will right themselves if planted the wrong way up). Soak bulbs overnight and add lots of leafmould to their planting holes. Watered well on planting, they should be kept as dry as possible during dormancy, using a cloche or dry mulch to protect them in a cold winter.

   A. nemorosa: plant bulbs horizontally just below ground level. Soak them if buying dry but buying in pots ready to plant is much easier. Mark where they are with grit.

Anthemis When it finishes flowering, cut right back to base to encourage strong basal growth. It will lose all its charm otherwise. It needs winter protection in cold areas.

Arabis (rock cress) Cut any remaining flower stems back. Take out any reversions on variegated plants.

Armeria (thrift, sea pink) With its flowering period ending, it can be trimmed and divided now (or in spring) if it is spreading everywhere. Avoid planting where it will get a dump of fallen leaves on it in autumn.

Aruncus dioicus Cut back woody stems and apply a humus-rich mulch over the crown.

Aster (now mostly classified as Symphyotrichum or Eurybia) Deadhead early flowers to help those that follow – impossible to do throughout the season but in the early stages it helps. Ensure tall ones, like the red *Aster novae-angliae* 'Andenken an Alma Pötschke', are well staked, as, once collapsed, their charm and abundance are lost (as are the pleasures of the plants they collapse over).

Astrantia major Cultivars divide easily now – some may be having a late flowering so wait to divide these in spring. If the soil is dry, pot up divisions in deep pots to plant out later. Cut dried up flowers and old leaves down to base.

Aubrieta Take cuttings; tug, rather than cut, a piece out of the rosette of foliage, so that the piece, preferably with about 7 cm/3 inches of brown stem, has a little heel which can be dipped in rooting hormone. Plant it in 50:50 grit and compost and keep cool.

Auricula Auriculas divide well in September when it is a bit cooler. See June for details.

Azalea see Rhododendron below

Basil Harvest the plants, cutting them down to the base or bring them inside as they will not survive the first frost.

Begonia Reduce watering as top growth dies back. As flowering ends and before the first frost, stop watering and, if potted, lay them on their sides. When the foliage has died, remove any remains and compost from the tuber to store dry and frost-free over winter.

Brugmansia (was called Datura) Now, as the leaves start to go yellow, it is time to consider pruning overgrown plants. The RHS advice is to try to keep them at 1.25–1.5 m/4–5 ft for best repeat flowering. They can be cut hard to within 2.5 cm/1 inch of old wood, creating over time a framework to which to cut back. If grown as a standard (see March), cut everything back to the top of the stem each year.

Take cuttings from these prunings. Using non-flowering stems, cut pieces into manageable lengths (a few inches) on the diagonal just below a node and place them in a glass of water; within a week tiny roots should appear. Pot these on in seed compost and provide some bottom heat until shoots appear. Then pot them to grow on under cover until next spring. Remember that brugmansia is poisonous.

Buddleia Continue to deadhead, especially the late flowering *Buddleja* × *weyeriana*. If planting new buddleia,

loosen the roots and plant a little lower than it was in the pot, pruning two or three of the lower shoots back to two buds to encourage bushiness round the base from the start.

***Camassia quamash, C. leichtlinii* subsp. *suksdorfii* 'Alba' and others** There are several different varieties and it is important to select one suitable for the situation. In a flower bed they may need support, while in long grass they have to remain unmown between April and July. In grass pull back the turf and plant in large groups of at least twenty-five; do not worry about individual holes for each bulb. They are better left to multiply as they do not like disturbance.

Campanula
- *Campanula lactiflora*: cut down to the base when flowering has finished.
- *C. takesimana* 'Elizabeth': they appear to shift about because of their invasive nature. Dig up and replant every three years to keep fresh and vigorous.

Cephalaria gigantea When they are finally over in early September, cut the stems right down to base and tidy the leaves but leave some in place.

***Cirsium rivulare* 'Atropurpureum'** When flowering has finally finished, cut the whole lot down to the bottom rosette of leaves and new growth will appear. Left uncut, the leaves get increasingly tatty.

Clematis This is an excellent time to plant clematis – see 'Clematis' in April for planting notes – but do not prune newly planted clematis until February. Tie in established clematis so they do not blow around. Give them all a final potash-rich feed and mulch well.

Colchicum (autumn crocus) Wear gloves when handling as all parts are poisonous. If plants are bought that are just about to flower, enjoy them inside until the flowers are over and then plant the bulbs (in rich fertile soil) before the leaves appear. The drier the soil, the deeper they need to be (about 12 cm/ 5 inches).

Coreopsis (tickseed) Do not cut perennial coreopsis right back when they have finished flowering (hopefully for the second time if you cut them back in July). Leave some cover to protect the crown during winter.

Corydalis Having planted them about 5 cm/2 inches deep, mark them well – until they are established, they are easy to dig up and lose.

Crown imperial (*Fritillaria imperialis*) This bulb will benefit from being planted in early September while the soil is warm. Plant 30 cm/12 inches deep, the same apart, at a slight angle so the water does not settle on them (and rot them) and on a bed of sharp sand or gravel. More gravel on top will mark their position. If any bulbs failed to flower well last spring, replant them now in improved gritty soil (they very often do not flower in their first year so give them at least two years before doing this). They may take a couple of years to flower again.

Cyclamen Though they do not need regular feeding, a sprinkling of bone meal and some additional mulch would be good where *Cyclamen hederifolium* flowers are shortly to appear and where *C. coum* tubers are resting.

Cymbidium (orchid) Bring plants under cover, keeping cool overnight (11–14°C is ideal). Water very sparingly, ideally using rainwater, once every week or two from now until May (the end of the flowering period). Protect from direct sunlight (a north windowsill is good) and check for pests such as red spider mite

or a lurking slug. If you detect signs – graininess on the back of the strappy leaves would be a clue – use Provado Ultimate Bug Killer or a biological control. See the entry for red spider mite in June. Feed once a month with orchid fertilizer following the advice on the label. You could use a potash-rich feed from now until the end of October, then change to a balanced feed from November to February and a nitrogen-rich feed from March to June, but this could be too much to manage. (If this regime is adopted, apply these feeds at half strength every three consecutive waterings and flush out the plant on the fourth.) Always let the plant drain well afterwards. McBean's Orchids, the oldest orchid nursery in the country, has been the source of much helpful information.

Daphne Sulphate of potash now will promote hardiness and good buds next year. Writing about *Daphne × transatlantica* 'Eternal Fragrance', John Massey, owner of Ashwood Nurseries in the West Midlands, recommends we 'gently brush over it to remove any old flowers which could rot and die back into the plant (like a caress to thank it for flowering on and off since spring)'. I love the idea of this caress.

Delphinium Feed with a potash-rich fertilizer such as Tomorite as the plants start their last flourish.

Echeveria If frosts are forecast, bring pots of these succulents into the greenhouse or put in a cold frame.

Echinacea purpurea (coneflower) Despite their reluctance to be divided, every four years, now or in May, divide them to maintain vigour. Water well beforehand to make the move a bit easier. They are unsocial plants that resent competition so give them space.

Erythronium (dog's tooth violet)
Spread leafmould over the area of established plants. New tubers can be planted up to early October. They are quite fragile and must not dry out before they are in the ground. Plant 10 cm/4 inches deep with some potash rich fertilizer, humus and sharp sand, arranging them 10–15 cm/4–6 inches apart in groups.

Escallonia Once flowering is over, prune to the size or shape you want, taking out one or two stems from the base only if necessary. It seems better as a dense shrub so a haircut with shears would be fine.

Eschscholzia (California poppy) This diminutive vivacious poppy propagates easily from seed collected when the pods are just about to crack. They can be sown now and again in April or May on very gritty soil.

Eucalyptus (gum) Autumn is a good time to plant (though in cold parts of the UK this is better done between April and June). The RHS advises not to incorporate manure in the hole, not to stake and not to plant a tree over 1 m/ 39 inches tall or its top will grow faster than its roots. Unstaked, it rocks in the wind and grows stronger roots (like most trees). Mulch around it to keep weeds at bay. Use root trainers for seedlings as it resents root disturbance. In the ground it should need watering only for the first couple of years.

***Euonymus europaeus* (spindle)** It is likely to get attacked by aphids at this time of year; spray if necessary with a soft soap solution.

Euphorbia: late summer flowering (spurge) Deciduous euphorbias will need to be cut down to ground level now or next month.

Euphorbia griffithii: cut back flowering shoots to ground level. Wear gloves as the sap is an irritant.

E. marginata: remove the flower stems when over, leaving its pretty white variegated leaves.

E. mellifera (honey spurge): take out the finished flowers and their stems right to the bottom, removing any other stems that look miserable but taking care not to remove new flower stems. It will regenerate well if pruned hard: there may be lots of new growth in the centre. Red spider mite can be a big problem; Helen Yemm in the Saturday *Telegraph*, whose articles are compulsive reading, suggested that it was possible to use a high pressure hose to get rid of them (I daresay a few leaves would be lost in the process). For biological control see the red spider mite entry in June.

E. sikkimensis: snip off spent flowers to gently tidy up.

***Filipendula rubra* 'Venusta' (meadowsweet)** Reduce its height so that its root is not loosened by wind rock in autumn.

Foxglove (Digitalis) Cut back to near the ground when any second flush is over. Plant out foxgloves grown from seed into dappled shade and moisture retentive, well-drained, light soil, giving them each a lot of space (they get fungal diseases when planted too close). If the soil is heavy add some compost to the top few inches to encourage the fibrous roots to spread. *Digitalis ferruginea* and *D. lanata* are two that like it hot and gritty. Water in well and feed with a balanced liquid fertilizer (seaweed extract would be excellent) now and once again in four weeks.

Freesia Cut back the flower stems. Lift the corms when foliage has turned yellow, keeping only the newest (plump) ones, and store in a dry mulch to plant again from April or May.

Gladiolus murielae (flowering August–October)

Fritillary This bulb benefits greatly from being planted early because it needs warm soil to get going. Sprinkle chilli powder on them to keep squirrels off. Cut the grass as short as possible where they are growing to allow for easier bulb planting and to show them off well next year. If planted on a slope, put them near the top so that seedlings gravitate downwards. Anna Pavord suggests that to get them to naturalize in grass, it might be easiest to start them off in pots – five in a 10 cm/ 4 inch pot – and when the leaves first show in spring, plant out the pots-full avoiding disturbance of their roots. Choose the right species for the situation – some like it well drained, others prefer a moist meadow.

Gardenia Stop the monthly feeding and gradually reduce (but maintain) watering over winter.

Gaura lindheimeri Leave on all top growth for winter protection and autumn colour. Each flower only lasts a day but it goes on producing flowers for ages.

Geranium Cutting back will prevent the unsightly outbreaks of mildew which can afflict them.

Geum (avens) Some, like *Geum* 'Scarlet Tempest', may still be flowering; on others cut back all the faded flowers and damaged foliage – the foliage will rejuvenate.

Gillenia trifoliata **(Bowman's root)** It can be divided now but its autumn foliage is so good and its seed heads are worth keeping, so I prefer to divide it in spring.

***Gladiolus murielae* (was called *Acidanthera bicolor* and *G. callicanthus*)**
Continue to feed with a liquid fertilizer such as seaweed extract or Tomorite during their flowering period. Maintain the moisture level of the soil. Pull off the tubes of flowers that have gone over.

***Gleditsia triacanthos* (honey locust)**
Prune now to prevent bleeding. When it is young, prune as a clear standard, taking off side shoots and shoots from the base, allowing it to branch only when it gets to over 2 m/7 ft. Keep a clear ring of soil around the tree, water well and stake when new to keep upright and anchor the roots. Gleditsia does not mind root restriction so copes well in tight spaces, making good street trees. When pruning a mature tree, continue to keep the trunk clear of new growth, take out crossing, misplaced or spindly branches, any that are overcrowding the crown and any that are hanging down too low and spoiling the shape, always cutting back to a neat junction with another branch. If renovation is needed spread it over a few years, never taking out more than 25 per cent of the canopy in one year.

Helenium Continue to deadhead and, when finally over, cut stems in half to help prevent mildew.

Helianthus (annual sunflower) A mention of the annual sunflower as opposed to the perennial: as the leaves and stalks turn brown, gather and bin them. It is better to grow annual sunflowers in a different place each year.

Heliopsis Continue to protect from slugs and deadhead regularly to prevent it seeding. Cut down to the ground when finally over.

Helleborus × hybridus As new roots are being formed, mature hellebores can be divided into large pieces, each with a growth point and good roots. A serrated knife may be needed. Replant immediately, adding a lot of humus to the planting hole, feed with Fish, Blood and Bone, and mulch with spent mushroom compost or leafmould. Keep an eye out for seedlings. Cut out any leaves that have a network of black veining. They may sulk for a year after division.

Cut dead flowers off *H. argutifolius* and *H. foetidus* if not done in spring. Look out for their seedlings. These species do not divide.

Hemerocallis (daylily) Divide in September or October when the foliage is less vibrant. Dig up a clump, shake off the soil and reduce leaves to a third of their length. Pull apart to make smaller pieces, each with leaves and roots. Cut the leaves into a fan shape as once frosted they get slimy and are harder to deal with. Replant each fan with its own roots at least 30 cm/12 inches apart.

Hepatica They can be divided now if not done in spring. Pot on seedlings, separating them carefully. Grow on for a year before planting out.

***Hesperantha coccinea* 'Major' (was called Schizostylis) (kaffir lily)** Kept really moist and with the flower spikes removed as they go over, it will flower well into November.

Hibiscus syriacus Leaves may start turning yellow even before the flowers have finished. Do not worry.

Hippeastrum (amaryllis) Bring them in from dormancy if outside, letting them dry out completely. Do not feed, just tidy them.

Hollyhock (Alcea) Cut down to 15 cm/ 6 inches after flowering, and mulch. Though considered biennials, they will last three or four years, so if they need transplanting (they become close together in time and then get mildew), do so now ensuring the soil is really moist as you lift and replant them. The younger they are, the less they get rust, so if replanting older ones place them behind late summer flowering plants (like penstemon) to cover their lower leaves.

Honeysuckle (Lonicera) See July for pruning twining honeysuckles in order to deal now with *Lonicera × brownii* 'Dropmore Scarlet', *L. etrusca,* and *L. periclymenum* 'Graham Thomas', whose flowering will have finished.

Hornbeam (*Carpinus betulus*) Trim hedges now and then leave for the rest of the year. A favourite garden tree is *Carpinus betulus* 'Frans Fontaine' with spectacular late autumn colour. If this needs to be shaped, it should be done by early September.

Hosta There are two good times to divide hostas: as shoots first appear and now, after flowering but before they die down. Plant the divisions into a deep organic mulch.

Hydrangea
- *Hydrangea macrophylla* (including *H. serrata*): do not be tempted to cut the heads off these fading hydrangeas. The dead flowers give vital protection over winter for the tender buds below them.
- *Hydrangea quercifolia*: these hydrangeas do not need pruning but their beautiful flower heads do not die gracefully, so deadhead in order not to spoil the look of the lovely scarlet foliage that follows.

Iris unguicularis Feed with a potash-rich fertilizer such as Tomorite to strengthen its flower power. If clumps are old this is a good time to divide, though they like congestion and will not flower well next year. Otherwise, just snip out old foliage and let it be.

Juniper: shrubby Pluck the tips off the shoots – twice a year ideally – to give the plant a thick covering of shoots rather than long, thinly covered branches. See also March.

***Knautia macedonica* (red scabious)** Cared for, it will go on giving pleasure for another month. It is well worth it.

***Lathyrus grandiflorus* (everlasting pea)** Cut down the yellowing growth and provide a dry mulch. New shoots will appear in spring.

Laurel: cherry and Portuguese (*Prunus laurocerasus, P. lusitanica*) Give the last prune of the year in early September. *P. lusitanica* is excellent as a clipped, clear-stemmed standard. All parts are extremely poisonous.

Lavender: French (*Lavandula stoechas*) French lavender is not fully hardy. Deadhead now and, in due course, overwinter in a frost-free greenhouse, kept almost dry and well ventilated.

***Leucanthemella serotina* (autumn ox-eye, giant daisy)** Like many daisies, they are daylight sensitive so will not flower until there is *less* than eight hours of daylight – this may be why they are not bursting into flower. They need moisture in the ground to thrive (and to prevent mildew).

***Leucanthemum × superbum* (shasta daisy)** Cut to the ground when flowering is finished.

***Leucojum vernum* (spring snowflake)** Bulbs can be soft when they arrive so plant them quickly. Anna Pavord recommends starting them in pots and planting them out in spring.

Lewisia Feed once with a potash-rich fertilizer to strengthen the foliage before winter, making them less likely to rot. Chempak 4 would be suitable.

Liatris spicata Keep deadheading. When the flower spikes are finally over, cut them down to the bottom. As the plant disappears, mark its position well.

Lily Always deadhead lilies but leave at least half the stem standing. As the plant dies down (in pots and the ground), add a fresh topdressing. They need autumn and winter to establish a good root system, so September and October are good months for planting. They hate being waterlogged so somewhere that remains a puddle after rain is no good (or a pot without good drainage). Plant the bulbs the moment they arrive, adding grit, a slow-release fertilizer and leafmould to the planting hole. Surrounding the bulb with sand discourages slugs. Check planting depths as species vary. Mostly plant bulbs to a depth of two and a half times the height of the bulb, but if it grows roots from its stem (as opposed to the plate of the bulb), as *Lilium longiflorum* does, plant deeper. *L. candidum*, on the other hand, likes being very close to the soil surface. Mark where they are so they are not sliced by a spade. They are better not moved, but if a clump needs dividing do it a month after flowering is finished. Ideally, they like their base in the shade and their heads in full sun, so planting them amongst low growing shrubs works well. Some shade in the afternoon too would be ideal.

Soil is an issue; some, such as *L. henryi*, *L. martagon* and *L. regale*, are fine with alkaline soil (martagon lilies actually prefer it). Trumpet and Asiatic lilies, including *L. longiflorum*, prefer it acidic. A few like *L. speciosum* cannot do alkaline at all, so resort to containers where the soil is unsuitable.

Lilies in pots: plant 5 cm/2 inches apart (in John Innes No. 3) with 10 cm/4 inches of soil above them, adding a slow release fertilizer and grit, with more grit on the top. The pot should be big enough to hold lots of soil beneath the bulb. Raise the pot on to feet. Planted in plastic pots, they can be dropped into the border to fill a hole, the ugly pot hidden by foliage.

Lily of the valley (*Convalaria majalis*) September is a good time to divide them. They need this every four to five years to keep flowering well. Water the clump a few days beforehand, then dig down well below the base of the plant, lift and tug apart, replanting in smaller clumps with the top of the root just below the soil surface. If dealing with an individual root and 'pip' (growing point), soak first, then plant so the tip of the root (which has no top or bottom) is just below the surface. Mulch over the whole area with leafmould and compost mixed together. Nothing else grows through the mat they form. Every part is poisonous to humans and pets.

Limonium platyphyllum (statice) Cut the flower stems right down when they are over.

Lobelia cardinalis, L. × speciosa Slugs love the purple leaved varieties most. Deadhead down to the first node in the leaves for another flower. Do not cut down when they are over – leave until spring. They will need a dry winter mulch, around but not over the base.

Lupin As aphids overwinter in the plants, cut them down to the ground now.

Lychnis coronaria (rose campion) They finish flowering about now; cut back by two-thirds unless wanted to seed.

Mathiasella bupleuroides Cut back any remaining flowered stems to a low growth point.

Matteuccia struthiopteris (shuttlecock fern) This lovely vase shaped fern is most effective when not crowded by its offspring. The young, which come from spreading rhizomes, can easily be removed to plant on; controlling the space between the ferns enables them to look their best.

Meconopsis (Himalayan poppy)
Cover the crowns with 5 cm/2 inches of leafmould (plus a few slug pellets).

Melianthus major It comes out of its summer reverie and has another growing spurt in early autumn. If it was not cut down at the start of the year, it may well need some discreet staking by now.

***Morina longifolia* (whorlflower)** The lovely whorlflower is hardy but dislikes winter wet, so add some grit around the thistle-like basal leaves. Use the seed as soon as ripe (planted in individual modules in very gritty compost), but do not cut all the seed heads down as they look good in early winter. It has a tap root so will not move happily.

Mulberry (Morus) Young trees need any corrective pruning done now; see November for established trees.

Muscari (grape hyacinth) Plant bulbs now, 10 cm/4 inches deep, 5 cm/2inches apart, in a place that will have shade later in the year – under deciduous trees or shrubs is good. *Muscari armeniacum* is a menace in a flower bed.

Narcissus (daffodil) One of the first spring bulbs to go in, plant the moment they arrive, 10–15 cm/4–6 inches deep (two and a half times their height or even deeper in dry soils). To achieve an unregimented effect, cast them on to the ground and plant where they land. Add bone meal to the planting hole and grit if drainage is poor.

Nerine bowdenii The leaves die away before the flowers emerge next month.

Keep them exposed to good light and ventilation, continuing the regular feeding and watering between now and spring.

Phalaenopsis (moth orchid) At the end of the month, stop any regular feeding. Reduce watering over winter. A few weeks of cooler (16–18°C) conditions now help to initiate flower buds (a higher temperature is needed for buds to open).

Phlox paniculata They need cutting back in early autumn, lifting and moving now if necessary. Variegated phlox tend to revert to green if moved so avoid doing so if possible.

***Physalis alkekengi*, now called *Alkekengi physalis* (Chinese lanterns)** If becoming invasive, dig a trench round it to stop the roots in their tracks. For flower arranging, cut the stems and lay them out to dry as the calyces begin to colour.

***Pontederia cordata* (pickerel weed)** Cut back leaf stems of this water plant as they start to collapse; they have a high cellulose content that will otherwise disperse into the water.

Potato Get to maincrop potatoes before the slugs do. Leave dug up potatoes on the soil briefly to dry and to check for pests, blight or sogginess. Store soon, soil-free, in a hessian or paper sack in a cool, dark, airy place to stop them sprouting or turning green.

Potentilla Whenever the shrubby *Potentilla fruticosa* has finished flowering it can be given a haircut.

***Primula beesiana*, *P. bulleyana*, *P. denticulata* (drumstick primula), *P. florindae*, *P. 'Inverewe'* (and other Candelabra primulas), *P. pulverulenta*, *P. vialii* and others** They quickly become very crowded – divide, replanting immediately, before the ground turns cold.

Do this in the shade as the roots will dry out in the sun. Watch out for vine weevil grubs, which love primulas; if found, the soil must be cleaned before replanting. There is still time to water in nematodes, which will get rid of them.

Privet Give it a final prune before winter.

Pyracantha On an established plant, all side shoots can be shortened to two or three leaves but avoid the ripening berries.

Rhododendron and Azalea Clear all weeds around them and give them a light mulch around their canopies to prevent more weeds appearing and to conserve moisture. Do not take the mulch over the root ball and ensure there is no pile-up of mulch over time; it is a frequent cause of death for young plants.

Rhododendrons are surface rooting so must not be planted deep. They should ideally be at least 2 m/7 ft from a tree, which otherwise takes up precious moisture. Almost all need acid soil (pH 3.0–6.0) with plenty of organic matter, but Millais Nurseries produce a range of small and neat rhododendrons grown on the 'Inkarho' rootstock that are happy in alkaline soils. I was thrilled with this discovery and now grow many. Good drainage is essential. Plant in a wide rather than deep planting hole (there need only be about 5 cm/2 inches of composted soil beneath the root ball) so the roots can splay outwards, not down. The top of the root ball should be level with or even just above soil level (with no possibility then of the lowest stems being buried). Use ericaceous compost with lots of leafmould or composted pine needles (absolutely not animal manure) and a small dose of superphosphate fertilizer in the planting hole. Water using rainwater, not tap.

Rhubarb Resist tidying old plants as autumn progresses – let the leaves die back naturally.

Robinia pseudoacacia 'Frisia' Its branches can snap off easily in wind so prune back now anything that might be caught. Its suckers are a nuisance and should be removed.

Rose Remove and bin leaves that are yellowing from black spot and gather debris off the ground. The latter half of September is the best time to take hardwood rose cuttings. Choose a pencil-thick piece of this year's healthy firm growth. Trim to 15–20 cm/6–8 inches, cutting beneath a leaf bud; remove all but two top leaves; to encourage faster rooting, nick the stem at the lowest eye, which will go below the soil level. Dip the bottom 5 cm/2 inches into hormone rooting powder and put the bottom third of the cutting into a 50:50 mix of grit and compost. Leave *in situ* for eighteen months.

Sage, culinary (*Salvia officinalis, S.o. 'Purpurascens'*) Harvest the leaves of the culinary sage and dry them in shade – take a third off and then leave alone until next year.

Salvia This is the last chance to take cuttings of *Salvia confertiflora, S. elegans, S. fulgens, S. leucantha, S. splendens* 'Van-Houttei' and other tender salvias which come in next month. It is so well worth doing. Use very gritty compost.

S. sclarea var. *turkestanica* is a very architectural biennial that does not need staking. Deadheading stops it going to seed, but I would let it seed, then collect and sow the seeds to plant out in spring.

Sanguisorba (burnet) Divisions can be done now. Lift the clump and, with a sharp knife, cut into two or three pieces, each with a good root. Plant at the same depth as previously and water in very well. Trim the leaves and shoots back by a third to help them get established. Young plants as well as divisions take a while to get going.

A liquid feed of seaweed will deter mildew on *Sanguisorba menziesii.* Otherwise, cut off affected leaves and remove the flower stems as they go over. Other sanguisorbas (such as *S. canadensis*) have catkin-like flowers which do not die particularly prettily. Rubbing these flowers off, leaves a good seed head behind. The *S. officinalis* seed heads are all worth keeping over winter unless it is becoming invasive, in which case remove them.

Saxifrage This (and early summer) is a good time to ease off gently a number of rosettes from the cushion of saxifrage, potting them into 2:1 damp compost and sharp sand; cover them with a cloche or plastic to establish. If setting them directly in a raised bed or rockery, position them out of the direct sun and give them a thick mulch of grit.

Selinum wallichianum Having flowered for months, cut off the flower heads and foliage as they start to fade and then mulch. Its long taproot makes it difficult to move. New plants are better grown from seed.

Smyrnium perfoliatum **(alexanders)** Its black seeds, best sown fresh, can be broadcast now. Years ago I sowed some with great care in a patch cleared of ivy, forgot about them and three years later spotted a patch of glorious yellow-green in dappled sunlight. In a garden setting it is easy enough to control, but it is currently illegal to plant in the wild.

Strawberry When the strawberries are finally over (perpetual varieties go on longer than the summer ones but with smaller flushes), tidy up the beds, removing old foliage and straw. Over the space of three years, change the whole bed over, renewing the stock and, if space allows, move the strawberries to another bed to avoid any build-up of soil diseases.

Sweet woodruff (*Galium odoratum*) It spreads merrily so slice bits off with a spade, shaping the remainder and using the offcuts to make new areas. Water them in well. It is so useful in deep shade but tends to scorch in direct sunlight.

Teucrium chamaedrys **(wall germander)** This diminutive aromatic evergreen shrub makes a good hardy 'hedge' in really gritty soil. Cut the pink flowers and stems back after flowering, not cutting into old wood.

Thalictrum delavayi **(meadow rue)** Cut this late summer flowering species right back after flowering. Mark the position of all thalictrums; as they start into growth so late, they are easily damaged when forking the bed.

Tibouchina urvilleana Bring under cover, potting on into good loam-based compost. The petals can stain so beware. Continue to feed until flowering is over.

Tithonia rotundifolia **(Mexican sunflower)** Flowering July to October, it needs deadheading regularly but carefully as the stems are hollow just below the bloom.

Tomato Remove more leaves to get stubborn tomatoes to redden up. They will also ripen on a warm windowsill. A banana beside them speeds things up.

Tradescantia (Andersoniana Group) It makes big clumps so divide now; it will respond enthusiastically to care. Cut back leaves to encourage fresh growth in spring.

Verbena The perennial *Verbena hastata* should be cut down now flowering is over. Leave the leaf growth in place to protect the crown over winter. *V. bonariensis* should be left standing. It will self-seed, which is usually very welcome.

Vine (grape) (grown under glass)

Some leaves may need to be removed to ripen grapes. Keep the greenhouse fairly dry so that they do not split. Resist picking them the moment they are fully coloured – they need to hang a bit longer for the sugars to develop. To avoid problems for years to come, resist cropping vines in their first two years and on established vines just pick one bunch per lateral.

Wallflower: biennial (*Erysimum cheiri*)

While the soil is still warm, this is the traditional time to plant out, deeply and firmly, biennial wallflowers grown from seed. Planting closely protects them against wind rock.

Walnut Formative pruning of walnut trees and the removal of large branches should be done now in early autumn to avoid bleeding sap in spring and decay from winter pruning cuts.

White rosebay willowherb (*Chamaenerion angustifolium* 'Album') (was called Epilobium)

This non-invasive willowherb is pretty until about now when all its seed heads need to be cut off low. Pull out any that have intruded where they are not wanted and leave other roots in.

Yew A sprinkling of bone meal along its roots will strengthen root development. By mid-September aim to give a final prune to yew. Much later than this, newly cut stems may be caught by cold weather and create brown patches. Even so, as yew will regenerate from old wood, these patches can be grown out, which is why it is usually the last of the evergreens to be pruned. When I was visiting Levens Hall in Cumbria in April to see their outstanding topiary, the gardeners had only just finished the yew pruning, which started when the gardens closed to the public in October – so whatever the rule book says, if there is a lot of yew, it just has to be fitted into the time available.

Ceratostigma willmottianum, (flowering August–November; see April for its post-winter care).

OCTOBER

In this glorious time of year, it is good to be methodical. Start with areas where trees hang over beds, dealing with them before leaf fall. Move on to lawns, finishing their autumn care before they too get covered by mushy leaves. Then turn to borders before plants disappear for months, checking labels, taking in tender plants and putting stakes around those that will need winter protection. Pamper all that continue to flower, ensuring they are supported and deadheaded. Unlike June's stampede of colour, now the occasional but measured burst brings such satisfaction.

AREAS TO CONSIDER

Annuals If there is space and time, start sowing hardy annuals – such as eschscholzia, larkspur, orlaya – browse catalogues as well as garden centres. After germination all they need is light and to be kept just above freezing. Prick out all seedlings early, as soon as two seed leaves show, to minimize disturbance.

Bedding plants Plant out winter and spring bedding plants: pansies and primroses are the obvious ones for winter, daisies, forget-me-nots and wallflowers for spring.

Bees They need pollen as they prepare for winter; ivy, now in flower, is a good source of nectar. Salvia also has high-protein pollen so do not be hasty cutting back flower heads.

Borders Before starting, have a plastic sheet to work off, a wheelbarrow of potting compost and lots of empty pots to take divisions, tools, a connected hose, labels and pen. Resist digging except to remove weeds and lift perennials, but always improve the soil where a hole is made. Use a board to reach the back. Clear spent annuals, divide and replant summer perennials that have got too big or are declining in vigour, deadhead what is still in flower, and dispose of any plants affected by mildew. Cut off the tallest stems of any (now over) late flowering shrubs to prevent wind rock; do not cut back anything slightly tender (salvia and penstemon are prime examples), any grasses, anything grey or woolly leaved, anything with a square stem (water collects and freezes in the stem and can kill the crown) or, of course, any winter/early spring flowerers. Leave about 15 cm/6 inches on all perennials being cut down to give some winter protection and to mark where they are (these stubs will be cut right back in spring). What I strive for is a balance between dull disorder and clinical tidiness: not to be overwhelmed by the chaos of everything collapsing but achieving enough winter shape for the garden not to look too manicured. It is an enjoyable editing process that continues throughout autumn and winter.

Bulbs When planting spring bulbs (not tulips yet) place them towards the back of a bed rather than at the front so that their

Quince 'Meech's Prolific'

dying foliage will be hidden by summer plants. Lift tender bulbs that may not get through winter. If planting dry corms, soak them overnight. Rolling bulbs in chilli pepper or soaking them in a weak solution of water and paraffin for some minutes gives them a scent which puts off rodents.

Bulbs for Christmas Start them off now – see below for hippeastrum, hyacinth and paper-white narcissus.

Conifers This is a good month to plant and move conifers, while they are dormant.

Containers and pots Plant up containers with winter bedding, evergreens and spring bulbs. Move less hardy plantings to a sheltered corner.

Deciduous trees, shrubs and hedges These are best planted between now and December before the ground is frozen but when the plants are dormant.

Division When dividing, soak the division before replanting, incorporate bone meal in the new hole and improve the soil at the same time by adding compost, leafmould, well-rotted manure or gravel, depending on the condition of the soil's drainage, water retention and plant's needs.

Evergreens On a windy site, erect a windbreak round newly planted evergreens – they could otherwise lose their leaves before making any new roots and therefore not be able to take up water. Remove the windbreak in spring, by which time they will have adequate roots.

Feeding From now on, do not give plants (including the lawn) any nitrogenous fertilizer to encourage fresh growth as this will be caught by frost and open up the plant to disease.

Frost and wind protection By mid-October aim to have brought in all pots which might not tolerate hard frost. For shrubs that risk being damaged and dehydrated by wind, mulch to help maintain the moisture level in the soil and erect a wind barrier.

Fruit canes and fruit bushes Caned fruit, currants and gooseberries do well if planted now.

Fruit trees: free standing Collect fallen apples and pears and bin any with rot (do not compost). If pure wood ash is available put it round the trees as a source of potash.

Greenhouse Before it is filled with tender plants, clean the structure and glass with a soapy wash; it destroys unseen resident pests and maximizes the winter light.

Half-hardy plants Lift plants that could suffer over winter, cutting down just a little if that makes storage easier (they will be cut properly in spring). Keep the greenhouse just frost free; more harm than good will come to plants stored warm.

Herbs To collect seed, let them bolt. Cut off the whole seed head, shake into a paper bag and store cool and dry.

Honey fungus If a piece of bark at the base of the tree can be picked off (a healthy bark should not break off) and a white/cream layer of mycelium (fungal tissue) smelling of mushrooms is evident, it is not a good sign. The 'black bootlaces' can be hard to spot but may be visible – like black veins. Dieback, foliage discolouration, a depleted canopy, bleeding or splitting of the bark are also all indicators, as, of course, are fruiting bodies round the base of the tree. To help combat its spread (honey fungus cannot be cured but its spread can be arrested), keep the base of trees clear of competition and decompact the soil around them; ensure the buttresses of trees are above the soil level (clear the soil away if necessary). Honey fungus is widespread and will hit when the plant is stressed, so taking measures to keep trees healthy and their defence mechanisms turned on gives the best environment to avoid it (see Phytophthora in April). I lost alders, a swamp cypress and other trees affected by honey fungus and was greatly helped by Dr Glynn Percival in containing it. Trees in the surrounding area were all given a pure willow mulch after clearance of the infected trees.

Lawns Raise the mower blades for the last cuts of the year. Textbook treatment involves mowing the lawn, spiking it using a garden fork (lifting the turf a little each time), then aerating it with a hollow tine aerater and topdressing with a mixture of topsoil, sharp sand and leafmould (gently raking this into the tined holes) and, finally, feeding with an autumn lawn feed using a wheeled spreader (difficult to do by hand – and wear gloves if you try). Scatter lawn seed over any bare areas. Even if there is little time available, spiking the lawn and raking through it to gather the accumulated thatch would help a great deal.

Moss eradication can be done now too – see March. Should there be a problem with worm casts brush them off into those tined holes. Acidifying the soil with a sulphur product such as sulphur chips helps to prevent this problem; worms burrow deeper to avoid the acidity. Badgers seem deterred by cut onions.

Leaves Collect leaves into bin liners with holes for aeration or make a leaf pile in mesh netting. Avoid adding too many leaves to the compost pile as they take much longer to rot down. Leaves make an acidic soil improver while compost is slightly alkaline. Some leaves left under shrubs and hedges make homes for hibernating creatures. A scattering of leaves mown and left on the lawn will be taken down by earthworms.

Mulching To conserve moisture and warmth, mulch 5–7 cm/2–3 inches around plants, shrubs and trees over their root area (avoiding the stem/trunk) when the soil is wet but not freezing. A really heavy soil is better mulched in spring. Spare the crown of peonies, camellias and rhododendrons, which want to be buried no deeper than they already are.

Perennials While the soil is still warm new perennials can be planted to get established before winter sets in. See Borders above for cutting back.

Pruning Never prune when frost is forecast. Avoid pruning winter or early spring flowering shrubs, those that need the protection of their dead flowers/foliage over winter and those which will give good winter outline. Do not 'tidy up' evergreens: it is too late.

Seeds and berries Collect seeds on a dry sunny day straight into labelled brown paper bags (or take stems of seed heads and lay them out to remove the seeds). Allow seed to ripen on the plant before harvesting. Choose a strong healthy plant, not one that has gone early to seed, as using seed from a sick plant may perpetuate that gene. They must be completely dry before their final storage (5°C in a fridge is a good place), so if necessary hang up your packets of seeds somewhere dark and dry and without fluctuating temperatures, until there is no moisture left in them. Seeds from cultivars and F1 hybrids will not be like their parent: they do not 'come true'. Alpines need a period of cold so are good to sow now, as are berries from shrubs.

Tree moving Tree root pruning can be done in late October; this can help a tree to flower by encouraging new fibrous roots and facilitates the moving of a tree the following autumn. Dig a trench round the tree, cut through some roots and backfill.

Vegetables In areas that are not too wet, root vegetables can be left in the soil (such as beetroot, carrots, parsnips) but, otherwise, take them up and store, scrubbed clean, in layers in moist sand. The key thing now is to maintain the health of the soil, improving its structure and drainage, so cover with a thick layer of mulch and let the worms do the rest.

Woodland A classic tip learnt at Coton Manor Garden School in Northamptonshire was to work on woodland areas before leaf fall, removing weeds, dividing perennials and planting new stock when you can see where you are going. The fallen leaves will then provide a duvet of frost protection until late winter when they can be blown off and leafmould spread around the new bulbs emerging into the dappled sunlight.

PLANTS

Aconitum (monkshood) Cut down dead flower stalks before the leaves turn brown. They can be divided in autumn but spring division is probably best. Always wear gloves: they are so poisonous.

Aeonium Succulents in containers which have been out all summer should be brought into a frost-free greenhouse, porch or left protected on a sunny sheltered wall.

Agapanthus Stop the feeding this month. The flower buds for next year have formed deep inside the plant, so if you move one now you may lose some flowers next year.

Agave Protect from cold winds and pot up unrooted offsets in very gritty compost.

Alstroemeria (Peruvian lily) Let the stems and foliage die back naturally, then cut them to the ground. A thick dry mulch

of bracken, straw or Strulch will protect the fleshy root system (particularly important for those newly planted).

Amaryllis (Jersey lily) As it finishes flowering, it will need protection from hard frost though it is fairly hardy. The foliage will not die right back until next summer.

Amelanchier Provide leafmould up to the edge of the canopy but not up against the trunk. It prefers lime-free soil.

***Anemanthele lessoniana* (pheasant's tail grass)** This lovely grass is better not crowded. Do not cut it, but draw through with gloved hands or gently with a rake and it will perk up.

***Anemone hupehensis* (Japanese anemone)** Flower stalks can be cut back when they have faded as there is no second flowering, though seed heads provide some early winter interest. They dislike disturbance so avoid moving them; nonetheless, divide them now if they have spread too far.

Apple and pear: free standing Put grease bands round them (and their stakes) to deter the winter moth. Store apples in a cool, airy, dim place (3–7°C is ideal), removing all bruised fruit and ensuring none touch each other. Keep mid-season and late ripening fruit separate. If space is at a premium, they can be wrapped individually in glossy pages from supplements and placed in cardboard boxes, but they do not keep indefinitely. Gather up and bin diseased fruit and leaves. Keep an eye on ripening pears, picking as the skin begins to lighten and as they lift off in your hand. They ripen from the inside out, so by the time they are soft to the touch, they are rotten.

Aquilegia Cut the flowered stems right down and mulch lightly.

Argyranthemum frutescens (marguerite) Leave the foliage in place and, in the south, leave in the ground with a deep mulch. Elsewhere bring inside to keep just watered over winter. They may get through in cool, light storage, but cuttings should have been taken to replace the mother plant next year. If cuttings were not taken, keep a mother plant in a frost-free greenhouse over winter and do it in spring.

Artemisia: perennial Cut perennial artemisias such as 'Valerie Finnis' and 'Silver Queen' back to base in autumn and apply a good mulch of compost. Leave very woody perennials and the shrubby ones (such as 'Powis Castle') until spring when new growth appears.

Artichoke Cut away well-rooted offshoots and suckers and plant at the same depth as before into sunny, well-drained, fertile soil. The old stems should be cut right back. The crown and offshoots will need mulching thickly before winter.

Asparagus Cut the fronds down to 2.5 cm/1 inch when they have turned yellow but before the berries drop and the autumn winds rock the stems and disturb the crowns. This will be before the first frost. Bin rather than compost the ferns. If you salted the bed in March, you will probably have no weeds; otherwise, spray any deep-rooted weeds with a systemic weedkiller (glyphosate) and non-persistent weeds with a contact herbicide or winkle them out by hand, but the danger with hand weeding is that the asparagus roots will be damaged. Cover the bed generously with garden compost or spent mushroom compost. Complete with a layer of topsoil.

Aster (now mostly classified as Symphyotrichum): *Aster amellus*, *A. × frikartii* **'Mönch' (and others still belonging to the Aster genus),** *A. cordifolius, A. diffusus, A. ericoides, A. lateriflorus, A.* **'Little Carlow'**, *A. novae-angliae, A. novi-belgii, A. pilosum* var. *pringlei* **(all now known as Symphyotrichum) and** *A. divaricatus* **(now known as** *Eurybia divaricata***)** Allow them to expand fully. Cut down the stems from late October onwards when the flowers are finished. Leave the Amellus Group and *Eurybia divaricata* until spring to divide. Others can be divided now if desirable.

Astilbe Flower heads can be left on for winter interest. Otherwise, cut plants down to ground level. They need dividing every four years but this can be done in spring if not now.

Banana (Musa) Cut down after the first frost damage. Protect the rootstock with a deep mulch of straw or bracken. A piece of hessian or fleece pinned over this will stop it blowing away. I like Jungle Seeds's method of protecting their bananas in Oxfordshire: the stem is cut at 60 cm/24 inches and it and its roots are wrapped in hessian. The whole thing is then covered in an upturned plastic dustbin with holes cut in the side for ventilation. Uncovered the following April, *Musa basjoo* and *M. sikkimensis* proceed to make 1.75–2 m/6–7 ft of growth (though they will not flower or fruit in the UK).

Beech If planting a beech hedge where ground is quite boggy, consider using hornbeam instead, which does better than beech where the soil is moist. It does not hold on to its leaves through winter quite as well but is an excellent alternative.

Beetroot Lift any beetroot still in the ground and store with their leaves in a cool ventilated place or, cleaned of soil but with 15 cm/6 inches of stalk, laid in moist sand.

Bergenia (elephant's ears) To propagate, take rooted sections of the rhizomes and plant in gritty potting compost with the growing tip just above the soil. When planting bergenia, add bulbs such as crocus, scilla or snowdrops close by as they make good companions.

Blackberry With 'managed' blackberries, cut the stems which have fruited right down to the ground, tying into a fan shape the remaining stems – they will fruit next year. Cutting out all but three or four canes will lead to bigger fruit.

Box If the leaves are bronzy red it may mean the plant is still short of nutrients, so you could add some bone meal to a mulch of garden compost and fork it in gently around the roots without damaging them. It is, however, important not to overfeed at this time of year.

Broad bean Dig rich organic compost or manure into soil where broad beans are to be planted.

Brugmansia Stop feeding and start to reduce watering but do not let the plant dry out. It can go into a greenhouse, cool conservatory or cool room. Stephen Lacey again passes on excellent advice from a grower: it needs 5–10°C and good light over winter. Taking it in now should achieve flowers from about May/June. It is able to take a slight frost (to -4°C) but then will need to be cut down in spring to regrow from lower down the same trunk and will produce flowers in September. That might be the best option if it is a huge plant.

Buddleja alternifolia* and *B. globosa Cover the roots with dry mulch.

Canna Take out the old flower stems, divide clumps into smaller bits if they are huge, repot and then leave them (with all their leaves) to overwinter in a shed or frost-free greenhouse just keeping them minimally damp. Otherwise, cut the stems down a bit but leave a good leafy amount on the plant and, once inside, let the stems gradually wither, giving the rhizomes time to develop a bit more. When the stems have finally died back, cut everything away, wash off the old soil, dry the rhizomes in the light for a few days, then wrap individually in paper and store in a garage or cellar. Alternatively, put them in old wine boxes filled with dry compost, with the neck of the rhizomes just showing above the surface and keep them a tiny bit moist over winter in an unheated greenhouse or shed.

Catananche (cupid's dart) It can be cut down to about 15 cm/6 inches. It also does well as a dried flower, so the flowers now over could be left to dry *in situ* and then picked. A short-lived perennial, it is better treated as a biennial.

***Cautleya spicata* 'Robusta'** They need a good winter mulch when the leaves have turned yellow and died down.

***Cerinthe major* 'Purpurascens' (honeywort)** Collect the large black seeds for next year. Cut the plants down but leave *in situ* so that potential seedlings are not disturbed.

***Chelone obliqua* (turtlehead)** A lovely sturdy plant flowering just when needed in mid-autumn. When over, cut down to 15 cm/6 inches or leave for good seed heads.

Chive This is a good moment (as is March) to divide clumps before they disappear for winter.

Clematis: Group 2 *Clematis florida* in containers will need to be moved into a sheltered corner or a cold greenhouse – it does not need heat, just shelter. In a cold garden it will need fleece round the base.

Clematis 'Kaiu' (group 3, flowering July–October), climbing into *Sorbus vilmorinii*

Cleome (spider flower) Collect seeds for next year as fresh seeds are best for germination (see May).

Cobaea scandens (cup and saucer plant) It will not survive outside over winter so is best treated as an annual. Grown inside, it can be pruned after flowering to fit the space available.

Cornus Mulch the roots of all cornus with lots of organic matter keeping just clear of the stems.

***Cosmos atrosanguineus* (chocolate cosmos)** These will struggle to get through winter outside so cut down to about 20 cm/8 inches and take inside to overwinter. Otherwise, mulch well (even protecting with fleece).

Cotoneaster Clip away growth that obscures the berries. Prune prostrate cotoneasters to improve their appearance. Take out stems of *Cotoneaster horizontalis* that are growing away from its support so that it fans out neatly. All deciduous species can be pruned when the berries are finished.

Crocosmia (montbretia) Resist cutting away faded leaves until they are well and truly dead. If they are standing well, leave them over winter – the leaves can look golden in late autumn sun. They can, if wanted, be lifted anytime into November and dried off to overwinter as dry corms. Otherwise, mulch round the crown for frost protection. Seedlings often make poor plants so divide (and plant) in spring.

Crocus: spring flowering Plant this month in grass, in beds, under deciduous shrubs or densely in gravel (two hundred in a 90 cm/36 inch triangle would not be too many) – anywhere there is good drainage.

Dahlia Continue cutting the flowers down to the next flower bud and then down to the next pair of leaves – a new bud will form. When flowering is over, the tubers benefit from a period of dormancy in the soil so leave the plants standing as long as possible; the tubers will increase in size. Well-established tubers will do better left in the ground if temperatures do not fall much below 0°C. Species dahlias are always left in – some dry mulch, grit or straw will mark where they are. For most of us, it is a game of roulette: leave dahlias in and it will be the fiercest winter ever; lift them and it will remain balmy. If you are intending to take them in and use homemade compost for their storage, if possible bring the compost into the warmth to dry out in bags, ready to use for next month's dahlia storage. This is unnecessary if you are using bought compost, which will have had the excess moisture removed from it.

Delphinium Cut down to 45 cm/ 18 inches from the ground – no lower. During the dormant season, now until March, a monthly dose of liquid slug killer will help kill slug eggs.

***Dicentra spectabilis* (now called *Lamprocapnos spectabilis*) (bleeding heart)** Cut any remaining foliage right down to ground level.

Epimedium They can be divided now as well as after flowering. Pull the root ball apart, ensuring each bit has a few pink buds among the roots. Check divisions for signs of disease or vine weevil and bin them if there are any; otherwise pot them up, covering the surface with grit, to plant on when they have made good new roots. If planting new stock or very large divisions, use lots of leafmould in the planting hole. The European species (including *Epimedium* × *perralchicum*, *E.* × *rubrum*, *E.* × *versicolor*, *E.* × *warleyense*) appear tougher than the many daintily flowered Asian species (*E. grandiflorum* and its many cultivars). The Asian species do need more moisture retentive soil, so a winter mulch will help them.

It is traditional to cut away the old leaves of the ground-covering epimediums now so that when the flowers appear in spring they can be seen to the full. Doing it now means there is no chance of cutting off emerging flower stems. Even so, I prefer to do this in February, taking time to avoid the new stems in order to have the enjoyment of their very attractive ground-cover leaves over winter. Either way, do not remove the leaves of the entrancing 'Pink Elf', which may have reflowered in the last two months – it will flower early in the spring and the leaves will protect them from frost damage. Like many of the most delicate looking ones, it likes its home to remain intact over winter.

Eremurus (foxtail lily, desert candle) Protect with as dry a mulch as possible (Strulch is good). Mulch around, not over, anything visible. Protect from slugs.

Eryngium (sea holly) If foliage is tatty, remove it but protect the basal rosette with a dry mulch such as Strulch or bracken (they should be kept as dry as possible when dormant). Anything that can be left on will provide extra protection over winter and their seed heads can look good (the birds will also enjoy them). With deep taproots, eryngium do not move or divide well. All like full sun and most like dry, poorish soil though just a few, *Eryngium agavifolium* for one (also having terrific seed heads in winter), like moist, well-drained soil.

Eucomis (pineapple lily) By early October, with leaves floppy and flowers nearly over, remove spent flower stems and really yellow leaves but not those that still have some life as they are feeding the bulbs.

Euphorbia (spurge) Euphorbias should have the flowered stems cut off before winter, neatly to the base where there will be new growth. Some are late flowering and these must be done now or they become very woody. This is a good time to divide them.

Evening primrose (*Oenothera biennis*) Cut down to its basal leaves at ground level. The best way to propagate them is with seed sown *in situ* now; otherwise, sow in early spring under cover but they dislike root disturbance. They will take until the second year after sowing to produce their flowering growth.

Fennel: bronze (*Foeniculum vulgare* 'Purpureum') Remove dead stems of this perennial unless they are good enough to provide winter interest.

Francoa sonchifolia (bridal wreath) It does not like winter wet and may not get through a hard winter so would be safer inside.

Fuchsia: tender and standard They must not be frosted so during the month bring under cover (shed, garage, greenhouse) and maintain a minimum temperature of 5°C. Having watered a few days previously, trim to take their structure back by about half, taking off the long stems and crossing and twiggy branches to get a good shape for next year. Cut a little above a leaf so that if there is dieback this can be taken off in spring. Do not remove the remaining leaves as they will drop off in time and will meanwhile help the plant to transpire as well as give an indication to water content within the plant. Water approximately once a week to maintain very slight moisture only. Lockyer Fuchsias in Bristol is an excellent source of advice for the care of fuchsias.

Galtonia The withered flower stems can be cut down, but allow the leaves to turn yellow so that the goodness can return to the bulb. They can then be cut away and covered with a thick mulch; Anna Pavord suggests in her book *Bulb* that using mushroom compost will give them all they need: 'food, blotting paper and protection all at the same time'. Mark where they are with some grit so the bulbs do not get a fork through them. If, like me, you have galtonia in pots, bring them into a frost-free environment to overwinter.

Geranium maderense Cut off old flower stems and tatty looking leaves. In cold areas give it lots of protection, tuck it under the skirts of a shrub or bring it inside. If it dies it will probably have set seed elsewhere. Each plant is short lived but the generations keep going.

Gerbera Leaving in place the leaves and flower heads of the hardy gerbera (Everlast and Garvinea series) helps them to get through winter. Feed with a potash-rich fertilizer such as Tomorite and mulch. Should temperatures drop below -4°C they will need protection with fleece. Tender varieties need to be taken into warmth, kept moist but not overwatered.

Gladiolus They can be treated as annuals and started anew each year. Otherwise, when the leaves have turned yellow, dig up the plants (giving them a wide berth to avoid damaging the corms), remove the leaves and stems, clean and dry the corms and dust with sulphur. After two weeks, when the corms are dry, snap the new corms from the old, discarding the old (lower one) and storing the new, cold but frost free, away from mice, ready to plant out next spring. If gardening in the warm south, remove the foliage, then, leaving the corms in the ground, cover with a thick mulch; mushroom compost would be ideal. Every few years they have to be dug up anyway, as otherwise too many corms fight for the available nutrients and lots of foliage is produced with few if any flowers.

Gladiolus communis subsp. *byzantinus* can safely be left in the ground and will spread. They can be planted now, 10–15 cm/ 4–6 inches deep, in very gritty soil, ideally where other plants will support them.

Gypsophila (baby's breath) Cut flower stems down to the ground. With the exception of *Gypsophila* 'Rosenschleier', they dislike winter wet so provide them with a dry mulch to get through winter.

Hawthorn For a neat hawthorn hedge give it a final prune before winter.

***Helianthus*, including 'Lemon Queen' (perennial sunflower)** Cut the finished stems down to the ground, check over for weeds and mulch.

Hemerocallis (daylily) Remove any remaining dead foliage and mulch for the winter.

Hepatica If the foliage is looking tatty it can be cut or it can go through winter as it is. Sprinkle bone meal incorporated in a mulch of garden compost or leafmould around the plants to give them care over the coming winter.

Hippeastrum (amaryllis) Start existing bulbs back into growth by cutting off any old leaves and topdressing with 5 cm/ 2 inches of new compost. Water and feed. For new bulbs to be ready for Christmas flowering, they need to be planted by late October in compost (John Innes No. 2 plus grit at 3:1 is good). Place two-thirds of the bulb above the soil surface. Use a heavy pot so that it does not fall over, and one that is not greatly bigger than the bulb. If necessary rehydrate the bulb before planting by standing it on a glass with only its roots in the water. Plant it gently in the pot, taking care not to damage the roots. Keep warm and light, out of direct sunlight, watering on planting but afterwards only when it dries out. When leaves appear, water regularly but never let the bulb or roots sit in water. It will flower six to eight weeks after planting. If the bud appears too soon, move it into a cooler place. Turn the plant so the stem grows straight.

Holly (Ilex) This is a good time to plant holly. Buy big as, unlike most trees and shrubs, which do better planted small, hollies fare better if planted when at least 60–90 cm/24–36 inches high.

Hyacinth Plant specially prepared bulbs for Christmas in bowls filled with moist bulb fibre (using bulb fibre removes the need for drainage holes in pots), but potting compost, perlite and grit in equal measure will do well. Pack the bulbs in close, their tips showing above the top of the compost. Finish with a layer of grit. Different colours flower at slightly different times so it works best to have just one colour in a pot. Water and put in a cool dark place to root, just occasionally moistened until the top growth is about 7 cm/3 inches high. This will take six to eight weeks. When there is an anaemic looking bud, bring into the light and warmth.

Iris

- Bearded iris: check divisions made last month are still clear of soil on top of their rhizomes. A light mulch of mushroom compost, ensuring it does not cover the irises, would be good.
- *Iris pseudacorus*: cut – or strim – the dead foliage down and bin it. This rhizomatous iris spreads rapidly and will need a cull every few years.
- *I. sibirica*: the dying foliage can be removed. Some (such as *I.s.* 'Exuberant Encore') may have just reflowered, in which case a potash-rich feed (and watering if it is dry) will help them regain strength to flower well next year.

Itea ilicifolia Young plants need a good deep mulch in autumn.

Kirengeshoma palmata When flowering is over, flowered stems should be cut down to the base. Mulch well and mark as it will disappear.

Kniphofia (red hot poker) Remove faded flower spikes of *Kniphofia rooperi* and other mid-autumn flowering species and cultivars before they set seed. Frisk for snails. Give them all, whatever their season of flowering, a deep dry mulch (such as composted pine needles) around but not over the crown. For those not totally hardy, pull the leaves together and tie them over the crown.

Lemon tree (citrus) Move the lemon back to its winter home (conservatory/porch/greenhouse) as the warmth goes out of the air. Stop feeding with the nitrogen-rich proprietary feed used since March and reduce watering, letting the compost dry out slightly between waterings. Towards the end of October start using a proprietary citrus winter feed. Repot or topdress only in spring.

They need a winter temperature of 7–10°C and relatively high humidity. Central heating going on and off, low light and dry atmosphere are guaranteed to kill, so if there is no such luxury as a greenhouse, a south facing window, a draught-free porch or bright room with no heating would ideal. A tray of wet gravel under the pot helps to maintain humidity, but if the water level reaches the pot base the compost will stay soggy – probably fatal. Hand misting would be very helpful. Watch out for red spider mite and mealybug – do not let either get a foot in the door.

Lemon verbena Cut back by about half and take under cover for winter. Its roots must not freeze.

Lewisia These pretty rockery/alpine plants need lots of grit around their base rosettes. If not on very well-drained soil, a wire cage covered with a dry mulch could keep off the worst winter wet.

Lily Cut growth down to 2.5 cm/ 1 inch after the leaves have gone yellow, checking for lily beetle as you do so. They will linger under the leaves and then drop into the soil to overwinter. Bulbs can be left in their pots. If possible move the pots into a sheltered corner and wrap them in fleece. Try to keep the soil only just moist, so if the pot is under the overhang of the building so much the better. (The only snow I remove from pots is those of lily bulbs.) Have fleece or newspaper ready to lay on the pots if there is a very hard frost forecast but it should be removed soon afterwards.

Lime (Tilia) If planting a pleached barrier it will be necessary to get all round it to do the pruning; they do not work well if too close to a wall. *Tilia × euchlora* is good for pleaching as it does not attract aphids, although *T. cordata* is also often used as it is more restrained in its growth than other species.

Lobelia erinus (trailing and clump forming) Treat as an annual and throw them away now, as they are too tender to survive winter.

Magnolia This is a good time to plant, while the soil is still warm, but do not plant deep as they are generally surface rooting and need a wide shallow hole. Use lots of leafmould and avoid all fertilizers, which would burn their fleshy roots. Newly planted magnolia will need frost protection in due course around the roots or they will be lost in a hard winter.

Marigold, Mexican (*Tagetes limmonii, T. minuta*) This will now be in flower – deadhead it to champion its defeat of the ground elder (see July).

Medlar (*Mespilus germanica*) Either pick the fruit as its flesh softens and leave somewhere cool for a few weeks or leave on the tree until the fruits are 'belted' (blackened by frost). Once the skins are purplish black and the fruits are soft and smelling slightly of wine, they are ready to be made into jelly or baked.

Narcissus Paper-white narcissus can be planted now for Christmas, 2.5 cm/ 1 inch apart, just below the surface of bulb fibre mixed with horticultural grit or just tucked into pebbles and water. Keep cool and moist but not dark. They will take about eight weeks to flower. Anna Pavord has wonderful advice in her beautiful book *Bulb*: if, when the shoots are about 5 cm/2 inches high, the water around the pebbles is mixed with alcohol (rum, gin, vodka, not wine or beer) at a ratio of 9:1 water and alcohol, the roots will take up the alcohol and grow 40 per cent shorter but flower just as well, achieving better proportioned and less floppy stems.

Nerine Nerines benefit from a low-nitrogen feed when flowering is over. They flower best when bulbs are congested so do not split them unnecessarily.

Ophiopogon planiscapus 'Nigrescens' (black grass) Push dry mulch under the leaves.

Ornithogalum
- *Ornithogalum thrysoides* (chincherinchee): except in very warm parts of the UK, they need to be brought in for winter; pot up into compost with John Innes No. 2.
- *Ornithogalum umbellatum* (star of Bethlehem): plant 10 cm/4 inches deep early in the month in well-drained soil in sun or partial shade. They will spread.

Pansy: winter flowering (Viola) Early October is a good time to plant to avoid legginess. Pansies turn to face the sun so plant where they will look towards you; otherwise you just see their backs. They need deadheading almost immediately, and do it regularly. When making a selection, consider the pale or brightly coloured ones which show up beautifully in winter light, unlike the lovely moody purples and dark blues which can get lost. The smaller flowered ones are most vibrant en masse because they keep their heads held high. Mulch with bark to keep the petals clean from soil splashed up by rain.

Pelargonium Tender pelargoniums need to come under cover before frosts begin. Stop feeding, gradually reduce watering and cut back by a third to help airflow and to reduce the incidence of disease over winter. They will be cut further back in spring.

Peony
- Herbaceous: cut back established herbaceous peonies now (not after flowering), removing dead stems and foliage that has started to brown. Bin (never compost) the leaves. Peonies can be moved and divided between October and late January. Each division needs at least three buds. Put the lifted root ball

in the shade for a bit, to dry and divide more easily. They may sulk but will recover. Now is the best time to plant them (better than spring) – never more than 5 cm/2 inches below the surface. Do not mulch over the crown, which otherwise would add to the depth of the soil. Plant where the early morning sun will not fall on the flowers.

- Tree peony: Japanese tree peonies need little tidying up. On other tree peonies, flowered shoots can be cut back to new growth, and if stems are poor or straggly, they can be cut hard back to within 10 cm/4 inches of the ground – they should reshoot. Tree peonies flower best on one-year-old growth. Do not overwater, which is a major cause of failure. Feed established tree peonies with bone meal or potash-rich fertilizer as they are greedy feeders. Autumn is their planting time too, but move them only if really necessary, after the leaves have started to drop. Add loads of compost to a big planting hole. While herbaceous peonies go just 5 cm/2 inches deep, tree peonies need to be planted with their graft point (most are grafted) 10 cm/4 inches below the surface. If containerized, plant slightly deeper than in the pot.

Plectranthus argentatus This is a beautiful and useful container plant but it is very tender. In early October bring under glass and ease off the watering as they rot in cold, wet compost.

Plumbago auriculata Its glorious blue flowers should continue until about October in a conservatory. A heavy prune when flowering is over will maintain its shape and encourage new growth for next season. Feed after pruning with a balanced fertilizer, water and mulch.

Poppy: oriental (Papaver orientale) Oriental poppies are better planted in

autumn than spring. They propagate from root cuttings; place these outside in a cold frame or protected area over winter.

Quince (Cydonia) The fruits hanging in abundance on a 'Meech's Prolific' quince tree look like great golden pears straight from a fairy tale. Pick them before they start to fall (when they will be over-ripe) and store, cool, not touching and well away from apples, for up to six weeks. They will scent the room. (See November.)

Rhododendron and Azalea If planting now, see September for advice. It is hard to resist clearing up leaves that have been shed beneath them because they look untidy in a small garden, but Millais Nurseries suggest they are the best mulch for these shallow rooted woodland plants unless the leaves are diseased.

Rhus typhina (sumach) Though it has fabulous autumn colour, it sends up a forest of suckers. These need to be removed when young by digging down, finding the connecting root and severing it.

Rose
- If wind rock is likely to be a problem, prune any tall, ungainly stems of repeat flowering shrub roses down by a third to an even height. Otherwise, leave them and once flowering and smaller roses alone.
- On alkaline soil the use of Sulphur Soil twice yearly helps to lower the pH to a suitable level (6.5) for roses and helps deter the recurrence of black spot. On neutral soils apply once yearly now.

Rosemary Give rosemary a dose of a potash-rich fertilizer such as Tomorite to strengthen it in winter.

Rudbeckia (black-eyed Susan) It can be divided most easily after flowering is finished; pull apart and replant small sections with a sprinkling of bone meal.

***Ruscus aculeatus* (butcher's broom)**
This native winter evergreen is long lived and totally tolerant of dry shade, but its glossy red berries need sunshine to look anything but dull. Move, if necessary, to a brighter place.

Salvia: hardy Towards the end of October consider salvia protection, most of which, however, will be done in November. Treat salvias that are staying outside like penstemons: to keep them healthy, cut back just to a lower leaf joint beneath the flowers as they finish flowering, but do not cut any salvias hard back, however hardy – even those being taken in. This will be done in late spring. Cutting back into bare wood or hard pruning now is usually fatal. Mark all salvias left in the ground; some do not come back into leaf until early summer when other things may be smothering them. *Salvia patens* tubers should really be lifted like dahlias but perhaps because winters have got warmer, they seem to survive left in the ground even here in Derbyshire. Know where they are as they are so easy to plant over. (See November.)

Sansevieria (mother-in-law's tongue) Reduce watering, doing so only when the compost is entirely dry. Irregular watering – underwatering then excessively watering – creates corky patches on the leaves, so watch out. Those with variegated leaves need a little more heat (minimum of 10°C) than plain-leaved varieties (minimum 8°C).

Santolina (cotton lavender) Cut back hard every year to stop it flopping over. Old wood cannot be treated so fiercely, so do this from year one.

Sempervivum (houseleek) They are usually fine outside so long as they are in well-drained soil; push more grit under their rosettes to prevent rot.

Sidalcea It really dislikes winter wet so provide a dry mulch of bracken or Strulch.

Snowdrop To treat snowdrops with added care, clear any leaves covering the resting bulbs and sprinkle bone meal and potash on the soil, then add a layer of leafmould.

Solomon's seal (*Polygonatum × hybridum*) Cut back to base. The muddle of roots can be divided and the soil mulched with leafmould and lots of grit. Some rhizomes could go in a pot to plant elsewhere in spring. Ensure the pot has rich compost and is also well covered with grit.

Sweet pea This is an excellent time to sow seeds in deep pots or root trainers. Protect them from mice, who love both seed and seedling. Roger Parsons, who holds a National Collection of Sweet Peas, advises us that soaking seeds can reduce germination. He says that nicking or chipping seeds is a personal preference (but he does not consider it necessary). Seeds should be only lightly covered in multipurpose compost with added John Innes, watered in well and then not watered again until after germination. To germinate they should be given only a very little heat or they will become soft; mollycoddling does them no good. A windowsill or uncovered propagator on very low heat would work well. Once germinated, they should be kept in a cool greenhouse, cold frame or cold windowsill in good light until there are three to four pairs of leaves, when they can be transferred to the individual pots in which they will stay until they are planted out. Put them out on sunny winter days, and if a cold frame is available, put them in it providing extra protection within the frame if it becomes very cold. A little frost is fine. Do not nip out the tips of autumn sown sweet peas; Roger Parsons explains that they will develop side shoots naturally if grown hard enough. (Later sown seeds will need pinching out – see March/April.)

Tarragon Cut down and cover with a thick dry mulch – like other members of the artemisia genus, it dislikes soggy soil.

***Tricyrtis formosana* (toad lily)** Black spots on leaves are natural. Continue to deadhead until flowering is over as they will form flowers lower down the stem. When they have finished allow them to die back naturally. Give the crowns a deep dry winter mulch and mark their position.

Tulbaghia Mulch well to help these rhizomatous perennials through winter. A thick layer of spent mushroom compost would do well for them. They grow well in pots, too, where their lack of hardiness can be better accommodated by bringing the pots under cover.

Viola cornuta Violas will be exhausted from their long flowering period. Cut them back in early October removing all flowering stems, buds and straggly foliage; leave just the late summer growth in the crown of the plant. Mulch around them with fresh compost for the winter.

Wallflower: biennial (*Erysimum cheiri* cultivars) Bare-root bundles of plants of the biennial wallflower *Erysimum cheiri* can be bought to plant out immediately, to flower from March to May; they will be called names like 'Fire King' or 'Vulcan', 'Scarlet Bedder' or 'Sunset'. If growing with tulips, get the wallflowers in now and put the tulips in next month. As soon as you can, pinch out top growth to avoid legginess.

A view over autumn beds towards Melbourne Pool including the aster *Symphyotrichum novae-angliae* 'Lye End Beauty', *Salvia splendens* 'Van-Houttei' and *Helianthus* 'Lemon Queen'

NOVEMBER

As daylight hours shorten and the lowering sun touches plants now brown and fawn – turning them momentarily into golden forms – evergreens and the structure of the garden become increasingly evident as its bones. The coming of winter is a time for catching leaves, metaphorically even if not literally (though what fun that was as a child): every accomplishment this month pays dividends in the spring.

AREAS TO CONSIDER

Alpines Grit round collars of alpines and the removal of dying leaves will help prevent rotting and slug damage.

Annuals Pots or trays of plants need to be kept just moist and under cover in the coldest months, while seedlings left outside will need fleece protection in fierce weather.

Bare-root plants This is the start of the season for bare-root planting – see Planting below.

Borders The editing process, started in October, continues with weeding and forking through the beds to undo surface compaction. Leave alone asters, *Gillenia trifoliata*, grasses, *Phlomis fruiticosa*, rudbeckia, *Verbena bonariensis* – they all give shape to the garden. Protect from sogginess salvias, eryngiums and grey leaved plants – anything that needs really well-drained conditions.

Heavy clay soil can be improved by adding well-rotted farmyard manure, leafmould or sharp sand over the top. Where areas of soil are bare, turn them over with a fork to aerate the ground, bringing pests to the surface, but avoid

breaking up the clods – they allow water to penetrate more easily and the lumps will be broken down naturally during winter. Water may well puddle on ground left as a fine tilth.

Bulbs This is tulip planting time. Late in the month, cut the grass when dry enough where bulbs are planted in preparation for their spring appearance (except where autumn flowering crocus and colchicum are growing). A layered pot of bulbs is easy to do, the latest bulb to flower going in the bottom and the earliest at the top. Use a terracotta pot as it will not freeze as fast as a plastic one. For three different bulbs, the bottom could be at 20 cm/8 inches, the next two layers 7 cm/3 inches apart, finishing with a covering of compost and a layer of grit, but do not worry too much about their spacing – they can be packed into close layers (but not touching each other or the side of the pot) and will find their way through each other's roots. Use compost mixed with leafmould, perlite and grit so that it drains well. Put a piece of broken pot over the hole at the bottom of the pot to keep the drainage clear. Raise the pot off the ground with bricks or pottery feet. Winter pansies in the compost of the top layer will give colour now and can stay there as the bulbs grow through them.

Carpinus betulus 'Frans Fontaine' (hornbeam) and *Cotinus coggygria* 'Flame' (smoke bush)

Compost heaps and leaf piles Set aside leafmould from previous years that is ready to use, to make space for the new dump of leaves. Do not compact the leaf collection as it needs air circulation to rot down well. This is a cold and therefore slower process than compost heaps, which need the build-up of heat – they are two quite different processes. Garden compost and spent mushroom compost are slightly alkaline, leafmould and composted pine bark, slightly acidic.

Containers and pots Raise containers left outside on to pottery feet or bricks. This allows rainwater to drain out and stops the compost becoming waterlogged and thereby rotting the roots. The surface can be mulched with grit. Put bubble wrap or hessian round those which may crack. When plants are no longer actively growing, stop feeding and do not overwater – do so only if the top layer of compost dries out.

Ferns Resist the urge to cut off dead fronds of deciduous ferns. It would be better to fold them over the crown for a few months' winter protection.

Frost and wind protection In three out of four years it seems that the garden is perfectly fine without the bother of much protection; then there is a bitter year and plants are lost, or there is so much rain that they drown in soggy soil. Err on the side of caution: at the very least, give wind protection to the many shrubs that are borderline and add grit around those which hate wet.

Fruit trees: free standing Give established fruit trees an organic winter tree wash to control overwintering pests if they were affected this year. Grease bands (easily available from garden centres) round fruit trees will help prevent winter moth damage.

Green manure Field beans can be planted as a green manure to be incorporated in March, fixing nitrogen in the soil.

Hedges From now until March plant bare-root hedges including yew. Prune deciduous hedges if necessary.

Lawns and long grass Mow when dry enough, to benefit early bulbs. Give the lawn a winter feed if it is looking yellow; a feed rich in phosphate and potash with added nutrients including, if the ground is chalk or limestone, added sulphur would be good. There are many products available: Nutralawn for autumn/winter (with or without added sulphur) is one. Leaves are most easily mown on the lawn and collected with the grass cuttings.

Leaves We leave sycamore and plane tree leaves out of the leaf pile as they are so slow to rot.

Mulch Any mulch on soil is usually better than nothing – the ideal would be well-rotted garden compost mixed with two-year-old leafmould. The worms take most of it down into the soil and anything left on top is forked in during spring. Where a dry mulch is called for, straw, Strulch, composted bark or bracken is good. In woodland areas use leafmould (never animal manure).

Perennial meadow It needs a last cut of the year when it starts to look rank. It might still be looking good, and indeed the seed heads may provide a welcome decoration to the garden in winter, especially in frost. Cut it down when it no longer has any pictorial value. It is important to compost cuttings before they rot on the soil, thereby returning nutrients to it (and by now all the seed will have fallen out so there is no point in leaving it even a few days).

Perennials Finish dividing perennials before the soil gets cold and wet. Protect tender perennials that cannot come inside with straw or bracken (or their own leaves). Cut back plants that have flopped, look leggy or where there is a cushion of fresh growth at the bottom so that they can overwinter successfully. For exceptions such as salvias and penstemons, many of which are not entirely hardy, see below.

Planting The season of bare-root planting is from now until March and is the best time to plant most deciduous trees, fruit trees, fruit bushes, hedging plants, roses and shrubs. The roots must be kept moist and should be soaked before planting. When planting shrubs or trees, trim any very long roots, dig a rectangular hole at least three times the diameter of root spread and about 30 cm/12 inches deep (probably no more) and place the roots on small mound of soil within the hole so that they spread out evenly. Before covering the root ball, if a stake is needed put it in the planting hole at a 45-degree angle on the side of the prevailing wind (see also Trees below). If on a slope, it may also be worthwhile incorporating a length of tubing with its opening a few inches above the soil line to enable watering to be directed straight to the roots. The top of the root ball should be at the surface of the final soil level. Firm the soil in gradually, first incorporating some bone meal, keeping the stem absolutely stable. Water well to settle the roots even if the soil seems very moist.

Pruning Pruning can be done on those deciduous trees and shrubs which are not going to flower in the first half of next year.

Seeds November is a good time to sow members of the Apiaceae (umbellifer) family like anthriscus, astrantia, orlaya and pimpinella. They need to be sprinkled on

Acer palmatum 'Sango-kaku'

to a tray of seed compost, covered with grit and left outside for a few frosts, then brought inside to germinate.

Shrubs November to March is the right time to move deciduous shrubs; water and mulch well when moved and water regularly thereafter.

Trees: staking and care Stakes need a buffer between tie and tree to avoid rubbing. Check stakes are not too tight but firm enough to prevent wind rock. Clear grass and weeds from around trunks to about 1 m/39 inches in diameter, particularly on young trees where they compete for nutrients. Cover the circle of ground under the canopy with mulch combined with a slow release fertilizer, leaving a small margin clear around the trunk. (See Phytophthora in April.)

Viburnum beetle The viburnum beetle lays its eggs in dead twigs so cut out any dead material and bin.

Wildlife Hidden where it does not intrude, some fallen fruit and stacked logs, a pile of leaves and a stack of hollow stemmed plants make a wildlife haven.

PLANTS

Abutilon Fleece those in pots – in the ground they seem to get through winter if protected from strong winds. If, as is preferable, they can be taken under cover, prune to the shape required and keep relatively dry.

Achillea (yarrow) Cut flowering stems near to ground level.

Actaea simplex (was called Cimicifuga) If *Actaea simplex* has been flowering, the towering spikes will be over. Either cut them down to the base or, if they are still standing well, leave for winter outline for a while but mulch well as they need plenty of moisture. Division, which they dislike, is best done in spring.

Aeonium Keep the roots very dry over winter months when they are resting. Some leaves will drop.

Agapanthus The leaves of deciduous hardy agapanthus will turn yellow. Cut them away with any old stems, just above the ground, water if necessary and mulch with 15cm/6 inch of composted bark. This will protect next year's buds. They need well-drained soil or they will rot, but otherwise they will be fine outside in all but the very coldest parts of the country. The hardy evergreen agapanthus (such as the Headbourne varieties) should also be fine – just tuck a dry mulch in and out of their base growth, not cutting back the leaves at all.

Those in pots will find cold weather harder to deal with: ideally they should be brought under cover but otherwise add grit to the soil surface, then a dry mulch and fleece the pot. Whether evergreen or deciduous, water well before mulching. Any evergreen plants brought inside will need the light of a shed or garage window and should be watered very sparingly from now until March. Deciduous ones can be kept quite dry and can go under the bench as they do not need light.

Agastache (giant hyssop) The hardy ones like *Agastache* 'Black Adder' should get through winter but the crowns need a deep mulch. Any growth should be left standing for extra protection. Bring tender varieties in under cover.

Amsonia tabernaemontana Cut down to ground level now the autumn colour has finished.

Anemone
- *Anemone × hybrida* (such as 'Honorine Jobert') (Japanese anemone): take root cuttings any time from now to January. Do not disturb for a few years after planting, though eventually they may become invasive. The flower stems can be cut to the ground when they finish, but their winter outline is agreeable for a while.
- *Anemone nemorosa* (windflower): to encourage spread, you can, now they are dormant, gently fork them up and break the rhizomes into pieces with a bud on each piece. Add leafmould to the soil, then place the rhizomes horizontally on the surface and quickly cover with a layer of compost so they do not dry in the process.

Apricot The dormant season from now until February is a good time to plant. Prune soon after planting, shortening the main leader by a third and any side shoots to 7 cm/3 inches. Chris Bowers's online guide to growing apricots, as trees and fan trained, is a valuable source of reference.

Arundo donax Cut to the ground unless the brown stems are wanted, in which case cut down in April.

Auricula They need to be kept on the dry side during their winter dormancy to avoid rot.

Bamboo Add grit around the plant to help drainage throughout winter. Some canes can be removed to give the clump better freedom of movement. A small trench round the edge of the bamboo reveals where runners are making their escape – this could help control undesirable spread.

Baptisia australis (blue wild indigo) Cut down the foliage of this spreading, dark blue summer perennial when it has blackened.

Blackcurrant New blackcurrants should be planted 5 cm/2 inches lower than they were in the nursery, then all stems cut to 2.5 cm/1 inch above the ground to encourage shoots from the base. They need sun and rich soil, while red and whitecurrants can deal with some shade. Do not grow blackcurrants in proximity to pines: both are host to white pine blister rust, which, while not serious for currants, is very serious for pines.

Blueberry Now is a good time to plant. They need well-drained soil as soggy conditions are unpopular, though they like a period of cold. On established plants remove a little of the old wood to keep in good shape.

Brassica: broccoli, cabbage, cauliflower Cover with horticultural fleece, supporting it several inches above the plants to keep pigeons off. Remove old leaves.

Broad bean Sow directly into the soil, 15 cm/6 inches apart, and cover the seeds with a raised fleece under which they can hunker down until growth starts in spring.

Buddleja davidii and cultivars They are brittle, so reduce winter wind damage by cutting a third off each stem.

Camellia Protect those in pots with hessian or bubble wrap as the roots will get much colder than they would in the ground (or move the pots into an unheated building).

As with the spring flowering camellias, *Camellia sasanqua* does not normally need pruning, but it can be done immediately after flowering is finished. Overgrown shoots can be shortened to a well-placed bud and other growth can be thinned, leaving alone any that are well placed. Harder pruning to renovate *C. sasanqua* should be done in the spring (see April). Feed after flowering with an ericaceous fertilizer and again in early spring but do not overfeed. Repot when pot bound using a John Innes ericaceous compost.

Cardiocrinum giganteum (giant lily) We cut down our now 2m/7ft-high flower stems and dry them off inside, keeping them in an umbrella stand to tease people about their identity.

Offsets need dividing during dormancy between November and early February. Smaller offsets are best grown on in pots in a cold frame until they have reached 5–7 cm/2–3 inches in diameter when they can better survive deep frost. Plant the biggest offsets with lots of organic mulch dug in, spacing them at least 75 cm/30 inches apart so the leaves will have space to flourish. From *The Genus Cardiocrinum: Its Identification and Cultivation* by Philip Bolt comes the following delightful quote: 'On that day, having dug a sizable hole and added some leaf mold and sand, the famed gardener [Miss Jekyll] also tossed in a freshly killed rabbit.' Whatever the feed – and Fish, Blood and Bone is somewhat easier – the planting hole does need to be big: as big as a football and full of compost, soil and fertilizer. This will be the only time it is fed. Position the tip of the bulb or offset just below the soil. It will take some years to flower, though the leaves are lush and lovely in themselves. Rich, cool, deep, well-drained loamy soil is the key to success. Although the bulbs prefer acidic conditions, they grow happily in neutral to slightly alkaline soil. Liking water in summer, they hate to be soggy in winter. Mulch around the clump – it will appreciate the enriched soil – but do not mulch over the nose of the crown lest the tips rot. Bulbs cope with temperatures down to -10°C, though smaller offsets are better planted into pots if it could be this cold. (Large offsets can be planted in pots too, but unlike in the soil, they will need a less rich medium and liquid feeding – and almost certainly will need support when they produce stems.)

Seeds can be collected as capsules open in late November. They will take five to seven years to reach flowering: an exercise in patience. Sow in trays of damp seed compost, spreading extra grit or sharp sand on top to hold the moisture at surface level and stop the seeds blowing away and getting soggy. Put them in the shade or a cold frame. They should be protected from excessive wet but kept moist. They will germinate after two cold winters (about sixteen months). When they have formed a true leaf, they can be potted up.

Philip Bolt's article in *The Plantsman* (December 2017, available on the RHS website) is the source of much fascinating advice.

Chaenomeles (Japanese quince)
Prune established plants now, cutting the current year's shoots back to two buds. It flowers on two-year-old wood and this stimulates the dormant flower buds.

Chrysanthemum
Cut down the stems after flowering finishes and mulch the crowns. They can be taken out over winter, trimmed down to 23 cm/9 inches with basal growth removed and put into a box of dry compost in the cold frame. If they are going back in the same place, prepare next year's bed by adding plenty of rich compost (well-rotted manure can be added) to boost fertility and improve drainage.

Citrus trifoliata (syn. *Poncirus trifoliata*) (Japanese bitter orange)
It needs only an occasional light trim; avoid pruning off the flower buds. Once tumbled into, it is never forgotten – it has immensely fierce thorns and makes a very strong boundary plant.

Clematis
- **Group 2**: every three or four years give clematis in this group a harder cut (to about waist height) to maintain leafiness lower down. Tie in the remaining growth to protect from wind damage.
- **Group 3**: to tidy late flowering clematis as they go over, cut down to chest height, tying in remaining stems to avoid wind damage. The full prune will be done in February or March.

Clerodendrum bungei
Cut down to the ground or leave alone, depending on the desired height. They will grow to about 1.25m/4 ft if cut down, clumping up to 2.5 m/8 ft if left alone. Suckers (which flower well) can be removed if out of place.

Cordyline
Protect against winter cold; to stop snow gathering on the tender growing point in the crown of the plant, bundle the leaves and tie together. Older plants are very wind resistant, which makes them very useful on roundabouts but also statuesque in gardens. Young plants may need staking for a while.

**_Coronilla valentina_ subsp. _glauca_
'Citrina'** Should you obtain one of these
uplifting plants, I read that it is best put
in a container for the winter and then
planted out (like the cuttings, see July)
after the danger of frost has passed. In
subsequent years it will survive winters
perfectly well in a sheltered spot.

Crinum × powellii The crown needs
protection from waterlogging: use straw.
Do not try to lift them as they hate root
disturbance. Any in containers could
come in under cover.

Crown imperial (_Fritillaria imperialis_)
A mulch of spent mushroom compost
would be good – fertile, alkaline soil is key
to their success.

Cymbidium (orchid) When flower spikes
emerge – sometime between November
and May, they may need supporting –
each one might last for two months. As
they fade, cut the stems down to 5 cm/
2 inches. If the night-time temperature is
too hot, the flower spikes may turn yellow
as they grow, so keep room temperature
at 11–14°C.

Dahlia In warmer areas where they are
left in the ground, cut down to about
10 cm/4 inches above the ground
after frost has blackened the leaves; a
thick layer of mulch secured in place
with chicken wire will provide winter
protection. If lifting them, also wait until
after the leaves are frost-blackened and
then cut stems to about 15 cm/6 inches
above the ground. Ease the tubers out,
wash off excess soil, trim off fine roots,
label (vital!) and store upside down in a
frost-free place to allow the sap to drain
out. When the tubers are dry, dust with
flowers of sulphur to prevent rot and put
in boxes of dry compost, sand or sawdust,
leaving stems exposed. Store them cool
and frost free in a shed, garage or under
greenhouse staging with a sack draped

over them, maintaining a temperature
of around 4°C. We use compost dried in
advance for this purpose, enabling us just
to wet this compost when we start them
going again. An alternative is to leave all
the soil on them as they dry and keep
them like that in a darkened place until
May; this works just as well though is a bit
more greedy on space. When in storage,
check them once a month for rot (and
discard any that look bad). Dig well-rotted
manure into ground where dahlias will go
next year.

Daphne Mulch with leafmould. Daphne
does not grow well in containers as it likes
cool, moist, humus-rich soil and is not
fond of being restrained in growth.

Delphinium Do not cut them down close
to the ground; leave about 12 cm/5 inches
standing to help prevent rot to the crown,
over which it is a good idea to apply a dry
mulch: gravel, spent mushroom compost
or Strulch would do. A liquid slug
deterrent will deal with any overwintering
slug eggs.

**_Eccremocarpus scaber_ (Chilean glory
flower)** As flowering finishes, collect the
seed for more plants as it is not hardy.

Echinacea (coneflower) Dead stems can
be cut down to the ground or left to stand
over winter to provide good shape. Do not
mulch the crowns with anything wet as
they dislike soggy ground.

Erigeron karvinskianus (fleabane) This
self-seeding little daisy can flower from
June to October given sunshine. When it
is over, cut back for winter. In spring it can
have a closer shave.

Eucomis (pineapple lily) Cut off
remaining foliage when frosts have
touched them and cover with spent
mushroom compost, straw, bark or
compost. They need to be kept dry at the

roots, so unless they are on very well-drained ground, you could keep this in place with netting.

In cold areas, take them up and let the foliage die down naturally before storing them, dry but not dessicated, and frost free. Those in pots should come inside until March or April. When bulblets are the size of hens' eggs, break them off from the parent and grow them on, but do not give up on the mother bulb; it will become large and corky but continue to flower for some years. Much advice has come to me over the years from Chris Ireland-Jones at Avon Bulbs in Somerset.

***Euonymus phellomanus* (spindle tree)** On planting, give it space as it does not do well crowded by other plants.

Felicia (blue daisy) Overwinter pots in a cold greenhouse using gritty compost, keeping them only just watered. They are generally intolerant of damp.

Fig As leaves start to fall, remove all unripened fruit larger than a small pea as these will freeze, rot or cause dieback, not ripening next year. Only the tiny embryo fruit will develop and mature next season. Do not prune any of this year's growth as it is holding next year's fruit. Take figs in pots under cover – garage, shed or greenhouse – and keep the soil slightly damp. Mice like the bark when it is under cover so take measures to protect it.

Gentian Willow gentians continue flowering until the first heavy frost; the foliage then turns into mats of yellow leaves which when removed will reveal the tiny green shoots of next year's growth. These leaves can stay in place for now to protect this growth. Keep moist if there are dry spells in winter.

***Gladiolus murielae* (was called *Acidanthera bicolor* and *G. callicanthus*)** Reduce watering, allowing the corms to dry off before winter sets in. Let the foliage die back. The corms can then be taken out of their pots and dried off or left in the pots but taken under cover. In any case do not let the corms get too cold in storage (a cool room in the house or shed is fine provided it does not become an ice house). So store, not only frost free but mouse-proof, until spring. They will get bigger for a couple of years before new corms are required.

Gunnera manicata Mulch round the crown with grit and straw. Then cover the crown with its own leaves to protect from frost. The stalks act as stakes and keep the leaves from blowing off.

Hamamelis (witch hazel) Suckers can be a nuisance; they usually hold their leaves longer than the cultivar and grow straight up. Take them out at the base. When planting, ensure the graft union is not buried in order to reduce suckering.

Helichrysum (curry plant) Mulch with straw or Strulch to get it through winter happily.

Heliotropium arborescens These tender, gloriously scented plants, so good in containers, need a heated conservatory or greenhouse to get through winter with night temperatures at a minimum of 10°C. Keep moist but do not overwater. It is much easier to treat them as annuals unless a well-heated greenhouse is available.

***Helleborus niger* (Christmas rose)** Help it to flower by Christmas by covering it with a cloche to protect from strong winds.

***Hesperantha coccinea* (syn. *Schizostylis coccinea*) (kaffir lily)** As they finish flowering, protect the crowns with leafmould or a dry mulch and mark where they are as they will disappear completely before re-emerging in spring. Those in clay soil may be better overwintered somewhere dryer with lots of grit dug in as they dislike cold clayey winter wet, even though they need moisture to flower. (I hedge my bets and move a few now.)

Hoheria sextylosa, H. sextylosa 'Stardust' and H. 'Glory of Amlwch' They may enjoy protection round the roots over winter (my evergreen *H. sextylosa* regrew after being cut down by frost, just as the deciduous hoheria are likely to do). Should major pruning be needed, do it now, but this is not usually necessary. If cutting a major branch, do an undercut first so that the bark of this aptly named 'ribbon wood' is not stripped back.

Hosta Remove dead or dying foliage to avoid crown rot and mulch the crown with bark.

Houttuynia (orange peel plant) Provide a deep winter mulch, especially on wet soils.

Hyacinth Protect bulbs with a layer of straw or other dry mulch which can be removed in early spring.

Hypericum (St John's Wort) Leave *Hypericum* × *inodorum* standing for winter as the berries look good. *H.* 'Hidcote' can be shaped for winter outline as desired.

Hyssopus officinalis Leave the faded flower stems as long as they look good over winter.

Imperata cylindrica 'Rubra' (Japanese blood grass) This grass needs a protective mulch in winter. It is not 100 per cent hardy.

Lavatera (mallow) Reduce the likelihood of wind and snow damage by cutting a third off each stem.

Leptospermum scoparium (New Zealand tea tree) It is not reliably hardy; place protection round its base for winter.

Lespedeza thunbergii After its lovely fountain of flowers is over, cut back lightly, leaving hard pruning until spring.

Leyland cypress (× *Cuprocyparis leylandii*) Plant about now (from containers not bare-root). If intended as a hedge, plants should be 45–60 cm/18–24 inches apart. Keep well watered and weed-free. Pinch out growing tips to make them bushier.

Libertia Mulch around the plant to give it some frost protection.

Macleaya Cut down to the base. The foliage may keep its good looks a bit longer when out of the wind.

Medlar (*Mespilus germanica*) This is a good time to shape a young tree if needed (but leave old trees alone). Cut off, to an outward facing bud, a third of last year's growth on branches growing from the main framework and any misplaced shoots that crowd the centre, back to two buds.

Melianthus major This lovely foliage plant may flop in the first hard frost. Do not despair as it will usually push up again from the root. Give it the best chance with a deep dry mulch of fern fronds or straw. If some stalks and leaves remain erect, leave them in place to provide protection for the rest of the plant. In warmer parts of the country, it may well stay standing, in which case do not cut it down as it could well flower in March.

Mint For fresh mint over winter, dig up a plant, take a few good roots, lay them in a pot and cover with compost. Water and put on a warm windowsill. Seeds can also be sown now.

Monarda (bergamot) Cut back to a few inches above the soil and mulch. They are late into growth so label well to avoid digging over them.

Mulberry (Morus) Do any pruning needed on established trees now. This would be the time to pollard it if that was wanted. *Morus alba* 'Pendula' is lovely for a small garden; out of place growths can be cut off now and its skirt lifted slightly for spring bulbs to dance around it.

Muscari (grape hyacinth) A winter dressing of bone meal will help the bulbs produce better flowers next year.

Nemesia Nemesia, not being hardy, needs to be potted up and kept under cover over winter, cool and slightly moist.

Nepeta (catmint) Cut back to make a neat clump, leaving stems about 15 cm/6 inches long. Leaving top growth *in situ* over the winter protects the crown in freezing weather. Mulch around the clumps.

Nerine Now is a good time to plant the bulbs (immediately on arrival), ensuring roots are spread out and some of the bulb is above the soil. Do not plant anywhere near narcissi, a death knell for the nerines. They often do not flower well in their first year. Research the right position first time as, when they have formed a clump, they hate being disturbed and like congestion. Bulblets can be removed when they appear, to be propagated in a cold greenhouse. Protect from excessive winter rain or the bulbs may rot; this is easier if they are in pots.

Nicotiana (tobacco plant) *Nicotiana sylvestris* and *N. alata* sometimes reshoot from their rootstock after a mild winter so do not dig them up, but cut them down to base when finished and provide a dry mulch.

Olive Olives need a fluctuation in day and night temperature with three months of winter cold below 10°C to flower well. Those kept warm in winter or which have been outside for a long time in freezing temperatures will not flower (or fruit). Overwintering them in a cold greenhouse or well-lit porch is ideal, where they will need only minimal watering. Left outside, move the pot, if possible, to a sheltered corner. Wrap it well and raise it on bricks to stop the root ball sitting in wet and freezing. Trees planted in the ground need shelter and summer warmth.

Parthenocissus Virginia creeper and Boston ivy can be renovated now. Any pruning needs to be done before Christmas. Both are strong growers and need support until well established. After two years they will need to be kept within bounds and out of gutters, with wanted new shoots tied in and unwanted cut out. Grown hungry, they do not get too thick. *Parthenocissus henryana* is beautiful for a small garden, much less invasive than its Boston ivy or Virginia creeper cousins and it tolerates a north wall. Try blu tack to keep it up until it self-clings.

Peach, nectarine and almond Trees which are kept dry by having a shelter built over them are significantly protected from peach leaf curl (and they also then have some winter protection). The sides will have to be opened for pollinating insects. The cover needs to be left in place until May.

Penstemon Penstemons must not be cut down until late spring. Remove any tall flower spikes but leave the top growth on. They need the protection of all their leaves over winter.

Perovskia (Russian sage) Reduce by about a third against wind rock but leave full pruning until spring.

Persicaria amplexicaulis, P. bistorta, P. milletii, P. polymorpha (bistort)
Cut back when their long flowering season is over. They can be divided now or in spring. They tend to get big so provide them with space to flourish. They dislike drying out. The huge, dramatic _P. polymorpha_ will collapse and just needs cutting at base; remember where it is, as it looks totally dead until the moment it is totally alive again.

Phormium Should dramatic looking flower stems have been produced on mature specimens, they need to be cut down before they collapse and rock the roots. Provide a deep dry mulch for winter round the base and between the leaves with leafmould or bark. If it is a slightly tender variety like _Phormium_ 'Dazzler' or _P._ 'Sundowner', draw up the leaves into a tall tube shape and wrap with fleece, but not so well that moisture gets trapped in the bundle and rots it.

Phygelius Mulch well to protect against frozen ground.

Pimpinella major 'Rosea' (pink cow parsley) Its taproot makes it difficult to move. Leave it firmly where it is but cut it right down now.

Pittosporum Protect the less hardy varieties from frost and winter winds.

Protea A deep mulch of pine needles or straw is the best protection over winter if they are going to stay outside. There is much advice easily available online. Usually overwintered inside, they should be kept well ventilated. High humidity can cause fungal problems to which they are very sensitive.

Pulmonaria (lungwort) In early winter, before the new flower stems begin to grow, cut back the leaves using shears; they have a strong central rib that make them difficult just to pull off (bin the leaves as they often have mildew). Mulch around the crown with leafmould if possible.

Quince (_Cydonia oblonga_) The longer the fruit is left on the tree the better the taste, but pick before they start dropping, keeping only undamaged ones, storing them for up to two months to further improve their flavour. They must not touch (or be wrapped like apples can) so it is no good leaving them in a bucket under the kitchen table, which is often as far as mine get. Lay them out on an airy place such as a windowsill. Their scent and taste in apple crumble or jam is wonderful.

Rhubarb Remove and bin dead leaves (never put them on the compost heap as they, like potato leaves, are poisonous). Put a deep mulch of organic matter round the crowns but keep the crown itself exposed to frost; this breaks dormancy and helps to get a good crop next year. Every five years, between November and early March, mature crowns need to be divided. Find the buds in the soil and split into chunks using a spade, getting four to five buds and roots on each bit. Replant 1 m/39 inches apart in soil enriched with loads of garden compost, making sure that the top of the clump is just above soil level. November to March is also the optimum time for planting rhubarb – Ken Muir's website has much detail.

Romneya coulteri (California tree poppy) Mulch around and between the stems. Do not cut it down now, although its rather attractive seed heads can be taken off if some tidiness is called for.

Rose
- Mulch with the best organic mulch you can procure, taking it right up to the rose about 5 cm/2 inches deep. Do this when the soil is wet but not frozen.
- Rose planting: plant bare-root roses

between November and March (containerized roses can be planted anytime). A soil with good anchorage that holds nutrients well and a pH up to 6.9 is best (anything above pH 7.5 is too high). Prepare the ground in advance, digging in well-rotted manure (fresh manure burns the roots) or a soil improver – both can be bought in bags from garden centres or online. If using bone meal, mix it well into the soil – otherwise it and mycorrhizal fungi, good to add round the roots, cancel out each other. Soak bare-root (and container) roses in water before planting, always adding a bucketful afterwards even if the ground is wet. The knuckle where the roots meet the shoots should be 5 cm/2 inches under the soil. Ensure the soil gets round the roots and is then well tamped down. For good air circulation, do not plant closer than about 35 cm/15 inches to a wall or less than 45 cm/18 inches from another rose unless it is a very upright one. If a rose must be moved, do it now, cutting back by half, taking as much of its soil with it as possible.

- Replacing roses in the same site: having made the wrong choice myself, I would advise others to grow something other than roses for four years before replanting, but there are two other options. You can sterilize the soil – growing and incorporating Caliente mustard green manure can be very effective for this – or change the soil to a depth of only 35 cm/15 inches, incorporating mycorrhizal fungi in the planting hole and keeping the soil in top condition by mulching on a regular basis so that there is a good level of nutrients. The frequently quoted idea of using a biodegradable cardboard box to plant in is no easier than changing the soil. The difficulty with the advice we have followed for years, to 'change the soil to two spits depth', is that the replacement soil soon becomes anaerobic: with the

structure of the old soil removed, the new soil becomes compacted, airless and unproductive. It is also difficult to find suitable new replacement topsoil.
- Roses on rope swags: if roses are wanted along swagging ropes, use ramblers not climbers as ramblers tend to have more flexible growth. Do not choose any that are too vigorous.

Salvia Many salvias survive below freezing temperatures provided their feet are not in heavy clay where they stay wet, cold and damp: everything they hate. Planted with lots of grit so they are well drained, most shrubby ones should be all right. They will all benefit from a dry mulch around their base and in between their stems to protect roots over winter – bracken, fern leaves or Strulch would be good (not leafmould), anything to stop too much wet getting in – and then perhaps a wrap of fleece. Allow the tops of all salvias to die back naturally to provide winter cover. With *Salvia uliginosa*, for example, put a considerable layer of dry mulch over the roots but do not cut down the stems (except a little to stop wind rock).

Borderline hardy and tender salvias, like *S. confertiflora*, *S. discolor*, *S. elegans*, *S. leucantha* and *S. splendens* 'Van-Houttei', must come into a shed, garage or cool greenhouse over winter. Pot them up, not cutting them back any further than the base of the old flower stems, into a compost and perlite mix (40:60). Water only enough to stop them dying of thirst; misting is good as it stops the roots getting soaked. A fan set to 'blow' not 'heat' also helps to keep humidity down. They should be kept above 4°C. *S. patens* and other tuberous salvias can be lifted and stored like dahlias. As they dislike winter wet, it is safer to take them up in soil which is not well draining.

Saxifrage
- Autumn flowering (*Saxifraga fortunei*): keep the clumps well mulched; they

are borderline hardy and need to be protected from being frozen.

- Evergreen, perennial, rosette forming: remove faded foliage and flowers after frost and mulch but do not cut back hard. Sheltered, cool, shaded conditions are fine but not frost pockets, waterlogging or lots of competition from other plants.

Sedum (now called Hylotelephium) (stonecrop) Leave the seed heads on, at least for the start of winter.

Solanum Even the blue 'Glasnevin' variety needs some protection over winter. The white variety, *Solanum laxum* 'Album', is hard to get through winter outside without considerable protection of its roots. Grown under cover, it attracts red spider mite very easily.

Stokesia Their dislike of wet soils calls for as dry a mulch as possible.

Streptocarpus (Cape primrose) Reduce watering and stop feeding from now until spring. Keep frost free and in the light.

Teasel (*Dipsacus fullonum*) When the tall stems of teasel are brown and striking a wonderful silhouette, move them to wherever they look best – it is astonishing that they can be moved and stay standing.

Tulip The best time to plant tulips is mid November. The deeper the bulb, the less likely it is to be eaten by predators and the more likely it is to reflower, so have about 15 cm/6 inches of soil above the bulb with some grit and bone meal mixed into the area under it. Heavy soil will need even more washed sand or grit in the planting holes. Slugs eat the shoots beneath the surface so protect against them regularly. To flower a bit later, bulbs can be planted on their sides. All species tulips reflower from year to year and many Darwin hybrids are perennial. 'Ballerina' and 'Burgundy', 'Queen of Night' and 'Spring Green' are four which safely reflower, though in subsequent years they are never quite as beautiful as the first. For tulips in pots plant even deeper (15–20 cm/6–8 inches) and put wire mesh over the top to stop squirrels digging them out. Aquilegia will cover the dying leaves of tulips if planted together.

Verbena Verbenas need a dry winter mulch round their crowns. Do not cut them back but mulch round crowns while letting them die back naturally. If the stem of *Verbena bonariensis* collapses, cut down by two-thirds but not down to the ground.

Veronica After the first frost, cut plants down to 2.5–5 cm/1–2 inches from the ground, mulching around them.

Zantedeschia

- *Zantedeschia aethiopica* (arum lily): these zantedeschia, hardy enough to overwinter outside, will have their leaves blackened by frost. These need to be cut off and the crowns then covered with a dry mulch such as straw or bracken, pinned down with chicken wire to stop it blowing off. For very cold gardens expecting deep frosts, treat zantedeschia like dahlias, bringing the tubers in, drying them off and storing them in a garage/ shed or under the greenhouse shelving.
- *Z. rehmannii* or other tender zantedeschia (calla lily): these need to be lifted before the first frost; bring under cover to dry off and overwinter frost free in trays of compost.

DECEMBER

The calmness that envelopes the garden as plants settle into dormancy is in wonderful contrast to the energetic preparations for Christmas going on inside. Leaves on borders will be pulled down by worms, skeletal stems will provide a home and cover for insects and unscattered seed will be welcome food for birds. And, joy, soil that sticks to boots is best left quite alone.

AREAS TO CONSIDER

Annual meadow When there are no more flowers or seed heads to enjoy, if the area needs to be tidied you can clear it and treat perennial weeds. There is, however, no hurry to do this as cultivation invites more weed seeds into the ground and makes April's job harder.

Cuttings: hardwood The stock of many plants can be increased using ripe growth made this year; climbers, shrubs, trees and vines are all candidates. Try cornus with coloured stems, currant, fig, fuchsia, honeysuckle, hydrangea, mulberry, philadelphus, viburnum, vine, willow: there are endless possibilities. See glossary for detail.

Evergreens As a rule of thumb, do not prune evergreens in winter, but see September for comments on winter pruning of yew.

Frost protection By Christmas, ensure everything in the ground that is remotely tender or that will suffer from wind – worse, really, than snow – is protected with mulch, straw, its own leaves, fleece, bubble wrap, the boughs of some cut yew or whatever you have to hand. Ensure, too, that alpines and other plants which

hate winter sogginess have extra grit to help drain excess moisture away from the crowns; even put a temporary plastic cover over them if a deluge is expected. Ensure pots that are left outside are on feet, pulled into a sheltered corner if possible and wrapped with hessian or bubble wrap.

Greenhouse and cold frame Bubble polythene inside will help to keep it frost free but retaining some good light remains very important. Remove any leaves with grey mould. Keep a can of rainwater at room temperature for azaleas, citrus and orchids and one of tap water too.

Hosepipes Store away from frost and protect outside taps with bubble wrap.

Leaves Leaves on paths and lawns should be cleared, and so should leaves fallen amongst the crowns of herbaceous perennials, where snails will lurk, and among plants such as lavender and thyme around which the free movement of air is important. And when leaf fall is truly over, even if you do little else, blow the leaves from where the emerging snowdrops and aconites are to appear.

Ponds Remove barley straw placed as algae controls and put on the compost

Skimmia japonica subsp. *reevesiana*

heap; remove any submersible pumps (or run them every two weeks except in frosty weather). Keep the surface from freezing over completely (see January).

Pruning Do not prune unnecessarily, but focus only on those specimens which have outgrown their allotted space. Leave alone plants and shrubs that have good frost protection like hydrangeas as well as grey and silver plants and shrubs that would rather be in the Mediterranean, espaliers, cordons, stoned fruit and, of course, conifers and evergreens. Most important, leave alone those which flower next spring and early summer and have already produced the wood on which to do so. Acers, birch, laburnum, all vines and other trees whose sap rises early in the year will need to be pruned before this starts to happen. See individual entries below.

Snow Tie up the fastigiate trees such as Irish yew, Italian cypress and *Juniperus communis* 'Hibernica' which are beautiful grown like sentinels, so that snow does not weigh down the boughs and spoil their slim profile. Flexi-Tie works very well. Do not knock snow off plants except where its weight is going to damage the structure. To do so will do much more harm than leaving it to melt naturally.

Trees with winter berries A light trim now, taking off shoots for decoration, will be excellent, but resist pruning shoots which have not carried fruit.

Wildlife Feed hedgehogs with a proprietary food or good quality cat food (not bread and milk). Feed birds with high energy foods like fat balls and sunflower seeds and keep bird baths full and unfrozen.

PLANTS

Acer (maple) Other than the snakebark maples (such as *Acer davidii*), which should be pruned in late summer, any pruning on acers should be done in December and early January to avoid bleeding sap, which starts to rise early into the new year. Prune any stems with dieback to healthy wood and cut out any crossing or badly placed branches. Be sensitive to the tree's graceful shape.

A. negundo **(box elder) and its cultivars** On two-year-old or older plants grown as shrubs, cut back last year's growth hard to get juvenile, larger leaves. If it is grown as a tree, clear the stem of lower branches as it gets bigger, or stool or pollard to a short length of trunk for excellent coloured stems next year.

Acers in containers Move into a sheltered spot and keep soil moderately moist. They can go into a garage for protection as they do not need light while dormant.

Agave americana Protect by moving under cover or wrapping the base extremely well against winter cold.

Anemone blanda, A. nemorosa If there is a shortage of leafmould over their area, a 2.5 cm/1 inch deep mulch is helpful.

Apple and pear: free standing Sometime between now and the end of February, apple and pear trees need pruning. Remove dead/dying/crossing and vigorous branches growing towards the centre, aiming for a goblet shape. The majority of apple trees are spur-fruiting varieties so cut the branch leaders back by a third of their length. Then cut back the side shoots coming off them (the 'laterals') to five or six buds from the base of the shoot. This will encourage more fruiting spurs. There are some (not so many) tip bearers and partial tip bearers (including Worcester Pearmain, Bramley's Seedling, Discovery). These can have an old branch or two cut out each year but the leading shoots are, for obvious reasons, left unpruned. For identification purposes, the fruit buds (as opposed to leaf buds) are downy, so downy buds on tips of shoots are fruit buds and should not be pruned. If rejuvenating a tree, it is best to completely remove only one large branch a year to prevent a mass of water shoots.

A circle of leaf mulch, pure willow mulch or spent mushroom compost around trees cleared of competing weeds and grass deters pests and reduces competition for nutrients. Leave space between trunk and mulch. Remove, with the small piece of wood by which they were attached, any mummified fruit remaining on the branches, and bin.

If small black or pale yellow eggs of aphids are spotted round the dormant buds or stems, give the tree a winter wash to remove them.

Artemisia 'Powis Castle' This shrubby artemisia will need protection in a cold winter.

Bamboo Ensure pots of bamboo do not dry out.

Bay trees in containers Protect from severe frosts – the root ball in particular. Wrap the pots and mulch the soil surface with straw, bracken, Strulch or deep compost.

Berberis Deciduous berberis such as *Berberis thunbergii* can have one stem in five removed at the base in winter to stimulate new growth. Resist clipping it, however, as you will be taking off the growth that produces next year's flowers. Evergreen and semi-evergreen berberis not yet pruned because of berries can be clipped as soon as the berries have been taken. For a compact shape, remove some long stems if necessary to achieve the desired size. Clean secateurs after use as they can carry virus.

Bergenia (elephant's ears) Remove old leaves and mulch. *Bergenia* 'Eric Smith' has brilliant winter colour.

Birch (Betula) Prune before Christmas to avoid bleeding sap. Take off lower branches on a young tree when removal is not going to leave too great a scar on the beautiful trunks. Scrubbing the trunks with a stiff brush and washing up liquid or a power jet washer so that they shine in the winter light is not a high priority but very satisfactory. To achieve a multi-stemmed tree, the easiest way is to plant three standard trees with clear trunks in one hole.

Chrysanthemum After flowering is really over, cut down and provide a dry mulch to keep the hardy varieties going over winter.

Cornus
- *Cornus kousa*: it does not appreciate pruning, but if work needs to be done, do it in early winter. Sometimes the lower branches need to be removed and now is a good time to do it.
- Cornus grown for winter stem colour: see Cuttings above – they are the easiest of all.

Cotoneaster As berries finish, trim back branches to the desired shape.

Crab apple (Malus sylvestris) Avoid hard pruning. *Malus floribunda* (unless shrubby from the start) should be grown with a clear stem and then allowed to branch at the crown; about now take out congested growth and crossing branches. *M.* 'Evereste', *M. hupehensis* and others grown as small spreading trees should have congested stems taken out but not pruned as hard as an apple. Some (including *M. tschonoskii*, which has such lovely autumn colour) are better not pruned at all. 'Comtesse de Paris' (a wonderful cultivar that hangs on to its yellow fruit into the new year), 'John Downie' (with its red/orange fruit) and many other wonderful cultivars need any pruning to be completed by February. Most crab apples need formative pruning in their first two years and then just shaping. Reference to a pruning book now would be useful.

Dahlia Check those in storage – if beginning to shrivel, give a soaking of water. If showing signs of rot, throw them out. Ensure those left in the ground are still well protected.

Dicksonia antarctica Stuff the crown with straw, wrap the top fronds over the crown, and secure it in place with fleece wound round and round. The crown does not mind cold but it does mind winter wet. Air circulation is important to prevent the tip rotting. The advice of the gardeners at West Dean in Sussex is to give them warm feet with a thick mulch of leaves as well as crown wrapping.

Dryopteris (buckler fern) Provide a light dry mulch avoiding the crown. Its tatty fronds will give it winter protection.

Fig (*Ficus carica*) Protecting the tips of branches on trees outside is important when it is really cold. Clive Simms suggests in his *Nutshell Guide* that lengths of foam pipe lagging might do the job, which is a clever idea. An alternative is to wrap the bare branches in fleece and pack with straw behind and between the branches, all kept in place with mesh or netting (but not plastic – too humid). We leave ours in the ground, open to the elements, getting a good crop when winter is mild but almost none when frost has killed the tips.

Garlic Traditionally planted on the shortest day (21 December) and harvested on the longest (21 June), this works well unless the soil is heavy and holds water, in which case wait until spring or plant in modular trays and leave in a cold frame until early spring. Protect when they first sprout until the roots get a grip or birds may pull them out.

Geranium (cranesbill) Clear dead leaves from the crowns to prevent rot and mulch around them, leaving any short, stubby top growth that may remain.

Hazel (Corylus) Traditionally hazel is coppiced in December every three to five years. Hard pruning will, of course, affect the production of next year's flowers and nuts but will provide a copious number of canes. This is an excellent time, too, to gather hazel for use in supporting perennials and climbers. These should be cut before mid-January when the catkins start to appear. Left after March the wood starts ripening and becomes less pliable. Store the canes in a cool dry place to extend their life beyond two to three years. If the hazel is not nutting well, another plant nearby is probably needed as, while most are self-fertile, they do better cross-pollinated.

Helleborus
- *Helleborus argutifolius, H. foetidus*: as the flowers appear on these evergreen hellebores, tidy up the old foliage and dead stems.
- *H. × ericsmithii*: it likes sun and well-drained soil so is slightly different to *H. × hybridus*, which does better in shade. It could be grown in deep pots where the soil is heavy clay. Cut off any scruffy leaves now.
- *H. × hybridus* (lenten rose): John Massey, owner of Ashwood Nurseries in the West Midlands, breeders of the most ravishing hellebores, cuts the leaves off his at Christmas. Doing

Hydrangea paniculata, left unpruned until February to provide winter interest

so now lessens the risk of cutting off nascent flower stems. Bin rather than compost the leaves. Mulch around them (with some bone meal or chicken manure mixed in) using leafmould, spent mushroom compost or bark before the new stems get into gear. If you are unlucky to have mice around, they love eating the flower buds as they emerge so a deterrent may be needed.

• *Helleborus niger* (Christmas rose): harder to please than many others, it needs lots of leafmould, shelter, heavy soil and tender loving care – and very often does not flower at Christmas.

Hippeastrum (amaryllis) Such a lovely Christmas present: keep in good light at 15–18°C. Do not let water stand in the saucer. Increase watering as growth develops. When it has produced a flower, give a weekly dose of a potash-rich fertilizer such as tomato feed until the leaves start to die down, still keeping it watered. This feed will help the bulb build up nutrients for next year.

Holly (Ilex) Holly is one of the few plants that clip well after a frost, so is not damaged by berries cut for decoration.

Hornbeam (Carpinus) Hornbeam hedges can be tidied up and mulched provided the ground is not frozen.

Hyacinth Bring those being forced for Christmas into a light but cool room on 1 December unless top growth is less than than about 5 cm/2 inches, in which case leave them a few more days.

Hydrangea The blue and red hydrangea colours of *Hydrangea macrophylla* and *H. serrata* are affected by the soil pH. Cream hydrangeas are not affected by pH. All white-flowered *H. macrophylla* and *H. serrata* turn pink or red in limey soil, while *H. arborescens* 'Annabelle' and her sisters remain green/cream and white and fade to light brown, never pink. Ground limestone or chalk scattered around hydrangeas in winter enhances the red; apply about 80 grams per square metre. Keeping them blue is harder: the addition in spring, before the buds form, of a blueing agent (containing aluminium sulphate) helps the blue to be bluer on soil which is neutral or slightly acid, but aluminium sulphate will not work at all on alkaline soil. The only way to have a blue hydrangea when there is any lime present in the soil is to grow it in a pot with ericaceous compost. But the only hydrangea small enough to be pot-grown is *H. serrata* – and Sally Gregson advises us that even this will outgrow the biggest pot in five years.

Iris
- Bearded iris: over the winter remove (and bin) dead leaves on the irises, keeping the bed free of weeds. Once entwined with perennial weeds they are difficult to manage.
- *Iris unguicularis*: remove some foliage to reveal better the sweetly scented pale blue flowers.

Laburnum Prune before Christmas to avoid sap bleeding from wounds.

Lily Pots of lilies left outside are better put on their side in winter so that the bulbs do not get too wet and drown. But check the soil does not become totally dried out. Pots of lily bulbs left standing are the only pots from which I remove snow.

Magnolia Newly planted magnolias can be killed by a hard winter. Their roots are very shallow and soft so protect them well.

Pampas grass (Cortaderia) The crown of a young plant needs protecting (established ones look after themselves).

Pansy: winter flowering (Viola) Dead head. Remove and burn leaves with spots, blotches or fuzzy grey mould as they will infect healthy plants. Avoid watering from above. Feed with a potash-rich fertilizer.

Phalaenopsis (moth orchid) If it is in flower, water weekly with tepid water, letting it gush through the pot and allowing the excess to drain away before putting it back on its saucer. While in flower, feed weekly with a specialist orchid fertilizer. A warm east-facing windowsill seems a perfect place. When it has finished flowering, cut off the stem(s) to three nodes from the bottom and repot in orchid compost, cutting off dead roots. Some roots will stay above the soil level and the lowest leaves should rest on the compost. Let it rest for the rest of the winter, watering only to prevent it drying out totally.

Phlomis If it snows it would be a kindness to gently knock the snow off the rather brittle stems.

Photinia davidiana, P. villosa 'Palette' Unlike *P. × fraseri*, these should be pruned in dormancy, cutting out wayward branches.

Pieris A mulch of composted pine needles, pine bark or bracken would be good.

Plum Remove and bin any mummified fruits that indicate brown rot.

Poinsettia (*Euphorbia pulcherrima*) Undo it from its shop wrapping as soon as you can. Keep away from direct sunlight, draughts, radiators and fires but in a bright place. To prolong its display, keep the flower at a steady daytime temperature of 15–18°C and 13–15°C at night time. Water only when the surface has dried out a little, and then do so by standing it in a bowl at room temperature until it has rehydrated. If you want to keep it going after Christmas, feed with a potash-rich fertilizer.

Rheum palmatum They need to be tidied up in midwinter to remove any dead-looking pieces of root. Then mulch with compost around the outer edges but keep it away from the rhizomes, which would rot if covered with a heavy layer. Although they need copious amounts of water in summer, during winter they must not become waterlogged; so, if they are near water – where they do so well – ensure that the rhizomes will not be drowned. Unless they have grown far too big for their space, they can remain undivided for years. See March for division.

Rose David Austin Roses begin their rose pruning at Christmas provided the weather is not freezing. They have more ground to cover than most people, but if you want to get on with the job, there is no harm starting now on climbers, ground cover, patio and shrub roses (see February).

Sophora Prune before Christmas to avoid sap bleeding from the wound.

Sorbaria sorbifolia Remove suckers to keep it a good shape.

Vine (grape) (grown under glass)
Much advice is available from the RHS, pruning books and elsewhere on growing grapes. On a greenhouse/conservatory vine, leave the main 'rod' intact, tied to a horizontal wire so that in spring the buds all along it are stimulated into growth by the rising sap. On a really cold day before Christmas, do the winter prune; done later, the vine will bleed. Follow the tip of each side shoot off the rod back to the junction with the previous year's growth and remove new growth to within 2.5 cm/1 inch or two buds of that junction. Then cut the spurs off the side shoots back to a single bud each. Do this every year. Established grape vines can have their bark scraped in December to avoid the use of pesticides. Scraping the bark (without exposing the green cadmium beneath) removes mealy bugs and mites which enjoy overwintering under the bark. After doing this, the greenhouse needs a thorough clean.

Vitis coignetiae This vigorous deciduous climber will probably need to have some stems cut out to control its size, so cut back hard now – before Christmas – to avoid bleeding sap. Take hardwood cuttings to propagate.

LEFT *Miscanthus sinensis* 'Gracillimus'. Leave the flower heads standing for winter interest. See March for cutting it down.

OVERLEAF *Allium spaerocephalon* (flowering July–September)

INDEX OF PLANTS AND THEIR CARE DURING THE YEAR

Bold text refers to an entry in the introductory section, 'Areas to consider', in each month.
Orange boxes refer to care suggested in that month.

PLANT	January	February	March	April	May
Abelia			43		
Abeliophyllum distichum (white forsythia)		25	43		
Abutilon				68	92
Acacia dealbata (mimosa)					92
Acanthus (bear's breeches)	15		43		
Acer (Japanese maple)	15			69	
Acer campestre (field maple)	16				
Acer davidii and other snakebark maples					
Acer negundo					
Acers in containers				69	
Achillea (yarrow)			43		92
Achimenes (hot water plant)				69	
Aconitum (aconite, monkshood)			43		92
Actaea (was Cimicifuga) (bugbane)					
Actinidia kolomitka		25			
Aeonium				69	
Agapanthus			43	69	
Agastache (giant hyssop)		25			
Agave americana			43		
Ageratina					
Ajuga (bugle)			43		
Akebia quinata (chocolate vine)					92
Alchemilla (lady's mantle)					
Alkanet *(Pentaglottis sempervirens)*					
Allium					93
Aloe					93
Alpines	13		39		
Alstroemeria (Peruvian lily)			44	69	
Amaryllis belladonna (Jersey lily)				69	
Amelanchier		25			93
Ammi majus, A. visnaga			44		

June	July	August	September	October	November	December
	135				202	
115			169			
			169			214
		152				
						214
115						214
	135		169		202	
			169			
		152	169	186		
	135		169		202	
		153		186	202	
	135			186	202	
		153			202	
				186		214
115		153				
	135					
	135					
	135					
	135		169			
					199	
	135		169	186		
				186		
				186		
			170			

PLANT	January	February	March	April	May
Amsonia tabernaemontana					
Anchusa					
Anemanthele lessoniana (pheasant's tail grass)					93
Anemone blanda, A. coronaria, A. nemorosa and others					93
Anemone hupehensis, A. × hybrida (Japanese anemone)	16			70	
Anemopsis californica					
Annual meadow (for perennial meadow see P)	13			65	89
Annuals: hardy and half hardy			39	65	89
Anthemis					93
Anthriscus sylvestris 'Ravenswing'					93
Antirrhinum (snapdragon)					93
Apple and pear: cordon and espalier					
Apple and pear: free standing	16	25			93
Apricot		25			
Aquilegia					94
Arabis					
Aralia			44		
Arbutus unedo (strawberry tree)		26			
Argyranthemum frutescens			44	70	
Armeria (thrift)					94
Artemisia				70	
Artichoke, globe					
Arum italicum subsp. *italicum* (lords and ladies)	16				
Aruncus dioicus					
Arundo donax				70	
Asparagus	16		44	70	
Aster (most now called Symphyotrichum or Eurybia)		26	44		
Astilbe	16			70	
Astrantia major			44	70	
Aubrieta					94

June	July	August	September	October	November	December
	135				202	
115			170			
		153		186		
			170		202	214
		153		186	202	
		153				
						213
113	133	151		183	199	
115			170			
		153				
	135					
	135					
		153		186		214
115		153			202	
115				186		
			170			
115		154		187		
			170			
115	136			187		215
115				187		
			170			
					203	
116	136			187		
116	136	154	170	187		
				187		
	136		170			
			170			

PLANT	January	February	March	April	May
Aucuba japonica			45		
Auricula		26			94
Azalea - see Rhododendron					
Ballota pseudodictamnus				70	
Bamboo			45		94
Banana				70	
Bare-root plants	13				
Baptisia australis (blue wild indigo)		26	45		
Bark	13				
Basil					94
Bay (*Laurus nobilis*)	16			70	
Bedding plants					89
Beech		26			94
Bees					
Beetroot				70	94
Begonia	16		45	71	
Berberis					94
Bergenia (elephant's ears)		26		71	95
Biennials					89
Bindweed and black bryony					
Birch	16				
Blackberry					
Blackcurrant		26			
Black spot and mildew				65	
Bluebell				71	
Blueberry		26		71	
Borders		23			
Box		27	45	71	95
Box diseases: control and preventative measures			39		89
Brachyglottis (was Senecio)				71	
Brassica: broccoli, cabbage, cauliflower		27		71	
Broad bean	16	27			95
Broom (Cytisus, Genista)					
Brugmansia (was called Datura)			45		

June	July	August	September	October	November	December
116			171		203	
					203	215
				187		
					199	
	136				203	
116			171			
116	136					215
				183		
		154		187		
				183		
	136			187		
116			171			
						215
				188		215
			167			
	133					
		154				215
				188		
116					203	
116		154			203	
113	133			183	199	
116	136	154		188		
	136				203	
	136			188	203	
117		154				
117			171	188		

PLANT	January	February	March	April	May
Brunnera				71	
Buddleja alternifolia					
Buddleja colvilei, B. crispa, B. globosa			46		
Buddleja davidii and cultivars, *B. × weyeriana, B. × fallowiana*			46		
Bulbs	13		40	65	90
Bulbs for Christmas					
Bupleurum fruticosum				71	
Calamagrostis		27			
Callicarpa bodinieri (beauty bush)				71	
Caltha (kingcup)				71	
Calycanthus			46		
Camassia			46		
Camellia and *C. sasanqua* (autumn flowering camellia)			46	72	
Campanula (bellflower)			46		95
Campsis × tabliabuana 'Madame Galen'		27			
Canna	16		48		
Cardiocrinum giganteum (giant lily)	16		48		
Cardoon		27			
Carex		27			95
Carpenteria californica					95
Caryopteris			48		
Catalpa		27			
Catananche (cupid's dart)					
Cautleya spicata					
Ceanothus: deciduous			48		
Ceanothus: evergreen, spring and autumn flowering				72	
Centaurea					
Cephalaria					95
Ceratostigma				72	
Cercidiphyllum		27		72	
Cercis canadensis		27			97
Cerinthe major 'Purpurascens'					

June	July	August	September	October	November	December
117						
	136			188		
		154		188		
		154	171		203	
113		151	167	183	199	
			167	184		
			171			
117	137	154			203	
117	137		171			
117	137	155		188		
		155			203	
		155				
	137					
117						
				188		
		155		188		
117		155				
	137					
118			171			
	137					
118				188		

PLANT	January	February	March	April	May
Chaenomeles (Japanese quince)		28	48		
Chamaecyparis lawsoniana				72	
Chasmanthium		28			
Chelone obliqua (turtlehead)					
Chelsea chop, Chelsea heave, Chelsea thin					90
Cherry: acid (morello) and sweet		28		72	
Cherry: ornamental (see also Prunus)				72	97
Chimonanthus praecox (wintersweet)		28			
Chive				72	
Choisya					
Chinodoxa					97
Chrysanthemum		28	48		97
Cirsium rivulare					
Cistus					
Citrus trifoliata (Japanese bitter orange)					
Clematis Group 1		28	48	72	97
Clematis Group 2		28	48	72–73	
Clematis Group 3		28	49	72	
Cleome					97
Clerodendrum		28		73	
Climbers		23		65	
Cobaea scandens (cup and saucer plant)		29			97
Colchicum and autumn flowering crocus				73	
Cold frame					90
Comfrey (Symphytum) and comfrey juice fertilizer					97
Compost	13	23		65	
Conifers			40	66	
Containers, pots and hanging baskets	13		40	66	90
Convolvulus cneorum				73	
Cordyline	17				97

June	July	August	September	October	November	December
	137				204	
118		155				
				188		
118		155				
118	137					
118				188		
118						
118		155			204	215
118	138		171			
118		155				
					204	
119			171			
119	138		171	188	204	
119	138		171		204	
		155		189		
					204	
				189		
119	138		171			
	133				200	
			167	184		
113	133	151		184	200	
		155				
					204	

PLANT	January	February	March	April	May
Coreopsis					98
Cornus canadensis (creeping dogwood)				73	
Cornus grown for ornamental foliage (e.g., *C. alba* 'Elegantissima')			49		
Cornus grown for showy bracts (e.g., *Cornus florida, C. kousa*)	17			73	
Cornus grown for winter stem colour (eg *C. alba* 'Sibirica')			49	73	
Coronilla					98
Correa (Australian fuchsia)			49		
Corydalis			49		
Corylopsis					98
Cosmos				73	98
Cosmos atrosanguineus (chocolate cosmos)					
Cotinus (smoke bush)			49		
Cotoneaster				73	98
Courgette					
Crab apple (Malus)					
Crambe cordifolia				73	
Crinodendron hookerianum (lantern tree)					
Crinum × powellii				73	
Crocosmia (montbretia)			50		
Crocus: spring flowering				74	
Crown imperial (*Fritillaria imperialis*)			50	74	98
Cunninghamia lanceolata					98
Cupressus sempervirens (Italian cypress)					98
Cuttings (also see glossary for specific methods)	13				90
Cutting garden				66	
Cyclamen		29			
Cymbidium (orchid)	17		50	74	98
Cytisus battandieri (now called Argyrocytisus)		29			
Daffodil - see Narcissus					

June	July	August	September	October	November	December
	138		172			
				189		
119				189		215
				189		215
	138				205	
		155				
	138		172			
	138					
				189		
		157				
				189		215
119	138	157				
	139					215
	139					
	139					
					205	
				190		
				190		
			172		205	
113	133					213
	139		172			
		157	172		205	
119						

PLANT	January	February	March	April	May
Dahlia			50	74	98
Daphne			50		
Deadheading and cutting back				66	90
Deciduous trees, shrubs and hedges		23			
Delosperma					
Delphinium			50		98
Dendrobium (orchid)	17				
Deschampsia		29			
Deutzia					99
Dianthus (garden pink and carnation)					99
Diascia				74	
Dicentra, including *D. spectabilis* (now called *Lamprocapnos spectabilis*) (bleeding heart)			51	74	99
Dichelostemma ida-maia					
Dicksonia antarctica			51		99
Dierama (angel's fishing rod)				74	
Dipelta					
Division			40		
Doronicum (leopard's bane)				74	99
Dryopteris				74	
Eccremocarpus scaber (Chilean glory flower)			51		
Echeveria					99
Echinacea (coneflower)			51		99
Echinops (globe thistle)					
Edelweiss (*Leontopodium alpinum*)					99
Edgeworthia (paper bush)		29	51		
Elaeagnus: deciduous			51		
Elaeagnus: evergreen				74	
Enkianthus			51		
Epimedium (bishop's mitre)		29			99
Eranthis hymelis (winter aconite)				75	
Eremurus (foxtail lily/desert candle)			51		99

June	July	August	September	October	November	December
119	139	157		190	205	216
			172		205	
113	133	151				
				184		
119						
119	139	157	172	190	205	
	139					
120	140	157				
120		157				
	140			190		
120						
						216
120						
			167	184		
	140					
						216
	140				205	
			172			
		157	172		205	
		157				
	140					
	140					
				190		
120		157		190		

PLANT	January	February	March	April	May
Erica arborea (tree heath)			52		
Erigeron (fleabane)			52		
Eryngium (sea holly)	17			75	
Erythronium (dog's tooth violet)			52		99
Escallonia				75	
Eschscholzia (California poppy)					
Eucalyptus (gum tree)		29			
Eucryphia			52		
Eucomis (pineapple lily)				75	
Euonymus alatus, E. europaeus, E. phellomanus (spindle tree)	17				
Euonymus fortunei, E. japonica: evergreen					100
Euphorbia (spurge)			52		
Evening primrose (Oenothera)					
Evergreen trees, hedges and shrubs	14			66	
Eurybia divaricata - see Aster (*Aster divaricatus*)					
Exochorda (pearl bush)					100
× Fatshedera				75	
Fatsia japonica (castor oil plant)					101
Feeding of plants			40		
Felicia (blue daisy)					
Fennel				75	
Ferns		23		66	
Festuca glauca (fescue)		29		75	
Fig			52	75	
Filipendula rubra (meadowsweet)		30			
Flowers of sulphur				66	
Forsythia				75	
Foxglove (Digitalis)			52		
Francoa sonchifolia (bridal wreath)			52		
Freesia				76	
Fremontodendron 'California Glory'			52		

June	July	August	September	October	November	December
120						
	140				205	
	140			190		
			173			
			173			
			173			
			173			
	140			191	205	
			173		206	
120			173	191		
				191		
113			168	184		213
113	134	151		184		
	140				206	
121		158		191		
					200	
121		158			206	216
		158	173			
		151				
121	140	158	173			
	140			191		
			173			
121		158				

PLANT	January	February	March	April	May
Fritillary				76	101
Frost and wind protection	14		40		
Fruit bush and fruit cane	14		41		
Fruit tree: fan/espalier	14				90
Fruit tree: free standing with and without stones	14	23	41		91
Fuchsia: hardy and tender species		30	52	76	
Gaillardia					101
Galega (goat's rue)		30			
Galtonia candicans			52		101
Gardenia				76	
Garlic		30			101
Garrya elliptica (silk tassel bush)			52		
Gaultheria mucronata					
Gaura lindheimeri				76	
Gentian		30		77	
Geranium (cranesbill)			53		101
Geranium maderense					
Gerbera					101
Geum (avens)			53		
Gillenia			53		
Gladiolus					101
Gladiolus murielae (was called *Acidanthera bicolor*)				77	
Gleditsia triacanthos (honey locust)					
Goldenrod (Solidago)					
Gooseberry	17				
Gorse					
Grasses		23	41	66	91
Green manure			41		
Greenhouse	14		41		91
Grisellinia				77	
Ground elder					
Gunnera					101
Gypsophila (baby's breath)					101

June	July	August	September	October	November	December
		158	174			
				184	200	213
113				184		
		151				
113	134	151		184	200	
121				191		
		158				
	140					
				191		
	140		174			
	140					216
	140					
	140					
	141		174			
121					206	
121			174			216
				191		
				191		
121			174			
			174			
		158		192		
122		158	175		206	
			175			
122		158				
122						
122						
			168		200	
	134	151	168	184		213
122						
					206	
	141			192		

PLANT	January	February	March	April	May
Hakonechloa		30			101
Halesia (snowdrop tree)		30			
Half-hardy plants over winter					
Hamamelis (witch hazel)		30			
Hardening off					91
Hawthorn	17				
Hazel (Corylus)	17			77	
Heather (Erica, Calluna)			53		102
Hebe			53	77	
Hedges	14	24	41		91
Helenium				77	102
Helianthemum (rock rose)					
Helianthus (sunflower: annual and perennial)				77	
Helichrysum italicum (curry plant)				77	
Helictotrichon sempervirens				77	
Heliopsis				77	
Heliotropium					102
Helleborus			53	77	
Hemerocallis (daylily)			53		
Hepatica		30		78	
Heptacodium miconioides		30			
Herbs			41		
Hesperantha (syn. Schizostylis) (kaffir lily)				78	
Hesperis (sweet rocket)					
Heuchera and × Heucherella			53		
Hibiscus					102
Hippeastrum (amaryllis)	19		54		
Hippophae rhamnoides (sea buckthorn)				78	
Hoheria sexstylosa and *H.* 'Glory of Amlwch'					
Holly (Ilex)		31			
Hollyhock (Alcea)					
Honey fungus					
Honeysuckle			54		102

June	July	August	September	October	November	December
				184		
					206	
122				192		
		158				216
		158				
	141	158				
113	134	151	168		200	
122	141		175			
	141					
122	141		175	192		
					206	
122			175			
					206	
	141		175		206	216
122	141		175	192		
			175	192		
114	134	152		184		
			175		206	
122	141					
	141					
122			175			
122			175	192		217
		158				
	141				207	
122		158		192		217
123	141		175			
				184		
	142		176			

PLANT	January	February	March	April	May
Hornbeam (Carpinus)					
Hosepipes					
Hosta				78	102
House plants				66	
Houttuynia cordata (orange peel plant)					
Hyacinth	19				
Hydrangea aborescens, H. paniculata		31			102
Hydrangea anomala subsp. *petiolaris, H. aspera, H. quercifolia*			54		102
Hydrangea macrophylla, H. serrata				78	102
Hypericum (rose of Sharon, St John's Wort)		31	54		
Hyssopus officinalis (hyssop)				79	
Iberis (candytuft)					102
Impatiens walleriana (busy lizzie)					102
Imperata cylindrica 'Rubra' (red baron grass)				79	
Indigofera			54		
Iochroma australe				79	
Ipheion			55		
Iris, bearded: rhizomatous	19		55		
Iris graminea, I. sibirica, I. unguicularis, Pacific coast: rhizomatous	19		55		102
Iris laevigata, I. pseudacorus, I. versicolor: pond margins			55		
Iris danfordiae, I. historioides, I. reticulata, Dutch: bulbous		31			
Itea ilicifolia				79	
Ivy		32		79	
Jacob's ladder (*Polemonium caeruleum*)			55		
Jasminum			55		103
Juniper			55		
Kalimeris incisa					103
Kalmia latifolia					

June	July	August	September	October	November	December
			176			217
						213
		159	176		207	
			168			
123					207	
				192	207	217
		159	176			
			176			217
	142				207	
					207	
	142					
123					207	
		159				
		159				
123	142	159		193		218
		160	176	193		218
		160		193		
123		160				
				193		
123						
		160				
			176			
	142					
123	142					

PLANT	January	February	March	April	May
Kerria japonica					103
Kirengeshoma palmata					103
Kolkwitzia amabilis					
Knautia macedonica (red scabious)				79	
Kniphofia (red hot poker)					103
Laburnum					
Lamium (dead nettle)					
Lathyrus grandiflorus (everlasting pea)					
Lathyrus vernus (see Sweet pea for *L. odoratus*)				79	
Laurel (*Prunus laurocerasus, P. lusitanica* (for *L. nobilis* see Bay)			56		
Lavatera			56		
Lavender and *Lavandula stoechas* (French lavender)				79	103
Lawns and long grass	14	24	41		91
Layering of shrubs			41		
Leaves	14				
Lemon tree (Citrus)	19		56	79	103
Lemon verbena			56		103
Leptospermum scoparium					
Lespedeza thunbergii					103
Leucanthemella serotina (autumn ox-eye, giant daisy)			56		
Leucanthemum				79	
Leucojum vernum and *L. aestivum*				79	
Lewisia					103
Leycesteria formosa (pheasant berry)			56		
Leyland cypress (× *Cuprocyparis leylandii*)					104
Liatris			56		
Libertia				79	
Ligularia				80	
Lilac	19				104
Lily - and lily beetle	19	32		80	104

June	July	August	September	October	November	December
				193		
		160				
	142	160	176			
123				193		
123						218
	142					
			176			
123			176			
					207	
124	142	160	176			
114	134		168	185	200	
				185	200	213
124				193		
				193		
	142				207	
					207	
			176			
	142		176			
124			176			
			176	193		
	142	160			207	
124			177			
					207	
		161				
124						
124	143	161	177	193		218

PLANT	January	February	March	April	May
Lily of the valley					104
Lime (Tilia)		32			
Limnanthes douglasii (poached egg plant)		32		80	
Limonium platyphyllum (statice)					
Liquidambar (sweet gum)		32			
Liriodendron tulipifera (tulip tree)			56		
Liriope				80	
Lithodora diffusa 'Heavenly Blue'				80	
Lobelia cardinalis, L. × speciosa: perennial			56		104
Lobelia erinus: trailing and clump forming annual					
Lobularia (sweet alyssum)					104
Lonicera nitida				80	
Lotus hirsutus (now called *Dorycnium hirsutum*)				80	
Lovage					
Lupin				80	
Luzula nivea				80	
Lychnis chaledonica					
Lychnis coronaria					
Lythrum salicaria					
Macleaya					104
Magnolia			57		104
Mahonia				81	
Malva moschata					104
Marigold (Tagetes)				81	
Marjoram (Origanum)					
Mathiasella bupleuroides	20		57		
Matteuccia struthiopteris (shuttlecock fern)					
Meadow planting - see Annual meadow and Perennial meadow					
Meconopsis (Himalayan poppy)			57		
Medlar					

June	July	August	September	October	November	December
			177			
	143			193		
	143		177			
	143					
			177			
		161		194		
124		161				
124						
124	143		177			
	143					
	143					
	143		177			
	143	161				
					207	
	143			194		218
124		161				
124	143			194		
125						
125			177			
			177			
125	144		178			
				194	207	

PLANT	January	February	March	April	May
Melianthus major			57		
Metasequoia glyptostroboides (dawn redwood)					
Milium effusum 'Aureum' (Bowles's golden grass)					
Mint					104
Miscanthus			57		104
Mistletoe		32			
Molinia		32			
Monarda (bergamot)					104
Morina longifolia					
Morning glory (*Ipomoea tricolor*)				81	
Mulberry				81	
Mulching	24	42			
Muscari				81	
Myrtle (*Myrtus communis*)				81	
Nandina domestica			57		
Narcissus		32		81	104
Nasturtium and *Tropaeolum speciosum*				81	
Nectaroscordum siculum			57		
Nemisia					104
Nepeta (catmint)					
Nerine					105
Nettle					
Nicotiana (tobacco plant)		33			
Nigella damascena (love-in-a-mist)					
Olearia				81	
Olive			57	82	105
Omphalodes			57		
Onion			58		
Ophiopogon planiscapus 'Nigrescens' (black grass)				82	
Ornithogalum (chincherinchee and star of Bethlehem)					105
Osmanthus					
Osmunda regalis (royal fern)			58		

June	July	August	September	October	November	December
			178		207	
		161				
	144					
	144				207	
125	144				208	
	144		178			
	144		178		208	
	134			185	200	
	144		178		208	
		161				
		161	178	194		
125						
					208	
	144				208	
	144	161	178	194	208	
125						
125	144	161			208	
125						
125						
125					208	
	144					
				194		
				194		
125						

PLANT	January	February	March	April	May
Osteospermum					105
Pachysandra			58		
Pampas grass (*Cortaderia selloana, C. richardii*)		33			105
Panicum		33			105
Pansy: winter flowering (Viola)	20	33			
Parahebe					
Parrotia persica (Persian ironwood)		33			
Parsley			58		105
Parthenocissus					
Passion flower (Passiflora)		33			105
Paths			42		
Paulownia (foxglove tree)		33			
Pea			58		105
Peach, nectarine and almond		33	58		105
Pelargonium		33	58	82	
Pennisetum					105
Penstemon				82	105
Peony: herbaceous			58		106
Peony: tree		33			106
Perennial meadow (for annual meadow see A)				66	
Perennials	14			67	91
Perovskia			58		106
Persicaria (bistort)			58		
Pests				67	
Petunia					
Phalaenopsis (moth orchid)	20		58		
Phalaris (gardener's garters)					106
Philadelphus					
Phlomis			59		106
Phlox			59		107
Phormium				82	
Photinia × fraseri			59		107
Photinia villosa, P. davidiana 'Palette'					
Phygelius				82	

June	July	August	September	October	November	December
						218
				194		218
	144					
		162				
	144				208	
127					208	
	144			194		
		162			208	
				194		
				195		
114		152	168		200	
114			168	185	201	
					208	
	145				209	
114	134	152				
127		162				
			178			218
		162				
	145					
		162				218
	145	162	178			
					209	
		162				
						218
		162			209	

PLANT	January	February	March	April	May
Physalis alkekengi (Chinese lanterns)				82	
Physostegia (obedient plant)					107
Physocarpus opulifolius				82	
Phytophthora				67	
Pieris			59		107
Pimpinella major 'Rosea'					
Pine					107
Pittosporum				82	
Planting				67	91
Plastic plant pots		24			
Plectranthus argentatus					107
Plum				82	
Plumbago auriculata		33			
Poinsettia					
Pollarding		24			
Polystichum				83	
Ponds	15		42		91
Pontederia cordata				83	
Poppy			59		107
Potato	20		59		107
Potentilla fruticosa (shrub) and clump forming potentilla			59		
Primula		33		83	107
Privet (Ligustrum)	20			83	
Protea				83	
Pruning	15		42	67	
Prunus (ornamental cherry)	20				107
Pulmonaria (lungwort)					108
Pulsatilla (Pasque flower/ Easter flower)			59		
Puschkinia - see Scilla					
Pyracantha			59		108
Quince (*Cydonia oblonga*)			59		
Raspberry: summer and autumn		33-34	60		
Redcurrant and whitecurrant		34			108
Red orache (*Atriplex hortensis* var. *rubra*)					

June	July	August	September	October	November	December
			178			
	145					
						218
127					209	
127		162			209	
			168		201	
				195		
127	145					218
				195		
						218
	134		168			213
			178			
	146			195		
127	146		178			
	146		178			
	146	162	178			
127			179			
					209	
	134			185	201	214
					209	
			179			
		162		195	209	
127		163				
127	146	163				
		163				

PLANT	January	February	March	April	May
Red spider mite					
Rhamnus alaternus (Italian buckthorn)				83	
Rheum palmatum			60		
Rhododendron and Azalea			60		108
Rhubarb	20				108
Rhus thyphina				83	
Ribes (flowering currant)					108
Robinia pseudoacacia 'Frisia'					
Rodgersia				83	
Romneya coulteri (California tree poppy)	20			83	
Rose		34	60	83	
Rosemary					108
Rubus thibetanus, R. cockburnianus, R. biflorus		35			
Rudbeckia (black-eyed Susan)				84	
Rue				84	
Ruscus aculeatus (butcher's broom)					108
Russian vine (*Fallopia baldschuanica*)				84	
Sage, culinary (*Salvia officinalis, S.o.* 'Purpurascens')				84	
Salix: tree, shrubby and grown for winter colour (willow)	20		60		
Salvia: hardy, half hardy and frost tender				84	
Sambucus (elder)		35			
Sanguisorba (burnet)			61		109
Sansevieria				84	
Santolina (cotton lavender)				85	
Sarcoccoca (Christmas box, sweet box)					109
Saxifrage					109
Scabious				85	
Scilla and Puschkinia		35			
Schizophragma				85	
Sedum (now called Hylotelephium)			61		109

June	July	August	September	October	November	December
114						
	146					
	146					218
127	146	163	179	195		
			179		209	
				195		
			179			
					209	
127	146	163	179	195	209	219
	147			195		
	147					
	147			195		
		163				
				196		
			179			
	147					
128	147	163	179	196	210	
			179			
				196		
	147			196		
128			180		210	
	147					
	147					
					211	

PLANT	January	February	March	April	May
Seeds, seed storage and berries		24	42	67	92
Seedlings and self-sowers			42		
Selinum wallichianum					
Sempervivum (houseleek)					
Senecio					
Sequoia sempervirens 'Adpressa' (coastal redwood)		35			
Shallot		36			
Shrubs				68	
Sidalcea			61		
Sisyrinchium					109
Skimmia					
Slugs and snails				68	
Smyrnium perfoliatum (alexanders)					
Snow	15				
Snowdrop (Galanthus)	20		61		
Solanum crispum 'Glasnevin' and *S. laxum* 'Album'	20			85	109
Solomon's seal (*Polygonatum × hybridum*)			61		109
Sophora					
Sorbaria sorbifolia		36			
Sorbus					
Spinach		36			
Spiraea: spring flowering					109
Spiraea japonica, S. canescens			62		
Spruce					109
Stachys byzantina (lamb's ears)			62		
Stachyurus praecox				85	
Staking and supporting plants			42		92
Stephandra incisa					
Stephanotis floribunda					109
Sternbergia lutea (autumn daffodil)					110
Stipa		36	62	85	
Stokesia					

June	July	August	September	October	November	December
114	134	152		185	201	
			168			
			180			
		163		196		
128						
	148					
		152			201	
	148			196		
128						
		152				
			180			
						214
		164		196		
		164			211	
				196		
	148					219
		164				219
129						
	148					
	148					
		164				
		164				
	135					
	148					
		164				
	148				211	

PLANT	January	February	March	April	May
Strawberry	21		62		110
Streptocarpus (Cape primrose)			62	85	110
Styrax (snowbell tree)		37			
Succulents				68	
Sweet cicely (*Myrrhis odorata)*					
Sweetcorn				85	
Sweet pea (*Lathyrus odoratus*)	21	37	62	85	110
Sweet william (*Dianthus barbatus)*				85	
Sweet woodruff (*Galium odoratum*)					110
Symphoricarpos (snowberry)					
Tamarix (tamarisk)				85	
Tanacetum				85	
Tarragon					
Teasel (*Dipsacus fullonum)*					
Teucrium chamaedrys (wall germander) and *T. fruticans*				85	
Thalictrum (meadow rue)				86	110
Thuja plicata					110
Thyme					
Tiarella (foam flower)				86	
Tibouchina urvilleana	21				
Tithonia (Mexican sunflower)					
Tomato			62	86	110
Topiary	15				
Trachelospermum				86	
Tradescantia Andersoniana Group: hardy					
Trees: planting and staking and moving	15			68	92
Trees grown for autumn/ winter berries			42		
Tricyrtis formosana (toad lily)				86	
Trillium (Trinity flower)		37	62		
Trollius (globeflower)				86	111
Tulbaghia violacea				86	
Tulip		37		86	111

June	July	August	September	October	November	December
129	148	164	180			
					211	
			169			
129						
129		164				
129	148	164		196		
			180			
		164				
129						
	148					
129				197		
					211	
			180			
	148		180			
		164				
	148					
129						
129			180			
129			180			
129	148	164	180			
	135					
		164				
	149		180			
				185	201	
						214
				197		
	149	165				
129						
		165		197		
130					211	

PLANT	January	February	March	April	May
Turf				68	
Uvularia (merrybells)			63		111
Valerian (Centranthus)					
Vegetables	15	25	42	68	
Veratrum					
Verbascum			63	86	
Verbena: perennial				86	
Veronica			63		
Veronicastrum				86	
Viburnum beetle					92
Viburnum × bodnantense, V. farreri (winter flowering)			63		
Viburnum: deciduous spring/summer flowering					
Viburnum: evergreen/semi-evergreen		37			111
Viburnum plicatum					
Vinca				86	
Vine, grape (under cover)		37	63	86	111
Vine weevil					
Viola cornuta					
Vitis coignetiae					
Wallflower				86	
Walnut					
Waterlily (Nymphaea)				87	
Watering		25			
Weedkilling					
Weeds/weeding		25		68	
Weeping pear (*Pyrus salicifolia* 'Pendula')	21				
Weigela				87	
White rosebay willowherb (*Chamaenerion angustifolium* 'Album')					
Wildlife	15				
Winter bedding		25			
Winter damage to plants					92
Wisteria		37			111

June	July	August	September	October	November	December
			169			
	149					
114			169	186		
130		165				
		165				
	149		180		211	
130					211	
	149					
114					202	
130						
130						
	149					
130		165	181			219
114						
130				197		
		165				219
130	149		181	197		
			181			
	149					
115	135	152				
115						
		152				
	149					
131						
	149		181			
					202	214
	149	165				

PLANT	January	February	March	April	May
Woodland					
Xanthoceras sorbifolium		37			
Yew			63	87	
Yucca					111
Zaluzianskya ovata (night scented phlox)					
Zantedeschia (arum lily and calla lily)				87	
Zenobia pulverulenta					
Zinnia					111

The sculpture *Chelsea Morning*, by Helen Sinclair, appears to cartwheel exuberantly down a lawn edged with *Rosa* 'Blanche Double de Coubert', *Malus tschonoskii*, standards of *Prunus jonandrum* and pillars of Irish yew.

June	July	August	September	October	November	December
				186		
131		165	181			
131		165				
131	149	165			211	
	149					

Agapanthus Headbourne hybrid outside the study window
(flowering July–August)

GLOSSARY

Acid – soil with a pH below 7 (the neutral point of a range 1–14).

AGM – an 'Award of Garden Merit' (AGM) is given by the RHS to plants of all kinds, including fruit and vegetables, which, after trials, are proved to perform exceptionally well. Awards are reviewed regularly.

Alkaline – soil with a pH value above 7 (the neutral point of a range 1–14).

Annual – a flower that grows, seeds and dies in one growing season.

Apical dominance – the bud at the top of the stem can inhibit growth of side shoots. Apical dominance is arrested by removing the growing tip and also by taking a stem (such as on a rose) from the vertical towards the horizontal so that side shoots are produced.

Balanced fertilizer – a fertilizer containing a balanced mix of nutrients: nitrogen, phosphorus and potassium (denoted as NPK). Examples include Fish, Blood and Bone, Chempak 3 and Vitax Q4.

Balanced liquid fertilizer – faster acting than granular fertilizers, examples include liquid Growmore, liquid Miracle Gro All Purpose and Maxicrop Seaweed Extract.

Bare-root – a plant lifted from the open ground, usually in winter, with little soil attached to the roots. The converse is a container grown plant.

Basal cutting – a cutting with short stem and young leaves taken in late spring and summer from a shoot at ground level. Chrysanthemums and delphiniums are good candidates.

Base dressing – the incorporation of fertilizer into the soil or pot before planting.

Davidia involucrata 'Sonoma' (handkerchief tree), whose white bracts appear in May

Biological control – the control of pests or weeds using another organism: for example, nematodes to control vine weevil or parasitic wasps to control soft scale insects.

Biennial – a plant that grows one year and flowers and sets seed the next: in other words, requiring two growing seasons.

Bone meal – an organic, **slow release fertilizer** made of powdered cattle bones providing an important source of phosphorus.

Botrytis – a grey mould commonly found in humid conditions on petals, buds, foliage and fruit, causing decay of the soft tissue.

Bottom heat – warmth from a source placed beneath the plants, usually from a propagator or from electric cables coiled beneath gravel on a greenhouse bench.

Bract – a modified leaf at the base of a flower. It may be small, even scale-like, or large and brightly coloured as on ornamental cornus or davidia.

Bud burst – the period of time when new buds begin to swell, indicating the end of the dormant period.

Bulbil – a small bulb-like organ that grows in the axil of a leaf and stem or sometimes on a flower head.

Bulblet – a small bulb attached to its parent which, when removed, becomes an **offset**.

Calyx (plural calyces) – the entire protective whorl of sepals enclosing flower buds. The sepal is the often petal shaped protective covering of a bud; it then supports the flower as it opens.

Chicken manure – poultry manure, widely available as an organic fertilizer, is usually sold in a pelleted form. It is high in nitrogen but also contains some phosphates (phosphorus) and a little potash (potassium). It should not be used round **ericaceous** plants.

Chit – particularly relevant to potatoes, the action of putting tubers in the light to encourage them to sprout before planting.

Cold frame – a box-like structure with a transparent lid that can be propped open or closed, in which potted plants are given protection while stored outside.

Compost (garden compost) – decayed organic matter used to feed the soil and improve soil structure. Plant material (excluding pernicious weeds), woody trimmings, grass clippings and vegetable waste are the usual ingredients. Some cardboard and non-coloured paper can be added. It has a pH on the alkaline side of neutral. See also **potting compost**.

Controlled release fertilizer – usually in the form of inorganic pellets, mixed into compost to release nutrients over a period of time – more nutrient is released when the soil is warmer, so that the feed corresponds to the plant's growing needs.

Coppice – the cutting down of woody plants to just above ground level to encourage multi-stem growth.

Cordon – usually applied to a line of fruit trees which, planted at an angle, are restricted by careful training and pruning to grow as single stems with spurs.

Cormous – a plant growing from a corm: a round, underground storage organ which is replaced annually (as in crocosmia, for example).

Crown – the growing point of a plant where roots and shoots meet, usually just below the ground or at ground level.

Culm – stem of a grass, particularly used when referring to live bamboo shoots.

Cultivar – a cultivated plant (one that is not found in the wild) that maintains all the characteristics that distinguish it from the species to which it belongs. Cultivars do not come true from seed so have to be **vegetatively propagated**.

The cultivar name is written in the vernacular while **genus** and **species** are always in Latin.

Dieback – death from damage or disease of branches/shoots starting at the tip and going back towards the trunk.

Dioecious – having male and female flowers on separate plants. Both sexes must therefore be grown if berries/fruit are desired.

Dormancy – a period when all growth stops and there is very low metabolic activity.

Drip line – an imaginary circle on the ground around a tree/shrub which reflects the furthest reach of the canopy.

Earth up – the process of piling up soil around the growing stems of potato plants to prevent tubers being exposed to light, when they turn green and become inedible.

Ericaceous – belonging to the Ericaceae family; plants that require acid soil for good growth.

Ericaceous plant feed – a fertilizer suitable for plants requiring or prefering acid (lime-free) soil: for example, Chempak or Doff ericaceous fertilizers or Gro-sure Ericaceous Plant Food.

Espalier – the training of a tree, shrub or vine along a wall or free standing, having one main stem off which selected laterals are trained into any shape but usually horizontally. This system tends to produce an increased amount of blossom, fruit and berries.

Fertilizer – nutrients (see **NPK** below) added to the soil or potting compost to nourish the plant.

F1 hybrid – the first generation of seed produced by crossing two pure-bred plants, each having different and desirable qualities. These are passed on to the seed. F1 hybrids are vigorous and produce high yields, but their seeds do not come **true** to the parents.

Fireblight – a bacterial fungus affecting the Rosaceae family; indications are leaves, particularly at the tips of branches, hanging limp and brown any time from the beginning of the growing season.

Fish, Blood and Bone – an example of an organic fertilizer where all three major nutrients (nitrogen, phosphorus and potassium) are well balanced for healthy plant growth.

Floribunda – usually applied to a rose that has a long blooming season and large dense clusters of small flowers.

Flowers of sulphur – powdered pure yellow sulphur applied to soil over a number of years. It gradually induces better autumn colour by lowering the pH of the soil.

Foliar feed – the technique of applying a liquid fertilizer directly on to the leaves using a spray gun; the leaves absorb the nutrients through their **stomata** and epidermis (the outer layer of the leaf/stem).

Fungicide – an organic or chemical spray to kill fungal spores. There are many on the market. Bayer Fungus Fighter, Rose Clear Ultra, Fungus Clear Ultra are just a few. Home-made remedies giving some short-term control include 1 tablespoon bicarbonate of soda or dishwasher soap (without bleach or degreaser) to a gallon of water.

Genus – the classification of a group of species that are botanically similar. The genus is the first Latin name given to a plant; the second name (the **species**) is also in Latin.

Graft union – the point on a root, shoot or branch where two plants have been intentionally joined together.

Green manure – a crop which, when mature, is turned back into the soil to improve and nourish it. Examples include clover, lupin, mustard and phacelia.

Hardening off – the process of preparing a plant to acclimatize to life outside. Plants are moved out from under cover to somewhere sheltered, out of wind and direct sunlight for short times every day. The length of time spent outside is increased until plants are 'hardened off' and can be left out overnight. The process may take up to two weeks.

Hardwood cutting – a length of stem taken during dormancy (mid-autumn to mid-winter) from the current season's growth of a woody plant, to root in a pot or the open ground. To make a cutting, take 15–30 cm/6–12 inches from the lowest part of this year's growth for the strongest growth hormones. Slope the cut just above a bud so that water runs off. Remove any soft tip growth and bury the cutting vertically into a slit in the ground or into pots of well-watered 50:50 compost and perlite. Bury up to the tip for a single stemmed cutting or, for a multi-stemmed cutting, to about two-thirds of the length. Pots should be left outside, labelled, until the following autumn.

Hardy – a plant able to withstand the normal rigours of winter. In the UK, the ability of plants to withstand excessive cold, wind and water is denoted by the letter H followed by a number up to 7 (the higher the number, the hardier the plant). H3 is considered not hardy enough to remain outside in winter in most of the country. A reverse system of numbering hardiness is used in the USA: the lower the zone number, the hardier the plant.

Herbaceous perennial – a plant that, having no woody stem, loses its growth down to the crown when its growing season is over but whose roots remain alive to regrow for a number of years.

Honeydew – the secretion of aphids and scale insects as they suck on the leaves of plants.

Humus – the organic content of the soil made from decayed plant matter. It is moved around by micro-organisms.

Hybrid tea – a classification for a group of roses characterized by long straight stems, pointed buds, usually one flower to a stem and a good fragrance.

Involucre – a ring of **bracts** around the base of a flower head or flower cluster. They are very evident on euphorbias.

John Innes – formulae included in **loam** based composts, one especially suitable for seedlings and young plants (JI No. 1), another for potting on plants and houseplants (JI No. 2), and JI No. 3 for established pots and vigorously growing plants like tomatoes. There is also an **ericaceous** John Innes compost.

Lateral – a side growth off the main shoot.

Layering – the process of enabling shoots to form roots in the ground by pinning them down while still attached to the parent.

Leader – a main stem of a plant.

Leafmould – decayed leaves which, taking at least a year to decompose, are then used to improve the soil. Slightly acidic, leafmould helps to hold moisture and increases microbial activity when incorporated in the soil. It is an excellent **soil conditioner**.

Loam – a soil that contains clay, sand and silt in more or less equal quantities.

Misting – spraying leaves with a handheld sprayer to avoid soaking the compost.

Module – individual cells in a tray, each one able to take one or two seeds. A hole in the bottom is necessary in order to push out the compost at planting time.

Monocarpic – a plant that flowers, sets seed once and then dies. It may live for a number of years before flowering.

Monoecious – separate male and female flowers but on the same plant (see **dioecious**).

Monospecific – a genus which has only one species.

Mulch – a covering (often 5 cm/2 inches deep), usually of organic material, spread over the soil surface: garden compost, leafmould, composted or chipped bark, spent mushroom compost, composted pine needles and well-rotted farmyard manure are typical examples. All these inhibit weed growth, conserve moisture and prevent soil erosion. Taken down into the soil by earthworms, the mulch releases nutrients to plants and improves the soil structure by increasing its porosity and microbial activity. A mulch is never dug in. A grit or pebble mulch will do much of the above but contains no nutrients.

Mushroom compost – spent mushroom compost is a good **soil conditioner**, increasing the water holding capacity and adding nutrients. It contains straw and horse/poultry manure. As it is slightly alkaline, its use should be avoided on ericaceous plants. Its high salt level can build up over time.

Mycorrhiza – fungi that concentrate phosphorus and other minerals at the roots of plants in exchange for sugars, starches and amino acids; they are beneficial to plant growth.

Nematode – a parasitic worm or 'phylum', active during the warmer months. When watered into the soil it targets specific pests such as vine weevil.

Nitrogen (N) – supports green leafy growth.

Nitrogen-rich fertilizer – organic examples include Dried Blood, Hoof and Horn and nettle juice. Sulphate of ammonia is an inorganic highly nitrogenous feed.

Nodal cutting – a cutting taken just below a leaf joint (**node**) where growth hormones are most concentrated.

Node – the points on a stem from which leaves, branches or aerial roots may grow.

NPK – a rating system (which should be found on the labels of fertilizers) to describe the balance of **nitrogen (N)**, **phosphorus (P)** and **potassium (K)** in the product.

Osmocote – a readily available example of a **controlled release fertilizer**.

Offset – small bulb produced at the base of the parent bulb. Also a young plant developing close to the stem of the parent.

Perennial – a plant that lives for more than two years and usually much longer.

Perlite – a neutral, sterile, granular medium made from volcanic rock which is added to seed and potting composts to lighten the soil and improve air circulation and drainage.

Pesticide – a contact or systemic insecticide. Usually sold as a spray, a contact pesticide (for example, pyrethrum) will kill insects when absorbed through the body of the pest. A systemic pesticide (for example, Provado Ultimate Bug Killer) will move through the tissue of the plant on which it has been sprayed, retaining longer residual protection against insects that are feeding on it (see **Systemic insecticide** below). Pesticides should only be applied in the early morning or evening to minimize risk to beneficial insects and they must be kept away from ponds and all water courses.

pH – the measure from 0 to 14 of acidity and alkalinity levels in soil. The lower the number the more acidic it is; pH7 is considered 'neutral'. Most plants grow well in soil with a pH between 6 and 7.5.

Phosphorus (P) – supports strong cell development and water retention in plants resulting in good root and shoot development.

Phosphorus-/phosphate-rich fertilizer – organic examples include bone meal, fish bone meal, bat guano and rock phosphate. Inorganic fertilizers include superphosphate, triple superphosphate and ammonium phosphate. Rock phosphate (and, it is now thought, bone meal too) will not break down in alkaline soils (those with a pH above 7).

Phostrogen – formulation of an all-purpose plant fertilizer as a water-soluble powder and normally applied as a solution in water (liquid feed). Many brands are available.

Pinch out – to remove the growing tip of the shoot to encourage side shoots.

Pleach – to entwine branches of a line of trees or shrubs to create a screen or hedge (often done with clear stems to above head height).

Plug plants – usually annuals, sold as very young plants in individual modules, to be grown and potted on again before being planted out.

Pollard – the annual cutting back of branches to an established framework on the main trunk of a tree.

Potassium (K) – promotes flowering, fruiting and taste; it also regulates water retention and improves resistance to disease and plant hardiness.

Potassium-/potash-rich fertilizer – organic examples include comfrey juice and seaweed products; inorganic examples include Tomorite (liquid), Chempak Rose Feed (soluble), sulphate of potash (granular).

Potting compost – may be soil based or contain little or no soil, have **John Innes** added or not added. It is usually bought in bags as a multipurpose mix or prepared specifically for **ericaceous** plants, seed sowing, cuttings, containers or hanging baskets.

Predatory mite – an organism (bought online) that is used as a biological control of harmful mites usually found in the greenhouse.

Pricking out – carefully lifted seedlings, held only by a leaf, transplanted immediately into individual pots to be grown on before being planted out.

Renovate – to prune hard to rejuvenate a shrub that has got too large or old.

Reversion – applies to shoots and leaves that revert from an intended variegation to plain green, white or pale yellow.

Rhizome – a horizontal underground or above ground swollen stem that stores water for the plant.

Rod – the single cordon of a grape vine, planted one end of a greenhouse/ conservatory and trained parallel with the roof ridge. The fruiting spurs will grow off the rod.

Root cutting – cutting taken from roots, normally during winter. The plant is eased out of the soil and one or two roots, 5–7 cm/2–3 inches long, cut away, the top and bottom identified with a horizontal cut at the top and a slanted cut at the bottom. The mother plant is replanted before its roots dry out. Cuttings are inserted vertically round the edge of a small pot using a dibber so that the tops are level with the surface of the compost; they will not grow if the wrong way up. Thin roots can be placed horizontally on a seed tray, covered with 1 cm/½ inch of a 50:50 mix of compost and grit. Watered well, they are then kept in the light but out of direct sunlight.

Scarify – to vigorously rake over a lawn to remove **thatch** growing through the grass.

Seed leaves – the first pair of leaves (sometimes more than a pair) produced by the germinating seed. For a time the leaves may remain within the seed coat above the soil but will soon emerge as true leaves.

Semi-ripe cutting (also called soft-tip cutting) – a cutting 10–15 cm/ 4–6 inches long taken midsummer to early autumn from a plant whose stems have ripened (that is, hardened) but still have soft tips. Examples include box, choisya, cistus, heather, hebe. Remove the lower leaves and pinch off any soft tips. Dip the bottom of the cutting in hormone rooting powder. Dib pencil-size holes in modules of 50:50 compost and grit, insert and water well. The cuttings should not touch each other. They do best given some bottom heat and covered, out of direct sunshine until they are rooted. They can then be put in a **cold frame** or kept in the shade, pinched out as they grow ready to be planted out the following spring.

Sequestrene – a tonic (not a feed) for acid loving plants growing in alkaline conditions. The tonic unlocks the iron in the soil which is otherwise unavailable in alkaline soil. An indication of need is yellowing (chlorotic) leaves.

Silver leaf – a fungal disease that infects through wounds, often those made by pruning cuts. Apples, apricots, cherries and plums are particularly susceptible.

Slow release fertilizer – a fertilizer that releases a small amount of nutrients over the course of time; examples include bone meal, Fish, Blood and Bone and Miracle Gro Slow Release.

Soft scale – limpid-like insects, usually first seen as lumps and bumps on leaves and stems, that suck the sap from plant tissue while excreting a **honeydew** that is colonized by another fungus – sooty mould. Soft scale can be picked off by hand, controlled using a parasitic wasp, sprayed using an insecticide or, on larger specimens, washed off with a **winter tree wash**.

Softwood cutting – a cutting taken from spring to early summer before the stem has begun to firm. Candidates include hydrangea, osteospermum, pelargonium and salvia. Take a non-flowering shoot; cut just below a **node** so it is about 10 cm/4 inches long. Remove half the leaves and plant into a 50:50 mix of perlite and multipurpose compost. Label, keep moist and warm (bottomless, lidless plastic bottles work as individual propagators if space is at a premium). If under a plastic bag, prevent the cuttings touching the sides. Grey leaved plants will not need covering. If using hormone rooting powder, cover just the cut, not the sides of the cutting.

Soil conditioner – organic matter (see **mulch**) that will improve the soil structure by increasing its porosity, moisture retentiveness and level of micro-organisms. Unlike a mulch, it is usually dug in. Commercial products are available online and at garden centres if home grown options are unavailable.

Sooty mould – a black mould, formed as a by-product of **honeydew** excretions from sap sucking insects, that covers the top surfaces of (usually glossy) leaves. It can be washed off laboriously by hand using soapy water. A **systemic insecticide** will kill the insects from which it derives. The mould weakens the plant by blocking sunlight from the leaves.

Species – a group of closely related plants within a **genus**; the second Latin name in a plant's binomial.

Spur – a short branch off a main branch usually carrying clusters of flower buds, then fruit.

Standard – a single stemmed tree or shrub with a clear stem.

Stomata – microscopic pores which open and close on the surface of a leaf through which gasses and water vapour pass. They often close in hot weather to preserve water.

Stool – a multi-stemmed plant cut down to about 5 cm/2 inches.

Strulch – a mineralized wheat-straw mulch available online, used to suppress weeds and maintain warmth in the soil. Useful around plants needing a dry winter mulch. It does take a few years to be broken down into the soil.

Succession planting – as used in the flower garden, a planting scheme which provides continued interest through the seasons with plants growing to maturity as their neighbours are cut back.

Sulphate of potash – a mixture of potassium (K) and sulphur which encourages flower and fruit development and helps to build a plant's hardiness and resistance to disease.

Superphosphate – a high concentration of phosphorus (P), an insoluble mineral in short supply in the soil, which encourages strong root development and the ripening of fruit.

Systemic insecticide – an insecticide that is absorbed by the plant tissue to kill the insects that feed on it. It cannot be 'washed off' so it is essential to read the label to ensure it is suitable for edible plants such as tomatoes. Examples include Provado Ultimate Bug Killer and Bug Clear Ultra (there are many others).

Taproot – the primary vertical root of a plant which goes deeply into the soil.

Tender – a plant that may be damaged by temperatures below 5°C.

Thatch – dead grass and moss through which the blades of grass grow.

Tine – used in relation to spiking a lawn with a fork or hollow tiner to improve aeration and drainage.

Tomorite – an example of an inorganic potash-rich liquid fertilizer.

Topdressing – covering over the top layer of soil without digging it in.

True – a plant raised from seed that has virtually identical characteristics to its parents.

Truss – a cluster of flowers (or fruit), for example on rhododendrons and tomatoes.

Turgid – the state of a plant's cells when they are full of water.

Vegetative propagation – reproducing a plant by cuttings, division, grafting or layering. It allows for no genetic diversity.

Vermiculite – a light, clean, moisture retentive and sterile medium made from mica, used as an addition to seed and potting composts.

Water shoots – vigorous sappy shoots growing straight up from older branches, usually following a wound or extensive pruning.

Winter tree wash – a wash consisting of plant oils diluted with water, made into a spray and applied to fruit trees to reduce fungal spores and overwintering eggs of pests such as aphids, woolly aphids and winter moth.

Wood ash – alkaline ash from wood burners, fires or bonfires where only wood has been burnt. When wet, the potash leaches out so it must either be stored dry (and it becomes less potent with time) or be used immediately on the compost heap, around fruit trees and fruit canes or in the vegetable garden (especially around brassicas).

RECOMMENDED REFERENCES

In the text I frequently advise readers to obtain more detailed advice. The following books would be a helpful collection to have.

Essential Pruning Techniques, George Brown, revised and expanded by Tony Kirkham (Portland: Timber Press, 2017)

Royal Horticultural Society A–Z Encyclopedia of Garden Plants, 4th edn, ed. Christopher Brickell (London: Dorling Kindersley, 2016)

Royal Horticultural Society Essential Gardening Techniques, ed. Christopher Brickell (London: Mitchell Beazley, 2002)

Royal Horticultural Society Pests and Diseases, Pippa Greenwood and Andrew Halstead (London: Dorling Kindersley, 2018)

Royal Horticultural Society Propagating Plants, ed. Alan Toogood (London: Dorling Kindersley, 2006)

Royal Horticultural Society Vegetable and Fruit Gardening, ed. Michael Pollack (London: Dorling Kindersley, 2008)

PREVIOUS PAGES A romantic planting (July): *Rosa* 'Florence Mary Morse', *R.* 'Champagne Moment' and other roses, with pennisetum, molinia and veronicastrum, still to flower.

COMMON & LATIN NAMES

Many English common names are used in the Index (pages 222–63). For example, honeysuckle is used rather than Lonicera, box rather than Buxus, lime rather than Tilia. However, there are many occasions where the Latin name is given because it is familiar: for example, Helleborus rather than Christmas rose, Pulmonaria rather than lungwort. For plants that are identified by their Latin name, this list gives the English equivalent where it exists, to facilitate its reference in the Index.

Also included are a few instances where a very familiar Latin name such as Senecio is now no longer used, but this list will guide the reader to its current approved name: in this case to Brachyglottis.

Acidanthera	*Gladiolus murielae*
Aconite/monkshood	Aconitum
Aconite, winter	*Eranthis hyemalis*
Alexanders	Smyrnium
Alkanet, green	*Pentaglottis sempervirens*
Alyssum, sweet	*Lobularia maritima*
Amaryllis	Hippeastrum
Angel's fishing rod	Dierama
Angel's trumpet	Brugmansia
Arum lily	*Zantedeschia aethiopica*
Australian fuchsia	Correa
Autumn crocus	Colchicum
Autumn daffodil	Sternbergia
Avens	Geum
Baby's breath	Gypsophila
Bear's breeches	Acanthus
Beauty bush	Callicarpa
Bellflower	Campanula
Bergamot	Monarda
Bishop's mitre	Epimedium
Bistort/bistorta	Persicaria
Black-eyed Susan	Rudbeckia
Black grass/lilyturf	Ophiopogon
Blanket flower	Gaillardia
Bleeding heart	Dicentra

Blue daisy	Felicia
Boston ivy	Parthenocissus
Bowles's golden grass	*Milium effusum* 'Aureum'
Bowman's root	Gillenia
Box-leaved honeysuckle	*Lonicera pileata*
Bridal wreath	Francoa
Buckler fern	Dryopteris
Buckthorn, Italian	Rhamnus
Bugbane	*Actaea simplex*
Bugle	Ajuga
Burnet	Sanguisorba
Bush clover	*Lespedeza thunbergii*
Busy lizzie/balsam	Impatiens
Butcher's broom	*Ruscus aculeatus*
California poppy	*Eschscholzia californica*
California lilac	Ceanothus
California tree poppy	*Romneya coulteri*
Calla lily	*Zantedeschia rehmannii*
Callicanthus	*Gladiolus murielae*
Campion	Lychnis
Candytuft	Iberis
Cape primrose	Streptocarpus
Carnation	Dianthus
Castor oil plant	× Fatshedera
Catmint	Nepeta
Cherry	Prunus
Chilean glory flower	Eccremocarpus
Chincherinchee	*Ornithogalum thrysoides*
Chinese lanterns/physalis	*Alkekengi physalis*
Chocolate cosmos	*Cosmos astrosanguineus*
Chocolate vine	*Akebia quinata*
Christmas box/sweet box	Sarcoccoca
Christmas rose	*Helleborus niger*
Cimicifuga	*Actaea simplex*
Clary sage	*Salvia viridis*
Climbing hydrangea	*Hydrangea petiolaris*
Coastal redwood	*Sequoia sempervirens*
Columbine	Aquilegia
Comfrey	*Symphytum officinale*
Coneflower	Echinacea
Cornflower, perennial	Centaurea
Cotton lavender	Santolina

Crab apple	*Malus sylvestris*
Cranesbill	Geranium (hardy)
Crinum lily	*Crinum × powellii*
Crown imperial	*Fritillaria imperialis*
Culver's root	Veronicastrum
Cup and saucer plant	*Cobaea scandens*
Cupid's dart	Catananche
Currant, flowering	Ribes
Curry plant	*Helichrysum italicum*
Cypress	Chamaecyparis
Daffodil	Narcissus
Daisy bush	Olearia
Daisy, Mexican/fleabane	Erigeron
Daisy, ox-eye/marguerite	*Leucanthemum vulgare*
Daisy, giant/autumn ox-eye	Lecanthemella
Daisy, shasta	*Leucanthemum × superbum*
Datura	Brugmansia
Dawn redwood	Metasequoia
Daylily	Hemerocallis
Dead nettle	Lamium
Desert candle/foxtail lily	Eremurus
Dog's tooth violet	Erythronium
Dogwood	Cornus
Dusty miller	Senecio
Easter flower/pasque flower	Pulsatilla
Eastern redbud	*Cercis canadensis*
Elder	Sambucus
Elephant's ears	Bergenia
Eupatorium	Ageratina
Everlasting pea	*Lathyrus grandiflorus*
False mallow	Sidalcea
Fescue	Festuca
Flame thrower	*Tropaeolum speciosum*
Flowering currant	Ribes
Foam flower	Tiarella
Foxglove tree	Paulownia
Foxtail lily/desert candle	Eremurus
Gardener's garters	Phalaris
Germander	Teucrium
Giant hyssop	Agastache
Giant lily	Cardiocrinum
Globeflower	Trollius

Globe thistle	Echinops
Glory of the snow	Chinodoxa
Goat's rue	Galega
Golden marguerite	*Anthemis tinctoria*
Grape	see under Vine in index
Grape hyacinth	Muscari
Gum	Eucalyptus
Hair grass (tufted hair grass)	Deschampsia
Heath, tree	*Erica arborea*
Heavenly bamboo	Nandina
Himalayan poppy	Meconopsis
Honey locust	*Gleditsia triacanthos*
Honeywort	*Cerinthe major*
Hortensia hydrangea	*Hydrangea macrophylla*
Hot water plant/Cupid's bower	Achimenes
Houseleek	Sempervivum
Italian cypress	*Cupressus sempervirens*
Japanese anemone	*Anemone × hybrida*
Japanese angelica tree	Aralia
Japanese bitter orange	*Citrus trifoliata*
Japanese quince	Chaenomeles
Jersey lily	*Amaryllis belladonna*
Jerusalem cross	*Lychnis chaledonica*
Jerusalem sage	*Phlomis russeliana*
Joe Pye weed	*Eupatorium purpureum*
Kaffir lily	Hesperantha
Katsura tree	*Cercidiphyllum japonicum*
King cup/marsh marigold	Caltha
Knapweed	Centaurea
Lacecap hydrangea	*Hydrangea serrata*
Lady's mantle	*Alchemilla mollis*
Lamb's ears	Stachys
Lantern tree	Crinodendron
Laurel, Portuguese	*Prunus lusitanica*
Laurel, cherry	*Prunus laurocerasus*
Laurel, spotted	*Aucuba japonica*
Lawson's cypress	*Chamaecyparis lawsoniana*
Lenten rose	*Helleborus × hybridus*
Leopard's bane	Doronicum
Lilyturf	Liriope
London pride	*Saxifraga × urbium*
Loosestrife	Lythrum

Lords-and-ladies	Arum
Love-in-a-mist	*Nigella damescena*
Lungwort	Pulmonaria
Mallow	Lavatera/Malva
Maple	Acer
Marguerite	Argyranthemum
Marguerite	*Leucanthemum vulgare*
Marsh marigold/kingcup	Caltha
Meadowsweet	Filipendula
Meadow rue	Thalictrum
Medlar	*Mespilus germanica*
Merrybells	Uvularia
Mexican sunflower	Tithonia
Mexican orange blossom	*Choisya ternata*
Michaelmas daisy	Aster
Mimosa	*Acacia dealbata*
Mock orange	Philadelphus
Monkshood/aconite	Aconitum
Montbretia	Crocosmia
Mophead hydrangea	*Hydrangea macrophylla*
Mother-in-law's tongue	Sansevieria
Mountain ash	Sorbus
Mullein	Verbascum
Mugwort/masterwort	Astrantia
Navelwort	Omphalodes
Night scented phlox	*Zaluzianskya ovata*
Ninebark	Physocarpus
Obedient plant	Physostegia
Oleander	Elaeagnus
Orange peel plant	Houttuynia
Orchid	Cymbidium/Dendrobium/Phalaenopsis
Ox-eye daisy	Leucanthemella
Paper bush	Edgeworthia
Pearl bush	Exochorda
Periwinkle	Vinca
Pernettya	Gaultheria
Persian ironwood	Parrotia
Peruvian lily	Alstroemeria
Pheasant berry	*Leycesteria formosa*
Pheasant's tail grass	*Anemanthele lessoniana*
Physalis/Chinese lanterns	*Alkekengi physalis*
Pickerel weed	*Pontederia cordata*

Pineapple broom	*Cytissus battandieri*
Pineapple flower	Eucomis
Pink	Dianthus
Pink cow parsley	Pimpinella
Poached egg plant	*Limnanthes douglasii*
Poncirus trifoliata	*Citrus trifoliata*
Poppy, California	*Romneya coulteri*
Poppy, Himalayan	Meconopsis
Pussy willow/goat willow	*Salix caprea*
Pyrethrum	Tanacetum
Queen Anne's lace	*Anthriscus sylvestris* 'Ravenswing'
Quince, Japanese	Chaenomeles
Red baron grass	Imperata
Red hot poker	Kniphofia
Red scabious	*Knautia macedonica*
Rock cress	Arabis
Rock rose	Cistus/Helianthemum
Rose of Sharon	Hypericum
Rowan	Sorbus
Royal fern	*Osmunda regalis*
Russian sage	Perovskia
Sage	Salvia
Schizostylis	Hesperantha
Sea buckthorn	*Hippophae rhamnoides*
Sea holly	Eryngium
Sedge	Carex
Senecio	Brachyglottis
Shasta daisy	*Leucanthemum × superbum*
Shuttlecock fern	*Matteuccia struthiopteris*
Silk tassel bush	*Garrya eliptica*
Smoke bush	Cotinus
Snapdragon	Antirrhinum
Snowberry	Symphoricarpos
Snowdrop tree	Halesia
Snowflake	Leucojum
Soft shield fern	Polystichum
Speedwell	Veronica
Spider flower	Cleome
Spindle	Euonymus
Spotted laurel	*Aucuba japonica*
Spring snowflake	*Leucojum vernum*
Spring bitter vetch, vetchling	*Lathyrus vernus*

Spurge	Euphorbia
St John's wort	Hypericum
Star jasmine	*Trachelospermum jaminoides*
Star of Bethlehem	*Ornithogalum umbellatum*
Statice	Limonium
Strawberry tree	*Arbutus unedo*
Stonecrop	Sedum
Sumach	Rhus
Summer snowflake	*Leucojum aestivum*
Sunflower	Helianthus
Sweet gum	Liquidambar
Sweet rocket	*Hesperis matronalis*
Tea tree	Leptospermum
Thorow-wax	Bupleurum
Thrift/sea pink	Armeria
Tickseed	Coreopsis
Toad lily	Tricyrtis
Tobacco plant	Nicotiana
Tree fern	*Dicksonia antarctica*
Tree heath	*Erica arborea*
Trinity flower	Trillium
Tulip tree	Liriodendron
Turtlehead	Chelone
Virginia creeper	Parthenocissus
White forsythia	Abeliophyllum
Whorlflower	*Morina longifolia*
Woodrush	Luzula
Wild indigo	Baptisia
Willow	Salix
Wintersweet	*Chimonanthus praecox*
Witch hazel	Hamamelis
Windflower	Anemone
Yarrow	Achillea

OVERLEAF A quiet, still garden – a new year

NOTES

OVERLEAF From the cottage garden through the greenhouse arch: *Rosa* 'Cécile Brünner' on left,
R. multiflora 'Grevillei' and *R*. City of York on right (all flowering June–August)